Hans-Herbert Kögler's
Critical Hermeneutics

Also Available from Bloomsbury

Hermeneutics After Ricoeur, John Arthos
Relational Hermeneutics: Essays in Comparative Philosophy,
ed. Paul Fairfield and Saulius Geniusas
Hermeneutics and Phenomenology: Figures and Themes,
ed. Saulius Geniusas and Paul Fairfield
Erich Fromm's Critical Theory: Hope, Humanism, and the Future,
ed. Kieran Durkin and Joan Braune

Hans-Herbert Kögler's Critical Hermeneutics

Edited by Ľubomír Dunaj and Kurt C.M. Mertel

BLOOMSBURY ACADEMIC
LONDON • NEW YORK • OXFORD • NEW DELHI • SYDNEY

BLOOMSBURY ACADEMIC
Bloomsbury Publishing Plc
50 Bedford Square, London, WC1B 3DP, UK
1385 Broadway, New York, NY 10018, USA
29 Earlsfort Terrace, Dublin 2, Ireland

BLOOMSBURY, BLOOMSBURY ACADEMIC and the Diana logo are trademarks of Bloomsbury Publishing Plc

First published in Great Britain 2022
This paperback edition published 2023

Copyright © Ľubomír Dunaj, Kurt C.M. Mertel, and Contributors, 2022

Ľubomír Dunaj and Kurt C.M. Mertel have asserted their right under the Copyright, Designs and Patents Act, 1988, to be identified as Editors of this work.

Cover design by Charlotte Daniels
Cover image: Lifestyle balance concept with balanced equilibrium
Illustration (© Panther Media GmbH / Alamy Stock Photo)

All rights reserved. No part of this publication may be reproduced or transmitted in any form or by any means, electronic or mechanical, including photocopying, recording, or any information storage or retrieval system, without prior permission in writing from the publishers.

Bloomsbury Publishing Plc does not have any control over, or responsibility for, any third-party websites referred to or in this book. All internet addresses given in this book were correct at the time of going to press. The author and publisher regret any inconvenience caused if addresses have changed or sites have ceased to exist, but can accept no responsibility for any such changes.

A catalogue record for this book is available from the British Library.

A catalog record for this book is available from the Library of Congress.

ISBN: HB: 978-1-3502-2863-4
PB: 978-1-3502-2867-2
ePDF: 978-1-3502-2864-1
eBook: 978-1-3502-2865-8

Typeset by RefineCatch Limited, Bungay, Suffolk

To find out more about our authors and books visit www.bloomsbury.com and sign up for our newsletters.

Contents

Preface   vii

Introduction   *Ľubomír Dunaj and Kurt C.M. Mertel*   1

Part One   Critical Hermeneutics as Social Theory

1. The Case for a Critical Hermeneutics: From the Understanding of Power to the Power of Understanding *Simon Susen*   7
2. Power, the Body and Reflexivity. Hans-Herbert Kögler's Hermeneutics in the Context of Critical Sociology *Rainer Winter*   71
3. Naturalizing Kögler *Stephen Turner*   87

Part Two   Recognition, Cosmopolitanism, Religion

4. The Moral Stance, Our Moralizing Nature, and the Hermeneutic and Empathic Dimension of Human Relations *Karsten R. Stueber*   105
5. Dialogue, Cosmopolitanism, and Language Education *Werner Delanoy*   123
6. Secularity, Religion, and Dialogue: Rethinking the Conditions of the Possibility for Genuine Complementary Learning *Paul Healy*   139
7. The Limits of Interreligious Hermeneutics and the Need for Alternative Understanding *John C. Maraldo*   159

Part Three   Toward a Critical Hermeneutics of the Present

8. The Ontology of the Present and the Tasks of a Future Sociology *Frédéric Vandenberghe*   181
9. Cherche pas à Comprendre: Cosmopolitan Hermeneutics in Difficult Times *William Outhwaite*   195
10. Playing More Seriously: An Enactivist Critique of Kögler's Critical Reflexive Dialogue *Lauren Swayne Barthold*   215
11. Dialogue in a Polarized World—Is There a Way Out? *Randi Gressgård*   231

Conclusion
    Social Ontology, Dialogic Recognition, and Contemporary Challenges:
    A Reply. *Hans-Herbert Kögler*   249

List of Contributors   291
Index   295

Preface

Ľubomír Dunaj and Kurt C.M. Mertel

Is domination omnipresent and our ability to emancipate ourselves from power relations limited? How much transformative power does philosophy have? Can philosophy contribute to the improvement of the human condition and, therefore, retain a broader socio-cultural relevance? Is it really the case that philosophers nowadays are rather impotent to successfully resist *diabolum* as many cynical postmodern critics today tend to argue? Is there no moral progress at all? Are we doomed to moving in an eternal circle of minor successes and major disasters? And what about other cultures, nations, and civilizations outside of "the West?" Do they hold potential keys to contributing to the solution of global problems, or are they condemned to sharing the same fate? To be sure, we now face tremendous difficulties in attempting to answer the questions above. In a time like ours, belief in dialogue and the strength of the better argument is consistently confronted with skeptical scorn. Indeed, we may now say that the nonlinear character of historical development requires a certain modesty in the search for answers, that history has taught us too much optimism can sometimes bring more harm than good.

We would like to stress from the outset a shared premise that animates the volume as a whole, viz. that any viable contribution to the project of a critical theory of society must avoid two extremes: the hyperbolic belief in the unlimited power of philosophical reason and inevitable moral and societal progress on the one hand, and, on the other, the wholesale rejection of rational argumentation and reason-giving as attainable ideals of moral and civilizational advancement. In accordance with Hans-Herbert Kögler's lifelong project, in which he skillfully integrates resources and insights from both philosophical hermeneutics and Frankfurt School critical theory, among others, we recognize that any critical theorist is always embedded in a historical, societal, and cultural context which in turn is permeated by relations of power. Hence, she always makes use of concepts and assumptions produced by that context. As a result, our essential social situatedness must become the methodological point of departure when trying to diagnose and criticize social pathologies. This, in turn, rules out the possibility of attaining an absolutely authoritative or privileged perspective "from nowhere," i.e., that of a super-rational observer. The contextual character of all understanding, however, does not mean that a critical stance towards existing concepts, categories, methods, power relations, etc. and, therefore, the possibility to overcome them immanently, is unavailable or impossible. On the contrary, as Kögler's work has convincingly shown, such a stance must neither lead to an ultimately disempowering moral relativism, nor to "the end of philosophy." It rather represents a necessary point of departure for genuine philosophical inquiry and social criticism.

Milan Kundera's novel *Immortality* (French 1990, English 1991), published two years before Kögler's first major publication *The Power of Dialogue* (German 1992, English 1996/99), not only provoked us to rethink the questions mentioned at the outset. It also expresses a certain *Zeitgeist* that appears to be particularly influential in the last three decades. According to the novel's protagonist, professor Avenarius, no revolution has ever been successful in the fight against *diabolum* due to its uncanny ability to absorb any movement or organization directed against it. For Kundera's figure, this leads to the following predicament: either we simply accept defeat and give up our noblest ideals; or we cultivate an "inner revolt" that can be occasionally expressed in individual acts of rebellion by heeding the call of our own personal moral imperative. Now our task here can neither be to assess the adequacy of professor Avenarius' observations nor to evaluate the results of his "inner revolt"—e.g., jogging through the streets of Paris at night, puncturing tires in order to protest against the aesthetic devastation of cities and the destruction of the environment. Rather, we suggest that there is a third path opened up by Kögler's critical hermeneutics. Kögler would neither subscribe to the overall defeatist position of Kundera's fictive figure nor to his rather peculiar form of personal revolt, while being, like Kundera, skeptical of the comprehensive revolutionary pretentions of the classical Marxist model as well as of Jacobinian pretensions to the absolutely new (society, culture, economy, etc.). We suspect this to be owed to his training as a Frankfurt School critical social theorist, informed by his original reflections on the hermeneutic nature of dialogue and self, developed in conversation with Gadamer, Foucault, Mead, and Rorty, and of course Habermas, among others. Indeed, Kögler's critical hermeneutics teaches us that reflexive self-distanciation from our natural "lifeworld" is the precondition for a critique not only of our own individual self-conduct, but also of societal mis-developments. Consequently, it provides the starting point for a process of transformation whose aim is the "good life" for all, however it be defined, and however utopian this might sound in the current climate; and while we would be remiss to ignore the creative character of professor Avenarius's individual "solution" in his struggle against *diabolum*, Kögler's critical hermeneutics provides a much-needed *theoretical* horizon that combines analysis with hope. Indeed, as this volume bears testimony, it provides a creative, *collective* way forward by enabling us to disclose modes of non-conformist agency, both individual and collective, embedded within the complex, manifold layers of social life.

For many readers cognizant of the current challenges to democracy posed by neoliberal global capitalism, religious and far right extremism, environmental and public health crises, etc., such an undertaking may appear naïve or idealistic. But is this so because we have indeed become hopelessly cynical, or are we just disappointed by the apparent lack of moral and institutional progress in various aspects of human affairs? This volume provides neither easy consolations nor self-congratulatory platitudes to oppose such tendencies; it certainly does not offer a new "philosophy of history" which will re-affirm the inevitability of progress; rather, it provides sober but constructive observations on social ontology and its current predicament, characterized by paradoxical societal developments. Whatever the reader's ultimate judgment, we are proud of the essays collected in this book, which—all with a view to opening new horizons for social criticism—critically and productively engage with Hans-Herbert Kögler's critical hermeneutics. We express our gratitude to all the authors for their illuminating and rich contributions towards such a hermeneutic reconceptualization of social critique; and especially to Hans-Herbert Kögler for his willingness to reply to each contribution in a uniquely dialogical manner, i.e., in a way that not only addresses the particular claims of his interlocutors but also helps to indicate future directions of research.

Introduction

Ľubomír Dunaj and Kurt C.M. Mertel

In light of the multitude of contemporary global crises (political, social, environmental, etc.), the project of a critical theory of society has been struck with an urgency that has stimulated a process of self-transformation and renewal. This can be recognized on two fronts: intellectual and institutional. On the one hand, the tradition has become more pluralistic in recent years, embracing a wider range of figures and theoretical and methodological approaches—including poststructuralism, post-colonial, and gender theory, among others—thereby expanding its "canon" and the theoretical tools at its disposal. As a result, Critical Theory is gradually becoming a more inclusive and global enterprise. On the other hand, Critical Theorists have sought to enhance the institutional scope, visibility, and profile of Critical Theory within the academy worldwide.[1] These developments, in turn, indicate that Germany, the birthplace of the "Frankfurt School" tradition of Critical Theory, is no longer the epicenter of theoretical innovation, thereby opening up space for voices from the "periphery" to make a substantive contribution to mainstream debates. Nevertheless, there remains much room for progress: the necessary critical dialogue with situated forms of theory and praxis emanating from developing regions such as East and Southeast Asia, MENA, and Africa, has not yet taken place in earnest due, in part, to the lingering Eurocentric biases of some of its predominant theoretical approaches (e.g., the Kantian and Marxist-Hegelian models). The project of "globalizing" Critical Theory, therefore, remains in its incipient phase.

Against this background, cutting-edge research in Critical Theory must be in touch with and be capable of doing justice to the abovementioned "de-colonizing" or "globalizing" trends if it is to make an effective intervention in the diagnosis and critique of the social dynamics of an increasingly globalized and multi-polar world. In this regard, the theoretical approach of Hans-Herbert Kögler, viz. *critical hermeneutics*, provides a particularly fruitful foundation for a multi-disciplinary, cosmopolitan emancipatory enterprise capable of satisfying the aforementioned desiderata. Trained in the Frankfurt School tradition under the supervision of Jürgen Habermas, Kögler articulated a novel conception of Critical Theory in his much-cited *The Power of Dialogue: Critical Hermeneutics after Gadamer and Foucault*. Indeed, since the publication of the English version in 1996, critical hermeneutics has inspired scholars the world over from a variety of disciplines and theoretical approaches.[2]

While the contemporary landscape in Critical Theory is, within the appropriate post-linguistic turn and postmetaphysical setting, largely divided between Kantian, Marxist-Hegelian, and Foucauldian-Nietzschean approaches, critical hermeneutics cannot be easily subsumed under these general categories. Its distinctiveness, in a nutshell, consists in its novel re-appropriation and fusion of philosophical hermeneutics and Foucauldian genealogy, while preserving the basic insights of the so-called "communicative turn" in Critical Theory initiated by Habermas. The core concept of a dialogical understanding, which captures the insights of the linguistic turn in philosophy, is transformed beyond the idea of an "event of tradition" (Gadamer) or a validity-oriented communicative action (Habermas) to encompass our essentially reflexive attitude toward others and being in general. The reconstruction of our background understanding as encompassing a subjective self-relation, a distinct symbolic pre-understanding, and a social structuration through power relations fuses hermeneutics with poststructuralist insights to create the first systematic "critical hermeneutics" since Paul Ricoeur's early pioneering thought. An essential aspect of critical hermeneutics is thus its account of the defining feature of selfhood, viz. reflexivity, as socially situated, embodied, and linguistically articulated, permeated by power, but yet critical and creative. This, in turn, not only opens the path for a fruitful inter-disciplinary approach, but most importantly makes cross-cultural dialogue with *concrete cultural traditions* as essential to the project of Critical Theory. Hence, retaining the inter-disciplinary and empirically informed character of the Frankfurt School tradition, critical hermeneutics expands the field of Critical Theory's "learning process" by initiating an essential and unavoidable dialogue with the rich field of cultural studies. In this vein, Kögler developed the normative implications of this approach toward an "ethos of dialogue," further grounded the critical reflexivity of interpretation into an account of socially acquired cognitive capabilities as grounds for a culturally grounded cosmopolitan self-consciousness, and reconstructed the hermeneutic concept of symbolic world-disclosure as the source for a truly non-ethnocentric and global conception of intercultural dialogue. In sum, in light of the aforementioned need to globalize Critical Theory by challenging its lingering Eurocentric biases, the relevance and fruitfulness of critical hermeneutics has never been greater.

As such, the aim of our collected volume, *Hans-Herbert Kögler's Critical Hermeneutics*, is precisely to capture the continued dynamism of critical hermeneutics by assembling an interdisciplinary group of leading theorists from various parts of the world. This volume provides the first comprehensive, cutting-edge engagement with the work of Hans-Herbert Kögler and his distinctive approach to critical theory. The contributors to the volume, representing a variety of disciplinary backgrounds and geographical contexts, enrich and expand the methodological, theoretical, and applicative scope of critical hermeneutics by addressing some of the most complex and pressing problems of contemporary global society. Hence, the book makes a distinctive contribution to the ongoing task of advancing the project of a critical theory of society by "globalizing" it, i.e., by opening it up to an inter-disciplinary and cultural learning process. The volume is organized along three thematic axes:

- critical hermeneutics as social theory;
- recognition, cosmopolitanism, religion;
- toward a critical hermeneutics of the present.

Part I: Critical Hermeneutics as Social Theory

The chapters in Part I reflect different disciplinary perspectives (Philosophy, Sociology, and Cultural Studies), and jointly contribute to the enrichment of critical hermeneutics through rigorous, systematic reflection on its core methodological commitments. Simon Susen's opening contribution provides an illuminating, comprehensive reconstruction of Kögler's critical hermeneutics as an autonomous paradigm within critical theory, highlighting both the advantages it offers and the challenges it faces in the diagnosis and critique of social misdevelopments. Rainer Winter's chapter draws inspiration from the Foucauldian dimension of Kögler's thought—particularly the hermeneutics of power and resistance—to argue for the importance of the notion of "obstinacy" for contemporary political thought, while equally pressing the importance of the body as a locus of critique. Finally, Stephen Turner's original contribution lies in its skillful juxtaposition of the basic premises of critical hermeneutics—regarding agency, empathy, dialogue, recognition, etc.—with some core insights and commitments of contemporary cognitive science, which makes plausible an alternative, naturalist grounding for critical hermeneutics.

Part II: Recognition, Cosmopolitanism, Religion

The chapters in Part II focus on re-evaluating and renewing some of the classic conceptual tools of Critical Theory from the perspective of critical hermeneutics, e.g., cosmopolitanism, intersubjectivity, empathy, recognition, and dialogue. In particular, they explore the nexus between intersubjectivity, understanding, empathy, and morality in a variety of contexts (political, educational, religious, etc.). Karsten Stueber's chapter breaks important ground in rethinking the relationship between naturalism and critical theory, particularly the naturalist foundations of the moral stance, through an appeal to Adam Smith's notion of empathy and Kant's *sensus communis*. Werner Delanoy's insightful chapter shows the way in which the notions of dialogue, drawn from critical hermeneutics, and cosmopolitanism can serve as pillars for a novel approach to foreign language education that makes it more suitable for an increasingly globalized modern world. Continuing the focus on dialogue, but moving from pedagogy to the public sphere, Paul Healy makes an important contribution to the contemporary debate on religion and politics by defending a hermeneutically informed model of dialogue that better captures the pre-conditions for mutual learning than its rivals (e.g., Habermas' postmetaphysical model). Finally, moving from the dialogue between religion in the public sphere to dialogue between religions, John Maraldo expands and enriches the notions of inter-religious hermeneutics and dialogue by moving beyond the relation to religious texts—taken as paradigmatic by Gadamer, Heidegger, and Ricoeur—and embracing inter-monastic dialogue and praxis.

Part III: Toward a Critical Hermeneutics of the Present

The chapters in Part III further contribute to the enrichment of the project of critical hermeneutics by introducing an essential *Zeitdiagnostische* dimension, as well as a variety of methodological and theoretical innovations. Hence, they show how critical hermeneutics can be fruitfully employed to address such pressing contemporary problems such as racism, right-wing populism, authoritarianism, and the Anthropocene. Frédéric Vandenberghe's chapter carefully reconstructs a reflexive approach to sociology informed by Kögler's moral and political philosophy in a way that makes it amenable to a critique of contemporary social and political problems, while overcoming the opposition between cultural and philosophical anthropology toward a more "humanist" critical hermeneutics. William Outhwaite's chapter deftly explores a deep problem that confronts critical hermeneutics today, viz. the prevalence of increasingly reflexive forms of anti-democratic politics that serve to polarize rather than contribute to collaborative solutions to social problems. Lauren Barthold takes a bold step toward the renewal of critical hermeneutics by challenging Kögler's approach and placing it in critical dialogue with contemporary enactivist approaches to the philosophy of mind, which ultimately leads to the reconstruction of the notion of dialogue in the direction of play/playfulness, as opposed to empathy. Gressgård's chapter demonstrates the continued relevance of critical hermeneutics by showing how it can help us to think beyond political polarization toward a diagnosis of a deeper problem of contemporary politics, viz. a reified "universal world" predicated upon racialized "death politics." Finally, in a genuine dialogical spirit, Kögler provides a careful reconstruction the core concerns of his interlocutors and meticulously crafted responses that will no doubt further current debates in critical theory far beyond the confines of this volume.

Notes

1 Perhaps the most striking example of such efforts is the multi-million research grant recently awarded to philosophers at UC Berkeley and Northwestern by the prestigious Mellon Foundation to establish the *International Consortium of Critical Theory Programs*. Its mandate is to promote cooperation between Critical Theory programs worldwide, particularly in the Global South, and the general profile of Critical Theory, as manifested by the recent establishment of the journal, *Critical Times: Interventions in Global Critical Theory*.
2 Kögler has since further developed and explicated his approach and its diverse facets in four authored or co-edited books and more than eighty journal articles and book chapters. For further details, see https://hansherbertkoegler.domains.unf.edu.

Part One

Critical Hermeneutics as Social Theory

1

The Case for a Critical Hermeneutics

From the Understanding of Power to the Power of Understanding

Simon Susen

Introduction

The main purpose of this chapter is to examine the case for a critical hermeneutics. To this end, the analysis draws on the work of the contemporary social philosopher Hans-Herbert Kögler[1]—arguably, one of the most influential representatives of critical hermeneutics in the late twentieth and early twenty-first centuries. The chapter is divided into four parts:

The first part focuses on Kögler's engagement with Pierre Bourdieu's plea for an *epistemological break*, suggesting that it obliges us not only to rethink the role of the paradigms of understanding and explanation in the humanities and social sciences, but also to re-examine the concept of power, especially if determinist and fatalist accounts of social life are to be rejected. The second part centers on Kögler's *hermeneutics of power*. It maintains that the exercise of power involves varying degrees of relationality, agency, mediacy, efficacy, and experientiality. Building on this assumption, it will become clear why the critical study of power cannot be dissociated from a sustained concern with domination and resistance. This insight, which lies at the core of Kögler's critical hermeneutics, paves the way for a shift in perspective from "the understanding of power" to "the power of understanding." The third part explores the idea of *critical theory as critical hermeneutics*, positing that every hermeneutically constituted background comprises three key spheres: a symbolic sphere, a practical sphere, and a subjective sphere. Their socio-ontological significance can be elucidated by reference to three—hermeneutically inspired—themes: theory and agency, hermeneutic reflexivity and dialogic subjectivity, and the "me" and the "I." The fourth part offers some *critical reflections* on important issues arising from Kögler's project, notably with regard to its limitations and shortcomings.

The chapter concludes by asserting that Kögler's critical hermeneutics raises valuable epistemological and methodological questions, whose relevance is illustrated in the far-reaching challenges that the humanities and social sciences face in the twenty-first century.

I. The Epistemological Break: Between Understanding and Explanation

Drawing on the work of Bourdieu, Kögler analyzes the idea of an *epistemological break*. An epistemic rupture of the sort endorsed by Bourdieu obliges us to examine the relationship between the paradigm of understanding [*Verstehen*] and the paradigm of explanation [*Erklären*].[2] Both paradigms have had a significant impact on the development of the humanities and social sciences since the "methodological dispute" [*Methodenstreit*].[3] As Kögler emphasizes, however, Bourdieu's plea for an epistemological break also requires us to grapple with "the methodological question concerning *power*."[4] The issue with which we are confronted, then, involves the relationship between "the self-understanding of social actors"[5] and "the explanatory claims of social-scientific theory,"[6] including the degree to which *any* kind of knowledge-seeking engagement with the world is permeated by power dynamics. From a Bourdieusian perspective, critical social scientists—insofar as they are committed to adopting "a skeptical posture towards the operative self-understanding of social agents"[7]—need to undertake a "double epistemological break."[8] Let us consider the main assumptions underlying this two-step venture.

i. The First Break

The first break consists in a decisive rupture with what may be described as *phenomenological subjectivism*. The problem with this approach is that, as a sociological method, it is confined to "an explication of the familiar and unthematized knowledge of the social world."[9] Epistemic accounts based on this strategy are "phenomenological" in that they intend not to rise above the "pregiven meaning phenomena"[10] but, in a rather modest fashion, "to make this level accessible in its internal coherence."[11] The principal reason this methodological framework is firmly embedded in the paradigm of *understanding* is that, far from pursuing the goal of "a theoretical transcendence of the self-understanding"[12] obtained by those immersed in quotidian interactions, it is aimed at "an internal disclosure of the (largely unthematically familiar) semantic implications."[13] On this view, major insights can be acquired from studying everyday constructions of meaning and identifying them as the key source of world disclosure enjoyed by human beings.

Critical sociology à la Bourdieu, however, has a strong *objectivist* component in that it *questions* the validity of "the original self-understanding[s]"[14] in which ordinary agents tend to remain trapped. This radical break with common-sense perceptions, assumptions, and representations generated in people's lifeworlds reflects a shift from the paradigm of understanding to the paradigm of explanation and, correspondingly, a change in focus from the *phenomenological* level of an *interpretive* sociology to the *ontological* level of an *explanatory* sociology.

In short, we are faced with two different types of knowledge: *phenomenological* knowledge and *objectivist* knowledge.[15] The former endeavors "to make explicit the truth of *primary experience* of the social world,"[16] allowing for the creation of a sense of *familiarity* not only with one's environment but also, crucially, with the categories and presuppositions constructed and mobilized when attributing meaning to the confluence of factors shaping one's existence. The latter attempts to shed light on "the *objective relations* ... which structure practice and representations of practice"[17] and whose underlying logic, since it is not immediately obvious to the epistemically "naïve" observer, needs to be *uncovered* by the critical social scientist. Thus, in order to carry out a decisive break with the taken-for-granted and tacitly shared assumptions that have the power to "give the social world its self-evident, natural character,"[18] it is necessary to draw upon the terminological tools, epistemological insights, conceptual devices, methodological strategies, and empirical data provided by critical social science.

Pursuing this "uncovering mission,"[19] it becomes possible to engage in the process of a "distanciated construction,"[20] whereby collectively generated, implicitly shared, and intuitively mastered meanings and presuppositions are converted into an object of scrutiny. An "objectivist sociology,"[21] designed to pursue this goal, aims to *transcend* "the symbolic horizon of the participants"[22]—that is, of those who, by virtue of their everyday actions and interactions, make the production and reproduction of the social world possible in the first place. This "enlightening ambition"[23] manifests itself in a "strategy of disclosure,"[24] capable of exposing the objective conditions underlying symbolically mediated actions and experiences. On this account, common-sense perceptions, conceptions, representations, and understandings are always *potentially* common-sense misperceptions, misconceptions, misrepresentations, and misunderstandings. For their primary function is to provide social life with (effectively reassuring) degrees of stability, solidity, and predictability, rather than with (possibly disconcerting) degrees of fragility, questionability, and illegitimacy. A "structuralist argumentation"[25] draws attention to the largely "*deceptive* force of the self-understanding,"[26] relied upon by ordinary agents, and to "the *objective* regularities and structures of the agents' social world,"[27] whose underlying complexity they fail to grasp when going about their everyday lives.

ii. The Second Break

The second break consists in a decisive rupture with what may be described as *structuralist objectivism*. The problem with this approach is that, as a sociological method, it is restricted to a one-sided analysis of social structures *without* "linking them again to their correlative *praxis*."[28] The task of a genuinely reflexive sociology, however, is to offer "a *mediation* of the self-understanding of the agents with the objective conditions of symbol systems"[29]—that is, a "mediation between phenomenological and objectivist perspectives"[30] and, hence, between the *internal* point of view, formed through everyday experiences in the lifeworld, and the *external* point of view, developed on the basis of rigorous social-scientific inquiry. The intimate relationship between social structures and social practices is essential to the very possibility of human coexistence: the viability of society depends on its members' largely unconscious, and yet *active*, compliance with and reproduction of historically contingent sets of *rules*, by which normatively codified forms of life are governed.

The study of gift exchange may serve as an example, especially when contrasting Claude Lévi-Strauss's structuralist explanation with Marcel Mauss's phenomenological interpretation. In the former, the emphasis is placed on the hidden mechanisms regulating practices of reciprocity and reversibility. In the latter, the meanings attached to these processes by knowledge-generating subjects take center stage. The double epistemological rupture envisaged by Bourdieu, however, purports to take both the structural *and* the phenomenological aspects of social life into account, thereby permitting us to comprehend "the *real functioning*"[31] of the implicit principles underpinning interactional dynamics, such as gift exchanges. In order for the second epistemological break to be successful, it is vital to relate the "theoretical abstract of objectivist knowledge back to praxis-inherent thought and action"[32]—that is, the *external* knowledge about structures examined by a social-scientific observer back to the *internal* knowledge acquired through a person's self-understanding.

A genuinely comprehensive social theory, therefore, must seek to grasp "the *dialectical* relations between the objective structures to which the objectivist mode of knowledge gives access and the structured dispositions within which those structures are actualized and which tend to reproduce them."[33] *Social* agents occupy different *social* positions and acquire different *social* dispositions within different *social* fields. It is through the largely unconscious and intuitive knowledge embedded in, and mobilized by, their habitus that they are equipped with a "feel for the game"[34]—that is, with the practical capacity to decipher, to respond to, and to cope with the praxeological imperatives thrown at them, as they navigate the social world by inhabiting different sets of field-specific contexts and constellations.

Thus, the habitus serves as "the mediator between structure and praxis."[35] The habitus is a positionally determined and dispositionally constituted apparatus of perception, appreciation, and action. In other words, it makes those immersed in social life look at, attach meaning to, and interact with reality in a particular manner—and, crucially, *not* do so in another manner. It permits agents not simply to follow *rules*,[36] but, rather, to employ a range of *strategies* when positioning themselves in relation to others and mobilizing their dispositions in a way that allows them to pursue their field-contingent *interests*. Given the preponderance of social objectivity, permeating even the seemingly most autonomous forms of human subjectivity, *strategies*—far from being reducible to "the genuine product of acting subjects"[37]—are "the objectively effected result of general structures"[38] and, hence, of social constellations. These constellations are as relationally organized and spatiotemporally variable as the symbolically constituted discourses constructed to sustain them.

If, however, we buy into the logic of determinist reductionism, then we are left with a kind of "second-order sociological objectivism,"[39] which suggests that the relative autonomy and consciousness of human agents is hardly more than "the deceptively necessary semblance of a deeper, causally efficacious truth or social reality."[40] On this account, conflicts and struggles between individuals and/or social groups are strategically motivated confrontations "not of the actors themselves but of the corresponding habitus formations."[41] Indeed, such a reductive theory portrays human subjects, including their ostensibly most creative and improvisational practices, as mere epiphenomena of underlying power structures at work "behind their backs."

iii. Beyond Determinism and Fatalism

Kögler accuses Bourdieu of endorsing an explanatory position that may be described as *social determinism*.[42] According to the arguably bleak picture painted by Bourdieu's conceptual framework, human life is a permanent struggle for socially relevant—notably material, symbolic, reputational, and financial—resources. Kögler holds Bourdieu responsible for making a case for a "two-step approach"[43] that, effectively, "places itself *outside* any possible *power-critical praxis*"[44] performed by ordinary *actors*, rather than *agents*.[45] The act of "understanding" [*Verstehen*], in the sense of an epistemically valuable capacity allowing subjects to make sense of reality in a meaningful and insightful fashion, "has no role to play within the strong and theoretically *totalizing* explanatory claim of this [i.e. Bourdieu's] theory."[46]

From Kögler's point of view, Bourdieu's approach endeavors to explain "*all* thought and action as the expression of largely implicit dispositions,"[47] which are reduced to mere products of power structures, asymmetrically distributed resources, and inequitably allocated positions. Following the reductive rationale behind this "ontological model,"[48] one is led to believe that "*every* statement or action is per se the product of unconscious structures within the framework of power relations."[49] Put differently, we are faced with a theoretical account in which, owing to its totalization of power as the overriding force *determining all* social practices, it is impossible "to extract any meaning from the necessary counterconcepts to power, namely subjective freedom and reflexive awareness."[50]

It appears, then, that "the dialectic between subjective meaning and objective structures (or between understanding and explanation)"[51] is dissolved in favor of "an explanatory objectivism"[52] that tends to reduce almost every single aspect of the social world—including species-constitutive features—to an epiphenomenon of underlying power relations. By underestimating, if not denying, the epistemic significance of the interpretive, explanatory, and reflexive capacities of ordinary actors, including their various forms of understanding and self-understanding, "Bourdieu prevents the conception of power from being corrected or revised in light of *empirical-hermeneutic experiences* with another's meaning and praxis contexts."[53] It is the task of Kögler's critical hermeneutics not only to take these experiences seriously but also, in a more general sense, to unearth the foundational role they play in the construction of normatively codified forms of life.

Kögler insists, therefore, that, as an explanatory strategy, a truly critical hermeneutics must be "unfolded as *complementary* to the internal understanding of meaning,"[54] in order to do justice to "the analytical difference between self-understanding and power structure"[55] and, by implication, between the reflexive capacities of ordinary actors and the relations of inequality they experience, to a greater or lesser degree, in particular social fields. Kögler contends, however, that Bourdieu is guilty of "bracketing (via his two-step methodology) the self-understanding of the agents in such a way that the resulting account of objective structural conditions is longer amenable to dialogic mediation with symbolic orders."[56] In such a power-driven universe, determined by the constant struggle for socially relevant resources, it appears that, ultimately, every human action is motivated by "economically conceived habitus strategies."[57] Ironically, this means that Bourdieu, despite his fierce critique of rational-choice and rational-action theories, effectively subscribes to a sociological version of instrumentalist economism.[58]

What appears to predominate in such a *fatalist* conception of the social is "an objectifying will to explanation,"[59] whose proponents do "not believe it necessary to engage in a potentially self-problematizing conversation with the other,"[60] even less so if its epistemic horizon is reduced to doxa and common sense.[61] The desideratum of a critical hermeneutics à la Kögler, by contrast, is committed to fostering the idea of a social science oriented towards realizing the ideal of "dialogic openness to difference"[62] and recognizing "disparate world perspectives."[63] In essence, this project aims to combine the paradigms of understanding and explanation. Such an undertaking facilitates "a hermeneutically sensitive mediation of the *interpretive* understanding of other (and thus self-contrastive) symbolic orders with an *explanatory* approach that allows one to go beyond or to get beyond the other's (and one's own) respective self-understanding."[64] The cross-fertilization of interpretive and explanatory ambitions can be achieved "*without* either methodologically or ontologically absolutizing power."[65] This is not to ignore the pivotal role that *power* plays in the material and symbolic organization of *social reality*; this is to posit, however, that the latter cannot be reduced to a mere product of the former.

iv. Towards a Hermeneutic Analysis of Power

A hermeneutic analysis of power, as proposed by Kögler, needs to accomplish the following: instead of detaching the interpreter from power relations *as if* he or she were situated *outside* the horizon of the social, it sheds light on the degree to which "power constrains and operates on *her [or his] own symbolic horizon*."[66] Such a hermeneutically informed approach, therefore, seeks "to expose the potential effects of power that operate behind the back of *one's own* preunderstanding,"[67] rather than exclusively behind the backs of the subjects it studies. Particularly fruitful in this respect are "intercultural-interpretive encounters with foreign or unfamiliar meanings,"[68] since these oblige everyone involved in generating epistemic practices—that is, both experts and laypersons, social scientists and ordinary actors, observers and participants, outsiders and insiders—to call the validity, acceptability, and applicability of hitherto taken-for-granted assumptions into question. In brief, "hermeneutic unfamiliarity"[69] can be a source of, rather than an obstacle to, epistemic insight. Far from laying claim to "any extracultural, objective, or transcendental perspective,"[70] this critical framework aims to embrace "the natural unfamiliarity of unfamiliar naturalness for a hermeneutically sensitive, explanatory approach to power relations."[71]

Based on the previous reflections, Kögler spells out that a hermeneutic conception of power draws attention to three pitfalls:

1. The concept of power should not be employed as "a *totalizing* category."[72] It would be erroneous—as, according to Kögler, is the case in Bourdieu's "one-sided ontological framework"[73]—to conceive of *every* social practice "as the operation of power or as an outlet for strategic relations."[74] The fact that all social practices, structures, and constellations are *power-laden* does not mean that all of them are also *power-driven*.[75]

2. The concept of power should not be used as "a *transcendental* category."[76] It would be misleading to assume that every form of understanding or self-understanding is explicable by reference to a monolithic architecture, the ontological basis (and ubiquitous feature) of which is "power." Granted, *power*—as an underlying force—may be present "within one's own *preunderstanding*,"[77] even when the symbolic resources of the latter are mobilized in order to make sense of the social impact of the former. According to Kögler, however, a comprehensive theory of power must proceed, at once, inductively and deductively:

> ... the category of power must be *specific* enough to discriminate power practices from social practices, while still *general* enough to grasp the particularities and structures of various power contexts.[78]

In short, power has *universal* features that manifest themselves in *particular* ways within relationally constituted, and hence spatiotemporally contingent, contexts. Given its typological elasticity and constitutive malleability, the "universality" of power, which pervades distinct sets of socio-historical constellations, is only *quasi*-transcendental.

3. The concept of power should not be referred to as a *determinist* category—that is, it should not be "*directly determined* as the counterconcept to truth."[79] If one makes the mistake of portraying power as "a negative category of verification,"[80] then one runs the risk of pretending that "one's own symbolic order"[81] could be "made immune to criticism."[82] In *real* life, "power" and "truth" presuppose and permeate, rather than contradict, one another. This does not mean that one determines [*bestimmt*] the other; it means, however, that they condition [*bedingen*] one another. Just as different language games are played in different forms of life, different systems of meaning are embedded in different regimes of power. The interplay between discourse and power is always as open as the contingency of social history itself.

The epistemic benefits derived from "hermeneutic and self-distanciating encounter[s] with unfamiliar meanings"[83] can hardly be overstated. As a methodological strategy, critical hermeneutics permits us, as knowledge-seeking entities, "to uncover constitutive power effects precisely where we were previously accustomed to seeing nothing but 'reality'"[84] as a seemingly "factual" given. This "reality," however, is tantamount to an ensemble of constantly shifting meanings, upon which we draw—and which we (re)construct—when relating to, making sense of, and acting upon the objective, normative, and/or subjective dimensions of our existence. In the next part, let us consider the main features of Kögler's hermeneutically informed analysis of power.

II. Hermeneutics of Power à la Kögler

Building on the preceding reflections, Kögler presents an outline of a hermeneutically informed analysis of power. This undertaking, which draws on key Foucauldian insights, is guided by three principal objectives: (1) to avoid any kind of "ontological reduction to power,"[85] (2) to provide a critical analysis of the "productive effects of power,"[86] and (3) to develop a framework capable of grasping "the always-particular self-understanding"[87] achieved by human subjects.

In Kögler's eyes, Michel Foucault's work is useful when pursuing the aforementioned objectives, not least because, unlike Bourdieu, he does *not* propose an effectively "totalizing 'theory of power.'"[88] Emphasizing the spatiotemporally contingent constitution of *all* social constellations, Foucauldian approaches dismiss the idea of advocating context-transcending accounts of power. In this spirit, Foucault's work offers, at best, conceptual devices and methodological tools—rather than a "theory," let alone an "ontology"—of power.[89]

Kögler concedes that in some of Foucault's writings, especially in his *earlier* works, "power" is portrayed as "the ontological basis of history, knowledge, and subjectivity."[90] We may add, however, that the context-dependent, and hence historically contingent, constitution of power *is* stressed in most of Foucault's intellectual interventions and reflected, unambiguously, in his shift from "archaeological"[91] to "genealogical"[92] studies. Especially in his *later* contributions, Foucault conceives of both knowledge and subjectivity as crucial dimensions of human experience, which are irreducible to relations, let alone systems, of power.[93] Motivated by this conviction, Kögler aims to integrate "basic Foucauldian concepts and methods into the framework of a critical hermeneutics,"[94] which—to his mind—represents a cross-fertilizing move through which "any reduction of meaning and critical subjectivity to 'power' is in fact conceptually excluded."[95] This project, in other words, takes seriously the species-constitutive features of "hermeneutic experience"[96] and, by doing so, prevents us from falling into the trap of realizing a "hypostatization of power,"[97] which is equivalent to a crude form of socio-ontological reductionism. The central assumptions that undergird this hermeneutic perspective will be examined in the following sections.

i. Power

According to Kögler, power is *neither* "the exclusive ontological substrate of social relations"[98] *nor* "the metaphysical ground of every symbolic or social meaning, every action or possible knowledge."[99] If this is true, then it is not possible to infer the constitution of particular social orders, including the material and symbolic elements that sustain them, from a foundational type of power, which imposes itself, in a monolithic manner, on every single aspect of human reality. Kögler does not deny that our practices are bound up with power as much as power is bound up with our practices. Still, the omnipresence of power does not prove its omnipotence.

As stressed by Kögler's critical hermeneutics, "world and power principally disclose themselves to us through a multistranded interpretive framework."[100] While the symbolic realm is inevitably infused with power relations, it is not necessarily determined by them. Since every form of understanding is situated in a hermeneutically constituted horizon of preunderstandings, the former cannot escape the overt or hidden power dynamics shaping the treasure of semantic resources provided by the latter. To the extent that "[u]nderstanding cannot be assured a preunderstanding that has always already evaded structures of domination,"[101] it is vital to uncover "the nonconscious strains of power"[102] permeating *any* kind of symbolically mediated mode of attributing meaning to the world.

In line with Foucault's approach, Kögler rejects any attempts to portray power as a "localizable"[103] force that can be "possessed"[104] by particular individual or collective actors—for instance, by members of a specific social group, based on class, ethnicity, gender, age, (dis)ability, and/or any other key sociological variable.[105] From the perspective of critical hermeneutics, such an account is problematic—not only because it understates the complexity of power relations, but also because it may "make it all too easy for the critic of power to place herself in a position illusively 'outside power.'"[106]

If, however, a scholar declares to stand in firm "solidarity with the struggle of the oppressed"[107] (defined in economic, cultural, ethnic, political, sexual, generational, mental, physical, or any other socially relevant terms) or if a researcher—following the Bourdieusian spirit—seeks "to grasp power relations completely objectively through a theoretical break,"[108] then they also run the risk of failing to acknowledge, let alone to problematize, their "own entanglement in power contexts, which unavoidably permeate the largely implicit preunderstanding and the interpretations put forward"[109] when studying reality in a *seemingly* "scientific," "disinterested," and "systematic" fashion. To be clear, social-scientific accounts of particular aspects of reality may be conceptually sophisticated, methodologically rigorous, and empirically substantiated. This does not mean, however, that these accounts—including the social conditions under which they are produced—are devoid of power relations.

To a greater or lesser extent, we are all accomplices of power.[110] If all social relations are power relations and if, furthermore, we are all situated in social relations, then we are all immersed in power relations. Hence, it is imperative to stress the *relational* constitution of power. As a relationally contingent force, power cannot be reduced to a "property" or "possession,"[111] ascribed to particular individual or collective actors, let alone to an all-encompassing "fundamental principle"[112] by means which *every* social phenomenon can be explained. Instead, power should be conceived of as "a specific social relation,"[113] established between "individuals, groups, or social institutions"[114]—that is, a multilayered reality that, at the same time, "cuts across these groupings"[115] and is irreducible to one overriding element. On this view, power should be regarded "neither as direct force nor as a consensual relation,"[116] but, rather "as the indirect efficacy of actors working on the experience of other actors."[117]

According to this—hermeneutically inspired—definition, the exercise of power involves varying degrees of (1) *relationality*, (2) *agency*, (3) *mediacy*, (4) *efficacy*, and (5) *experientiality*. To be exact, the exercise of power is contingent upon the following:

1. the capacity to participate in the construction of social relations;
2. the capacity to relate to, to act upon, and to shape reality in a purposive manner;
3. the capacity to exert influence on somebody or something by virtue of context-specific means and strategies, irrespective of whether these are employed consciously or unconsciously;
4. the capacity to have a certain degree of impact on the material and/or symbolic organization of reality;

5. the capacity to affect the ways in which other subjects experience reality, including the ways in which they experience—and, crucially, do *not* experience—the ways in which power is, or is not, exercised by themselves and/or others.

In many cases, the exercise of power entails the misrecognition of power, notably by those affected, if not governed, by it.[118] The exercise of power may occur openly or covertly, consciously or unconsciously, deliberately or unwittingly. Yet, it always requires the "recognition of the other as a free subject,"[119] even when this freedom is sought to be undermined or denied. From a Foucauldian perspective, "power relations logically presuppose the freedom of the subjects,"[120] but the former—especially when they are converted into relations of domination—"tend to arrest and negate precisely this dimension of individual self-determination."[121]

Paradoxically, the more individual or collective subjects are sought to be deprived of their *freedom* by a particular exercise of *power*, the more the latter only reinforces the agential strength of the former. Freedom constitutes "a complementary and, as it were, immanent condition of power relations."[122] Just as the exercise of power depends on the actualization of freedom, the actualization of freedom hinges on the exercise of power. The "intrinsic connection between the operation of power and the realization of freedom"[123] lies at the core of human forms of life. The moment an "operative power relationship . . . is no longer capable of being made fluid by the agents"[124] involved in its production and reproduction, it is converted into a state of *domination*.[125]

ii. Power and Domination

Drawing on the previous insights, Kögler insists on the *bottom-up*, *circular*, and *reversible* constitution of power:

- Given its *bottom-up* constitution, "power comes from below."[126] Even the most abstract modes of *macro-power* exerted by the two main domains of the *system*—that is, the state and the market—are rooted in quotidian forms of *micro-power* exercised by interacting subjects in the *lifeworld*.[127] The former manifest themselves in the predominance of instrumental, strategic, and functionalist types of reason in modern society.[128] The latter emanate from the foundational role of communicative reason, enabling subjects to engage in purposive, normative, and expressive speech acts and thereby to contribute to the symbolically mediated and discursively regulated construction of sociality.[129]
- Given its *circular* constitution, "power is principally dispersed throughout, and implanted within, the social body."[130] Hence, it is not only irreducible to "the product of a localizable subject of power,"[131] but, moreover, it cannot be indefinitely retained in one particular social space or be indeterminately monopolized by one specific actor or group of actors. Just as actors circulate, so do both the power dynamics and the power structures within and through which they navigate the social world.
- Given its *reversible* constitution, power is never forever.[132] In fact, to the degree that power relations are not "causal-nomological but intersubjective-symbolic,"[133]

they are always, at least in principle, amendable and rescindable. Not even the seemingly most consolidated power relationships, including those that can be characterized as forms of domination, contain "an a priori fixed structure or causality that absolutely determines"[134] the outcome of every action taking place within their parameters. Since power structures are normative orders,[135] they are never "ontologically fixed and causally irreversible"[136] but, on the contrary, always potentially criticizable, challengeable, and changeable.

In systems of domination, every attempt is made to undermine, if not to eliminate, the dimension of reversibility, notably by "establishing a firmly united world picture that joins together 'reality' and social hierarchy,"[137] as is often the case in the construction of dominant ideologies, designed to defend and to justify the status quo in accordance with the interests of the most powerful.[138] Indeed, when "fixed and stabilizing *structures of domination*"[139] are in place in a given context, these "always already press individuals and collective subjects into a determinate pattern of thinking, acting, and perceiving,"[140] in such a way that the legitimacy of the hegemonic system of power is reinforced. The very possibility of building effective power relations presupposes the existence of subjects enjoying an actual or potential degree of freedom.[141] Paradoxically, however, in systems of domination "this potentially expandable freedom"[142] is sought to be weakened, if not eradicated.

Following the preceding reflections, we are confronted with an intricate scenario: on the one hand, "*positions* of power and domination that have crystalized into fixed *positionalities*";[143] on the other hand, "an open and fair *struggle*, a direct conflict between *competing* interest groups or individual agents."[144] This relationship is dialectical in the sense that, as a tension-laden affair, it drives social developments—irrespective of whether these are experienced as "progressive" or "regressive," "emancipatory" or "repressive," "empowering" or "disempowering." It is impossible, however, to grasp the complexity of this dialectic without taking into account the pivotal role played by normative—and, hence, symbolic—orders in the construction of social life, including systems of domination:

> Structures of domination are built into the symbolic order itself; they belong structurally though not consciously to the world-view into which a subject qua socialization and culturalization is integrated.[145]

Thus, power relations, including those that result in forms of domination, are always already part of the symbolically constituted background horizon upon which we draw, and in which we are situated, when seeking to make sense of the objective, normative, and/or subjective dimensions of our existence. In Gadamerian terms, this means that we must "always already presuppose a linguistic world picture and linguistic competence."[146] While these may lurk in the background, they are vital to our performative capacity to inhabit symbolically mediated social roles in our lifeworld and to accomplish this in a more or less meaningful fashion.

Considering the legitimizing power of hegemonic ideologies, "the synthetic and identity-conferring power of domination . . . stems from its fusion with an implicitly authorized understanding of reality,"[147] which provides the established social order with a viable degree of legitimacy and thereby makes it "appear to correspond to the natural order"[148] of things. Hence, this "synthesizing capacity"[149] of efficient modes of domination ensures that the *social order* is effectively presented as a *natural order* by virtue of the normalizing force of a corresponding *symbolic order*, which defines the parameters underlying "the holistic character of our world-disclosure."[150]

In this context, Kögler proposes to draw an *analogy* between, on the one hand, the *sociological* distinction between "*domination structure* and *power struggle*"[151] and, on the other hand, the *linguistic* distinction between "*langue* and *parole*."[152] Just as "every power struggle and every open strategy are already engaged in a field of pregiven relations of domination,"[153] "every actualization of language during speech already presupposes a system of rules and structures."[154] In other words, inasmuch as the performative aspects of power-laden practices cannot be dissociated from the structural constellations underlying social domination, the executive dimensions of symbolically mediated utterances cannot be divorced from the grammatical conventions underpinning linguistic interaction. Both cases illustrate that the pursuit of human agency is, at once, made possible and constrained by degrees of structural determinacy.

Owing to the confluence of structure and agency in every aspect of human sociality, there is no getting away from the dialectic of reproduction and transformation in the daily construction of reality. Put in Foucauldian terms, "technologies of normalization and habitualization ... stand over against strategies of open conflict."[155] It is the task of critical social scientists to uncover the mechanisms that make subjects not only comply with behavioral, ideological, and institutional patterns of domination, but also contribute, in a productive fashion, to their efficacy by equipping them, on the basis of their symbolically mediated actions and interactions, with sustainable degrees of legitimacy.

Kögler reminds us, however, that, due to our hermeneutic resources, we are able not only to confirm but also to challenge the legitimacy of hegemonic practices, ideologies, and institutions. Because we possess the purposive potential of *Verstand*, the normative potential of *Vernunft*, and the evaluative potential of *Urteilskraft*, we have the capacity to create "*a space for reflection and action over against established interpretations and structures of domination*."[156] Owing to this capacity, the overt latency of emancipation inhabits the most consolidated systems of domination.

iii. Power, Domination, and Resistance

The concept of *resistance* captures the notion that actors have the capacity not only to contest established mechanisms of power and domination but also to engage in practices oriented towards subverting them. In every stratified form of social organization, "domination-reproducing power practices and the freedom struggles opposed to such practices"[157] reflect the dialectic of domination and emancipation. The fact that "the possibility of overthrow and the 'danger' of dissolution is built into even the most rigid of domination mechanisms"[158] indicates that social relations, including their seemingly most solidified variants, are never forever. Indeed, "no ever-so-perfect habitualization of subjects or installation of surveillance techniques is capable of saving a domination formation from its own potential transcendence."[159] The transcendence of immanence reveals the immanence of transcendence. The most powerful system of domination cannot annihilate this tension-laden potential, which is built into every human form of life.

Just as it is vital to recognize the *fragility* inherent in each set of social arrangements,[160] however, it is important to face up to the integrationist force of complex, rather than simple, modes of domination.[161] It is no accident that "power technologies aim at a transformation of individuals in such a way as to disarm their power-endangering potential for resistance and, at the same time, productively to redirect their psychical-organic energies to the benefit of the system."[162] Following this integrationist logic of co-optation, it becomes possible to instrumentalize resources of critique and resistance[163] in order to infuse systems of domination with more, rather than less, legitimacy.

Faced with the challenge of domination in its multiple variations, critical hermeneutics sets itself the ambitious task of helping "to break the spell of power-laden forms of identity, thereby opening up possibilities for reflexive self-determination and self-empowerment"[164] and, hence, reason-guided emancipation. This process permits subjects to break out of the straitjacket of social domination only to the degree that they are protagonists of their own destiny: the potential transformation of effectively disempowering identities "has to be left to the subjects themselves."[165] Their "reflexive identity,"[166] understood in the spirit of critical hermeneutics, "can never be fixed or determined but remains an open and ongoing process of self-construction."[167] A person's identity is not only in a constant state of flux but also a realm of contestation.[168] Just as it is open to change, it is open to questioning—not only "from the outside" by others, but also "from the inside" by the identity's carrier searching for meaning.

Self-fulfilment depends on one's capacity to challenge both the parameters and the contents of normalization that dominate in a given field *if* one's sense of self is at odds with the expectations dictated by the dominant forces of one's social environment.

> The struggle for one's own identity, for the recognition of oneself and for the closely linked possibilities of social self-realization, is thus a struggle against imposed, often deeply internalized symbolic typifications as well as against their material power basis. Resistance and critique set themselves against the use of individual- and group-ontologizing labels within the symbolic-practical economy of a culture or epoch. At the same time, however, the goal is to unfold a positive picture of one's own identity, which would free itself of the earlier, domination-laden connotations. Paradoxically enough, the struggle against individualizing classification is at the same time a struggle for the free recognition of one's individuality or cultural identity.[169]

In brief, if and when one's sense of self is, to a large extent, controlled by hegemonic modes of behavioral, ideological, and/or institutional functioning, it is through the disarticulation, and successive rearticulation, of one's identity that it becomes possible for somebody to regain a potentially empowering degree of autonomy.

iv. From the Understanding of Power to the Power of Understanding

While different structures of domination permeate different social relations, individuals are converted into corresponding subjects through "micropractices of power."[170] The most far-reaching macrophysics of power is inconceivable without a microphysics of power,[171] because all societal mechanisms of systemic steering (engineered "from above") are embedded in everyday processes of action and interaction in the lifeworld (performed "from below"). Kögler conceives of "[s]ocial power struggles"[172] as "an expression of that struggle against imposed patterns of thought, perception, and behavior that aims at a coercion-free and conscious self-realization"[173] pursued by autonomy-seeking subjects. This means that, according to his account, social struggles have a teleological outlook: resistance to social mechanisms designed to perpetuate relations of power and domination are "teleologically guided by the will to attain a good life"[174] and, by implication, by the ambition to transform the historical conditions leading to the emergence of a bad life.[175] For Kögler, this task involves taking on the challenge of emancipating oneself from the arbitrary authority of exogenously imposed identities and, instead, developing a sense of personal autonomy.

To the extent that "*[p]ower prevents human existence from corresponding to its own self-understanding*,"[176] it is, ultimately, a repressive force obstructing subjects to realize their purposive, co-operative, creative, and projective potential. Insofar as one's own cognitive and emotional universe is colonized by systemic imperatives of power and domination, however, "a certain break with the immediate self-understanding of the agents is necessary."[177] A rupture of this kind may be accomplished "through the hermeneutic experience of other epochs and foreign cultures."[178] By stepping outside one's own—socio-culturally specific—horizon, it becomes possible to question the validity of the taken-for-granted assumptions of one's own hermeneutic circle, which serves as an epistemic comfort zone.

Doxa—defined as taken-for-grantedness based on common sense[179]—can be "de-doxified" when those subscribing to it are exposed to the unexpected, unacquainted, and unfamiliar. By looking at the world through a largely or entirely unknown worldview, "the specificity and [presumed] coherence of one's own symbolic order can ... contrastively appear in a hitherto unfamiliar light."[180] One may not be aware of the existence, let alone the idiosyncrasy and contingency, of the symbolic order upon which one commonly relies when relating to, attributing meaning to, and acting upon the world in one's everyday life.

"This defamiliarizing effect [*Verfremdungseffekt*] with respect to symbolic world-disclosure makes possible a distanciation from the naïve and customary perspective of the speaker or actor."[181] It permits subjects to distance themselves from themselves by approaching, and putting themselves in the shoes of, others. Far from being reducible to a "socio-epistemic vacation," however, such a defamiliarizing endeavor involves "hard work," in the sense that it requires us to project ourselves into another—largely or entirely unfamiliar—horizon *without* imposing our own standards—as the ultimate yardstick by which to measure the objective, normative, and/or subjective validity of truth claims, rightness claims, and/or sincerity claims—upon another sociocultural setting.

Kögler introduces the idea of a *"quasi-functionalist perspective."*[182] This approach ensures that functional imperatives—such as systematic stability and efficiency— "always remain subject to the self-understanding of the agents"[183] engaged in their praxeological and institutional reproduction. At the same time, this critical method "starts from the experiential suffering of the subject,"[184] permitting the social scientist "to determine what, as power, structurally inhibits good living"[185] and, thus, prevents human beings from realizing their emancipatory potential.[186] In light of this deliberate emphasis on *"their* suffering"[187]—that is, the suffering as it is *experienced* by ordinary people in their everyday lives—the social analyst is encouraged *not* to focus primarily, let alone exclusively, on "power in itself."[188] Hence, instead of using the concept of power as a sociological category defined "from above," here its meaning is assembled "from below," by drawing on people's quotidian experiences.

In this sense, Kögler's critical hermeneutics is characterized by a strong *antiuniversalist* spirit: the "uniquely *hermeneutic* feature of [its] kind of power analysis is that no universal principle is introduced over against all contexts as the other of power."[189] Building on the experiences of socio-historically situated subjects, it conceives of "the concrete life projections of historical and cultural contexts ... as the specific antipodes of always-particular power practices and power constellations."[190] Kögler attempts to erect a hermeneutic bastion of hope and resistance by insisting on the pivotal role played not only by *historicity* but also by *individuality* in the construction of human realities:

> ... standing over against power ontologically is *human individuality*, which can never be completely integrated into symbolic frameworks of disclosure or practical rule systems. Rather, *the "essence" of individuality* consists precisely in *projecting itself anew*; in *developing innovative and different ideas about self, world, and society*; in *opposing the prevailing interpretations and practices*.[191]

In brief, one's sense of individuality—understood, literally, as the *indivisible* aggregate of one's idiosyncrasies—represents the crucial hermeneutic reference point when exploring the purposive, co-operative, creative, and projective capacities of the human subject.

Yet, the metaphysical notion of "the abstract and pure individual is just as empty and 'transcendental' in the bad sense as the concept of total or absolute power."[192] In order to avoid endorsing the misleading idea of a socially detached, entirely autonomous, and spatiotemporally free-floating subject, we need to recognize that "both power and individuality are ... always situated in symbolic orders, within which the antagonism between complete conformity to a system and individual self-realization is capable of first being ignited."[193] In other words, *social orders* are *normative orders* whose hermeneutic constitution is illustrated in the construction of *symbolic orders*, marked by the tension between the imposition of systemic heteronomy and the pursuit of experiential autonomy.

III. Critical Theory as Critical Hermeneutics

Kögler's proposal to conceive of his critical theory as a critical hermeneutics is an ambitious endeavor. Underlying this project is the supposition that "every interpretive act is made possible by a largely implicit preunderstanding."[194] This preunderstanding comprises three key spheres, which allow for the emergence of a hermeneutic *background*:

1. a *symbolic* sphere, which consists of an ensemble of beliefs, principles, and assumptions;
2. a *practical* sphere, which consists of acquired habits, conventions, and practices;
3. a *subjective* sphere, which consists of an accumulation of biographical events, personal experiences, and life stories.[195]

This three-dimensional conception of hermeneutic backgrounds permits us to grasp not only how power relations influence systems of understanding, but also how both the former and the latter can be called into question by virtue of critical forms of interpretation. More specifically, Kögler makes a case for a critical hermeneutics based on the concept of "*reflexivity-in-interpretation*,"[196] by means of which individuals can distance themselves from "the taken-for-granted background of symbolic assumptions and social practices."[197] It is through "the critical practice of *self-distanciation*"[198] that it becomes possible to cultivate a reflexive sense of self-understanding, enabling not only researchers and experts but also laypersons to obtain "an enlightened insight into usually hidden linkages between symbolic relations and social networks of power."[199]

Given the complexity, multiplicity, and polycentricity of social constellations, these linkages are irreducible to a merely functional relationship between an "ideological superstructure" and an "economic base."[200] It is important, however, to recognize the "double fact"[201] that (1) every symbolic act, including every interpretation, is "grounded in some particular context"[202] and (2) each of these contexts, serving as spatiotemporally variable settings of action and interaction, "may be permeated by hitherto-unrecognized power structures."[203]

In light of this "double fact,"[204] we are faced with a dilemma. On the one hand, it would be an epistemic illusion to pretend that, as knowledge-generating entities, we can occupy an "Archimedean, absolute standpoint or criterion"[205] from which to raise universally valid—and, hence, irrefutable—truth claims, rightness claims, and/or sincerity claims. On the other hand, if we accept that every assertion of epistemic validity is "necessarily situated"[206] in particular—that is, socio-historically contingent—circumstances and, by implication, "never pure, context-free, or absolute,"[207] then it is far from obvious how we can rely on the presuppositional standards that are implicitly or explicitly mobilized in a specific proposition, or set of propositions, without conceding, in a relativist fashion, that these may be normatively and/or subjectively variable and, thus, entirely arbitrary. In short, we are confronted with the tension between universalism and relativism.[208]

Kögler proposes to give "a dialogic response"[209] to this dilemma. To be precise, he seeks to "combine a contextual and pluralistic conception of meaning with a critical analysis of power"[210] by carrying out "a dialogic reconstruction of the interpretive effect of *self-distanciation*,"[211] based on a *socially reflexive* understanding of the objective, normative, and subjective aspects of one's existence by ensuring that "*the other* becomes the point of departure for critical insight into the self,"[212] including its way of relating to the world. By reconstructing "the other," notably his or her material and symbolic background, one gains access to "a critical foil from which to become, as it were, *one's own other*."[213] This intersubjectivist stance stresses the epistemic value of *perspective-taking*, especially with regard to discernments that "we could not have generated by ourselves,"[214] let alone as monological beings.

In Kögler's "dialogic model,"[215] two levels of analysis are crucial:

- At the *epistemic* level, the interpreter has to commence by identifying common concepts between him- or herself and "the other," before embarking on the more difficult exercise of differentiating the other's understandings and preunderstandings from his or her own through a dialogic process. By reconstructing basic symbolic forms, it becomes possible to relate them to the social practices in which they are embedded and which shape the subjects' world- and self-understandings. This kind of inter- and trans-subjective "hermeneutic encounter"[216] is potentially enlightening, due to its capacity to call the validity of taken-for-granted assumptions into question. For instance, a specific set of social practices, structures, and arrangements may be perceived as "empowering," "progressive," and "emancipatory" from one perspective, but as "disempowering," "retrograde," and "repressive" from another. Those subjects to whom they seem "natural," however, are invited to reflect on their justifiability, just as those to whom they appear "arbitrary" are compelled to grapple with their presumed legitimacy. The dialogic model encourages knowledge-generating subjects to engage in a dynamic process of inter- and trans-subjective *epistemic* perspective-taking, with the aim of rising above the limited horizon of their own background of intuitively accepted presuppositions.
- At the *ethical* level, "subjects are dialogically constituted as autonomous cosubjects,"[217] who, by definition, have the right to develop, to defend, and to live in accordance with "their own conceptions of self-realization."[218] Of course, these conceptions may be undermined or supported, weakened or strengthened, constrained or amplified by the social settings in which subjects are situated. The serious mistake the external interpreter must not make, however, is to impose his or her own worldview on "culturally disparate contexts,"[219] without taking into consideration "the other's concrete self-understanding and ethical vision."[220] For Kögler, this is not to posit that, as an external interpreter, one has a license to embrace a cynical, let alone fatalist, attitude "that would treat oppression in other contexts simply as a different form of life."[221] This is to contend, however, that it remains essential for the hermeneutically oriented interpreter to endorse a "contextually sensitive"[222] approach that is sociologically reflexive, in the sense that it allows for "a culturally grounded pluralism of forms of self-realization."[223] In order to pursue this "*critical-hermeneutic* objective,"[224] it is imperative to ensure that those advocating different conceptions of truth, justice, and beauty by

mobilizing divergent background assumptions enter into a *reflexive* dialogue—that is, an inter- and trans-contextual conversation in which the impact of power relations on the production, circulation, and reception of truth claims, rightness claims, and sincerity claims is exposed and problematized, rather than ignored, let alone denied.

In brief, *the interpretive practice of critical dialogue allows for enhanced degrees of self-realization and self-determination, based on epistemically and ethically motivated forms of self-reflection and self-distanciation.* It is the task of critical hermeneutics to facilitate this endeavor. When doing so, however, it "never equates truth with power,"[225] validity with legitimacy, or justifiability with authority.[226] The principal goal of "reconstructing power-laden symbolic forms is to open up subjects a more self-determined mode of life,"[227] thereby contributing to their self-realization. On this account, the Nietzschean and Foucauldian hypothesis of a "will to power"[228] is not meant to refer to "an ontological metatheorem"[229] by means of which every social practice, structure, or constellation can be deduced from one overarching vitalist force, which manifests itself in a constant struggle for asymmetrically distributed resources. Rather, in Kögler's critical hermeneutics, it reflects "the interpretive decision to methodologically side with the oppressed,"[230] the substantive decision to give a voice to the voiceless, and the normative decision to empower the disempowered.

This project is suspicious of both *socio-ontological romanticism*,[231] which portrays lifeworlds as pure realms of pristine intersubjectivity, and *socio-ontological fatalism*,[232] which suggests that power is "the real and only ground of social life."[233] Indeed, instead of "reducing the whole of the social world to the gray of everlasting and ever-renewed forms of power,"[234] Kögler's approach pursues an emancipatory path permitting subjects "to reopen a space for critical reflection within which [they] can reconceptualize their identities by seeing their taken-for-granted selves as social constructions of power,"[235] whose normative constitution they are invited to call into question and, if desired, to subvert. Such a perspective, far from downgrading human subjects to "power dupes,"[236] regards them as purposive, co-operative, creative, and projective actors[237]—capable not only of producing and reproducing power relations, but also of challenging and transforming them.

Building on the previous insights, let us explore three themes that are central to the conceptual architecture of Kögler's program: first, *the relationship between theory and agency*;[238] second, *the relationship between hermeneutic reflexivity and dialogic subjectivity*;[239] and, third, *the relationship between the "me" and the "I."*[240]

i. Between Theory and Agency

Kögler strongly rejects any kind of reductionist approach that conceives of "truth (or subjective experience) as an epiphenomenon of some more real or basic dimension."[241] In fact, one may add that reductive accounts of this sort—which are based on a combination of determinism, epiphenomenalism, and positivism—may be described as *Vulgärfunktionalismus* ("vulgar functionalism"), in the sense that they presume "a radical separation between theory and agency, between what the theorist can objectively know and what the subjects are exposed to in their situated lives,"[242] between experts and laypersons, between the educators and the still-to-be-educated, between the enlighteners and the still-to-be-enlightened.

According to extreme versions of this dichotomous view, the difference between the two perspectives can be described as follows: the former is "nonsituated," "undistorted," "objective," "nonbiased," "analytical," "rational," "enlightened," and "fact-based"; the latter is "situation-laden," "distorted," "subjective," "biased," "interpretive," "emotional," "trapped," and "deluded." On this account, it is the task of critical social science to transcend the hermeneutically constrained horizon of ordinary people, who are "symbolically imprisoned in contextual meaning frameworks"[243] (which make them misperceive, misrepresent, and misinterpret reality) and "practically constrained by objective social forces beyond their understanding and control"[244] (which make them reproduce, reinforce, and relegitimize reality).

Critical hermeneutics à la Kögler, however, "regards this razor-sharp distinction between theorist and agent as a methodological fiction,"[245] endorsing a "dialogic approach"[246] instead. This alternative strategy pursues "a discursive mediation"[247] between different epistemic levels and, above all, builds on "the self-understanding of the situated subjects themselves."[248] Thus, rather than devaluing and inferiorizing the epistemic accomplishments of ordinary actors, it not only takes them seriously but also acknowledges that their symbolically mediated practices constitute the very foundation of communicatively sustained lifeworlds.

The reconstruction of the social world—including its symbolic dimensions—must be realized "in close co-operation *with* the subjects,"[249] rather than *above*, let alone *without*, them. Just as we must discard any kind of objectivist reductionism, we must avoid its subjectivist counterpart. Indeed, the "thesis of the background"[250] is based on the supposition that "subjects think and act on the basis of a largely implicit and unreflective preunderstanding,"[251] whose constitutive elements, and whose effects on their ways of attributing meaning and relating to the world, are largely beyond their control. This does not mean, however, that their background assumptions do not serve a central socio-ontological function. On the contrary, they "preorient and implicitly guide individual subjects"[252] as "*meaningful* premises,"[253] which are "intuitively understood"[254] and enable them to make sense of their existence and environment.

To the degree that ordinary actors tend to rely on the background structure of their habitualized ways of perceiving, appreciating, and interpreting different aspects of the world, "*the outsider*"[255] takes on the role of an external figure capable of obtaining *a reflective understanding of a largely unreflective preunderstanding*. The things that may appear "evident and natural"[256] require a considerable degree of "'explanation' and reconstruction"[257] for external and uninitiated interpreters. Hence, "the outsider" finds him- or herself in an epistemologically advantageous position in that he or she can thematize and problematize "what the insider accepts without thinking."[258] What remains largely implicit, unconscious, and unrecognized to the latter is more likely to be rendered explicit, conscious, and recognized by the former. This is not the case because "outside" interpreters find themselves in an epistemically "superior" position; rather, this is the case because their "natural unfamiliarity with the other context makes it necessary to explicate assumptions hidden within this very context."[259] The result is a process of *defamiliarization*, whereby hitherto unquestioned background assumptions become an object of critical reflection.

Kögler insists, however, that the experience of *unfamiliarity* can have an epistemologically illuminating effect for both external interpreters *and* situated agents, since *both* sides can learn from each other by questioning the things they usually take for granted, irrespective of whether they do so as experts or as laypersons. In addition, he maintains that it would be erroneous to associate the paradigm of *interpretation* exclusively with the *symbolic* sphere and the paradigm of *explanation* exclusively with the *practical* sphere. We are, therefore, confronted with an epistemic "duo-scenario," based on the paradigms of interpretation and explanation: the former "requires a first-person or 'hermeneutic' approach,"[260] in order to understand [*verstehen*] and to grasp [*nachvollziehen*] the subjective, perspectival, and experiential constitution of the daily pursuit of meaning; the latter requires a second-person or "functional" approach, in order to explain [*erklären*] and to elucidate [*aufklären*] the objective, causal, and relational nature of the underlying structures shaping, if not determining, the course of social life.[261]

Still, Kögler repudiates this distinction, since—to his mind—it is founded on the simplistic assumption that, at the *symbolic* level, subjects "know what they really think and intend to do,"[262] while, at the *practical* level, the underlying causes, as well as the consequences, of their actions are embedded in structural patterns whose complexity escapes "the intuitive horizons of participants situated in social life."[263] Dislodging the conceptual architecture of this dualistic framework, Kögler is adamant that the pervasiveness of our lifeworld-specific backgrounds operate "at both the symbolic and the practical level"[264]—and, one may add, at the subjective level. Human subjects "organize their explicit thoughts as well as their action-oriented intentions on the basis of largely implicit interpretive schemes,"[265] which are part of their inner world, to which they have privileged access.

The symbolic, practical, and subjective spheres that constitute human forms of life depend on, overlap with, and permeate one another. Symbolic orders, which underpin different patterns of interpretation, are "shared within the context of established social practices"[266] and, for their reproduction, "do not require explicit thematization by the subjects,"[267] unless they are out of sync with the objective constraints of the world and/or with the subjective needs of individuals, in which case they may have to be revised and reconfigured. Interpretive schemes, which are transmitted through symbolic orders, are embedded in behavioral, ideological, and institutional modes of functioning.[268] Paradoxically, they are "at once known and unknown to the subjects":[269]

- They are *practically* "known" to them, in the sense that, through their *sens pratique*,[270] they draw on them in a largely intuitive, unconscious, and unreflective manner, when navigating different spheres of the social world.
- They are *theoretically* "unknown" to them, in the sense that they tend to take them for granted and, through their *sens théorique*,[271] problematize them only in exceptional circumstances—notably in individually or collectively experienced moments of crisis and/or in discursively motivated processes of argumentation.

Kögler's dialogic strategy, then, endeavors to combine and to cross-fertilize the world- and self-understandings of ordinary actors with those generated by reflexive researchers, who engage in the "reconstruction of hidden features"[272] shaping the symbolic, practical, and subjective spheres in which they find themselves immersed. Drawing on the distinction between "*interpreting hidden meaning structures* and *reconstructing hidden practices*,"[273] Kögler maintains that these are "inscribed in the dialectic between *interpreter/outsider* and *agent/insider*."[274] Both the symbolic and the practical levels of analysis are crucial in this respect:

1. At the *symbolic* level, it is the interpreter's task to grapple with "implicit, deep-seated ontological assumptions"[275] held by the agents under investigation. The "horizon of intelligibility"[276] formed by these assumptions provides a "ground of possibility"[277] whose main function consists in making specific sets of beliefs, principles, values, and convictions appear "rationally acceptable"[278] to those who subscribe to them, even—or, arguably, especially—if they do so unconsciously. The problem with a structuralist reading of the social is that it conceives of the symbolic sphere as "a realm sui generis,"[279] as if it were entirely detached from the subject's self-understanding, thereby reifying it into "an autonomous sphere of existence."[280] A reductive approach of this sort fails to account for the fact that the symbolic infrastructure upon which subjects draw in their everyday activities—although it operates "behind their backs"—always remains "tied to their self-understanding"[281] and, hence, contingent on their hermeneutic capacity to attribute meaning to the world.[282] Moreover, such a short-sighted view entails the risk of constructing relatively "arbitrary patterns of symbolic relations,"[283] which are projected *upon* the lifeworld by the external interpreter, rather than produced *within* the lifeworld by the agents themselves.

   If both the forms and the contents of our hermeneutic approaches depend largely, if not exclusively, on the theoretical decisions made by external interpreters, then the interpretive schemes upon which we rely in our analysis are marked by "the total arbitrariness of the 'explanatory' framework[s]"[284] imposed upon human lifeworlds from the ostensibly "objective" point of view generated by creative minds from "the outside."[285] In order for hermeneutic accounts of symbolic spheres to be empirically substantiated and dialogically constituted, they cannot be based on theoretical frameworks designed by external interpreters; rather, they "require—at least ideally—the consent of the subjects thereby interpreted."[286] In other words, they can succeed in capturing the subjects' underlying preconceptions and preconceptualizations only to the degree that "these very subjects ... recognize themselves and their self-understanding in the reconstructions."[287]

   Unlike Donald Davidson[288] and Jürgen Habermas,[289] Kögler does not posit that this reconstruction process must be oriented towards, let alone attain, "a substantive consensus,"[290] following some kind of teleological logic.[291] While it is true that shared meanings and common concepts are employed "as bridgeheads to enter into dialogue with others,"[292] the hermeneutic encounter that unfolds as a "differentiating process,"[293] based on the contrast between different epistemic horizons, renders it possible to make hitherto implicit background assumptions explicit. It is the task of the interpreter to reconstruct the taken-for-granted assumptions at work behind the agents' backs. Agents, however, need to "recognize these reconstructions as capturing the basic meaning of their explicit beliefs,"[294] in order for the interpretations provided by "the outsider" to enjoy both epistemic validity and social legitimacy in the eyes of "the insider."

2. At the *practical* level, it is important to cast light on the relationship between the critical interpreter and the situated agent. One of the main advantages of the dialogic method is that, through the "open reconstruction of symbolic orders,"[295] it avoids erecting an ethnocentric pecking order of culturally distinct forms of life, according to which some socio-ontological infrastructures, along with their ideological superstructures, are superior (and/or inferior) to others. While critical hermeneutics is, by definition, a "contextually sensitive"[296] undertaking, it conceives of practical contexts not as horizons of intelligibility but, rather, as causal realms of "influence and application."[297]

The reason for this methodological decision is that symbolically mediated intuitions "cannot serve as criteria for a correct reconstruction of the structure and impact of the practices themselves,"[298] since their hidden causes and consequences tend to escape the agents' largely implicit horizons of perception, appreciation, and interpretation. The "'derealization' of symbolic forms"[299] performed by the external interpreter can uncover the concealed "correlations between symbolic assumptions and the social practices that undermine or contradict declared and taken-for-granted purposes and meanings."[300] In this sense, it may be described as a "double hermeneutics" leading to a form of "double enlightenment": both the interpreters and the agents obtain insightful knowledge from engaging in this dialogic mode of examining the link between symbolic realms and social practices.

Once again, it is worth stressing that the "dialectic between critical interpreter and situated agent"[301] cannot be captured by "[p]urely objectifying research programs"[302]—such as positivism, structuralism, functionalism, and systems theory. The main reason for this deficiency is that they fail to take "the *phenomenon of power*"[303] seriously, since both individual and collective experiences of exclusion, marginalization, oppression, exploitation, and/or domination are, at best, underestimated by or, at worst, omitted "from their conceptual-methodological framework."[304] Granted, ordinary agents may lack the necessary conceptual and methodological devices to grasp the multilayered functioning and typological variety, let alone the agential and structural complexity, of power relations. In order to reach a comprehensive understanding of the numerous ways in which power relations operate (notably as mechanisms of exclusion, marginalization, oppression, exploitation, and/or domination), it is vital to scrutinize how they are perceived, interpreted, and experienced by the agents contributing to, or affected by, their production and reproduction.

Kögler's critical hermeneutics, then, is based on what may be described as a "dialogic dialectic," suggesting that "the theorist" and "the agent" can, and should, work hand in glove: the theorist can help the agent to obtain a better understanding of *how* power functions; at the same time, the agent can help the theorist to acquire valuable insights into the degree to which structural constraints should, or should not, count as power.[305] Hence, critical hermeneutics à la Kögler argues that the challenge of interpreting both *symbolic* and *practical* presuppositions of situated agents requires both *the theorist* and *the agent* to commit to immersing themselves in "a distanciating learning experience."[306] This devotion to mutual engagement has two major implications:

- Participation in *critical dialogue* enables agents to undertake "a self-distanciation from their taken-for-granted beliefs and convictions."[307] By the same token, it permits "the theorist to avoid introducing misplaced conceptual schemes in an analysis of the other's background."[308] By reconstructing the symbolic orders in which agents find themselves immersed, all parties involved in the intersubjective exchange go through an enlightening process of *defamiliarization*: the "dialogic cross-reconstruction"[309] results in defamiliarization on both sides, meaning that *both* ordinary agents (who are situated in communicatively sustained lifeworlds) *and* theoretically informed and methodologically equipped interpreters (who are motivated by hermeneutically guided research interests) are obliged to reflect upon, and possibly to revise and to reconceptualize, their cognitive premises.
- Due to the *genealogical correlation* between *symbolic forms*, which are hermeneutically explicable, and *social practices*, which are historically localizable, it is possible to explore the extent to which the implicit background assumptions held by agents are inextricably linked to, and permeated by, "effects and functions of structural power."[310] Crucially, however, this genealogical reconstruction can, and should, *also* be carried out in relation to the interpreter's own spatiotemporal situatedness and underlying presuppositions.

In short, critical interpretation, understood in hermeneutic terms, can be considered "a process of a *truly reciprocal elucidation* of hitherto unthematized premises of meaning and action"[311]—a process that is viable only insofar as a purposive, co-operative, creative, and projective dialogue occurs between "interpretive theorist and situated agent."[312] The two sides, therefore, are immersed in a relationship of close interdependence:

- *The theorist requires the agent* to consent to the dialogic cross-reconstruction process in a reflexive and self-confident fashion. Only with such consent can (1) the "reconstruction of the other's hidden assumptions"[313] take place with, rather than without, everyone willingly involved in this process and (2) the "reconstruction of transsubjective social forces have any critical value,"[314] in the sense that ordinary people are regarded as sovereign entities—capable not only of speech and action, but also of reflection and self-justification.
- *The agent requires the theorist* to consent to the dialogic cross-reconstruction process in a non-patronizing and non-self-aggrandizing manner. Only with such consent can (1) "the theorist's unfamiliarity with the agent's background assumptions"[315] serve as a fertile ground for valuable insight obtained from direct exposure to behavioral and cognitive modes of functioning outside their comfort zones and (2) the theorist mobilize the conceptual tools and methodological

devices necessary to shed light on the underlying structures shaping the constitution and development of power constellations.

By means of a hermeneutically inspired dialogue between the two sides, a critical engagement with one another becomes possible, allowing both of them "to avoid arbitrary or ethnocentric distortions of the other."[316] Rather than subscribing to the short-sighted view that both agents and interpreters are equipped with a clear grasp of their own practices and assumptions, we need to recognize that a sustained dialogue between differently positioned subjects, across (adjacent or distant) epistemic horizons, can be a crucial source of insight and understanding.

ii. Between Hermeneutic Reflexivity and Dialogic Subjectivity

Let us turn to examining Kögler's conception of *the relationship between hermeneutic reflexivity and dialogic subjectivity*, of which the human subject—as a critical self—is a carrier. At the heart of Kögler's notion of "interpretive dialogue"[317] lies the concept of "reflexivity."[318] Indeed, one of the main aims of his critical hermeneutics is "the creation of a reflexive distance,"[319] permitting both "agents" and "theorists" to scrutinize the behavioral, ideological, and institutional modes of functioning in which they are immersed in a largely intuitive fashion. Kögler's "model of co-operative dialogue"[320] opens up new spaces for "critical self-reflection at the level of theory and at the level of agency."[321]

This approach is *horizontal* in that it seeks to promote "dialogue between members of different cultures and communities"[322] *without* erecting an epistemological hierarchy, in which some groups are *necessarily* and *unambiguously* more (or, indeed, less) insightful than others. Kögler's account, then, rejects the idea of a vertical distribution of cognitive resources and epistemic authority, according to which theorists, researchers, and experts find themselves in the hermeneutically privileged position of being able to "see through the distortions"[323] blindly reproduced by ordinary actors, who tend to rely on doxa and common sense as they navigate the social world.

Kögler's egalitarian model acknowledges that external interpreters—regardless of whether they are observers, researchers, or theorists—are *also* socially situated agents, who are "embedded in, and influenced by, [their] own unrecognized background assumptions."[324] At the same time, socially situated agents are "observers," "researchers," and "theorists" in the indigenous sense—that is, in the sense that they constantly "watch," "examine," and "analyze" key aspects of their lifeworlds. Such an egalitarian approach aims at the "*reflexive incorporation and differentiated fusion of both perspectives in one and the same agent.*"[325] The result of this "fusion of horizons"[326] [*Horizontverschmelzung*] is a genuine form of bridge-building between seemingly distant symbolic realms in which epistemic positioning takes place:

> Whereas the agent internalizes the perspective of the interpreting other in terms of theoretically informed self-perception, the theorist herself incorporates the perspectives of the agent and relates the reconstruction of the other's symbolic-practical context to her own lived experience. Thus, although analytically and initially there are two subject positions in a "real" dialogue, the *processual teleology*

of critical interpretation attempts a *distanciating fusion* of both perspectives in one and the same subject.[327]

The idea of "reflexivity-in-interpretation,"[328] however, is not meant to result in "a total self-objectification,"[329] let alone in one's artificial abstraction or alienation from one's context. Quite the reverse, it is aimed at unearthing and problematizing particular aspects of one's background "*in contrast to which* the subject develops herself as a critical and 'distinctive' self"[330] and through which the subject can develop a sense of identity. This is the point at which the *subjective* sphere and, with it, the constitution of *subjectivity* come into play.

Let us recall that, according to Kögler, every hermeneutic background has three main components: a *symbolic* sphere, a *practical* sphere, and a *subjective* sphere.[331] Subjectivity is constituted by the confluence of symbolic orders and practical structures, illustrating how the three aforementioned spheres are inextricably interrelated. In this sense, it would be erroneous to portray the subjective sphere as "a separate dimension or 'object domain' over against the other two realms."[332] Given its intrinsic connection to the symbolic and practical spheres, the subjective sphere should not be reified or hypostatized into "a distinct 'world' in and of itself,"[333] detached from the other "worlds" of human existence.

Granted, the subjective sphere enjoys a degree of "relative autonomy"[334] with respect to its contiguous two spheres. This does not mean, however, that it can be reduced to a completely separate realm, let alone an autopoietic system. Subjective elements of experience are an irreducible component of the human condition.[335] The subjectivities emerging from individual and collective experiences result in a person's "'ontological' distinctness,"[336] which is constantly being reconfigured though her "reflexive and specific stance of distanciation"[337] towards the symbolic and practical spheres in which she finds herself immersed *through*, rather than apart from, the socio-individuating power of her subjective sphere. We cannot relate to, let alone build on, our background without constructing, and potentially reconstructing, our subjectivity.

To be clear, Kögler dismisses any "naïve conceptions of individual freedom or choice"[338] that portray human subjects as largely, if not entirely, autonomous entities, equipped with free will.[339] The whole point of his critical hermeneutics is to insist that the symbolic, practical, and subjective spheres inhabited by human beings are, to a significant degree, structured "by the taken-for-granted features of their background."[340] Their intuitively guided participation in social life is made possible by the fact that, most of the time, subjects "do *not* reflectively analyze the background"[341] upon which they draw and upon which they depend—symbolically, practically, and subjectively.

Hermeneutic reflexivity, however, involves a process of *conscious distanciation*, whereby subjects embrace the opportunity "to see themselves at a distance from hitherto taken-for-granted aspects of their shared social life,"[342] including the culturally codified standards of their lifeworlds. This means that critical hermeneutics engenders a paradoxical constellation:

- On the one hand, it objectifies subjects at the "object level"[343] in a conceptually sophisticated, methodologically rigorous, and empirically substantiated fashion.

- On the other hand, it regards subjects as capable of relating to and acting upon—as well as of describing, analyzing, interpreting, explaining, and making value judgements about—the world at the "theory or reflection level."[344]

This apparent paradox can be considered "the very lifeblood of critical-hermeneutic self-constitution"[345]—that is, of the interpretive constitution permeating the lives of all subjects capable of speech and action. The human subject, far from being definable "in itself"[346] as an entirely autonomous and autopoietic being, exists in "the shared horizon of social meanings and practices,"[347] which *it shapes* as a purposive, co-operative, creative, and projective entity and by which *it is shaped* when absorbing both the agential and the structural components of its environment.

There are two levels of selfhood that are central to the construction of the subject: first, the *situated-biographical self*; and, second, the *reflexive-distanciated self*.[348] When subjects move from the first to the second level, they are converted into "an object of analysis and thematization."[349] By doing so, they distance themselves from their "lifeworldly, situated"[350] selves; in fact, this perspectival transition permits them to see their seemingly "natural selves" as social constructions—that is, as "a 'self'-relation grounded in a social situation"[351] of which they are part and which, so to speak, is part of them. Kögler's critical hermeneutics intends to contribute to this reflective process, encouraging agents to undertake "a radical break from the immediate self-understanding of situated subjectivity,"[352] by thematizing and problematizing their place in the world.

Thus, embracing a critical-hermeneutic attitude "opens up a transgressive space of self-creation that avoids deterministic or reductionist pitfalls"[353] and, instead, does justice to the complexity of the subject by comprehending "the self as a *relation* within social networks."[354] Kögler's relationalist account conceives of the "tension between the *situated* and the *distanciated* self"[355] as a source of "transgressive power,"[356] without which the very project of critical hermeneutics would be pointless. This tension, however, should not be equated with a bipolar dynamic between two mutually exclusive forces—that is, between individual autonomy and social heteronomy. Rather, it reflects a dialectical relationship that "has to be kept open."[357]

According to Kögler, there are two major currents of thought in which the aforementioned relationship has been conceptualized in an erroneous fashion.

- In the intellectual traditions shaped by *Hegel*[358] and *Marx*,[359] this reductive move occurs in simplistic interpretations of the relationship between "being" [*Sein*] and "consciousness" [*Bewußtsein*]. Here, "the gap between reflexivity and situatedness"[360] is being "sublated" [*aufgehoben*] by the subject's alleged capacity "to make fully transparent the external background conditions of [its] own social situation."[361] This view, however, underestimates the degree to which numerous dimensions of our situatedness in a specific historical context—far from ever being "absolutely transparent"[362] and intelligible—can never be explained in a conclusive manner and, on some levels, remain beyond our grasp.

- In the intellectual traditions shaped by *the later Heidegger*[363] *and Nietzsche*,[364] this short-sighted move manifests itself in what may be described as determinist conceptions of the subject, in which there is little, if any, room for human agency.

On this account, "reflexive subjectivity is nothing but the product of the (especially unhappy) Western tradition of metaphysics."[365] Insofar as both philosophical hermeneutics and poststructuralism tend to conceive of processes and structures as underlying forces that exert their influence "behind our backs," they understate the empowering role of "critical reflexivity,"[366] which consists in its capacity to convert human beings into protagonists of their "own condition of possibility"[367] by virtue of reason-guided agency.

Kögler's project is an attempt to combine and to cross-fertilize different aspects of reflexivity, notably the pivotal role it plays in making us aware of key features of our preunderstanding and practices, including the extent to which these lie beyond our control. Instead of portraying it as a monologically present attribute, however, reflexivity needs to be understood as *"dialogically constituted,"*[368] in the sense that it is only through the intersubjective engagement with others that it can be acquired and developed. The agent that comes into existence as a result of intersubjective encounters is not a wholly self-reliant "natural biographical self"[369] but, rather, a dialogically constituted being existing and evolving *"in a relation to others within these contexts."*[370] What emerges, then, is "a radically situated mode of reflexivity,"[371] which is the product of the various "horizons that have 'clashed' in dialogue"[372] and that, by doing so, have cross-fertilized each other.

Kögler proposes to take three main steps by which critical hermeneutics succeeds in *mediating between reflexivity and situatedness*:

1. Dialogic interpretation makes it possible to fuse "the subjective-reflexive stance with the abandonment of the self to an uncontrolled process of experience."[373] The dialogic attitude, which lies at the core of critical hermeneutics and reflects its intersubjectivist spirit, fulfils the role of "a consciously adopted ethos of interpretation."[374] The interpretive process itself, however, largely "escapes the control or predictive foresight of the subject."[375] Critical hermeneutics involves the fusion of being and consciousness, in which the latter cannot entirely anticipate, let alone determine, the challenges posed by the former.
2. Subjects can engage in processes of interpretation only insofar as they draw upon "a largely implicit, prereflective background understanding."[376] When exposed to largely or entirely unfamiliar patterns of thought and behavior, however, "a process of becoming reflectively aware of hitherto hidden assumptions and practices"[377] is set off. The experience of "other" modes of cognitive and behavioral modes of functioning can trigger invaluable dynamics of "critical self-reflection,"[378] which subjects are far less likely to perform when remaining caught up in their epistemic and executive comfort zones. The context-ladenness of reflexivity makes it "always already suited for situational relevance."[379] There is no such thing as "context-free" reflexivity or "socially detached" interpretation.
3. "The self" and "the other" are inextricably linked. This is not to suggest, however, that the former can be reduced to a mere effect of the latter, let alone to an epiphenomenon of a "transsubjective force"[380]—irrespective of whether it is defined in cultural, political, ideological, linguistic, economic, or any other

socially relevant terms. The main reason the self "is 'profiled' through an encounter with the other"[381] is that it evolves through "reflexive differentiation from its background context"[382]—a complex process that is inconceivable without the self's exposure to and experience of the perspectives held by other selves. Ultimately, this illustrates that, in the human world, there is no structurality without agency. The self is not subordinated to, let alone determined by, the other. The former is equipped with the capacity to draw, and to reflect, on the dialogic experiences it shares with the latter, allowing for self-constitution by virtue of co-constitution.

iii. Between the "Me" and the "I"

As Kögler reminds us, G. H. Mead has made valuable contributions to our understanding of selfhood, notably in terms of the relationship between, on the one hand, the *social, conformative, and conservative* aspects of the self (expressed in the development of *the "me"*) and, on the other hand, the *individuative, reflexive, and creative* aspects of the self (epitomized in the construction of *the "I"*).[383] Crucially, however, Mead conceives of human society as "a universal community of reflexive selves."[384] On this view, human subjects are capable not only of taking a critical distance towards the situation in which they find themselves, but also of embracing the role of active and imaginative participants in "a radically transcontextual community of interpreters,"[385] permitting them to engage in the daily exercise of perspective-taking when encountering, and trying to solve problems, with others.[386]

Kögler is eager to stress that his own approach is "both more modest and more dialogic in scope"[387] than the one developed by Mead. In essence, his version of hermeneutics conceives of "the critical self as a concretely distanciated product of reflection still tied to its context, albeit reflectively."[388] In brief, the self is a reflective and creative, as well as context-dependent and context-laden, entity capable of distancing itself *from* itself and its environment by looking *at* itself and its environment *through* itself and its environment. In this respect, Kögler insists on the *social* constitution of the self: unlike Husserlian[389] and Sartrian[390] approaches, which tend to portray the self as the ultimate "ground and source of meaning constitution"[391] and, by doing so, hypostatize the subject as "the source of the meaning-conferring act,"[392] Kögler proposes to follow a hermeneutic path that is inspired by structuralism and, consequently, recognizes the formative influence of the background of meanings.

This background, however, is a symbolically and practically constituted "realm of meaning distinctions that *delimit*, rather than *determine*, the possible space—both objective and subjective, that is, institutionally and in one's imagination—of subjective reinterpretations."[393] Kögler's account, then, does *not* advocate *determinist structuralism*, according to which subjects are largely, if not entirely, determined by their background. Rather, it defends what may be described as *agential structuralism*, in that it acknowledges everybody's capacity to reactivate and to revitalize shared meanings and assumptions *in their own way*—that is, by *combining* the social, conformative, and conservative force of the "me" with the individuative, reflexive, and creative power of the "I."[394]

Thus, the critical self à la Kögler embodies an "ethos of interpretation"[395] that is embedded in a "dialogic attitude,"[396] enabling those who embrace it to explore "their social 'genealogical' origin."[397] This change in perspective is expressed in a paradigm shift from "differentiation in itself"[398] to "differentiation for itself":[399] the former refers to the existence of a *social self*, whose identity is shaped by its environment; the latter designates the emergence of a *reflexive self*, which "becomes aware of its origins and *thereby* becomes the possible source of new identities"[400] articulating a sense of agency inherent in the purposive, co-operative, creative, and projective potential of humanity. What comes into being, as a result, is the insight that the sustained engagement in dialogic processes is essential to constructing emancipatory forms of life, in which it is "possible to expose hidden power practices without falling into the trap of ethnocentrism"[401] or, for that matter, any other—intersectionally constituted—type of social domination, such as classism, sexism, racism, ableism, or ageism. It is this context-sensitive and power-conscious reflexivity on which Kögler's critical hermeneutics "bases both its methodological project and its ethical hope,"[402] in the pursuit of the good life and, by implication, the rejection of the social conditions that obstruct its realization.

IV. Limitations and Shortcomings

This section offers some critical reflections on important issues arising from Kögler's project, notably with regard to its limitations and shortcomings.

(i) A crucial component that is missing from Kögler's undertaking is a systematic account of our *species-constitutive features*—that is, of the elements that make us human. Arguably, among these species-constitutive facets, which are intimately interrelated, are the following: culture, language, consciousness, self-awareness, selfhood, personhood, identity, subjectivity, agency, morality, aesthetic judgement, and reason—to mention only a few.[403] Undoubtedly, Kögler's work stands in the tradition of European humanism, notably its Kantian and Habermasian variants. Thus, Kögler conceives of subjects as reason-guided creatures—capable not only of speech and action, but also of reflection and self-justification. Owing to the purposive potential of *Verstand*, the normative potential of *Vernunft*, and the evaluative potential of *Urteilskraft*, human beings have the capacity to relate to, to interpret, and to act upon the world in a reason-guided fashion.

We develop, and learn to make use of, our *Verstand*, *Vernunft*, and *Urteilskraft* by engaging in processes oriented towards *Verstehen* [understanding] through *Verständigung* [communication]. Regardless of whether we reach an understanding in the ("soft") sense of *Verständlichkeit* [intelligibility] or in the ("strong") sense of *Einverständnis* [agreement], it cannot be divorced from intersubjectively established, symbolically mediated, and linguistically constituted processes of meaning construction.[404] We relate to the world by relating to one another as meaning-searching entities.

One of the principal problems with Kögler's approach, however, is that it tends to *overstate* the role of *language and reason*, including their pivotal role in dialogic processes, and to *understate* the role of *other attributes* that are (1) *species-constitutive* in that they make us human, (2) *species-distinctive* in that they distinguish us from other creatures, and (3) *species-generative* in that they permit us to shape the conditions of our existence. If critical hermeneutics focuses almost exclusively on the socio-ontological significance of language and reason, then it fails to do justice to the complexity and convergence of the *multiple* factors that define the human condition.

(ii) As illustrated in the previous sections, Kögler's analysis of *power* is insightful in many respects. Yet, it is also problematic on several counts.

1. Just as it is simplistic to suggest that Bourdieu's oeuvre presents a "totalizing 'theory of power,'"[405] it is far from uncontroversial to contend that Foucault's studies "should be viewed as tools for deciphering social power relations, not as a 'theory' or 'ontology' of power."[406]

    Bourdieu's conception of power is far more sophisticated than Kögler is willing to concede. Given the fine-grained and nuanced nature, as well as the breadth and depth, of Bourdieu's work, it would be erroneous to reduce his multifaceted ways of conceptualizing, and problematizing, power to a rigid framework that is based on a schematic field-habitus-capital triad.[407] This is not to deny that Bourdieu's critical sociology suffers from serious shortcomings—notably objectivist and determinist, if not fatalist, tendencies.[408] This is to recognize, however, that Bourdieu himself refers to his key concepts (including "field," "habitus," and "capital") as "heuristic devices,"[409] insisting that they should *not* be misinterpreted as "theories," let alone "slogans."[410]

    In a similar vein, it is worth pointing out that Foucault's writings, even if they may not have been intended to offer a "theory" or "ontology" of power, contain substantial elements that indicate that they deliver precisely this kind of outline: a fairly *systematic* theory of power, which portrays it as a *quasi-transcendental*—and, hence, ultimately *ontological*—force at work in *all* social relations. Indeed, drawing on Foucault's analysis, the following dimensions may be regarded as intrinsic features of power in general and of the way it operates in society in particular: ubiquity, productivity, relationality, intangibility, habituality, discursivity, corporeality, polycentricity, performativity, normativity, spatiality, temporality, disciplinarity, circularity, and transcendentality.[411] One may argue over their *theoretical* significance (in terms of how power is *conceptualized*) in Foucault's writings as well as their *empirical* significance (in terms of how power is *exerted*) in society. It is hard to deny, however, that they are central to Foucault's attempt to shed light on the pivotal role that power relations play in the construction of *all* human societies.

    Social theory may be defined as "the attempt to provide a conceptually informed—and, in many cases, empirically substantiated—framework designed to (a) describe, (b) analyze, (c) interpret, (d) explain, and (e) assess the constitution, the functioning, and the development of social reality, or of particular aspects of social reality, in a more or less systematic fashion."[412] Both Bourdieu and Foucault engage in an undertaking of this sort, but this does not mean that they propose "totalizing" (in the case of the former) or "non-ontological" (in the case of the latter) theories of power.

2. Ironically, Kögler appears to overstate "the power of power"[413] when asserting, for instance, that "*every power struggle* and *every open strategy* are already engaged in a field of pregiven *relations of domination*."[414] It is, at best, an exaggeration or, at worst, a misrepresentation to affirm that *all* power struggles and *all* strategic modes of action are embedded in relations of domination. This is not to downplay the significance, let alone the omnipresence, of power relations in social life. This is to acknowledge, however, that it is erroneous to assume that *all* power relations—including the struggles and strategically motivated actions taking place within them—are relations of domination.

Such a bleak view of the human world leads to *socio-ontological fatalism*,[415] a position from which Kögler aims to distance himself when accusing scholars such as Bourdieu of endorsing determinist accounts of reality. It is ironic, to say the least, that Kögler himself contends that relations of domination are an ineluctable state of affairs in *all* contexts in which power struggles and strategic actions unfold. The distinction between "power to" and "power over" is crucial in this regard:[416]

> The former designates an entity's capacity to do something and/or to act upon the world in a particular way. In this sense, it may be described as a *productive* form of power. The latter captures an entity's capacity to exercise influence, or even control, over something or somebody in a particular way and to a specific extent. In this sense, it may be interpreted as a *coercive* form of power.[417]

"Power to" can be defined as *the capacity of A to think or to do something in accordance with A's—consciously or unconsciously pursued—interests, needs, desires, beliefs, and/or convictions*. "Power over" can be defined as "*the capacity of A to motivate B to think or do something that B would otherwise not have thought or done*."[418] Strictly speaking, "power over" is always parasitical upon "power to," since the former would be inconceivable without the latter. In a more fundamental sense, "power to" is an ontological precondition for the emergence of social order: subjects need to be able to exert a minimal amount of "power to," in order to construct, and to reconstruct, both the symbolic and the material elements of their existence. By contrast, "power over"—although it may be immensely potent in terms of its impact on the objective, normative, and subjective facets of our lives—does not represent a *sine qua non* of human existence.

To a greater or lesser extent, "subjects have to be able to influence one another, in order to shape each other's interests, needs, desires, beliefs, and/or convictions."[419] This does not mean, however, that all modes of "power to" are obvious or latent versions of "power over." We can exert "power to" without converting it into, and without it being colonized by, "power over." In brief, whereas all relations of domination are permeated by relations of power, not all relations of power are permeated by relations of domination.

(iii) We may take Kögler's hermeneutically informed account of society to another level by positing that there are five socio-ontological conditions: (1) *relationality*, (2) *reciprocity*, (3) *reconstructability*, (4) *renormalizability*, and (5) *recognizability*.[420]

1. Society can come into existence only to the extent that its members *relate* to one another. It is made up of *relational* selves, who cannot exist in complete isolation from each other. As such, it constitutes a form of being-*with*-one-another [*Miteinandersein*].
2. Society can come into existence only to the extent that its members *reciprocate* one another. It is sustained by *reciprocal* selves, who relate to each other on the basis of quotidian actions, reactions, and interactions. As such, it constitutes a form of being-*through*-one-another [*Durcheinandersein*].
3. Society can come into existence only to the extent that its members *reconstruct* one another. It is created by *reconstructable* selves, who constantly invent and reinvent themselves as well as the realities by which they are surrounded. As such, it constitutes a form of being-*beyond*-one-another [*Jenseitsvoneinandersein* or *aufhebbares Sein*].
4. Society can come into existence only to the extent that its members *renormalize* one another. It is shaped by *renormalizable* selves, who attribute meaning and value to each other's, as well as their own, actions. As such, it constitutes a form of being-*about*-one-another [*Übereinandersein*].
5. Society can come into existence only to the extent that its members *recognize* one another. It is generated by *recognizable* selves, who seek acknowledgment, acceptance, and appreciation when establishing meaningful relationships with their fellow human beings. As such, it constitutes a form of being-*within*-one-another [*Ineinandersein*].

In short, society is a realm of human interconnections brought into existence by *relational*, *reciprocal*, *reconstructable*, *renormalizable*, and *recognizable* selves. It is based on networks of *sociality*, *mutuality*, *transformability*, *signifiability*, and *identity*, which allow for the emergence of individual and collective forms of engagement oriented towards the construction of meaning-laden realities.

(iv) Kögler has a tendency to deprecate seemingly "old," "already established," and "hegemonic" dimensions of social life, while idealizing purportedly "new," "alternative," and "counterhegemonic" ones. At the same time, one may get the impression that he effectively celebrates "the cult of individuality" in a quasi-essentialist fashion. In Kögler's critical hermeneutics, these two issues are intimately related, as illustrated in the following statement:

> ...*the "essence" of individuality* consists precisely in *projecting itself anew*; in *developing innovative and different ideas about self, world, and society*; in *opposing the prevailing interpretations and practices*.[421]

This view, however, is far from unproblematic. The fact that particular sets of behavioral, ideological, and/or institutional modes of functioning are *established*, *prevalent*, and/or *hegemonic* does not necessarily make them *retrograde, repressive, exploitative, or undesirable*. And the fact that particular sets of behavioral, ideological, and/or institutional modes of functioning are *emerging, marginal, and/or counterhegemonic* does not make them necessarily *progressive, inspiring, empowering, or desirable*. The latent demonization of "the hegemonic" is no less problematic than the a priori idealization of "the counterhegemonic." Hegemonic practices and structures *may or may not* contribute to different forms of social domination, just as counterhegemonic practices and structures *may or may not* contribute to different forms of human emancipation.[422]

In a similar vein, the "essence" of someone's individuality *may or may not* consist in "projecting itself anew." Different people develop different ways of combining the social, conformative, and conservative aspects of their "me" with the individuative, reflexive, and creative aspects of their "I."[423] Indeed, the idiosyncratic interplay between their "me" and their "I" is precisely what converts a living being into a person—that is, into a meaning-seeking creature with a sense of selfhood, a unique life story, and particular personality traits.

Kögler's project is not antithetical to a more complex picture of "the 'essence' of individuality,"[424] including the role it plays in the dialectic of domination and emancipation. A truly critical theory of society, however, needs to do justice to this complexity, instead of reproducing clichés about the power of individuality in the struggle with, within, and/or against hegemonic modes of sociality.

(v) Kögler provides a powerful account of the relationship between two—*seemingly* distant, if not incompatible—sides of knowledge production, which are often portrayed in terms of epistemic binaries, such as the following: ordinary people *vs.* scientists, laypersons *vs.* experts, agents *vs.* theorists, intuitive performers *vs.* critical interpreters, participants *vs.* observers, insiders *vs.* outsiders, the still-to-be-enlightened *vs.* the enlighteners—to mention only a few. Kögler is right to draw attention to the limitations and contradictions of a binary understanding of the epistemic universe prevalent in modern societies. Furthermore, he offers a persuasive critique of "epistemological breaks" à la Bourdieu—not only with respect to their tendency to paint a simplistic picture of a socio-epistemic divide that is less clear-cut and more blurred than its advocates suggest, but also with regard to their tendency to "inferiorize" the knowledge intuitively relied upon by "ordinary people" and to "superiorize" the knowledge reflectively generated by "scientists" and "researchers." This issue has been discussed by numerous commentators—often in terms of the relationship between, on the one hand, *"common sense," "doxa," and "ordinary knowledge"* and, on the other hand, *"critique," "reflexivity," and "scientific knowledge."*[425]

What is missing from Kögler's hermeneutics, however, is a systematic inquiry into the epistemological and methodological options with which we are confronted when making sense of the distinction between *ordinary knowledge* and *scientific knowledge*. Broadly speaking, there are three main options:[426]

- *Option 1:* The former is superior to the latter, because it is based on the "genuine" (individual and/or collective) experiences made by human actors in "real life." On

this view, the former provides a degree of perspectival authenticity that the latter, due to its socially detached constitution, fails to embrace, let alone to convey.
- *Option 2:* The latter is superior to the former, because it is—at once—empirically substantiated, methodologically rigorous, epistemologically reflexive, terminologically precise, and theoretically informed. On this view, the latter guarantees a degree of epistemic certainty that the former, owing to its inevitable reliance on everyday preconceptions, fails to strive for, let alone to achieve.
- *Option 3:* Little is to be gained from constructing a rigid epistemic hierarchy between the former and the latter. Although "ordinary knowledge" and "scientific knowledge" are qualitatively different, they reflect equally legitimate types of epistemic engagement with the world. Rather than opposing "ordinary" and "scientific" ways of attributing meaning to and acting upon reality, we should seek to cross-fertilize these—arguably complementary—modes of relating to the world. As laypersons, we can navigate our everyday lives and—whether we do so consciously or unconsciously—draw on scientifically established insights. As experts, we can study objective, normative, and/or subjective aspects of the world and take ordinary people—including their conceptions, as well as their misconceptions, of reality—seriously.

In short, from an epistemological point of view, there are both advantages and disadvantages to each side of the *epistemic divide*, which—given its multilayered and intersectional constitution—may be more accurately described as an *epistemic continuum*. The seemingly distortive aspects of knowledge production—such as bias, doxa, ideology, prejudice, background, milieu, etc.—permeate both "ordinary" *and* "scientific" modes of epistemic engagement. In other words, *all* forms of knowledge production are context-laden, value-laden, meaning-laden, perspective-laden, interest-laden, power-laden, and tension-laden.[427] This is reflected in the fact that "[t]he question of whether we consider a statement right or wrong depends not only on *what* is being said, but also on *who* says it *when*, *where*, and *to whom*"[428]—and, of course, *why* and *how*. Put in sociological terms, "*objectivity* ('What?') is—inevitably—a matter of *social authority* ('Who?'), *spatiotemporal contextuality* ('Where and when?'), and *interactional relationality* ('To whom?')"[429]—as well as *causality* and/or *intentionality* ("Why?") and *modality* ("How?").

Kögler makes a strong case for the idea that a *critical dialogue* needs to be established between different agents, who are—by definition—shaped by different backgrounds, equipped with different resources, placed in different positions, and situated in different realms of the universe. Such a noble undertaking, however, must not detract from the fact that these differences *do* imply that we live in an asymmetrically organized world of unequally distributed opportunities, in which our liberating sense of agency is significantly constrained by the coercive force of structurality. Surely, Kögler's project is not incompatible with this sobering insight. As defenders of his endeavor, however, we need to remind ourselves of a crucial hermeneutic tenet: every *understanding of reality* is contingent upon a symbolically mediated and historically transmitted background allowing for the *reality of understanding*.

Summary

The main purpose of this chapter has been to examine the case for a critical hermeneutics. To this end, the previous inquiry has cast light on several aspects of the work of Hans-Herbert Kögler, who may be considered one of the most prominent advocates of critical hermeneutics in the late twentieth and early twenty-first centuries. The first part has focused on Kögler's engagement with Bourdieu's plea for an *epistemological break*, drawing attention to its implications for the paradigms of understanding and explanation as well as for the critical analysis of power relations. The second part has centered on Kögler's *hermeneutics of power*. More specifically, it has discussed the relationship between power, domination, and resistance, emphasizing the pivotal role that each of these dimensions plays in the hermeneutic pursuit of understanding. The third part has been concerned with the idea of *critical theory as critical hermeneutics*, scrutinizing the confluence of the symbolic, practical, and subjective spheres of human existence. Their socio-ontological significance has been elucidated by reference to three themes: theory and agency, hermeneutic reflexivity and dialogic subjectivity, and the "me" and the "I." The fourth part has offered some *critical reflections* on important issues arising from Kögler's project, notably with regard to its limitations and shortcomings.

Notwithstanding its flaws, Kögler's critical hermeneutics represents a strong sociophilosophical program that raises valuable epistemological and methodological questions, whose relevance is illustrated in the far-reaching challenges that the humanities and social sciences face in the twenty-first century. The matters arising from the critical engagement with Kögler's program could hardly be more topical—among these are the following: the anthropocentric thesis of species-distinctiveness and human exceptionalism; the dialectic of "power to" and "power over," "empowerment" and "disempowerment," "emancipation" and "domination"; the foundations of the social, whose species-bonding universality transcends all spatiotemporally contingent forms of culturally codified particularities; binary epistemic categorizations, such as laypersons *vs.* experts, participants *vs.* observers, and insiders *vs.* outsiders. All of these issues, which—in one form or another—have been on the philosophical agenda for centuries, are here to stay. Kögler's critical hermeneutics is a strong reminder of the fact that genuinely reflexive dialogue across epistemic horizons is not an obstacle to but, rather, a prerequisite for the emergence of emancipatory practices—that is, of practices that enable us to reach an in-depth understanding of power through the power of understanding.

Notes

1   See, for example: Kögler (1990); Kögler (1992); Kögler (1994); Kögler (1996); Kögler (1996 [1992]); Kögler (1997a); Kögler (1997b); Kögler (2000); Kögler (2003); Kögler (2004 [1994]); Kögler (2005a); Kögler (2005b); Kögler (2011); Kögler (2012); Kögler (2013); Kögler (2019); Kögler, Pechriggl, and Winter (2019a); Kögler, Pechriggl, and Winter (2019b); Kögler and Stueber (2000a); Kögler and Stueber (2000b).

2   On the distinction between the paradigm of "explanation" [*Erklären*] and the paradigm of "understanding" [*Verstehen*], see, for instance: Apel (1971); Apel (1979); Bourdieu (1993b); Delanty (1997); Delanty and Strydom (2003); Dilthey (1883); Habermas (1970); Outhwaite (1986 [1975]); Outhwaite (1987); Outhwaite (1998); Outhwaite (2000); Susen (2011a); Susen (2011d); Susen (2013d: 326); Susen (2015a: 48 and 66–7).
3   On the "methodological dispute" [*Methodenstreit*], see, for instance: Lachenmann (1995); McCarthy (2001); Neemann (1993/1994); Susen (2015a: 48 and 66–7).
4   Kögler (1996 [1992]: 215–30, italics added).
5   Ibid., 220. Cf. Celikates (2009) and Susen (2011a).
6   Kögler (1996 [1992]), 220 (quotation modified).
7   Ibid., 220 (spelling modified).
8   On this point, see ibid., 220–6. See also, for instance: Bourdieu (1980: esp. 61); Bourdieu, Chamboredon, and Passeron (1968: esp. 46). On the centrality of this point, see, for example: Boltanski, Rennes, and Susen (2014 [2010]: 175–6, 178, 179–82, 182–5, 191, and 193–4); Robbins (1998); Susen (2007: 135–7 and 262); Susen (2011c: 376); Susen (2011e: 49–51, 69, 75–6, and 82); Susen (2011a: 449–51); Susen (2012b: 689, 692, 695–8, 699–701, 710–11, and 713–15); Susen (2013c: 205–6, 223–4, and 231–2*n*22); Susen (2013d: 333–5 and 339–41); Susen (2014 [2015]: 322–3 and 340*n*30); Susen (2016b: 62–6, 73–4, 80*n*118, and 82*n*151); Susen (2016c: 198–9 and 217–18).
9   Kögler (1996 [1992]: 220).
10 Ibid., 220.
11 Ibid., 220.
12 Ibid., 220.
13 Ibid., 220.
14 Ibid., 220.
15 See Bourdieu (1977 [1972]-a: esp. 3). See also Kögler (1996 [1992]: 221).
16 Bourdieu (1977 [1972]-a: 3, italics added). See Kögler (1996 [1992]: 221).
17 Bourdieu (1977 [1972]-a: 3, italics added). See Kögler (1996 [1992]: 221).
18 Bourdieu (1977 [1972]-a: 3). See Kögler (1996 [1992]: 221).
19 On this point, see, for example: Susen (2011e: 47, 49–51, 52, 56, 60–1, 63, 65–6, 69, 73–5, 77–8, and 82); Susen (2013a: 91 and 100*n*33); Susen (2014c: 617, 681, and 749); Susen (2015a: 73, 99, and 168); Susen (2016c: 198–9); Susen (2021c).
20 Kögler (1996 [1992]: 221).
21 Ibid., 221.
22 Ibid., 221.
23 See Susen (2011e: 76 and 82).
24 Kögler (1996 [1992]: 221).
25 Ibid., 221.
26 Ibid., 221 (italics added).
27 Ibid., 221 (italics added).
28 Ibid., 221 (italics in original).
29 Ibid., 221 (italics added).
30 Ibid., 224.
31 Ibid., 222 (italics in original).
32 Ibid., 222.
33 Bourdieu (1977 [1972]-a: 3, italics in original). See Kögler (1996 [1992]: 222). On this point, see also Kontopoulos (1993: 222–8).

34 On this expression, see, for example: Edgerton and Roberts (2014: 200); Grenfell (2013: 281); Paulle, van Heerikhuizen, and Emirbayer (2011: 147 and 150).
35 Kögler (1996 [1992]: 223) and Kögler (2011). On this point, see also, for instance: Bourdieu (1971); Bourdieu (1974 [1967]); Bourdieu (1977 [1972]-b); Bourdieu (1985); Bourdieu (1986); Bourdieu (2003); Bourdieu and Wacquant (1992a). See also, for example: Susen (2007: esp. 180–92 [Section ii, Chapter 7]); Susen (2011b: 179–81); Susen (2011c: 368–71, 376, 379, 382, 384–5, 389, 392–3, 393–7, 397–400, 403, and 409); Susen (2013b); Susen (2013c: 210, 214–15, 219, 222, 226, and 229); Susen (2013d: 324–5, 327, 331–2, 340, 344, 348–9, 354, 370, and 374); Susen (2014d: 95, 103, 105, and 110n8); Susen (2014 [2015]: 319–22, 325, 328–9, and 330); Susen (2016a: esp. 39, 30, 40, 41, 46, 60, 75, 81–6, and 94); Susen (2016b: 67 and 83); Susen (2016c: 207); Susen (2017a: 135, 140, 141–2, 146, and 148n14); Susen and Turner (2011: xviii, xxiii, xxv, and xxvi).
36 See Kögler (1996 [1992]: 223).
37 Ibid., 223.
38 Ibid., 223.
39 Ibid., 224.
40 Ibid., 224.
41 Ibid., 224.
42 On the issue of social determinism, see, for example: Gautier (2001); Habermas (2004); Inglis (2013); Quiniou (1996); Susen (2007: 13, 14, 150–2, 156, 158, 206–7, 225, 227n4, 239, 250, and 309); Susen (2013c: 203–4, 207, 209, 215–18, 220–1, 223, 225–6, and 228–9); Susen (2015a: 75, 100, 104, 129, 138, 139, 140, 160, 162, 163, 164, 295n26, and 311n4); Varela (1999).
43 Kögler (1996 [1992]: 224).
44 Ibid., 225 (italics added to "outside"; "power-critical praxis" is italicized in the original).
45 On a critical note, it may be worth pointing out that Kögler appears to use the terms *"agent(s)"* and *"actor(s)"* interchangeably. Yet, these terms should be carefully distinguished: the former tends to be employed by *Bourdieu (and Bourdieusian scholars)*, whereas the latter tends to be employed by *Boltanski (and Boltanskian scholars)*, indicating a paradigm shift from *"critical sociology"* (in which subjects tend to be portrayed as "agents," who are largely determined by the interplay between "field," "habitus," and "capital") to *the "pragmatic sociology of critique"* (in which subjects tend to be conceived of as "actors," who are equipped with critical and moral capacities). On this point, see, for instance, Susen (2014 [2015]) and Susen (2015c). Cf., for instance: Boltanski, Honneth, and Celikates (2014 [2009]); Celikates (2009); Susen (2011a).
46 Kögler (1996 [1992]: 225, italics added).
47 Ibid., 225 (italics in original).
48 Ibid., 225.
49 Ibid., 225 (italics in original).
50 Ibid., 225.
51 Ibid., 225.
52 Ibid., 225.
53 Ibid., 226 (italics added).
54 Ibid., 227 (italics in original).
55 Ibid., 227.
56 Ibid., 227.

57 Ibid., 227. On this point, cf. Bourdieu (1994) and Bourdieu, Boltanski, and de Saint Martin (1973). For a Foucauldian account of the relationship between "power" and "strategies," see Foucault (1980b).
58 On this problem, see, for instance, Susen (2007: 103–4, 155, 168n21, and 209). It should be noted that Bourdieu rejects—or at least claims to reject—both *mechanistic* economism ("mechanical causes") and *finalist* economism ("conscious ends"). See Bourdieu (1990 [1980]: 50): "Finalist economism explains practices by relating them directly and exclusively to economic interests, treated as consciously posited *ends*; mechanistic economism relates them no less directly and exclusively to economic interests, defined just as narrowly but treated as *causes*. Both are unaware that practices can have other principles than mechanical causes or conscious ends and can obey an economic logic without obeying narrowly economic interests. There is an *economy of practices*, a reason immanent in practices, whose 'origin' lies neither in the 'decisions' of reason understood as rational calculation nor in the determinations of mechanisms external to and superior to the agents." (Italics added.)
59 Kögler (1996 [1992]: 227).
60 Ibid., 227.
61 On this point, see, for instance: Bourdieu (1980: 113 and 244); Bourdieu (1982a: 10 and 34); Bourdieu (1984: 6); Bourdieu (1997: 21–6, 118, 120, 123, and 206); Bourdieu (1999: 334); Bourdieu, Chamboredon, and Passeron (1968: 30, 58, and 105); Bourdieu and Eagleton (1992). See also, for example: Accardo (1997: 49); Bonnewitz (1998: 80–2); Chauviré and Fontaine (2003: 40); Hamel (2000 [1997]); Holton (2000); Myles (2004); Ostrow (2000 [1981]: 302–8); Pinto (1998: 214, 216, and 243); Susen (2007: 24, 138–41, 146n16, 153, 157, 159, 160, 178, 191, 215, 223, 224, 225, 226, 243, 251, 252, 253, 267, 309, and 312); Susen (2011e: 50, 76, and 82); Susen (2013c: 204–5, 208, 209, 218, 219, 221, 223, 225, 227, 228, and 231n18); Susen (2013d: 332, 340, 349, 341, 355, 356, 364, and 372); Susen (2016b: 53, 55–6, 61–6, and 72–3); Susen (2017a: 136–7, 145, and 149n20); Wacquant (2004).
62 Kögler (1996 [1992]: 227). Cf. Kögler (2005b) and Kögler (2012).
63 Kögler (1996 [1992], 227).
64 Ibid., 227 (italics added).
65 Ibid., 227 (italics added).
66 Ibid., 229 (italics in original).
67 Ibid., 229 (italics in original).
68 Ibid., 229.
69 Ibid., 229.
70 Ibid., 229.
71 Ibid., 229.
72 Ibid., 229 (italics in original).
73 Ibid., 229.
74 Ibid., 229.
75 On this point, see, for example: Susen (2008a); Susen (2008b); Susen (2009a); Susen (2014a); Susen (2018c).
76 Kögler (1996 [1992]: 230, italics in original).
77 Ibid., 230 (italics added).
78 Ibid., 230 (italics in original).
79 Ibid., 230 (italics in original).
80 Ibid., 230.
81 Ibid., 230.

82 Ibid., 230.
83 Ibid., 230.
84 Ibid., 230.
85 Ibid., 230.
86 Ibid., 230.
87 Ibid., 230.
88 Ibid., 231.
89 See ibid., 231. See also, for example: Foucault (1983 [1982]); Kögler (1990); Kögler (1992); Kögler (1996); Kögler (2003); Kögler (2004 [1994]). In addition, see, for instance: Foucault (2001 [1961]); Foucault (2002 [1966]); Foucault (1979 [1975]); Foucault (1978 [1976]); Foucault (1985 [1984]); Foucault (1988 [1984]); Foucault (1980a); Foucault (1988); Foucault (2005 [2001]).
90 Kögler (1996 [1992]: 231). Cf. Habermas (1987 [1985]: 266–93).
91 See Foucault (2001 [1961]) and Foucault (2002 [1966]).
92 See Foucault (1979 [1975]), Foucault (1978 [1976]), Foucault (1985 [1984]), and Foucault (1988 [1984]).
93 See Kögler (1996 [1992]: 231). Cf. Foucault (1985 [1984], esp. 3–13).
94 Kögler (1996 [1992]: 231).
95 Ibid., 231.
96 Ibid., 231. Cf. Foucault (1983 [1982]). Cf. also Foucault (1985 [1984]), esp. Introduction.
97 Kögler (1996 [1992]: 231).
98 Ibid., 232.
99 Ibid., 232.
100 Ibid., 232.
101 Ibid., 232.
102 Ibid., 232.
103 Ibid., 233.
104 Ibid., 233.
105 On this point, see, for example: Susen (2008a); Susen (2008b); Susen (2009a); Susen (2014a); Susen (2018c).
106 Kögler (1996 [1992]: 233).
107 Ibid., 233.
108 Ibid., 233.
109 Ibid., 233.
110 On this point, see, for example: Susen (2008a); Susen (2008b); Susen (2009a); Susen (2012a, esp. 297); Susen (2014a); Susen (2018c: esp. 9–10); Susen (2020a: 5, 10, 14, 15, 28, 83, 134, 139–40, 179, 294, and 308). See also, for instance: Holloway (2005 [2002]); Holloway and Susen (2013).
111 See Kögler (1996 [1992]: 233).
112 Ibid., 233.
113 Ibid., 233.
114 Ibid., 233.
115 Ibid., 233.
116 Ibid., 233.
117 Ibid., 233.
118 See ibid., 233–4.
119 Ibid., 234. Cf. Kögler (2000), Kögler (2005b), and Kögler (2012). Cf. also, for instance: Alexander and Lara (1996); Brink and Owen (2007); Baynes (2002); Fraser

and Honneth (2003); Honneth (1995 [1992]); Honneth (2002); Honneth (2012 [2010]); Susen (2007: 192–8); Susen (2015a: esp. Chapter 5).
120 Kögler (1996 [1992]: 234).
121 Ibid., 234.
122 Ibid., 234.
123 Ibid., 234.
124 Ibid., 234–5.
125 See ibid., 235.
126 Ibid., 235.
127 On Habermas's account of the relationship between "lifeworld" and "system," see, for example: Habermas (1987 [1981]-a) and Habermas (1987 [1981]-b). See also, for instance: Apel (1992); Bohman (1989); Detel (2000); Hartmann (1985); Peters (1993: 557–60); Seemann (2004); Stikkers (1985). Furthermore, see, for example: Susen (2007: 61, 70, 71–3, 239, 245, 246, and 305); Susen (2009b: 84–5, 86–7, and 105–6); Susen (2010c: 108, 113, 117, and 119n31); Susen (2011d: 51).
128 See Habermas (1987 [1981]-a) and Habermas (1987 [1981]-b).
129 See Habermas (1987 [1981]-a) and Habermas (1987 [1981]-b).
130 Kögler (1996 [1992]: 235).
131 Ibid., 235. Cf. Foucault (1978 [1976]: esp. 92–3).
132 See, for example: Susen (2008a); Susen (2008b); Susen (2009a); Susen (2014a); Susen (2018c).
133 Kögler (1996 [1992]: 235). Cf. Kögler (2000), Kögler (2005b), and Kögler (2012).
134 Kögler (1996 [1992]: 235).
135 On this point, see Forst and Günther (2011a) and Forst and Günther (2011b). See also, for instance: Forst (2002 [1994]); Forst (2012 [2007]); Forst (2013); Forst (2013 [2003]); Forst (2013 [2011]); Forst (2014); Forst (2015a); Forst (2015b); Forst (2017); Forst, Hartmann, Jaeggi, and Saar (2009).
136 Kögler (1996 [1992]: 235).
137 Ibid., 236.
138 On this point, see, for example: Boltanski (2008); Bourdieu and Boltanski (1976); Bourdieu and Boltanski (2008 [1976]); Susen (2014d); Susen (2016c).
139 Kögler (1996 [1992]: 236, italics in original).
140 Ibid., 236.
141 See ibid., 236.
142 Ibid., 236.
143 Ibid., 236 (italics added).
144 Ibid., 236 (italics added).
145 Ibid., 236–7.
146 Ibid., 237.
147 Ibid., 237.
148 Ibid., 237.
149 Ibid., 237.
150 Ibid., 237.
151 Ibid., 237 (italics added).
152 Ibid., 238 (italics in original).
153 Ibid., 238.
154 Ibid., 238.
155 Ibid., 238.
156 Ibid., 239 (italics in original).

157 Ibid., 239.
158 Ibid., 240.
159 Ibid., 240.
160 On this point, see, for instance: Boltanski, Rennes, and Susen (2010); Boltanski, Rennes, and Susen (2014 [2010]); Cordero (2017a); Cordero (2017b); Susen (2015a: 166, 178, and 317n190); Susen (2017b); Susen (2020a: 37, 152, and 275–6); Susen (2020b: 315); Susen (2021c: 27, 30, and 46).
161 On the concept of "simple domination," see, for example: Boltanski (2008: esp. 149–58); Boltanski (2009: 186–90); Boltanski (2011 [2009]: 124–6). See also, for instance: Susen (2012b: 707–10); Boltanski, Rennes, and Susen (2014 [2010]: 188–90); Susen (2014c: 652–6); Susen (2016c: 212–15); Susen (2020a: 132); Susen (2021c: 48). On the concept of "complex domination," see, for example: Boltanski (2008: esp. 149–58); Boltanski (2009: 190–3); Boltanski (2011 [2009]: 127–9). See also, for instance: Susen (2012b: 707–10); Boltanski, Rennes, and Susen (2014 [2010]: 188–90); Susen (2014c: 652–6); Susen (2016c: 212–15); Susen (2020a: 132); Susen (2021c: 48).
162 Kögler (1996 [1992]: 241).
163 Cf. Callinicos (2006). Cf. also Browne and Susen (2014).
164 Kögler (1996 [1992]: 243).
165 Ibid., 243.
166 Ibid., 243.
167 Ibid., 243. Cf. Susen (2007: 192–8).
168 Cf. Susen (2007: 54–7 and 192–8) and Susen (2015a: 110–23).
169 Kögler (1996 [1992]: 244).
170 Ibid., 244.
171 On this point, see, for example: Susen (2008a); Susen (2008b); Susen (2009a); Susen (2014a); Susen (2018c).
172 Kögler (1996 [1992]: 244).
173 Ibid., 244 (spelling modified).
174 Ibid., 244.
175 On the idea of "the good life" [*gelingendes Leben*] in contemporary critical theory, see, for instance: Rosa (1998); Rosa (2005); Rosa (2010); Rosa (2012); Rosa (2013 [2010]); Rosa (2015 [2005]); Rosa (2016); Rosa (2019 [2016]). See also Susen (2020b).
176 Kögler (1996 [1992]: 244, italics in original).
177 Ibid., 244–5.
178 Ibid., 245.
179 Cf. Susen (2007: 138, 253, and 309). Cf. also Bourdieu and Eagleton (1992).
180 Kögler (1996 [1992]: 245).
181 Ibid., 245 (quotation modified).
182 Ibid., 245 (italics in original).
183 Ibid., 245.
184 Ibid., 245.
185 Ibid., 245.
186 Cf. Susen (2015b).
187 Kögler (1996 [1992]: 246, italics in original). On this point, see also, for instance: Bernstein (2005); Boltanski (1999 [1993]); Bourdieu (1999 [1993]); Charlesworth (2000); Eyerman, Alexander, and Breese (2011); Turner (2006).
188 Kögler (1996 [1992]: 246).
189 Ibid., 246 (italics in original).

190 Ibid., 246.
191 Ibid., 246 (italics added). On this point, see also Kögler's analysis of "the forestructure of understanding" in ibid., esp. 13, 86–9, 91–5, 100, and 105.
192 Ibid., 246.
193 Ibid., 246–7. Cf. Mead (1967 [1934]). Cf. also Susen (2010d) and Susen (2016e).
194 Kögler (1996 [1992]: 251).
195 See ibid., 251.
196 Ibid., 251 and 268 (italics added). On Kögler's conception of "reflexivity," see, for instance: Kögler (1992); Kögler (1996 [1992]); Kögler (1996); Kögler (1997a); Kögler (1997b); Kögler (2000); Kögler (2019); Kögler, Pechriggl, and Winter (2019b).
197 Kögler (1996 [1992]: 252).
198 Ibid., 252 (italics added).
199 Ibid., 252.
200 For excellent discussions of the Marxist distinction between "base" and "superstructure," see, for instance: de Lara (1982); Hall (1977); Jakubowski (1990 [1976]); Labica (1982); Larrain (1991 [1983]); Weber (1995). See also, for example: Susen (2007: 22, 72, 122, 126n9, 179, 180, 191, 210, and 227n4); Susen (2008a: 62–3 and 80); Susen (2008b: 146 and 164); Susen (2010a: 166, 172, 201, and 208); Susen (2010b: 267); Susen (2011b: 189, 193, and 194); Susen (2012a: 284, 299, and 302); Susen (2013d: 340–1); Susen (2014d); Susen (2014b: 340); Susen (2015a: 90, 91, 97, 99, 100, 101, 265, 295n27, 298n31, and 300n110); Susen (2015b: 1031); Susen (2016c: 202, 211, and 222); Susen (2017b: 116); Susen (2017c: 114–15); Susen (2017e: 6 and 64); Susen (2018a: 48); Susen (2020a: 102, 111, and 254).
201 Kögler (1996 [1992]: 252).
202 Ibid., 252.
203 Ibid., 252.
204 Ibid., 252.
205 Ibid., 252.
206 Ibid., 252.
207 Ibid., 252.
208 Cf. Susen (2015a: esp. Chapter 1).
209 Kögler (1996 [1992]: 253).
210 Ibid., 252.
211 Ibid., 252 (italics in original).
212 Ibid., 252 (italics in original).
213 Ibid., 252 (italics added).
214 Ibid., 252. Cf., for instance: Boltanski, Honneth, and Celikates (2014 [2009]); Celikates (2009); Susen (2011a).
215 Kögler (1996 [1992]: 253). On Kögler's conception of "dialogue," see, for instance: Kögler (1992); Kögler (1996 [1992]); Kögler (2000); Kögler (2005b); Kögler (2012).
216 Kögler (1996 [1992]: 253).
217 Ibid., 253.
218 Ibid., 253. On this point, see also ibid., Chapter 4, Section 4.3.
219 Ibid., 253.
220 Ibid., 253.
221 Ibid., 253. Cf. Jaeggi (2014) and Jaeggi (2018 [2014]).
222 Kögler (1996 [1992]: 253).
223 Ibid., 253.
224 Ibid., 253 (italics in original).

225 Ibid., 254.
226 Cf. Susen (2017d) and Susen (2018b).
227 Kögler (1996 [1992]: 254).
228 See ibid., 255. See Nietzsche (1967 [1930]). See also Foucault (1979 [1975]), Foucault (1980a), Foucault (1988), Foucault (2005 [2001]). Cf. Saar (2007), Saar (2010), and Saar (2013). Cf. also Erdmann, Forst, and Honneth (1990).
229 Kögler (1996 [1992]: 254).
230 Ibid., 255.
231 On the problem of "socio-ontological romanticism" (as well as "socio-ontological optimism," "socio-ontological utopianism," and "socio-ontological idealism"), see, for example: Coles and Susen (2018: 256 and 259); Susen (2007: 13–14, 22, 44n47, 54–5, 90, 115, 121–5, 218, 226, 239, 240, 250, 252–3, 260–1, 268, 270n21, 305, and 308); Susen (2011c: 373); Susen (2013c: 229–30); Susen (2013d: 325, 327, 333, 335, 343, 344, 354, 359–60, 361–4, 367, 372, and 373); Susen (2014c: 619, 642, 646, 647, 675, 709, and 734); Susen (2014d: 102, 105, and 108); Susen (2014 [2015]: 331–2); Susen (2015a: 180, 204, and 225); Susen (2015c: 181–2); Susen (2016b: 74–5); Susen (2016c: 222); Susen (2020c: 148 and 149); Susen (2020b: 334); Susen (2020d: 753 and 754–5). In addition, see, for instance: Brunkhorst (1997); Habermas (1987 [1981]-d); Lemieux (2014).
232 On the problem of "socio-ontological fatalism" (as well as "socio-ontological pessimism," "socio-ontological defeatism," and "socio-ontological nihilism"), see, for example: Coles and Susen (2018: 256); Susen (2007: 14, 22, 54, 217, 221–6, 239, 253, 267–8, 277, 304, and 312); Susen (2011c: 405); Susen (2013c: 229–30); Susen (2013d: 327, 328–9, 333, 362, and 373); Susen (2014c: 635, 675, 690, 705, 732, and 735); Susen (2014d: 103–4); Susen (2014 [2015]: 316, 326–7, and 332); Susen (2015a: 129, 219, 244, and 275); Susen (2015c: 157–8, 174, and 181); Susen (2016b: 74–5); Susen (2016c: 222); Susen (2020c: 146–7 and 148); Susen (2020b: 321 and 334); Susen (2020d: 736 and 738); Susen (2021c: 32 and 45). In addition, see, for instance: Boltanski (1998) Boltanski (1999–2000); Boltanski (2002); Boltanski (2011 [2009]); Boltanski (2012 [1990]); Boltanski and Chiapello (1999: esp. 27, 29, and 633–40); Boltanski, Honneth, and Celikates (2014 [2009]); Boltanski, Rennes, and Susen (2010); Boltanski and Thévenot (1999); Boltanski and Thévenot (2000); Bourdieu (1998).
233 Kögler (1996 [1992]: 255).
234 Ibid., 255.
235 Ibid., 255.
236 Ibid., 255.
237 Cf. Susen (2007: Chapter 10).
238 See Kögler (1996 [1992]: 256–66).
239 See ibid., 266–73.
240 See ibid., 273–5.
241 Ibid., 256.
242 Ibid., 256.
243 Ibid., 256.
244 Ibid., 256.
245 Ibid., 256.
246 Ibid., 257.
247 Ibid., 257.
248 Ibid., 257.

249 Ibid., 257 (italics in original) (quotation modified).
250 Ibid., 257.
251 Ibid., 257.
252 Ibid., 257.
253 Ibid., 257 (italics in original).
254 Ibid., 257.
255 Ibid., 257 (italics in original).
256 Ibid., 257–8.
257 Ibid., 258.
258 Ibid., 258.
259 Ibid., 258.
260 Ibid., 258.
261 Cf. Habermas (1988 [1967/1970]).
262 Kögler (1996 [1992]: 258).
263 Ibid., 258. Cf. Giddens (1977).
264 Kögler (1996 [1992]: 258).
265 Ibid., 258.
266 Ibid., 259.
267 Ibid., 259.
268 Cf. Susen (2016d: esp. 460–1 [Section ii]).
269 Kögler (1996 [1992]: 259).
270 Cf. Susen (2007: 94).
271 Cf. ibid., 94.
272 Kögler (1996 [1992]: 259).
273 Ibid., 259 (italics added).
274 Ibid., 259 (italics added).
275 Ibid., 259.
276 Ibid., 259.
277 Ibid., 259.
278 Ibid., 259.
279 Ibid., 259.
280 Ibid., 259.
281 Ibid., 260.
282 Cf. Celikates (2009) and Susen (2011a).
283 Kögler (1996 [1992]: 260).
284 Ibid., 260.
285 On this point, see ibid., 260 and 312n14.
286 Ibid., 260 (quotation modified).
287 Ibid., 260 (quotation modified).
288 See, for instance, Davidson (2001 [1984]), esp. Davidson (2001 [1984/1974]).
289 See, for instance, Habermas (1987 [1981]-a) and Habermas (1987 [1981]-b).
290 Kögler (1996 [1992]: 260). On this point, see ibid., Chapter 4.
291 See Foucault (2002 [1966]) and Löwith (1953). In addition, see Susen (2015a: Chapter 4).
292 Kögler (1996 [1992]: 260–1).
293 Ibid., 261.
294 Ibid., 261 (quotation modified). See also ibid., 313n18.
295 Ibid., 261.
296 Ibid., 261.

297 Ibid., 261. Cf. Kögler (1994).
298 Kögler (1996 [1992]: 261).
299 Ibid., 261.
300 Ibid., 261.
301 Ibid., 262.
302 Ibid., 262.
303 Ibid., 262 (italics in original).
304 Ibid., 262.
305 See ibid., 262.
306 Ibid., 262.
307 Ibid., 262.
308 Ibid., 262.
309 Ibid., 262.
310 Ibid., 263.
311 Ibid., 263 (italics in original).
312 Ibid., 263.
313 Ibid., 263.
314 Ibid., 263.
315 Ibid., 263.
316 Ibid., 263.
317 Ibid., 266.
318 Ibid., 266.
319 Ibid., 266.
320 Ibid., 266–7 (quotation modified).
321 Ibid., 267.
322 Ibid., 267.
323 Ibid., 267.
324 Ibid., 267.
325 Ibid., 267 (italics in original).
326 On the concept of the "fusion of horizons" [*Horizontverschmelzung*], see, for instance: Gadamer (1989 [1975]: 306–7, 374–5, 397, and 576); Gadamer (1982 [1976/1978/1979]: 111); Gadamer (2001: 43, 48–50, 56, and 113). See also Kögler (1996 [1992]: 14, 71, 72, 128–41, 147, 148, 170, and 285*n*20). Furthermore, see, for instance: Dawson (1998 [1983]: xvi and xxiv); Delanty (2009: 253); Jain (2016: 202 and 207); Susen (2015a: 211); Taylor (2002: 134–6 and 138–42); Vessey (2009); Vitkin (1995). In addition, see, for example: Dostal (2002); Gadamer (1998 [1983]); Grondin (2002); Habermas (1971); Harrington (1999); Harrington (2000); Harrington (2001); How (1995); How (1998); How (1985); How (2007); Mendelson (1979); Michelfelder and Palmer (1989); Outhwaite (1986 [1975]); Scheibler (2000); Wachterhauser (1994); Warnke (1987); Weinsheimer (1998 [1983]).
327 Kögler (1996 [1992]: 267, italics added).
328 Ibid., 251 and 268. On Kögler's conception of "reflexivity," see, for instance: Kögler (1992); Kögler (1996 [1992]); Kögler (1996); Kögler (1997a); Kögler (1997b); Kögler (2000); Kögler (2019); Kögler, Pechriggl, and Winter (2019b).
329 Kögler (1996 [1992]: 268).
330 Ibid., 268 (italics in original).
331 See ibid., 251.
332 Ibid., 268.
333 Ibid., 268.

334 Ibid., 268. On this point, cf., for instance: Susen (2007: 188–9, 213, 244, and 285); Susen (2011b: 177–8 and 186); Susen (2011e: 59, 70, and 77); Susen (2013c: 204, 207, 213, and 220); Susen (2013d: 331 and 362); Susen (2015a: 80, 81, 88, 101, 105, 129, and 266); Susen (2016a: 41, 43, 59–60, 83, and 105); Susen (2016c: 201–3); Susen (2017a: 116 and 120); Susen (2018c: 23–4 and 27).
335 On this point, cf. Foucault (1985 [1984]), esp. Introduction. For an analysis of the implications of Kögler's three-dimensional ontology, see Kögler (1990).
336 Kögler (1996 [1992]: 268).
337 Ibid., 268.
338 Ibid., 269 (spelling modified).
339 Cf. Susen (2007: 153–7).
340 Kögler (1996 [1992]: 269).
341 Ibid., 269 (italics added).
342 Ibid., 269.
343 Ibid., 269.
344 Ibid., 269.
345 Ibid., 269.
346 Ibid., 269.
347 Ibid., 269.
348 See ibid., esp. 269–70.
349 Ibid., 269.
350 Ibid., 270.
351 Ibid., 270.
352 Ibid., 270.
353 Ibid., 270.
354 Ibid., 270 (italics added).
355 Ibid., 270 (italics added).
356 Ibid., 270.
357 Ibid., 270.
358 See Hegel (1975 [1837]), Hegel (1977 [1807]), Hegel (1990 [1825–6]), and Hegel (1991 [1820]).
359 See Marx (2000/1977 [1844]), Marx (2000/1977 [1845]-a), Marx (2000/1977 [1845]-b), Marx (2000/1977 [1857–8/1941]), Marx (2000/1977 [1859]), and Marx and Engels (2000/1977 [1846]).
360 Kögler (1996 [1992]: 270).
361 Ibid., 270.
362 Ibid., 271.
363 See Heidegger (1949 [1946]) and Heidegger (1998 [1967/1976]). See also Heidegger (1992 [1989/1924]) and Heidegger (2001 [1927]).
364 See Nietzsche (1967 [1930]), Nietzsche (1992 [1887]), and Nietzsche (1999 [1886]).
365 Kögler (1996 [1992]: 271).
366 Ibid., 271.
367 Ibid., 271.
368 Ibid., 271 (italics in original).
369 Ibid., 272.
370 Ibid., 272 (italics in original).
371 Ibid., 272.
372 Ibid., 272.
373 Ibid., 272.

374 Ibid., 272.
375 Ibid., 272. On this point, see also ibid., Chapter 4, Section 4.1.
376 Ibid., 272.
377 Ibid., 272.
378 Ibid., 272–3.
379 Ibid., 273.
380 Ibid., 273.
381 Ibid., 273.
382 Ibid., 273.
383 See ibid., 273. On this point, see, for example, Mead (1967 [1934]: esp. 173–8, 192–200, 209–13, and 273–81). See also James (1890) as well as Susen (2010d). In addition, see, for instance: Aboulafia (1999); Athens (2002); Dews (1999); Gillespie (1984); Habermas (1987 [1981]-c); Habermas (1992 [1988]); Joas (1997 [1980]); Schubert (2006); Silva (2007b); Silva (2007a); Susen (2015a: 208).
384 Kögler (1996 [1992]: 273).
385 Ibid., 273.
386 Cf. Mead (1967 [1934]). On the concept of "perspective-taking," see, for instance: Susen (2007: 82); Susen (2015a: 221 and 223); Susen (2016b: 70); Susen (2017d: 352 and 357); Susen (2018e: 1287).
387 Kögler (1996 [1992]: 273).
388 Ibid., 273.
389 See, for example: Husserl (1931); Husserl (1970); Husserl (1972 [1939]); Husserl (2012 [1913/1931]). See also, for instance: Chelstrom (2013); Farber (1984); Myles (2004).
390 See, for example: Sartre (1939); Sartre (2003 [1958/1943]); Sartre (2007 [1946]); Sartre (2008 [1974/1972]); Sartre, Auster, and Davis (1978 [1977/1976]). See also, for instance: Archard (1980); Baert (2015); Boschetti (1988 [1985]); Bourdieu (1993a); Drake (2005); Flynn (1984); Leak (2006); Thompson and Thompson (1984).
391 Kögler (1996 [1992]: 274). Cf. Frank (1989 [1984]).
392 Kögler (1996 [1992]: 274).
393 Ibid., 274 (italics added).
394 Cf. Susen (2010d).
395 Kögler (1996 [1992]: 272 and 274).
396 Ibid., 274.
397 Ibid., 274.
398 Ibid., 274.
399 Ibid., 275.
400 Ibid., 275 (italics in original).
401 Ibid., 275.
402 Ibid., 275.
403 Cf. Susen (2020c: esp. 125, 131, 137, 138, 142, 144, and 147).
404 Cf. Susen (2018d: esp. 43, 49, 50, and 54). Cf. also Susen (2021a: esp. 372–3 and 382–4).
405 Kögler (1996 [1992]: 231).
406 Ibid., 231.
407 On this point, see Susen (2007: Chapter 7). Cf. Calhoun (1995).
408 On this point, see Susen (2007: Chapter 8). See also, for instance, Susen (2013c: esp. 220–30).

409 On this point, see Bourdieu (1985). See also, for instance: Grenfell (2013: 282); Robbins (2016: 7); Susen (2013d: 348–9); Thorpe (2011: 216).
410 On this point, see, for example, Bourdieu, Schultheis, and Pfeuffer (2011 [1999/2000]: 117, italics in original): "... all of these terms are often used in misleading ways, without really understanding what they stand for, and hence they become *slogans*. In reality, however, these concepts—these frameworks—are only *principles* for scientific work, which is usually of mere practical nature; they are *synthetic* or *synoptic* notions, which serve to provide research programmes with scientific *orientations*."
411 See Susen (2014a).
412 Susen (2015a: 5, italics removed from the entire quotation, numbering modified). Cf. Susen (2020a: 313–4). Cf. also Susen (2022: 122, 125, and 138).
413 On this point, see his self-critical reflections—for instance, Kögler (1996 [1992]: 254–6).
414 Ibid., 238 (italics added).
415 See previous note on "socio-ontological fatalism."
416 On the distinction between "power to" and "power over," see, for instance: Hearn (2014); Holloway (2002: 28–30 and 36–7); Holloway (2010: 9, 59, 62, 68, 85, 96, 98, 124, 128, 130–5, 199, 206, 209, 224–6, 232–3, 235, 246–9, 252, 261, 277n1, 277n2, 277n5, and 280n9); Holloway and Susen (2013: esp. 36); Saar (2010); Susen (2007: 21, 24, 32, 34, 65–6, 69, 70, 87–8, 94, 105, 118, 124, 125, 144, 183, 184, 186, 187, 191, 266–7, 281, 285, 286, 290, 292, 294, and 296); Susen (2008a: 59, 65, and 71–2); Susen (2008b: 142, 145, 151, and 155–7); Susen (2012a: 312); Susen (2014a); Susen (2015a: 52 and 117–18); Susen (2015b: 1029); Susen (2018c: esp. 6–7).
417 Susen (2018c: 6, italics in original).
418 Forst (2015b: 115, italics in original).
419 Susen (2018c: 6).
420 See Susen (2007: 192–8). See also Susen (2018c: 28–9 and 32) and Susen (2021b: 393).
421 Kögler (1996 [1992]: 246, italics added).
422 On this point, see, for instance, Susen (2016c: 220 [point 6]). Cf. Susen (2014d).
423 Cf. Susen (2010d).
424 Kögler (1996 [1992]: 246).
425 On the Bourdieusian distinction between "ordinary knowledge" and "scientific knowledge," see, for example: Bourdieu (1980: 24, 43–5, 48–50, and 61); Bourdieu (1982a: 10, 15, and 32); Bourdieu (1982b: 18–19); Bourdieu (1995: esp. 3–5 and 10); Bourdieu (1997: 119, 163, 217–18, and 225–6); Bourdieu (1999: 334–5); Bourdieu (2000); Bourdieu (2001: 15); Bourdieu, Chamboredon, and Passeron (1968: 27–49 and 100–2); Bourdieu and Eagleton (1992: esp. 117); Bourdieu, Schultheis, and Pfeuffer (2011 [1999/2000]); Bourdieu and Wacquant (1992b: 150); Bourdieu and Wacquant (1992c: 213). See also, for example: Boltanski, Rennes, and Susen (2010: 155–6); Boltanski, Rennes, and Susen (2014 [2010]: 597–8); Kögler (1996 [1992]: 220–7 and 229–33); Susen (2007: 135–7); Susen (2011a: esp. 450–8); Susen (2011c: 375–7, 378–80, and 403–5); Susen (2011e: 49–53, 73–5, and 81); Susen (2013c: 205–8 and 223–4); Susen (2013d: 333, 335, 339–41, and 378n158); Susen (2014d: 98–9); Susen (2014 [2015]: 322–4, 332–4, and 335); Susen (2014c: 634–5, 643, 647, 650, and 688); Susen (2015c: 167–70, 181–4, and 184–6); Susen (2016a: esp. 61–5); Susen (2016b: esp. 53, 55–6, 61–3, 66, 72, and 73–4); Susen (2017a: esp. 136–7 and 140); Susen (2021c: 43–6); Susen (2022: 122, 126–7, 132, 135, and 138); Susen and Turner (2011: xxi–xxii).

426 Cf. Susen (2012b: 713–15). Cf. also Susen (2022: 122, 126–7, 132, 135, and 138).
427 On this point, see Susen (2015a: 10). Cf. ibid., 71, 152, 174, 200, and 263.
428 Ibid., 10 (italics in original).
429 Ibid., 10 (italics in original).

References

Aboulafia, Mitchell (1999), "A (neo) American in Paris: Bourdieu, Mead, and Pragmatism," in Richard Shusterman (ed.) *Bourdieu: A Critical Reader*, Oxford: Blackwell, pp. 153–74.
Accardo, Alain (1997), *Introduction à une sociologie critique. Lire Bourdieu*, Bordeaux: Le Mascaret.
Alexander, Jeffrey C. and Maria Pia Lara (1996), "Honneth's New Critical Theory of Recognition," *New Left Review* 220: 126–36.
Apel, Karl-Otto (ed.) (1971), *Hermeneutik und Ideologiekritik*, Frankfurt am Main: Suhrkamp.
Apel, Karl-Otto (1979), *Die Erklären-Verstehen-Kontroverse in transzendental-pragmatischer Sicht*, Frankfurt am Main: Suhrkamp.
Apel, Karl-Otto (1992), "Normatively Grounding 'Critical Theory' through Recourse to the Lifeworld? A Transcendental-Pragmatic Attempt to Think with Habermas against Habermas," in Axel Honneth, Thomas McCarthy, Claus Offe, and Albrecht Wellmer (eds.) *Philosophical Interventions in the Unfinished Project of Enlightenment*, Cambridge, MA: MIT Press, pp. 125–70.
Archard, David (1980), *Marxism and Existentialism. The Political Philosophy of Satire and Merleau-Ponty*, Belfast: Blackstaff Press.
Athens, Lonnie (2002), "'Domination': The Blind Spot in Mead's Analysis of the Social Act," *Journal of Classical Sociology* 2(1): 25–42.
Baert, Patrick (2015), *The Existentialist Moment: The Rise of Sartre as a Public Intellectual*, Cambridge: Polity.
Baynes, Kenneth (2002), "Freedom and Recognition in Hegel and Habermas," *Philosophy & Social Criticism* 28(1): 1–17.
Bernstein, J. M. (2005), "Suffering Injustice: Misrecognition as Moral Injury in Critical Theory," *International Journal of Philosophical Studies* 13(3): 303–24.
Bohman, James (1989), "'System' and 'Lifeworld': Habermas and the Problem of Holism," *Philosophy & Social Criticism* 15(4): 381–401.
Boltanski, Luc (1998), "Critique sociale et sens moral. Pour une sociologie du jugement," in Tetsuji Yamamoto (ed.) *Philosophical Designs for a Socio-Cultural Transformation: Beyond Violence and the Modern Era*, Tokyo; Boulder, CO: École des Hautes Études en Sciences Culturelles; Rowman & Littlefield, pp. 248–73.
Boltanski, Luc (1999–2000), "Une sociologie sans société ?," *Le genre humain*, Hiver-Printemps: 303–11.
Boltanski, Luc (1999 [1993]), *Distant Suffering: Morality, Media and Politics*, trans. Graham Burchell, Cambridge: Cambridge University Press.
Boltanski, Luc (2002), "Nécessité et justification," *Revue économique* 53(2): 275–89.
Boltanski, Luc (2008), *Rendre la réalité inacceptable. À propos de "La production de l'idéologie dominante,"* Paris: Demopolis.
Boltanski, Luc (2009), *De la critique. Précis de sociologie de l'émancipation*, Paris: Gallimard.

Boltanski, Luc (2011 [2009]), *On Critique: A Sociology of Emancipation*, trans. Gregory Elliott, Cambridge: Polity.
Boltanski, Luc (2012 [1990]), *Love and Justice as Competences*, trans. Catherine Porter, Cambridge: Polity.
Boltanski, Luc and Ève Chiapello (1999), *Le nouvel esprit du capitalisme*, Paris: Gallimard.
Boltanski, Luc, Axel Honneth, and Robin Celikates (2014 [2009]), "Sociology of Critique or Critical Theory? Luc Boltanski and Axel Honneth in Conversation with Robin Celikates," in Simon Susen and Bryan S. Turner (eds.) *The Spirit of Luc Boltanski: Essays on the "Pragmatic Sociology of Critique,"* trans. Simon Susen, London: Anthem Press, pp. 561–89.
Boltanski, Luc, Juliette Rennes, and Simon Susen (2010), "La fragilité de la réalité. Entretien avec Luc Boltanski. Propos recueillis par Juliette Rennes et Simon Susen," *Mouvements* 64: 151–66.
Boltanski, Luc, Juliette Rennes, and Simon Susen (2014 [2010]), "The Fragility of Reality: Luc Boltanski in Conversation with Juliette Rennes and Simon Susen," in Simon Susen and Bryan S. Turner (eds.) *The Spirit of Luc Boltanski: Essays on the "Pragmatic Sociology of Critique,"* trans. Simon Susen, London: Anthem Press, pp. 591–610.
Boltanski, Luc and Laurent Thévenot (1999), "The Sociology of Critical Capacity," *European Journal of Social Theory* 2(3): 359–77.
Boltanski, Luc and Laurent Thévenot (2000), "The Reality of Moral Expectations: A Sociology of Situated Judgement," *Philosophical Explorations* 3(3): 208–31.
Bonnewitz, Patrice (1998), *La sociologie de P. Bourdieu*, Paris: Presses Universitaires de France.
Boschetti, Anna (1988 [1985]), *The Intellectual Enterprise. Sartre and "Les temps modernes,"* trans. Richard McCleary, Evanston, IL: Northwestern University Press.
Bourdieu, Pierre (1971), "Champ du pouvoir, champ intellectuel et habitus de classe," *Scolies* 1: 7–26.
Bourdieu, Pierre (1974 [1967]), "Der Habitus als Vermittlung zwischen Struktur und Praxis," in Pierre Bourdieu, *Zur Soziologie der symbolischen Formen*, Frankfurt am Main: trans. Wolf H. Fietkau, Suhrkamp, pp. 125–58.
Bourdieu, Pierre (1977 [1972]-a), *Outline of a Theory of Practice*, trans. Richard Nice, Cambridge: Cambridge University Press.
Bourdieu, Pierre (1977 [1972]-b), "Structures, Habitus, Power: Basis For a Theory of Symbolic Power," in Pierre Bourdieu, *Outline of a Theory of Practice*, trans. Richard Nice, Cambridge: Cambridge University Press, pp. 159–97.
Bourdieu, Pierre (1980), *Le sens pratique*, Paris: Minuit.
Bourdieu, Pierre (1982a), *Leçon sur la leçon*, Paris: Minuit.
Bourdieu, Pierre (1982b), "L'économie des échanges linguistiques," in Pierre Bourdieu, *Ce que parler veut dire. L'économie des échanges linguistiques*, Paris: Fayard, pp. 11–21.
Bourdieu, Pierre (1984), "Espace social et genèse des 'classes,'" *Actes de la recherche en sciences sociales* 52–3: 3–14.
Bourdieu, Pierre (1985), "The Genesis of the Concepts of 'Habitus' and 'Field,'" *Sociocriticism* 2(2): 11–24.
Bourdieu, Pierre (1986), "Habitus, code et codification," *Actes de la recherche en sciences sociales* 64: 40–4.
Bourdieu, Pierre (1990 [1980]), *The Logic of Practice*, Cambridge: Polity.
Bourdieu, Pierre (1993a), "A propos de Sartre . . .," *French Cultural Studies* 4(3): 209–11.
Bourdieu, Pierre (1993b), "Comprendre," in Pierre Bourdieu (ed.) *La misère du monde*, Paris: Éditions du Seuil, pp. 1389–1447.

Bourdieu, Pierre (1994), "Stratégies de reproduction et modes de domination," *Actes de la recherche en sciences sociales* 105: 3–12.
Bourdieu, Pierre (1995), "La cause de la science," *Actes de la recherche en sciences sociales* 106–7: 3–10.
Bourdieu, Pierre (1997), *Méditations pascaliennes*, Paris: Seuil.
Bourdieu, Pierre (1998), "A Reasoned Utopia and Economic Fatalism," *New Left Review* 227: 125–30.
Bourdieu, Pierre (1999), "Scattered Remarks," *European Journal of Social Theory* 2(3): 333–40.
Bourdieu, Pierre (1999 [1993]), *The Weight of the World: Social Suffering in Contemporary Society*, trans. Priscilla Parkhurst Ferguson [et al.], Cambridge: Polity.
Bourdieu, Pierre (2000), "Mit Weber gegen Weber: Pierre Bourdieu im Gespräch," in Pierre Bourdieu, *Das religiöse Feld. Texte zur Ökonomie des Heilsgeschehens*, herausgegeben von Franz Schultheis, Andreas Pfeuffer, und Stephan Egger, übersetzt von Stephan Egger, Konstanz: Universitätsverlag Konstanz, pp. 111–29.
Bourdieu, Pierre (2001), *"Si le monde social m'est supportable, c'est parce que je peux m'indigner"*. *Entretien avec Antoine Spire*, Paris: Éditions de l'Aube.
Bourdieu, Pierre (2003), "La fabrique de l'habitus économique," *Actes de la recherche en sciences sociales* 150: 79–90.
Bourdieu, Pierre and Luc Boltanski (1976), "La production de l'idéologie dominante," *Actes de la recherche en sciences sociales* 2–3: 4–73.
Bourdieu, Pierre and Luc Boltanski (2008 [1976]), *La production de l'idéologie dominante*, Paris: Demopolis / Raisons d'agir.
Bourdieu, Pierre, Luc Boltanski, and Monique de Saint Martin (1973), "Les stratégies de reconversion. Les classes sociales et le système d'enseignement," *Information sur les sciences sociales* XII(5): 61–113.
Bourdieu, Pierre, Jean-Claude Chamboredon, and Jean-Claude Passeron (1968), *Le métier de sociologue. Préalables épistémologiques*, Paris: Éditions de l'École des Hautes Études en Sciences Sociales / Mouton.
Bourdieu, Pierre and Terry Eagleton (1992), "Doxa and Common Life," *New Left Review* 191: 111–21.
Bourdieu, Pierre, Franz Schultheis, and Andreas Pfeuffer (2011 [1999/2000]), "With Weber against Weber: In Conversation with Pierre Bourdieu," in Simon Susen and Bryan S. Turner (eds.) *The Legacy of Pierre Bourdieu*, trans. Simon Susen, London: Anthem Press, pp. 111–24.
Bourdieu, Pierre and Loïc Wacquant (1992a), "Interest, Habitus, Rationality," in Pierre Bourdieu and Loïc Wacquant, *An Invitation to Reflexive Sociology*, Cambridge: Polity, pp. 115–40.
Bourdieu, Pierre and Loïc Wacquant (1992b), "Language, Gender, and Symbolic Violence," in Pierre Bourdieu and Loïc Wacquant, *An Invitation to Reflexive Sociology*, Cambridge: Polity, pp. 140–74.
Bourdieu, Pierre and Loïc Wacquant (1992c), "The Personal is Social," in Pierre Bourdieu and Loïc Wacquant, *An Invitation to Reflexive Sociology*, Cambridge: Polity, pp. 202–15.
Brink, Bert van den and David Owen (eds.) (2007), *Recognition and Power: Axel Honneth and the Tradition of Critical Social Theory*, Cambridge: Cambridge University Press.
Browne, Craig and Simon Susen (2014), "Austerity and Its Antitheses: Practical Negations of Capitalist Legitimacy," *South Atlantic Quarterly* 113(2): 217–30.
Brunkhorst, Hauke (1997), "Kritische Theorie als Theorie praktischer Idealisierungen," *Zeitschrift für kritische Theorie* 4: 81–99.

Calhoun, Craig (1995), "Habitus, Field, and Capital: Historical Specificity in the Theory of Practice," in Craig Calhoun, *Critical Social Theory*, Oxford: Blackwell, pp. 132–61.
Callinicos, Alex (2006), *The Resources of Critique*, Cambridge: Polity.
Celikates, Robin (2009), *Kritik als soziale Praxis. Gesellschaftliche Selbstverständigung und kritische Theorie*, Frankfurt am Main: Campus.
Charlesworth, Simon (2000), "Bourdieu, Social Suffering and Working-Class Life," in Bridget Fowler (ed.) *Reading Bourdieu on Society and Culture*, Oxford: Blackwell/Sociological Review, pp. 49–64.
Chauviré, Christiane and Olivier Fontaine (2003), *Le vocabulaire de Bourdieu*, Paris: Ellipses.
Chelstrom, Eric S. (2013), *Social Phenomenology: Husserl, Intersubjectivity, and Collective Intentionality*, Lanham: Lexington Books.
Coles, Romand and Simon Susen (2018), "The Pragmatic Vision of Visionary Pragmatism: The Challenge of Radical Democracy in a Neoliberal World Order," *Contemporary Political Theory* 17(2): 250–62.
Cordero, Rodrigo (2017a), *Crisis and Critique: On the Fragile Foundations of Social Life*, London: Routledge.
Cordero, Rodrigo (2017b), "In Defense of Speculative Sociology: A Response to Simon Susen," *Distinktion: Journal of Social Theory* 18(1): 125–32.
Davidson, Donald (2001 [1984/1974]), "On the Very Idea of a Conceptual Scheme," in Donald Davidson, *Inquiries into Truth and Interpretation*, 2nd Edition, Oxford: Oxford University Press, pp. 183–98.
Davidson, Donald (2001 [1984]), *Inquiries into Truth and Interpretation*, 2nd Edition, Oxford: Oxford University Press.
Dawson, Chris (1998 [1983]), "Translator's Introduction," in Hans-Georg Gadamer, *Praise of Theory: Speeches and Essays*, New Haven, Conn.: Yale University Press, pp. xv–xxxviii.
de Lara, Philippe (1982), "Superstructure," in Gérard Bensussan and Georges Labica (eds.) *Dictionnaire critique du marxisme*, Paris: Presses Universitaires de France, pp. 1106–11.
Delanty, Gerard (1997), *Social Science: Beyond Constructivism and Realism*, Buckingham: Open University Press.
Delanty, Gerard (2009), *The Cosmopolitan Imagination: The Renewal of Critical Social Theory*, Cambridge: Cambridge University Press.
Delanty, Gerard and Piet Strydom (eds.) (2003), *Philosophies of Social Science: The Classic and Contemporary Readings*, Buckingham: Open University Press.
Detel, Wolfgang (2000), "System und Lebenswelt bei Habermas," in Stefan Müller-Doohm (ed.) *Das Interesse der Vernunft: Rückblicke auf das Werk von Jürgen Habermas seit "Erkenntnis und Interesse"*, Frankfurt am Main: Suhrkamp, pp. 175–97.
Dews, Peter (1999), "Communicative Paradigms and the Question of Subjectivity: Habermas, Mead and Lacan," in Peter Dews (ed.) *Habermas: A Critical Reader*, Oxford: Blackwell, pp. 87–117.
Dilthey, Wilhelm (1883), *Einleitung in die Geisteswissenschaften. Versuch einer Grundlegung für das Studium der Gesellschaft und der Geschichte*, Erster Band, Leipzig: Duncker & Humblot.
Dostal, Robert J. (ed.) (2002), *The Cambridge Companion to Gadamer*, Cambridge: Cambridge University Press.
Drake, David (2005), *Sartre*, London: Haus.
Edgerton, Jason D. and Lance W. Roberts (2014), "Cultural Capital or Habitus? Bourdieu and beyond in the Explanation of Enduring Educational Inequality," *Theory and Research in Education* 12(2): 193–220.

Erdmann, Eva, Rainer Forst, and Axel Honneth (eds.) (1990), *Ethos der Moderne: Foucaults Kritik der Aufklärung*, Frankfurt am Main: Campus.
Eyerman, Ron, Jeffrey C. Alexander, and Elizabeth Butler Breese (eds.) (2011), *Narrating Trauma. On the Impact of Collective Suffering*, Boulder, Colo.: Paradigm.
Farber, Marvin (1984), *The Search for an Alternative: Philosophical Perspectives of Subjectivism and Marxism*, Philadelphia: University of Pennsylvania Press.
Flynn, Thomas R. (1984), *Sartre and Marxist Existentialism: The Test Case of Collective Responsibility*, Chicago: University of Chicago Press.
Forst, Rainer (2002 [1994]), *Contexts of Justice: Political Philosophy beyond Liberalism and Communitarianism*, trans. John M. M. Farrell, Berkeley, Calif.: University of California Press.
Forst, Rainer (2012 [2007]), *The Right to Justification. Elements of a Constructivist Theory of Justice*, trans. Jeffrey Flynn, New York: Columbia University Press.
Forst, Rainer (2013), "Zum Begriff eines Rechtfertigungsnarrativs," in Andreas Fahrmeir (ed.) *Rechtfertigungsnarrative. Zur Begründung normativer Ordnung durch Erzählungen*, Frankfurt: Campus, pp. 11–28.
Forst, Rainer (2013 [2003]), *Toleration in Conflict: Past and Present*, trans. Ciaran Cronin, Cambridge: Cambridge University Press.
Forst, Rainer (2013 [2011]), *Justification and Critique. Towards a Critical Theory of Politics*, trans. Ciaran Cronin, Cambridge: Polity.
Forst, Rainer (2014), *Justice, Democracy and the Right to Justification: Rainer Forst in Dialogue*, London: Bloomsbury.
Forst, Rainer (2015a), *Normativität und Macht. Zur Analyse sozialer Rechtfertigungsordnungen*, Frankfurt am Main: Suhrkamp.
Forst, Rainer (2015b), "Noumenal Power," *Journal of Political Philosophy* 23(2): 111–27.
Forst, Rainer (2017), "Noumenal Alienation: Rousseau, Kant and Marx on the Dialectics of Self-Determination," *Kantian Review* 22(4): 523–51.
Forst, Rainer and Klaus Günther (eds.) (2011a), *Die Herausbildung normativer Ordnungen. Interdisziplinäre Perspektiven*, Frankfurt: Campus.
Forst, Rainer and Klaus Günther (2011b), "Die Herausbildung normativer Ordnungen," in Rainer Forst and Klaus Günther (eds.) *Die Herausbildung normativer Ordnungen. Interdisziplinäre Perspektiven*, Frankfurt: Campus, pp. 11–30.
Forst, Rainer, Martin Hartmann, Rahel Jaeggi, and Martin Saar (eds.) (2009), *Sozialphilosophie und Kritik*, Frankfurt am Main: Suhrkamp.
Foucault, Michel (1978 [1976]), *The History of Sexuality. Volume 1: The Will to Knowledge*, trans. Robert Hurley, London: Penguin.
Foucault, Michel (1979 [1975]), *Discipline and Punish: The Birth of the Prison*, trans. Alan Sheridan, Harmondsworth: Penguin Books.
Foucault, Michel (1980a), *Power/Knowledge: Selected Interviews and Other Writings 1972–1977*, edited by Colin Gordon, translated by Colin Gordon [et al.], Brighton: Harvester Press.
Foucault, Michel (1980b), "Power and Strategies," in Colin Gordon (ed.) *Power/Knowledge: Selected Interviews and Other Writings, 1972–1977*, trans. Colin Gordon [et al.], Brighton: Harvester, pp. 134–45.
Foucault, Michel (1983 [1982]), "The Subject and Power," in Hubert L. Dreyfus and Paul Rabinow, *Michel Foucault: Beyond Structuralism and Hermeneutics*, with an afterword by Michel Foucault, Chicago: University of Chicago Press, pp. 208–26.
Foucault, Michel (1985 [1984]), *The History of Sexuality. Volume 2: The Use of Pleasure*, trans. Robert Hurley, London: Penguin.

Foucault, Michel (1988), *Politics, Philosophy, Culture: Interviews and Other Writings 1977–1984*, trans. Alan Sheridan and others, edited with an introduction by Lawrence D. Kritzman, London: Routledge.

Foucault, Michel (1988 [1984]), *The History of Sexuality. Volume 3: Care of the Self*, trans. Robert Hurley, London: Penguin.

Foucault, Michel (2001 [1961]), *Madness and Civilization: A History of Insanity in the Age of Reason*, trans. Richard Howard, with an introduction by David Cooper, London: Routledge.

Foucault, Michel (2002 [1966]), *The Order of Things: An Archaeology of the Human Sciences*, London: Routledge.

Foucault, Michel (2005 [2001]), *The Hermeneutics of the Subject: Lectures at the Collège de France, 1981–1982*, London: Palgrave Macmillan.

Frank, Manfred (1989 [1984]), *What is Neostructuralism?*, trans. Sabine Wilke and Richard Gray, foreword by Martin Schwab, Minneapolis: University of Minnesota Press.

Fraser, Nancy and Axel Honneth (2003), *Redistribution or Recognition? A Political-Philosophical Exchange*, trans. Joel Golb, James Ingram, and Christiane Wilke, London: Verso.

Gadamer, Hans-Georg (1982 [1976/1978/1979]), *Reason in the Age of Science*, trans. Frederick G. Lawrence, Cambridge, MA: MIT Press.

Gadamer, Hans-Georg (1989 [1975]), *Truth and Method*, 2nd Edition, translation revised by Joel Weinsheimer and Donald G. Marshall, London: Sheed & Ward.

Gadamer, Hans-Georg (1998 [1983]), *Praise of Theory: Speeches and Essays*, trans. Chris Dawson, New Haven, Conn.: Yale University Press.

Gadamer, Hans-Georg (2001), *Gadamer in Conversation: Reflections and Commentary*, edited and translated by Richard E. Palmer, New Haven: Yale University Press.

Gautier, Claude (2001), "La sociologie de l'accord. Justification contre déterminisme et domination," *Politix* 54: 197–220.

Giddens, Anthony (1977), "Habermas's Critique of Hermeneutics," in Anthony Giddens, *Studies in Social and Political Theory*, London: Hutchinson, pp. 135–64.

Gillespie, Alex (1984), "G. H. Mead: Theorist of the Social Act," *Journal for the Theory of Social Behaviour* 14(2): 19–39.

Grenfell, Michael (2013), "'Shadow Boxing': Reflections on Bourdieu and Language," *Social Epistemology* 27(3–4): 280–6.

Grondin, Jean (2002), "Gadamer's Basic Understanding of Understanding," in Robert J. Dostal (ed.) *The Cambridge Companion to Gadamer*, Cambridge: Cambridge University Press, pp. 36–51.

Habermas, Jürgen (1970), *Zur Logik der Sozialwissenschaften*, Frankfurt am Main: Suhrkamp.

Habermas, Jürgen (1971), "Zu Gadamers 'Wahrheit und Methode,'" in Karl-Otto Apel (ed.) *Hermeneutik und Ideologiekritik*, Frankfurt am Main: Suhrkamp, pp. 45–56.

Habermas, Jürgen (1987 [1981]-a), *The Theory of Communicative Action. Volume 1: Reason and the Rationalization of Society*, trans. Thomas McCarthy, Cambridge: Polity.

Habermas, Jürgen (1987 [1981]-b), *The Theory of Communicative Action. Volume 2: Lifeworld and System: A Critique of Functionalist Reason*, trans. Thomas McCarthy, Cambridge: Polity.

Habermas, Jürgen (1987 [1981]-c), "The Paradigm Shift in Mead and Durkheim: From Purposive Activity to Communicative Action," in Jürgen Habermas, *The Theory of*

Communicative Action. Volume 2: Lifeworld and System: A Critique of Functionalist Reason, trans. Thomas McCarthy, Cambridge: Polity, pp. 1–2.
Habermas, Jürgen (1987 [1981]-d), "The Concept of the Lifeworld and the Hermeneutic Idealism of Interpretive Sociology," in Jürgen Habermas, *The Theory of Communicative Action. Volume 2: Lifeworld and System: A Critique of Functionalist Reason*, trans. Thomas McCarthy, Cambridge: Polity, pp. 119–52.
Habermas, Jürgen (1987 [1985]), *The Philosophical Discourse of Modernity*, trans. Frederick Lawrence, Cambridge: Polity.
Habermas, Jürgen (1988 [1967/1970]), *On the Logic of the Social Sciences*, trans. Shierry Weber Nicholsen and Jerry A. Stark, Cambridge, MA: MIT Press.
Habermas, Jürgen (1992 [1988]), "Individuation through Socialization: On George Herbert Mead's Theory of Subjectivity," in Jürgen Habermas, *Postmetaphysical Thinking: Philosophical Essays*, trans. William Mark Hohengarten, Cambridge, MA: MIT Press, pp. 149–204.
Habermas, Jürgen (2004), "Freiheit und Determinismus," *Deutsche Zeitschrift für Philosophie* 52(6): 871–90.
Hall, Stuart (1977), "Rethinking the 'Base-and-Superstructure' Metaphor," in Jon Bloomfield (ed.) *Papers on Class, Hegemony and Party: The Communist University of London*, London: Lawrence and Wishart, pp. 43–72.
Hamel, Jacques (2000 [1997]), "Sociology, Common Sense, and Qualitative Methodology: The Position of Pierre Bourdieu and Alain Touraine," in Derek Robbins (ed.) *Pierre Bourdieu. Volume III*, London: SAGE, pp. 143–59.
Harrington, Austin (1999), "Some Problems with Gadamer's and Habermas's Dialogical Model of Sociological Understanding," *Journal for the Theory of Social Behaviour* 29(4): 371–84.
Harrington, Austin (2000), "Objectivism in Hermeneutics? Gadamer, Habermas, Dilthey," *Philosophy of the Social Sciences* 30(4): 491–507.
Harrington, Austin (2001), *Hermeneutic Dialogue and Social Science: A Critique of Gadamer and Habermas*, London: Routledge.
Hartmann, Klaus (1985), "Human Agency between Life-World and System: Habermas's Latest Version of Critical Theory," *Journal of the British Society for Phenomenology* 16(2): 145–55.
Hearn, Jonathan (2014), "On the Social Evolution of Power To/Over," *Journal of Political Power* 7(2): 175–91.
Hegel, Georg Wilhelm Friedrich (1975 [1837]), *Lectures on the Philosophy of World History. Introduction: Reason in History*, translated from the German ed. of Johannes Hoffmeister by H. B. Nisbet, with an introduction by Duncan Forbes, Cambridge: Cambridge University Press.
Hegel, Georg Wilhelm Friedrich (1977 [1807]), *Phenomenology of Spirit*, trans. A. V. Miller, with analysis of the text and foreword by J. N. Findlay, Oxford: Clarendon Press.
Hegel, Georg Wilhelm Friedrich (1990 [1825–6]), *Lectures on the History of Philosophy: The Lectures of 1825–1826*, edited by Robert F. Brown, trans. R. F. Brown and J. M. Stewart with the assistance of H. S. Harris, Berkeley, CA: University of California Press.
Hegel, Georg Wilhelm Friedrich (1991 [1820]), *Elements of the Philosophy of Right*, trans. H. B. Nisbet, edited by Allen W. Wood, Cambridge: Cambridge University Press.
Heidegger, Martin (1949 [1946]), *Über den Humanismus*, Frankfurt am Main: V. Klostermann.
Heidegger, Martin (1992 [1989/1924]), *The Concept of Time*, trans. William McNeill, Oxford: Blackwell.

Heidegger, Martin (1998 [1967/1976]), *Pathmarks*, edited by William McNeill, Cambridge: Cambridge University Press.
Heidegger, Martin (2001 [1927]), *Sein und Zeit*, 18. Auflage, Tübingen: Max-Niemeyer-Verlag.
Holloway, John (2002), *Change the World without Taking Power. The Meaning of Revolution Today*, London: Pluto Press.
Holloway, John (2005 [2002]), *Change the World without Taking Power. The Meaning of Revolution Today*, New Edition, London: Pluto Press.
Holloway, John (2010), *Crack Capitalism*, London: Pluto Press.
Holloway, John and Simon Susen (2013), "Change the World by Cracking Capitalism? A Critical Encounter between John Holloway and Simon Susen," *Sociological Analysis* 7(1): 23–42.
Holton, Robert (2000), "Bourdieu and Common Sense," in Nicholas Brown and Imre Szeman (eds.) *Pierre Bourdieu: Fieldwork in Culture*, Boston: Rowman & Littlefield, pp. 87–99.
Honneth, Axel (1995 [1992]), *The Struggle for Recognition: The Moral Grammar of Social Conflicts*, trans. Joel Anderson, Cambridge, MA: MIT Press.
Honneth, Axel (2002), "Grounding Recognition: A Rejoinder to Critical Questions," *Inquiry* 45(4): 499–519.
Honneth, Axel (2012 [2010]), *The I in We: Studies in the Theory of Recognition*, trans. Joseph Ganahl, Cambridge: Polity.
How, Alan (1995), *The Habermas-Gadamer Debate and the Nature of the Social*, Aldershot, Hants, England: Avebury.
How, Alan (1998), "That's Classic! A Gadamerian Defence of the Classic Text in Sociology," *Sociological Review* 46(4): 828–48.
How, Alan R. (1985), "A Case of Creative Misreading: Habermas's Evolution of Gadamer's Hermeneutics," *Journal of the British Society for Phenomenology* 16(2): 132–44.
How, Alan R. (2007), "The Author, the Text and the Canon: Gadamer and the Persistence of Classic Texts in Sociology," *Journal of Classical Sociology* 7(1): 5–22.
Husserl, Edmund (1931), *Ideas: General Introduction to Pure Phenomenology*, trans. W.R. Boyce Gibson, London: Allen and Unwin.
Husserl, Edmund (1970), *The Crisis of European Sciences and Transcendental Phenomenology. An Introduction to Phenomenological Philosophy*, trans. David Carr, Evanston: Northwestern University Press.
Husserl, Edmund (1972 [1939]), *Erfahrung und Urteil: Untersuchungen zur Genealogie der Logik*, 4. Auflage, redigiert und herausgegeben von Ludwig Landgrebe, Hamburg: F. Meiner.
Husserl, Edmund (2012 [1913/1931]), *Ideas: General Introduction to Pure Phenomenology*, trans. W.R. Boyce Gibson, with a new foreword by Dermot Moran, London: Routledge.
Inglis, David (2013), "Bourdieu, Language and 'Determinism': A Reply to Simon Susen," *Social Epistemology* 27(3–4): 315–22.
Jaeggi, Rahel (2014), *Kritik von Lebensformen*, Berlin: Suhrkamp.
Jaeggi, Rahel (2018 [2014]), *Critique of Forms of Life*, trans. Ciaran Cronin, Cambridge, MA: Harvard University Press.
Jain, Sheena (2016), "Worlds within and beyond Words: Bourdieu and the Limits of Theory," in Derek Robbins (ed.) *The Anthem Companion to Pierre Bourdieu*, London: Anthem Press, pp. 201–26.
Jakubowski, Franz (1990 [1976]), *Ideology and Superstructure in Historical Materialism*, trans. Anne Booth, London: Pluto Press.

James, William (1890), *The Principles of Psychology*, Volume 1. New York: Henry Holt.
Joas, Hans (1997 [1980]), *G. H. Mead: A Contemporary Re-Examination of his Thought*, trans. Raymond Meyer, Cambridge, MA: MIT Press.
Kögler, Hans-Herbert (1990), "Fröhliche Subjektivität: Historische Ethik und dreifache Ontologie beim späten Foucault," in Eva Erdmann, Rainer Forst, and Axel Honneth (eds.) *Ethos der Moderne: Foucaults Kritik der Aufklärung*, Frankfurt am Main: Campus, pp. 202–26.
Kögler, Hans-Herbert (1992), *Die Macht des Dialogs: Kritische Hermeneutik nach Gadamer, Foucault und Rorty*, J.B. Metzler: Stuttgart.
Kögler, Hans-Herbert (1994), "The Background of Interpretation. Ethnocentric Predicaments in Cultural Hermeneutics after Heidegger," *Internationale Zeitschrift für Philosophie* 2: 305–29.
Kögler, Hans-Herbert (1996), "The Self-Empowered Subject: Habermas, Foucault and Hermeneutic Reflexivity," *Philosophy & Social Criticism* 22(4): 13–44.
Kögler, Hans-Herbert (1996 [1992]), *The Power of Dialogue: Critical Hermeneutics after Gadamer and Foucault*, trans. Paul Hendrickson, Cambridge, MA: MIT Press.
Kögler, Hans-Herbert (1997a), "Alienation as Epistemological Source: Reflexivity and Social Background after Mannheim and Bourdieu," *Social Epistemology* 11(2): 141–64.
Kögler, Hans-Herbert (1997b), "Reconceptualizing Reflexive Sociology: A Reply," *Social Epistemology* 11(2): 223–50.
Kögler, Hans-Herbert (2000), "Empathy, Dialogical Self, and Reflexive Interpretation: The Symbolic Source of Simulation," in Hans-Herbert Kögler and Karsten R. Stueber (eds.) *Empathy and Agency: The Problem of Understanding in the Human Sciences*, Boulder, Colo.: Westview Press, pp. 194–221.
Kögler, Hans-Herbert (2003), "Situierte Autonomie. Zur Wiederkehr des Subjekts nach Foucault," in Stefan Deines, Stephan Jaeger, and Ansgar Nünning (eds.) *Historisierte Subjekte—Subjektivierte Historie: Zur Verfügbarkeit und Unverfügbarkeit von Geschichte*, Berlin: De Gruyter, pp. 77–92.
Kögler, Hans-Herbert (2004 [1994]), *Michel Foucault*, 2. Auflage, Stuttgart: J.B. Metzler.
Kögler, Hans-Herbert (2005a), "Constructing a Cosmopolitan Public Sphere: Hermeneutic Capabilities and Universal Values," *European Journal of Social Theory* 8(3): 297–320.
Kögler, Hans-Herbert (2005b), "Recognition and Difference: The Power of Perspectives in Interpretive Dialogue," *Social Identities* 11(3): 247–69.
Kögler, Hans-Herbert (2011), "Overcoming Semiotic Structuralism: Language and Habitus in Bourdieu," in Simon Susen and Bryan S. Turner (eds.) *The Legacy of Pierre Bourdieu: Critical Essays*, London: Anthem Press, pp. 271–99.
Kögler, Hans-Herbert (2012), "Agency and the Other: On the Intersubjective Roots of Self-Identity," *New Ideas in Psychology* 30(1): 47–64.
Kögler, Hans-Herbert (2013), "Unavoidable Idealizations and the Reality of Symbolic Power," *Social Epistemology* 27(3–4): 302–14.
Kögler, Hans-Herbert (2019), "Autonomie und Überschreitung. Bruchstücke einer Theorie der hermeneutischen Agency," in Hans-Herbert Kögler, Alice Pechriggl, and Rainer Winter (eds.) *Enigma Agency, Macht, Widerstand, Reflexivität*, Bielefeld: Transcript, pp. 81–112.
Kögler, Hans-Herbert, Alice Pechriggl, and Rainer Winter (eds.) (2019a), *Enigma Agency, Macht, Widerstand, Reflexivität*, Bielefeld: Transcript.

Kögler, Hans-Herbert, Alice Pechriggl, and Rainer Winter (2019b), "Einleitung: Das Enigma von Agency," in Hans-Herbert Kögler, Alice Pechriggl, and Rainer Winter (eds.) *Enigma Agency, Macht, Widerstand, Reflexivität*, Bielefeld: Transcript, pp. 7–34.

Kögler, Hans-Herbert and Karsten R. Stueber (eds.) (2000a), *Empathy and Agency: The Problem of Understanding in the Human Sciences*, Boulder, Colo.: Westview Press.

Kögler, Hans-Herbert and Karsten R. Stueber (2000b), "Introduction: Empathy, Simulation, and Interpretation in the Philosophy of Social Science," in Hans-Herbert Kögler and Karsten R. Stueber (eds.) *Empathy and Agency: The Problem of Understanding in the Human Sciences*, Boulder, Colo.: Westview Press, pp. 1–61.

Kontopoulos, Kyriakos M. (1993), *The Logics of Social Structure*, Cambridge: Cambridge University Press.

Labica, Georges (1982), "Base," in Gérard Bensussan and Georges Labica (eds.) *Dictionnaire critique du marxisme*, Paris: Presses Universitaires de France, pp. 93–6.

Lachenmann, Gudrun (1995), *"Methodenstreit" in der Entwicklungssoziologie*, Bielefeld: Universität Bielefeld, Forschungsschwerpunkt Entwicklungssoziologie, Working Paper, Issue 241.

Larrain, Jorge (1991 [1983]), "Base and Superstructure," in Tom Bottomore (ed.) *A Dictionary of Marxist Thought*, 2nd Edition, Oxford: Blackwell Reference, pp. 45–8.

Leak, Andrew N. (2006), *Jean-Paul Sartre*, London: Reaktion.

Lemieux, Cyril (2014), "The Moral Idealism of Ordinary People as a Sociological Challenge: Reflections on the French Reception of Luc Boltanski and Laurent Thévenot's *On Justification*," in Simon Susen and Bryan S. Turner (eds.) *The Spirit of Luc Boltanski: Essays on the "Pragmatic Sociology of Critique,"* London: Anthem Press, pp. 153–70.

Löwith, Karl (1953), *Weltgeschichte und Heilsgeschehen. Die theologischen Voraussetzungen der Geschichtsphilosophie*, 2. Auflage, Stuttgart: W. Kohlhammer.

Marx, Karl (2000/1977 [1844]), "Economic and Philosophical Manuscripts," in David McLellan (ed.) *Karl Marx: Selected Writings*, 2nd Edition, Oxford: Oxford University Press, pp. 83–121.

Marx, Karl (2000/1977 [1845]-a), "Theses on Feuerbach," in David McLellan (ed.) *Karl Marx: Selected Writings*, 2nd Edition, Oxford: Oxford University Press, pp. 171–4.

Marx, Karl (2000/1977 [1845]-b), "The Eighteenth Brumaire of Louis Bonaparte," in David McLellan (ed.) *Karl Marx: Selected Writings*, 2nd Edition, Oxford: Oxford University Press, pp. 329–55.

Marx, Karl (2000/1977 [1857-8/1941]), *"Grundrisse,"* in David McLellan (ed.) *Karl Marx: Selected Writings*, 2nd Edition, Oxford: Oxford University Press, pp. 379–423.

Marx, Karl (2000/1977 [1859]), "Preface to *A Critique of Political Economy*," in David McLellan (ed.) *Karl Marx: Selected Writings*, 2nd Edition, Oxford: Oxford University Press, pp. 424–8.

Marx, Karl and Friedrich Engels (2000/1977 [1846]), "The German Ideology," in David McLellan (ed.) *Karl Marx: Selected Writings*, 2nd Edition, Oxford: Oxford University Press, pp. 175–208.

McCarthy, George E. (2001), *Objectivity and the Silence of Reason: Weber, Habermas, and the Methodological Disputes in German Sociology*, New Brunswick, N.J.: Transaction.

Mead, George Herbert (1967 [1934]), *Mind, Self, and Society*, edited and with an introduction by Charles W. Morris, Chicago, London: University of Chicago Press.

Mendelson, Jack (1979), "The Habermas-Gadamer Debate," *New German Critique* 18: 44–73.

Michelfelder, Diane P. and Richard E. Palmer (eds.) (1989), *Dialogue and Deconstruction: The Gadamer-Derrida Encounter*, Albany, N.Y.: State University of New York Press.
Myles, John F. (2004), "From Doxa to Experience: Issues in Bourdieu's Adoption of Husserlian Phenomenology," *Theory, Culture & Society* 21(2): 91–107.
Neemann, Ursula (1993/1994), *Gegensätze und Syntheseversuche im Methodenstreit der Neuzeit*, 2 Bände, Hildesheim: Olms.
Nietzsche, Friedrich Wilhelm (1967 [1930]), *The Will to Power*, trans. Walter Kaufmann and R. J. Hollingdale, edited by Walter Kaufmann, New York: Random House.
Nietzsche, Friedrich Wilhelm (1992 [1887]), *Zur Genealogie der Moral: Eine Streitschrift*, mit einem Nachwort, einer Zeittafel zu Nietzsche, Anmerkungen und bibliographischen Hinweisen von Peter Pütz, 3. Auflage, München: Goldmann Verlag.
Nietzsche, Friedrich Wilhelm (1999 [1886]), *Jenseits von Gut und Böse: Vorspiel einer Philosophie der Zukunft*, Neuauflage, München: Goldmann Verlag.
Ostrow, James M. (2000 [1981]), "Culture as a Fundamental Dimension of Experience: A Discussion of Pierre Bourdieu's Theory of Human Habitus," in Derek Robbins (ed.) *Pierre Bourdieu. Volume I*, London: SAGE, pp. 302–22.
Outhwaite, William (1986 [1975]), *Understanding Social Life: The Method Called Verstehen*, 2nd Edition, Lewes: Jean Stroud.
Outhwaite, William (1987), *New Philosophies of Social Science: Realism, Hermeneutics and Critical Theory*, Basingstoke: Macmillan Education.
Outhwaite, William (1998), "Naturalisms and Antinaturalisms," in Tim May and Malcolm Williams (eds.) *Knowing the Social World*, Buckingham: Open University Press, pp. 22–36.
Outhwaite, William (2000), "Rekonstruktion und methodologischer Dualismus," in Stefan Müller-Doohm (ed.) *Das Interesse der Vernunft: Rückblicke auf das Werk von Jürgen Habermas seit "Erkenntnis und Interesse"*, Frankfurt am Main: Suhrkamp, pp. 218–41.
Paulle, Bowen, Bart van Heerikhuizen, and Mustafa Emirbayer (2011), "Elias and Bourdieu," in Simon Susen and Bryan S. Turner (eds.) *The Legacy of Pierre Bourdieu: Critical Essays*, London: Anthem Press, pp. 145–72.
Peters, John Durham (1993), "Distrust of Representation: Habermas on the Public Sphere," *Media, Culture & Society* 15(4): 541–71.
Pinto, Louis (1998), *Pierre Bourdieu et la théorie du monde social*, Paris: Albin Michel.
Quiniou, Yvon (1996), "Des classes à l'idéologie: déterminisme, matérialisme et émancipation chez P. Bourdieu," *Actuel Marx* 20, Deuxième Semestre: 117–34.
Robbins, Derek (1998), "The Need for an Epistemological 'Break'," in Michael Grenfell and David James, *Bourdieu and Education: Acts of Practical Theory*, London: Falmer Press, pp. 27–51.
Robbins, Derek (2016), "Introduction," in Derek Robbins (ed.) *The Anthem Companion to Pierre Bourdieu*, London: Anthem Press, pp. 1–15.
Rosa, Hartmut (1998), *Identität und kulturelle Praxis. Politische Philosophie nach Charles Taylor*, Frankfurt am Main: Campus.
Rosa, Hartmut (2005), *Beschleunigung. Die Veränderung der Zeitstrukturen in der Moderne*, Frankfurt am Main: Suhrkamp.
Rosa, Hartmut (2010), *Alienation and Acceleration. Towards a Critical Theory of Late-Modern Temporality*, Malmö: NSU Press.
Rosa, Hartmut (2012), *Weltbeziehungen im Zeitalter der Beschleunigung. Umrisse einer neuen Gesellschaftskritik*, Berlin: Suhrkamp.
Rosa, Hartmut (2013 [2010]), *Beschleunigung und Entfremdung: Entwurf einer kritischen Theorie spätmoderner Zeitlichkeit*, trans. Robin Celikates, Berlin: Suhrkamp.

Rosa, Hartmut (2015 [2005]), *Social Acceleration. A New Theory of Modernity*, trans. Jonathan Trejo-Mathys, New York: Columbia University Press.
Rosa, Hartmut (2016), *Resonanz. Eine Soziologie der Weltbeziehung*, Berlin: Suhrkamp.
Rosa, Hartmut (2019 [2016]), *Resonance: A Sociology of Our Relationship to the World*, trans. James C. Wagner, Cambridge: Polity.
Saar, Martin (2007), *Genealogie als Kritik. Geschichte und Theorie des Subjekts nach Nietzsche und Foucault*, Frankfurt am Main: Campus.
Saar, Martin (2010), "Power and Critique," *Journal of Power* 3(1): 7–20.
Saar, Martin (2013), *Die Immanenz der Macht. Politische Theorie nach Spinoza*, Berlin: Suhrkamp.
Sartre, Jean-Paul (1939), *Esquisse d'une théorie des émotions*, Paris: Hermann.
Sartre, Jean-Paul (2003 [1958/1943]), *Being and Nothingness. An Essay on Phenomenological Ontology*, translated by Hazel E. Barnes, introduction by Mary Warnock, with a new preface by Richard Eyre, London: Routledge.
Sartre, Jean-Paul (2007 [1946]), *Existentialism and Humanism*, New Edition, translation and introduction by Philip Mairet, London: Methuen.
Sartre, Jean-Paul (2008 [1974/1972]), *Between Existentialism and Marxism*, trans. John Matthews, London: Verso.
Sartre, Jean-Paul, Paul Auster, and Lydia Davis (1978 [1977/1976]), *Sartre in the Seventies. Interviews and Essays*, translated by Paul Auster and Lynda Davis, London: Deutsch.
Scheibler, Ingrid (2000), *Gadamer: Between Heidegger and Habermas*, Lanham, Md.: Rowman & Littlefield.
Schubert, Hans-Joachim (2006), "The Foundation of Pragmatic Sociology: Charles Horton Cooley and George Herbert Mead," *Journal of Classical Sociology* 6(1): 51–74.
Seemann, Axel (2004), "Lifeworld, Discourse, and Realism: On Jürgen Habermas's Theory of Truth," *Philosophy & Social Criticism* 30(4): 503–14.
Silva, Filipe Carreira da (2007a), "G. H. Mead: A System in a State of Flux," *History of the Human Sciences* 20(1): 45–65.
Silva, Filipe Carreira da (2007b), *G. H. Mead: A Critical Introduction*, Cambridge: Polity.
Stikkers, Kenneth W. (1985), "The Life-World Roots of Economy," *Journal of the British Society for Phenomenology* 16(2): 167–76.
Susen, Simon (2007), *The Foundations of the Social: Between Critical Theory and Reflexive Sociology*, Oxford: Bardwell Press.
Susen, Simon (2008a), "Poder y anti-poder (I–III)," *Erasmus: Revista para el diálogo intercultural* 10(1): 49–90.
Susen, Simon (2008b), "Poder y anti-poder (IV–V)," *Erasmus: Revista para el diálogo intercultural* 10(2): 133–80.
Susen, Simon (2009a), "Between Emancipation and Domination: Habermasian Reflections on the Empowerment and Disempowerment of the Human Subject," *Pli: The Warwick Journal of Philosophy* 20: 80–110.
Susen, Simon (2009b), "The Philosophical Significance of Binary Categories in Habermas's Discourse Ethics," *Sociological Analysis* 3(2): 97–125.
Susen, Simon (2010a), "Los movimientos sociales en las sociedades complejas," in Celia Basconzuelo, Teresita Morel, and Simon Susen (eds.) *Ciudadanía territorial y movimientos sociales. Historia y nuevas problemáticas en el escenario latinoamericano y mundial*, Río Cuarto: Ediciones del ICALA, pp. 149–226.
Susen, Simon (2010b), "The Transformation of Citizenship in Complex Societies," *Journal of Classical Sociology* 10(3): 259–85.

Susen, Simon (2010c), "Remarks on the Concept of Critique in Habermasian Thought," *Journal of Global Ethics* 6(2): 103–26.
Susen, Simon (2010d), "Meadian Reflections on the Existential Ambivalence of Human Selfhood," *Studies in Social and Political Thought* 17: 62–81.
Susen, Simon (2011a), "*Kritische Gesellschaftstheorie* or *kritische Gesellschaftspraxis*? Robin Celikates, *Kritik als soziale Praxis. Gesellschaftliche Selbstverständigung und kritische Theorie* (Frankfurt am Main, Campus Verlag, 2009)," *Archives Européennes de Sociologie / European Journal of Sociology* 52(3): 447–63.
Susen, Simon (2011b), "Bourdieu and Adorno on the Transformation of Culture in Modern Society: Towards a Critical Theory of Cultural Production," in Simon Susen and Bryan S. Turner (eds.) *The Legacy of Pierre Bourdieu: Critical Essays*, London: Anthem Press, pp. 173–202.
Susen, Simon (2011c), "Afterword: Concluding Reflections on the Legacy of Pierre Bourdieu," in Simon Susen and Bryan S. Turner (eds.) *The Legacy of Pierre Bourdieu: Critical Essays*, London: Anthem Press, pp. 367–409.
Susen, Simon (2011d), "Critical Notes on Habermas's Theory of the Public Sphere," *Sociological Analysis* 5(1): 37–62.
Susen, Simon (2011e), "Epistemological Tensions in Bourdieu's Conception of Social Science," *Theory of Science* 33(1): 43–82.
Susen, Simon (2012a), "'Open Marxism' against and beyond the 'Great Enclosure'? Reflections on How (Not) to Crack Capitalism," *Journal of Classical Sociology* 12(2): 281–331.
Susen, Simon (2012b), "Une sociologie pragmatique de la critique est-elle possible? Quelques réflexions sur *De la critique* de Luc Boltanski," *Revue Philosophique de Louvain* 110(4): 685–728.
Susen, Simon (2013a), "Comments on Patrick Baert and Filipe Carreira da Silva's *Social Theory in the Twentieth Century and Beyond*—Towards a 'Hermeneutics-Inspired Pragmatism'?," *Distinktion: Scandinavian Journal of Social Theory* 14(1): 80–101.
Susen, Simon (2013b), "Introduction: Bourdieu and Language," *Social Epistemology* 27(3–4): 195–8.
Susen, Simon (2013c), "Bourdieusian Reflections on Language: Unavoidable Conditions of the Real Speech Situation," *Social Epistemology* 27(3–4): 199–246.
Susen, Simon (2013d), "A Reply to My Critics: The Critical Spirit of Bourdieusian Language," *Social Epistemology* 27(3–4): 323–93.
Susen, Simon (2014a), "15 Theses on Power," *Philosophy and Society* 25(3): 7–28.
Susen, Simon (2014b), "The Place of Space in Social and Cultural Theory," in Anthony Elliott (ed.) *Routledge Handbook of Social and Cultural Theory*, London: Routledge, pp. 333–57.
Susen, Simon (2014c), "Luc Boltanski and His Critics: An Afterword," in Simon Susen and Bryan S. Turner (eds.) *The Spirit of Luc Boltanski: Essays on the "Pragmatic Sociology of Critique,"* London: Anthem Press, pp. 613–801.
Susen, Simon (2014d), "Reflections on Ideology: Lessons from Pierre Bourdieu and Luc Boltanski," *Thesis Eleven* 124(1): 90–113.
Susen, Simon (2014 [2015]), "Towards a Dialogue between Pierre Bourdieu's 'Critical Sociology' and Luc Boltanski's 'Pragmatic Sociology of Critique,'" in Simon Susen and Bryan S. Turner (eds.) *The Spirit of Luc Boltanski: Essays on the "Pragmatic Sociology of Critique,"* trans. Simon Susen, London: Anthem Press, pp. 313–48.
Susen, Simon (2015a), *The "Postmodern Turn" in the Social Sciences*, Basingstoke: Palgrave Macmillan.

Susen, Simon (2015b), "Emancipation," in Michael T. Gibbons, Diana Coole, Elisabeth Ellis, and Kennan Ferguson (eds.) *The Encyclopedia of Political Thought*, Vol. 3, Chichester: Wiley-Blackwell, pp. 1024–38.
Susen, Simon (2015c), "Une réconciliation entre Pierre Bourdieu et Luc Boltanski est-elle possible ? Pour un dialogue entre la sociologie critique et la sociologie pragmatique de la critique," in Bruno Frère (ed.) *Le tournant de la théorie critique*, Paris: Desclée de Brouwer, pp. 151–86.
Susen, Simon (2016a), *Pierre Bourdieu et la distinction sociale. Un essai philosophique*, Oxford: Peter Lang.
Susen, Simon (2016b), "The Sociological Challenge of Reflexivity in Bourdieusian Thought," in Derek Robbins (ed.) *The Anthem Companion to Pierre Bourdieu*, London: Anthem Press, pp. 49–93.
Susen, Simon (2016c), "Towards a Critical Sociology of Dominant Ideologies: An Unexpected Reunion between Pierre Bourdieu and Luc Boltanski," *Cultural Sociology* 10(2): 195–246.
Susen, Simon (2016d), "Scattered Remarks on the Concept of Engagement: A Socio-Philosophical Approach," *Philosophy and Society* 27(2): 459–63.
Susen, Simon (2016e), "Reconstructing the Self: A Goffmanian Perspective," in Harry F. Dahms and Eric R. Lybeck (eds.) *Reconstructing Social Theory, History and Practice*, Book Series: *Current Perspectives in Social Theory*, Volume 35, Bingley: Emerald, pp. 111–43.
Susen, Simon (2017a), "Hermeneutic Bourdieu," in Lisa Adkins, Caragh Brosnan, and Steven Threadgold (eds.) *Bourdieusian Prospects*, London: Routledge, pp. 132–159.
Susen, Simon (2017b), "Between Crisis and Critique: The Fragile Foundations of Social Life à la Rodrigo Cordero," *Distinktion: Journal of Social Theory* 18(1): 95–124.
Susen, Simon (2017c), "Following the Footprints of the 'Postmodern Turn': A Reply to Gregor McLennan," *European Journal of Cultural and Political Sociology* 4(1): 104–23.
Susen, Simon (2017d), "Remarks on the Nature of Justification: A Socio-Pragmatic Perspective," in Charlotte Cloutier, Jean-Pascal Gond, and Bernard Leca (eds.) *Justification, Evaluation and Critique in the Study of Organizations: Contributions from French Pragmatist Sociology*, Book Series: *Research in the Sociology of Organizations*, Volume 52, Bingley: Emerald, pp. 349–81.
Susen, Simon (2017e), "Reflections on Patrick Baert's *The Existentialist Moment: The Rise of Sartre as a Public Intellectual*," in Simon Susen and Patrick Baert, *The Sociology of Intellectuals: After "The Existentialist Moment,"* Basingstoke: Palgrave Macmillan, pp. 1–122.
Susen, Simon (2018a), "The Economy of Enrichment: Towards a New Form of Capitalism?," *Berlin Journal of Critical Theory* 2(2): 5–98.
Susen, Simon (2018b), "Justification," in George Ritzer and Chris Rojek (eds.) *The Blackwell Encyclopedia of Sociology*, 2nd Edition, Chichester: John Wiley & Sons, pp. 1–3.
Susen, Simon (2018c), "The Seductive Force of 'Noumenal Power': A New Path (or Impasse) for Critical Theory?," *Journal of Political Power* 11(1): 4–45.
Susen, Simon (2018d), "Jürgen Habermas: Between Democratic Deliberation and Deliberative Democracy," in Ruth Wodak and Bernhard Forchtner (eds.) *The Routledge Handbook of Language and Politics*, London: Routledge, pp. 43–66.
Susen, Simon (2018e), "Language," in Bryan S. Turner, Chang Kyung-Sup, Cynthia F. Epstein, Peter Kivisto, William Outhwaite, and J. Michael Ryan (eds.) *The Wiley Blackwell Encyclopedia of Social Theory*, Volume III, Chichester: John Wiley & Sons, pp. 1278–90.

Susen, Simon (2020a), *Sociology in the Twenty-First Century: Key Trends, Debates, and Challenges*, Basingstoke: Palgrave Macmillan.
Susen, Simon (2020b), "The Resonance of Resonance: Critical Theory as a Sociology of World-Relations?," *International Journal of Politics, Culture, and Society* 33(3): 309–44.
Susen, Simon (2020c), "Intimations of Humanity and the Case for a Philosophical Sociology," *Journal of Political Power* 13(1): 123–60.
Susen, Simon (2020d), "No Escape from the Technosystem?," *Philosophy & Social Criticism* 46(6): 734–82.
Susen, Simon (2021a), "Jürgen Habermas," in Peter Kivisto (ed.) *The Cambridge Handbook of Social Theory. Volume I: A Contested Canon*, Cambridge: Cambridge University Press, pp. 369–94.
Susen, Simon (2021b), "Civil Society," in Peter Kivisto (ed.) *The Cambridge Handbook of Social Theory. Volume II: Contemporary Theories and Issues*, Cambridge: Cambridge University Press, pp. 379–406.
Susen, Simon (2021c), "Mysteries, Conspiracies, and Inquiries: Reflections on the Power of Superstition, Suspicion, and Scrutiny," *SocietàMutamentoPolitica: Rivista Italiana di Sociologia* 12(23): 25–62.
Susen, Simon (2022), "Contemporary Social Theory," in Karim Murji, Sarah Neal, and John Solomos (eds.) *An Introduction to Sociology*, London: SAGE, pp. 121–141.
Susen, Simon and Bryan S. Turner (2011), "Introduction: Preliminary Reflections on the Legacy of Pierre Bourdieu," in Simon Susen and Bryan S. Turner (eds.) *The Legacy of Pierre Bourdieu: Critical Essays*, London: Anthem Press, pp. xiii–xxix.
Taylor, Charles (2002), "Gadamer on the Human Sciences," in Robert J. Dostal (ed.) *The Cambridge Companion to Gadamer*, Cambridge: Cambridge University Press, pp. 126–42.
Thompson, Kenneth and Margaret A. Thompson (1984), *Sartre. His Life and Works*, New York: Facts on File.
Thorpe, Chris (2011), "The Dual-Edged Sword of Sociological Theory: Critically Thinking Sociological Theoretical Practice," *Distinktion: Journal of Social Theory* 12(2): 215–28.
Turner, Bryan S. (2006), *Vulnerability and Human Rights*, University Park, Pa.: Pennsylvania State University Press.
Varela, Charles R. (1999), "Determinism and the Recovery of Human Agency: The Embodying of Persons," *Journal for the Theory of Social Behaviour* 29(4): 385–402.
Vessey, David (2009), "Gadamer and the Fusion of Horizons," *International Journal of Philosophical Studies* 17(4): 531–42.
Vitkin, Marina (1995), "The 'Fusion of Horizons' on Knowledge and Alterity: Is Inter-Traditional Understanding Attainable through Situated Transcendence?," *Philosophy & Social Criticism* 21(1): 57–76.
Wachterhauser, Brice R. (1994), "Gadamer's Realism: The 'Belongingness' of Word and Reality," in Brice R. Wachterhauser (ed.) *Hermeneutics and Truth*, Evanston, Ill.: Northwestern University Press, pp. 148–71.
Wacquant, Loïc (2004), "Critical Thought as Solvent of *Doxa*," *Constellations* 11(1): 97–101.
Warnke, Georgia (1987), *Gadamer: Hermeneutics, Tradition and Reason*, Cambridge: Polity.
Weber, Thomas (1995), "Basis," in Wolfgang Fritz Haug (ed.) *Historisch-Kritisches Wörterbuch des Marxismus (Band 2)*, Hamburg: Argument-Verlag, pp. 27–49.
Weinsheimer, Joel (1998 [1983]), "Foreword," in Hans-Georg Gadamer, *Praise of Theory: Speeches and Essays*, trans. Chris Dawson, New Haven, Conn.: Yale University Press, pp. vii–xiv.

2

Power, the Body and Reflexivity. Hans-Herbert Kögler's Hermeneutics in the Context of Critical Sociology

Rainer Winter

Introduction

In the following contribution, I would like to show how Critical Hermeneutics, as developed by Hans-Herbert Kögler, has deepened our understanding of how agents are anchored in social processes and of their capacity to critically reflect upon these contexts. Additionally, he succeeded in broadening the field of critical theory by combining the anti-positivistic procedure that is hermeneutics with a critical examination of the relations of power and dominance. In doing so, he also refined our understanding of agency and posited "self-empowerment" as an important aspiration.

I will begin by taking a closer look at the Frankfurt context in which Kögler developed Critical Hermeneutics. In the wake of Theodor W. Adorno's critique of positivism in sociology, various hermeneutical approaches were developed that drew on his work (2). Next, I will elaborate on the main features of Critical Hermeneutics (3). I will then contrast them with Pierre Bourdieu's sociology and his analysis of habitus that is rooted in the body, and I will ask where the limits of the hermeneutic reflexivity that Kögler postulated are located. Are there social compulsions and dispositions anchored in the body that cannot be uncovered, reflected and overcome through dialogue alone? Does it therefore make sense to combine Critical Hermeneutics with Bourdieu's reflexive sociology, which analyzes social fields and the relationships within them? (4) Lastly, I turn to the In-Depth Hermeneutics ("Tiefenhermeneutik") of Alfred Lorenzer, who regards the body not only as socially structured, but also as self-willed and resistant, because it represents a reservoir of longings and sensual inclinations that are not (no longer) attainable through language. Critical Hermeneutics can build on this in order to appreciate the potential of desire it postulates in a more nuanced way (5). A final reflection summarizes the vital importance of Critical Hermeneutics for an understanding of present-day power relations and subjectivity (6).

Critical Theory and Hermeneutics in Frankfurt

During the widely noted controversy over positivism in German sociology, Theodor W. Adorno (1969) joined forces with Jürgen Habermas to explain the characteristics and functions of a critical social theory in an intense debate with Karl Popper, Hans Albert, and others. Such a theory insists on the societal mediation of all phenomena, favors an epistemological process that does justice to their particular character, and is committed to a form of critique that articulates the suffering associated with the contradictions inherent to societal life. The critique should then be used as a starting point to develop the idea of a "right society." Following Adorno's untimely death, it was left to his students in the 1970s and 1980s to preserve and advance his findings and to translate them into critical social analyses. Central significance was attached to his justified skepticism toward well-established methodologies, which often inflict violence upon the phenomena to be investigated and yet fail to determine their very nature. In Frankfurt, in particular, scholars followed Adorno's example and developed methodologies, some of them critical.

For instance, Ulrich Oevermann (1983), a former assistant to Jürgen Habermas, presented his Objective Hermeneutics at the 1983 Adorno Conference in Frankfurt, describing an approach which, in his view, takes Adorno's methodological self-conception seriously insofar as it is guided by the principle of substantiality:

> ... which means, above all, that theory development and the progress of insight in sociology can only be safeguarded by concrete analyses that make the matter in question speak for itself, by clinging to it and, through this unbiased, radical engagement with the particular characteristics of the objects, arrive at a general understanding of social reality that is at once clarifying and critically transcending.
> Oevermann 1983: 234

However, Oevermann vigorously criticizes the use of the adjective "critical" to describe one's own actions, reproachfully describing this as an arrogant appropriation of an "additional moral quality" (Oevermann 1983: 283). In his understanding of Adorno the latter believed that "the critical content of science was precisely a function of the substantiality of analysis" (ibid.). This sweeping rejection of the conception of a critical theory clearly shows that Oevermann was influenced more by sociological positivism than by Horkheimer and Adorno. Still, he uses Adorno's insistence on the primacy of the object to develop his methodology, which surely cannot be described as critical in Adorno's sense. Even its original designation as Objective Hermeneutics – later Oevermann refers to it as Structural Hermeneutics—illustrates that he is concerned with a (post-)positivist version of hermeneutics. In Frankfurt, around the same time, the psychoanalyst and sociologist Alfred Lorenzer developed the critical methodology of "in-depth hermeneutics," which emerged in the context of a critical theory of the subject that Lorenzer had developed together with Klaus Horn, Helmut Dahmer, Thomas Leithäuser and others following Horkheimer and Adorno. He understood psychoanalysis itself as a critical theory, which he compared with the critical theory developed by Horkheimer following Marx (Lorenzer 2006). Both examine how phenomena are shaped by social contexts. Economic processes point to social conditions, individual life stories express social forms of life. The ultimate goal of any critical investigation is always to bring about a change in societal conditions (Lorenzer 2006: 91).

Unlike Oevermann, Lorenzer links directly to Horkheimer's (1937/1999) determination of critical theory. "As is the case in other fields, in psychoanalysis the purpose of change is not arbitrary. Psychoanalytical insight and therapeutic practice cannot strive—in a manner that preserves value-neutrality—to achieve successful psychological functioning under all circumstances. Psychoanalysis, too, should be oriented toward the goal of a 'right life'" (Lorenzer 2006: 91). Since the psychoanalyst as well as the critical theorist, however, are integrated into the prevailing conditions, they have no notion of a "right life" which would transcend the existing order and which they could use as a universal normative standard. Lorenzer is concerned with averting and overcoming the forms of life that make people ill. "Pushing through that which exists, the suffering of the analysand as a sensually experiencable contradiction against impositions of the existing order presses for the elimination of the intolerable . . . The notion of right life is thus replaced by the target fantasy of a less unbearable life" (Lorenzer 2006: 92). Aligned to this, we also have the in-depth hermeneutic cultural analysis developed by Lorenzer (1986), which represents a contribution to psychoanalytic social research. In literary texts and their reception, for example, it traces life concepts and figures of practice that were repressed, because they were not compatible with social values and norms.

Hans-Herbert Kögler studied philosophy at the University of Frankfurt in the 1980s. He received his doctorate in 1991 under Jürgen Habermas with his study "Die Macht des Dialogs. Kritische Hermeneutik nach Gadamer, Foucault und Rorty" (1992) [English modified version: The Power of Dialogue. Critical Hermeneutics after Gadamer and Foucault, 1996]. Max Horkheimer and Theodor W. Adorno do not feature at all in his doctoral thesis.[1] Critical Theory, meanwhile, is represented by Jürgen Habermas and Axel Honneth, and Kögler is henceforth in constant dialogue with their studies on the reflexive potential of language and the problematics of recognition.[2] The interpretation of the writings of Michel Foucault, to whom Kögler (2004) also dedicates a separate monograph well worth reading, emerges as central to his philosophical foundation of Critical Hermeneutics. He regards Foucault as a critical theorist. The analysis of the resistance, in particular, goes on to play an important role in his work. Against this backdrop, I will first reconstruct the main features of Critical Hermeneutics.

The Critical Hermeneutics Project

Kögler's point of departure is not the psychoanalytical situation as is the case with Alfred Lorenzer, a situation characterized by an asymmetrical communication structure (Winter 1986), but rather the dialogue based on equality, to which he assigns a critical and liberating function because it is unpredictable, surprising and innovative, and because it can call views and attitudes into question (Kögler 1996a: 4). His aim is to provide a more precise philosophical definition of this form of critical understanding, which should facilitate the questioning and overcoming of structures of power and domination, and to highlight its emancipatory power.

Gadamer (2013) showed that understanding is a fundamental condition of human life, in which our existence takes place and upon which sociality is constructed. Every interpretation is anchored in a preunderstanding by which it is determined. It is therefore not possible to escape the historically and culturally developed context of tradition, which has a transsubjective character (cf. Straub 1999: 257). In other words, there can be no neutral interpretations. The agent who understands is bound to a tradition and carries it on.

Gadamer (2013: 278ff.) emphasizes the important function of prejudices, which reflect past historical experience. They are, in his interpretation, not so much fallacies as background assumptions implicit in interpretation and understanding. Gadamer highlights ways in which the cultural experiences of the past shape the understanding of the present. And yet the agents actively and reflexively develop their own understanding of the past and present. Underlying assumptions can be made explicit and can be overcome. Every interpretation has the potential to transform the background upon which it is based. However, part of the background knowledge remains implicit. Gadamer believes that the perfect transparency of the historical and cultural conditions that define us is an illusion. Nevertheless, we can, for instance, reinterpret our lives and transform our self-conception. We will never, however, be able to detach ourselves entirely from our life situation and the tradition to which we are bound (Hoy 1994: 195).

Gadamer believes that understanding is linked to a conversation. After all, it is in conversations that we endeavor to understand our fellow human beings by seeking clarification when there is something we do not understand. This also applies to the cultural traditions in which we are embedded. "We can understand a text only when we have understood the question to which it is an answer"(Gadamer 2013: 378). Tradition engages us in a conversation that continues in perpetuity for humanity as a whole. However, it is not only a matter of understanding. "Rather, hermeneutical reflection implies that there is a process of self-criticism involved in all comprehension of the other or of another" (Gadamer 1997: 56). Here, Gadamer conceives of language as an enveloping medium in which the truth is expressed. The process of understanding is, however, never complete. It arises in a specific context and leads to new interpretations of a text when the context changes. As a result, our self-interpretations also change. New interpretations are the continuation of the previous history of interpretation.

Many interpreters note critically that Gadamer endowed tradition with an authority that cannot be circumvented. Habermas (1971: 156), for instance, criticized: "Dogmatic recognition of a tradition, and that means accepting the truth claim of this tradition, can of course only be equated with knowledge itself, if the tradition were to ensure an unconstrained and unrestricted agreement about tradition." He refers, among other things, to the In-Depth Hermeneutics of Lorenzer and the insight this brought forth that even an apparently reasonable agreement could be a form of pseudo-communication (ibid.: 152). Habermas (1971: 151) believes that the example of systematically distorted communication calls into question the basic assumptions of

Gadamer's hermeneutics. Moreover, Gadamer's view can also be considered extremely problematic in cases where a tradition legitimizes authoritarian rule. This is why he is accused of conservatism. David Hoy (1994: 196f.), meanwhile, is of the opinion that Gadamer's view should not be construed politically. Instead, it represents a methodological principle. Indeed, Gadamer repeatedly stresses that traditions can be challenged. He also notes that they are multidimensional and polyphonic.

Beyond this, Kögler (1996a) is of the opinion that the radical difference of forms of life must perforce be disregarded, if a linguistically constituted being is to be assumed which cannot be circumvented and which is intended to unite all. He is critical of Gadamer's concept of the fusion of horizons, which is based on the assumption that the events of being and truth are universal, uniform and conveyed through language. Against this backdrop, there can be no radical difference between forms of life and worlds of meaning, because tradition connects and unifies everything. Following on from Kögler (1996a), Jürgen Straub (1999: 271) argues that the hermeneutic theory of Gadamer "paves the way for nostrifying acts of appropriation of the foreign and empowerment of the other."

Kögler also rightly criticizes the fact that Gadamer is unable to see power relations that are not bound to meaning, but which nevertheless can have a significant influence on the self-conception of the interpreters. These can be discursive orders or surveillance systems as analyzed by Michel Foucault (1977, 1978). Their existence cannot be revealed in a conversation, but rather it requires an archaeological or genealogical exploration:

> Dialogic understanding can no longer proceed from the idea of a universal consensus or from the idea of prior being-in-the-truth; rather, it must pursue the more modest objective of seeking to make present one's own constraints through an understanding of the other, and of gaining knowledge of certain limits of the other through one's own perspective. Understanding becomes a reciprocal, critically challenging process with the other, but without the metaphysical guarantee of a comprehensive truth and without the further, albeit assured goal of a final consensus.
>
> Kögler 1996a: 84

Kögler seeks to investigate how meaning is constituted by power structures, as these penetrate and shape our preunderstanding. By analyzing and uncovering these processes, he hopes on „exposing the constraints on thought that are subject to an unconscious partnership with political and social power structures" (Kögler 1996a: 107). It must be assumed that the researcher's preunderstanding is also pre-formed by power. In view of this, Kögler justifiably asks how he can subject power-saturated structures of meaning to critical analysis. For this, the other person must first be recognized as an ontologically equal subject and his or her self-conception must be reconstructed (Kögler 1996a: 108). The critique is directed at forms of knowledge and thought that have not come about through dialogue, but rather at the dispositifs of power necessary for the formation of modern society and its capitalist economy, which Foucault (1977) analyzed and brought to mind in considerable detail. Kögler now proposes to reverse the principle of power and to use it as a basis for critical understanding:

> Inasmuch as understanding involves individualizing rather than normalizing, interpreting rather than objectifying, pluralizing rather than encompassing—in short, radically dialogic processes—we can free ourselves from our own potentially power-determined preunderstanding through an understanding of the other disclosed in this dialogic way. Through interpretive understanding, we transcend our own operative understanding of self and being and thus attain to a dialogically external perspective that, over against ourselves, makes possible radical critique: *we learn to see ourselves with the eyes of the concrete other.*
>
> Kögler 1996a: 109f.

The aim of Critical Hermeneutics is to make the agents more aware of the processes of disciplining, normalization and habitualization, as emphatically and systematically analyzed by Foucault, but also by Pierre Bourdieu (1984). Through these processes, they have become subjects subjugated to domination, who through understanding should now be empowered to distance themselves from themselves and from their views formed by power structures. "Precisely in this way does it become possible to give back to those agents that which dwells potentially within them: *a space for reflection and action over against established interpretations and structures of domination*" (Kögler 1996a: 239).

In light of this, Kögler (1996a: 239ff) considers the concept of resistance to be central to Foucault's work. Even though power practices reproduce and stabilize structures of domination, there will always be liberation struggles to oppose them. This allows for the transcendence of the disciplining and habitualization of the subjects.[3] What is now important for Kögler's perspective is that the hermeneutic critique of power relations is conveyed along with the agents' self-conception. "Indeed, in this manner, we are forced to understand the always-specific formations of power as contextually relative to their function in impeding the self-realization of the individuals, which, in turn, depends on the specific ideas, expectations, and utopias that the individuals take to be constitutive of an existence acceptable to them" (Kögler 1996a: 242).

Kögler concludes that power relations prevent the unconstrained and independent self-realization of agents in particular (Kögler 1996a: 244). Critical Hermeneutics aims to assist them in understanding and freeing themselves from the symbolic order and the practices of power that govern them. "To be sure, the general mark of 'power' is that an intended self-realization is functionally deflected by domination: standing over against power ontologically is human individuality, which can never be completely integrated into symbolic frameworks of disclosure or practical rule systems" (Kögler 1996a: 246). Using almost existentialist undertones, he emphasizes that agents can always reinvent themselves by modifying their understanding of themselves and others.

If it is the case that social power relations structure the symbolic, then what is "true" can also be determined by them (Kögler 1992: 294), as Foucault (1978; 1981) has shown. Kögler, however, strives to overcome the latter's power-monistic perspective by means of his radical orientation toward dialogue. In any given dialogue, the interpreter must assume the self-conception of the dialogue partners in order "to gauge from their resistance to certain conditions perceived as power that which is to be determined as domination in the other context" (Kögler 1992: 295). He can then endeavor to specify these relations of domination more precisely by including scientific analyses. The dialogue partner can question this objectification of his or her situation, reject it, or agree to it. The interpreter can also transform through the understanding of the other meaning, can perceive power relations and reach a new description of his/her understanding of the self and the world. "In terms of power, this act of understanding can accomplish two things: On the one hand, it reveals relationships of domination in the self-conception of the other and of oneself and, on the other hand, it uncovers power effects in the understanding of the other context of meaning itself" (Kögler 1992: 295). Based on a dialogical understanding of experiences and the inclusion of power analyses, Critical Hermeneutics pursues a critique of meaning. It follows "the notion of making people aware of deep-seated structures of meaning and power" (Kögler 1992: 300).

While Gadamer emphasizes the important function of prejudice and of the preunderstanding in an affirmative way, Kögler (1996b: 13) calls for a power-critical analysis of the "shared background of taken-for-granted assumptions" that is produced in the course of socialization and through social practices. Because these are shaped by power relations, the acquired "interpretive schemes" of perception and understanding, which are hidden and implicit, are defined by them:

> These schemata must be understood as unconscious patterns of meaning which give structured guidelines to the conscious self-reference of concrete individuals. The conscious intentionality of the subjects is thus based on unconscious forms of subjectivity ... Hence, the determination of subjectivity's power is a deeply ambivalent event: never completely absent, but also never fully determining.
> Kögler 2004: 194

This, however, restricts the cognitive horizon of the agents, their possibilities for reflection. Nevertheless, it is possible that the interpretative schemata are thematized and made explicit. Here Kögler introduces the concept of hermeneutic reflexivity: "The capacity to see through distorting and limiting schemes of understanding in order to determine one's life so as to realize oneself. The concept of hermeneutic reflexivity relates the radical situatedness of human understanding with the capacity of agents to thematize and explicate structural features of their socio-cultural background" (Kögler 1996b: 14). The objective of his hermeneutically sensitized critical theory is a "self-empowered subject."

Using this concept, Kögler believes that he can redress even the weaknesses of Foucault's analytics of power. The latter assumes that subjects are constituted thoroughly in power structures. Foucault fails to see that reflexivity is an essential part of the agents' lifeworld, according to Kögler (Kögler 1996b: 30). All the same, as Kögler (1996b: 32ff) states, Foucault assumes that those subject to the structures of domination have privileged access to their own life situation. This is why prisoners, those interned in psychiatric institutions, prostitutes, housewives, etc. ought to be listened to.

Kögler, for his part, deems it implausible that the marginalized and excluded might have "an adequate and complete understanding of the internal order and functions of power in their situations" (Kögler 1996b: 33). Surely, he is right in saying this. However, in my view, Foucault was merely concerned that the "outsiders" should be respected and given a voice in the discourse, despite the normalization and exclusion procedures. The articulation of their perspective cannot replace genealogical analysis, but must be communicated alongside it. As Kögler suggests, the "outsiders" do not have "epistemic authority" in Foucault's work (1996b: 33). Indeed, he would otherwise not have needed to carry out his historical investigations.

Kögler moves beyond Foucault and calls for a critical dialogue between the theorist and the agent, in which the mechanisms of power should be uncovered and reflected upon. "While itself situated in the modern context, critical hermeneutic theory argues that it can, in the dialogue with the subjects, reconstruct crucial and 'objective' features of the modern lifeworld" (Kögler 1996b: 34). In Kögler's view, this dialogue represents the method by which a "heightened self-awareness" and, subsequently, a "self-empowered subject" can be produced. "Critical hermeneutic theory should do no more than provide a tool for situated selves to use in recognizing and perhaps realizing hitherto invisible life-possibilities" (Kögler 1996b: 38).[4] What is decisive for Kögler's perspective is that agency is likely to be structured by power relations, but nevertheless, in the course of dialogue, a new self-conception can emerge through a reflexive examination of the other. This "enigmatic dimension of agency" allows a "reconstruction of situated and hermeneutically founded autonomy" (Kögler 2019: 81). It is in fact a matter of transgressing the given preunderstanding, since this was formed in a power relationship. "Rather, the self-determined action orientation, i.e., the situated autonomy, will itself emerge from the reflexive performance of resistance to power-determined relations of meaning" (Kögler 2019: 105).

Following George Herbert Mead (1967) and Axel Honneth (1995), Kögler insists that one's own self-identity is based on the recognition of the non-objectifiable other. It is contingent on a reciprocal adoption of perspectives and an openness to the other person's point of view (Kögler 2019: 106). By synthesizing the perceptions that others have of one ("me" according to Mead), a social self-identity is created that is open to different partners and that allows a flexible orientation for action. According to Kögler, the "enigma agency" is embodied in the category of "I" as defined by Mead. It symbolizes the instinctual structure of the human being, and is characterized by spontaneity and creativity. According to Kögler, this potential of desire renders action unpredictable. This potentially transgressive character could then become part of the self-identity through self-reflection. "In narrative-biographical reflection, I perceive my action in a given context as mine, and yet this *autonomous act of interpretation* can only take place in the social universe of shared meanings and practices" (Kögler 2019: 109).

So, for Kögler, the situated autonomy depends on the opportunities for development available to the concrete agency. His approach of a critical hermeneutic theory emphasizes that agents are anchored in social contexts. They are unable to design themselves freely, yet their actions are not fully determined by the contexts. They possess a desire. Reflection, criticism and dialogue can expand their margins of freedom. Similarly, Merleau-Ponty (1962) also believed that freedom is never absolute, but must be perceived as situated in the world. It is bound to situations which have their own rules and requirements, but which also afford certain opportunities.

Both Kögler and Merleau-Ponty differ from the voluntaristic idealism of Jean-Paul Sartre, who refuses to recognize the limitations of freedom. Yet Kögler's work also raises the question of the limits of hermeneutic reflexivity. Which power effects of structures of domination cannot be resolved and overcome through reflection or dialogue? I would like to lead into my considerations by first discussing Pierre Bourdieu's theory of habitus, which follows on from Merleau-Ponty (4). My aim is to further raise the profile of critical hermeneutic theory by revealing its breadth of scope and its possibilities.

Habitus as the Boundary of Hermeneutic Reflexivity

Following Merleau-Ponty, Bourdieu (2013) places the body and its dispositions at the very center of his observations. The term habitus refers to the unconscious formation of the body through history and society in the course of primary socialization. The body incorporates their objective structures, which become second nature. The social order inscribes itself into the physical dispositions, which are not immutable, but can be socially formed and shaped. Habitus is a

> system of lasting, transposable dispositions integrating past experiences, functions at every moment as a *matrix of perceptions, appreciations, and actions* and makes possible the achievement of infinitely diversified tasks, thanks to analogical transfers of schemes permitting the solution of similarly shaped problems and thanks to the unceasing corrections of the results obtained, dialectically produced by those results...
>
> Bourdieu 2013: 82f.

Through "regulated improvisations" (Bourdieu 2013: 78), the habitus generates forms of practice and practices which remain linked to the conditions of its origin, but allow creativity within this framework. The agents remain unaware that their actions have a meaning that extends beyond their intentions. Hence, Bourdieu (2013: 81) assumes that the actions of an individual or a group have an objective meaning that is independent of their subjective intentions. This meaning is only revealed when the objective relationships in which the individuals or groups are involved are analyzed. The members of a group or class incorporate the same social structures. The habitus thus embodies the position taken within the social structure (Bourdieu 2013: 82). "In short, the habitus, the product of history, produces individual and collective practices, and hence history, in accordance with the schemes engendered by history" (Bourdieu 2013: 82). Representing an enduring and stable system of dispositions of perception and classification, the habitus is responsible for the orderly nature of the social world.

The origin of these dispositions is usually not conscious, they become bodily phenomena through their incorporation. On this point Kögler states:

> ... Bourdieu defines the core of the habitus as practical and pre-conscious, even though its significance consists in providing a symbolic framework for intentional acts of expression. Habitus-formations are taken to be *embodied and non-cognitive* schemes that should not be conceived in terms of hidden rules or norms: their implicit organizing capacity simply accounts for regularities in social behavior, and no theoretical or reflexive account can ever fully grasp and elucidate them.
>
> Kögler 1997: 150

For Bourdieu (Bourdieu/Wacquant 1992: 127), the habitus represents the embodiment of that which is social. Social order is expressed in the bodily dispositions. In his opinion, the habitus is "the durable and transposable systems of schemata of perception, appreciation, and action that result from the institution of the social in the body (or in biological individuals) ..." (Bourdieu/Wacquant 1992: 126f.) which has been structured by a social field and therefore navigates within it. As a rule, a habitus is adapted to the logic of a field that represents a network of objective relations between people. For their part, the agents are not aware of the objective structure of relations (Bourdieu/Wacquant 1992: 97).

Bourdieu makes a point of emphasizing that the habitus also allows for change and transformation. "Habitus is not the fate that some people read into it. Being the product of history, it is an *open system of dispositions* that is constantly subjected to experiences, and therefore constantly affected by them in a way that either reinforces or modifies its structures. It is durable but not eternal" (Bourdieu/Wacquant 1992: 133). Bourdieu notes that the habitus can have a determining force first and foremost when its dispositions can manifest unchecked and unreflected (Bourdieu/Wacquant 1992.: 137f.). Then, unconscious acting will take place.

> This means that agents become something like ‚subjects' only to the extent that they consciously master the relation they entertain with their dispositions. They can deliberately let them ‚act' or they can on the contrary inhibit them by virtue of consciousness. Or, following a strategy that seventeenth-century philosophers advised, they can pit one disposition against another: Leibniz argued that one cannot fight passion with reason, as Descartes claimed, but only with "slanted wills" *(volontes obliques),* i.e., with the help of other passions.
>
> Bourdieu/Wacquant 1992: 137

In Bourdieu's view, this „is possible only with the support of explicit clarification" (Bourdieu/Wacquant 1992: 137). The socio-analysis or reflexive anthropology he developed can serve this purpose and can reveal the social illusions and myths within their role of stabilizing the dominant power structures. The habitus perceives the world it constructs as the only possible world. Its selective perception of options for action lends it a conservative force that leads to a reproduction rather than a transformation of that which exists. Sociology's duty is to uncover these processes which appear to be necessary and to stimulate sensitivity with regard to them. Bourdieu seeks to help social agents to see social determinants clearly by offering them "the means of a potentially liberating awakening of consciousness" (Bourdieu/Wacquant 1992: 215).

Both Critical Hermeneutics and reflexive anthropology share the same intention. The habitus can be thematized in the dialogue favored by Kögler, interpretative dispositions or schemes can become reflexively known and transcended (Kögler 1997). However, sociological and historical analyses of social fields and relations are needed in order to analyze and understand habitus formations in their genesis and in their effects. As Peter Zima (2020: 714) observes, there is a need for relational thinking that examines the interrelationships in the social sphere. Subsequently, this knowledge can be communicated through dialogue, which also helps to increase the hermeneutic reflexivity of the agents. Although the habitus will not be overcome by dialogue, it is possible to curb its unconscious acting, the free play of dispositions, by means of reflexivity. This can facilitate new perceptions and options for action. That which is social cannot be expelled from a body. All that can happen is that the dispositions become more flexible.

Consequently, Critical Hermeneutics should be linked not only with Foucault's analytics of power, but also with sociological analyses that examine and explain the social system of relations in which the agents are situated. For only then it can understand which practices are forms of resistance and what transformative significance they may have in the social field. Could they contribute to a transformation of domination structures, for example? Bourdieu emphatically shows that sociology is above all about exploring the social meaning, which does not arise from the intentions of the agents, but is instead determined by the relations in the social field.

The Self-Will of the Body. Enigma Agency in the Context of Alfred Lorenzer's In-Depth Hermeneutics

As Zima (2020: 730ff) argues, a habitus can be understood as "socialized subjectivity" or as an "individualized social structure" anchored in the body. What is missing in Bourdieu's sociological analysis of the body, however, is an analysis of its individuality. Kögler (2019) draws on Mead to identify the potential of desire as a source of change and agency that resists social expectations and impositions. This angle of Critical Hermeneutics can be expanded and deepened if we turn to Alfred Lorenzer's In-Depth Hermeneutics ("Tiefenhermeneutik"). When interacting with patients in his work as a psychoanalyst, he encountered unique individuals with different problems, who were nevertheless socially shaped through and through.

> The object of psychoanalytical insight is . . . the relationship between the individual and society, but *in* the individual—as an individual pattern of behavior, as a way of life of individual experience . . . renewal of the effort to convey psychoanalysis and critical social theory—along the central question of how the instinctual structure is socially produced.
>
> Lorenzer 2006: 104f.

Lorenzer, too, highlights the role of the body. For him, psychoanalysis understood in terms of the social sciences is a "hermeneutics of the body" (Lorenzer 2002: 59). In it the traces of life history, of earlier interactions, are inscribed. Lorenzer reformulates the Freudian concept of instinct and replaces it with that of the form of interaction. In doing so, he emphasizes that "the sociality of the human personality is anchored in the depths of the body" (Lorenzer 2002: 150). Corporeal and bodily desire is formed and socialized in interactions. For instance, the unconscious is initially brought forth in early sensual forms of interaction with the mother, which are not mediated by language, but are nevertheless socially formed. Social interactions become inscribed onto the body and give structure to future experiences and actions. "From the very beginning of life, socialization is simultaneously the approach of individuation in the development of an individual instinctual structure, which is produced in every ontogenesis" (Lorenzer 1981: 94). This, in Lorenzer's view, leads to an interlacing of human nature and all that is social.

The introduction of language gives rise to symbolic forms of interaction. Forms of interaction and language symbols are interlinked and become "conscious figures of practice" (Lorenzer 1981: 90). "If successful, the child's sensomotoric experience of the world is combined and unfolds with the collective's supra-individual experience of the world, which is stored in language" (Lorenzer 1981: 91). However, this also means that the rehearsed sensomotoric reactions are subjected to collective norms and values. This results in processes of repression, which Lorenzer (1970) defines as desymbolizations. Jürgen Straub (1999: 302) concludes:

> Repression is a kind of exclusion of behavior-determining 'forces' from the language, indeed from the wider field of the symbolic in general. We exclude those complexes of ideas and thoughts or plans of action and life that have proven to be incompatible with social norms, values and practices.
>
> Straub 1999: 302

The body, formed in the experiences of a subject, not only represents the social turned corporeal (Bourdieu/Wacquant 1992: 127), onto which domination has inscribed itself, but it also contains a willful potential for resistance that has arisen in interactions and can never be fully socialized. These are unconscious forms of interaction anchored in the body, which subversively elude language and its determining power, as Lorenzer pointedly states (Lorenzer 2002: 248).

He upholds Freud's insight that the inner nature is willfully structured. He thus complements Bourdieu's analysis of habitus, which assumes that the social penetrates the body, but does not further explicate the inner nature (cf. Wollenhaupt 2018: 250). While habitus and field fit together in Bourdieu's sense, the body does not merge with the field. It embodies concepts of life and forms of practice that are incompatible with existing relationships of power and domination, which are not recognized and which defy and challenge them. This is where Critical Hermeneutics, in conjunction with In-Depth Hermeneutics, now has the task of recognizing and developing the meaning of this subversive potential in a process of reflection and dialogue. In so doing, it can accomplish its self-imposed task of expanding cultural reflexivity and contributing to a situated autonomy.

Closing Remarks

The critical hermeneutic theory developed by Hans-Herbert Kögler, notably as a result of his work on Gadamer and Foucault, serves as a central methodology for the social and cultural sciences, which are geared to social critique. It focuses on the domination and power structures of the present, addresses and interprets them and attempts to destabilize, question and overcome them through reflection, dialogue and criticism. The aim is a "self-empowered subject."[5]

Kögler has conclusively demonstrated how hermeneutics, long regarded as conservative, can be rendered fruitful for critical theory. Critical hermeneutic theory is necessary to reveal and encourage the potential for resistance and willfulness or obstinacy in society and in the individual. It makes an essential contribution to the understanding of the enigma agency (cf. Kögler/Pechriggl/Winter 2019). Kögler's fundamental analyses are not only important for philosophy, but also for sociology, cultural studies, pedagogy, qualitative research, etc., provided that this research is not oriented "in a traditional way" in the sense of Max Horkheimer (1937/1999) or "in a positivist way" in the sense of Adorno. Ultimately, critical hermeneutic theory is concerned with critical theory in the tradition of the Frankfurt School.

Translated by Karen Meehan

Notes

1. In his contribution "Kritische Hermeneutik des Subjekts" [critical hermeneutics of the subject] (1999), he takes a detailed look at early critical theory and discusses its similarities and differences to cultural studies. In his view, both approaches explore the "symbolic construction of the subject by power" (ibid.: 196) and the question of how forms of resistance to existing power practices could be developed. Kögler seeks to show that Critical Hermeneutics can provide a theoretical framework that allows us to answer these questions. In doing so, it relies on the fact that "linguistic meaning simultaneously contains the potential of transgression and criticism of power" (ibid.: 228).
2. The fundamentally dialogical character of every theory formation is demonstrated by Peter Zima in "What is Theory?" (2007).
3. I exemplified this in my study "Die Kunst des Eigensinns. Cultural Studies als Kritik der Macht" [The Art of Obstinacy. Cultural Studies as Critique of Power] (2017). Cultural Studies examine the embeddedness of creativity in mundane practices and everyday uses that interpret symbolic forms, cultural objects and technologies "against the grain" or use them in a deconstructive way that deviates from the manual. This creative approach to the conflictual dynamics of everyday life is, according to my analysis, based on an art of obstinacy that does not primarily unfold in the struggle of arguments or as an expression of a universalizable rationality, but is often bodily integrated into common mundane practices.
4. In the field of qualitative research, it is mainly the methods of auto-ethnography and performance ethnography which, through self-analysis and a creative staging of life experiences, seek to adopt an innovative way of dealing with oneself in which one's own life is understood, interpreted and subsequently changed (Denzin 2003; Winter

2014). The aim is to create and extend a space for dialogue and debate with the intention of initiating and supporting personal and social change.

5   A discussion of this concept in the context of critical pedagogy (Kincheloe/McLaren/Steinberg 2011; McLaren 2015), which mainly follows on from Paulo Freire and the Frankfurt School, is still pending. For critical pedagogy, as for Kögler, the critical analysis of power relations and the strengthening of the agency of the subjects under their control is central. The "self-empowered subject" could be a model for critical pedagogy.

References

Adorno, Theodor W. (ed.) (1969), *Der Positivismusstreit in der deutschen Soziologie.* Neuwied: Luchterhand.
Bourdieu, Pierre (1984), *Distinction: A Social Critique of the Judgement of Taste.* London: Routledge and Kegan Paul Ltd.
Bourdieu, Pierre (2013), *Outline of a Theory of Practice.* Cambridge: Cambridge University Press.
Bourdieu, Pierre and Loic J.D. Wacquant (1992), *An Invitation to Reflexive Sociology.* Cambridge: Polity Press.
Denzin, Norman K. (2003), *Performance Ethnography. Critical Pedagogy and the Politics of Culture.* Thousand Oaks etc.: Sage.
Foucault, Michel (1977), *Discipline and Punish: The Birth of the Prison.* New York: Pantheon.
Foucault, Michel (1978), *The History of Sexuality, Volume 1.* New York: Pantheon.
Foucault, Michel (1981), "The Order of Discourse," in Robert Young (ed.), *Untying the Text: A Post-Structuralist Reader.* New York/London: Routledge & Kegan Paul, pp. 48–78.
Gadamer, Hans-Georg (2013), *Truth and Method.* New York: Bloomsbury.
Gadamer, Hans-Georg (1997), *Gadamer Lesebuch,* herausgegeben von Jean Grondin. Tübingen: Mohr.
Habermas, Jürgen (1971), "Der Universalitätsanspruch der Hermeneutik," in *Theorie-Diskussion Hermeneutik und Ideologiekritik.* Frankfurt a.M.: Suhrkamp, pp. 120–59.
Honneth, Axel (1995), *The Struggle for Recognition: The Moral Grammar of Social Conflicts.* Cambridge: Polity Press.
Horkheimer, Max (orig. 1937/1999), "Traditional and critical theory," in Matthew O'Connel (ed.) *Critical Theory. Selected Essays.* New York: Continuum.
Hoy, David Couzens (1994), "Critical Theory and Critical History," in David Couzens Hoy, and Thomas McCarthy, *Critical Theory.* Oxford, UK/Cambridge, USA: Blackwell, pp. 101–213.
Kincheloe, Joe L., Peter McLaren, and Shirley R. Steinberg (2011), "Critical Pedagogy, and Qualitative Research: Moving to the Bricolage," in Norman K. Denzin and Yvonna S. Lincoln (eds.), *The SAGE Handbook of Qualitative Research Fourth Edition.* Los Angeles et al.: Sage, pp. 163–78.
Kögler, Hans-Herbert (1992), *Die Macht des Dialogs. Kritische Hermeneutik nach Gadamer, Foucault und Rorty.* Stuttgart: Metzler.
Kögler, Hans-Herbert (1996a), *The Power of Dialogue. Critical Hermeneutics after Gadamer and Foucault.* Cambridge; London: MIT Press.
Kögler, Hans-Herbert (1996b), "The self-empowered subject. Habermas, Foucault and hermeneutic reflexivity," *Philosophy & Social Criticism,* 22 (4): 13–44.

Kögler, Hans-Herbert (1997), "Alienation as epistemological source: reflexivity and social background after Mannheim and Bourdieu." *Social Epistemology* Vol. 11, No. 2, pp. 141–64.
Kögler, Hans-Herbert (1999), "Kritische Hermeneutik des Subjekts. Cultural Studies als Erbe der Kritischen Theorie," in Karl H. Hörning and Rainer Winter (eds.), *Widerspenstige Kulturen. Cultural Studies als Herausforderung*. Frankfurt a.M.: Suhrkamp, pp. 196–237.
Kögler, Hans-Herbert (2004), *Michel Foucault*. Zweite Auflage. Stuttgart. Metzler.
Kögler, Hans-Herbert (2019), "Autonomie und Überschreitung. Bruchstücke einer Theorie der hermeneutischen Agency," in Hans-Herbert Kögler, Alice Pechriggl, and Rainer Winter (eds.), *Enigma Agency. Macht-Widerstand-Reflexivität*. Bielefeld: transcript, pp. 81–112.
Kögler, Hans-Herbert/Pechriggl, Alice/Winter, Rainer (eds.) (2019), *Enigma Agency. Macht-Widerstand-Reflexivität*. Bielefeld: transcript.
Lorenzer, Alfred (1970), *Sprachzerstörung und Rekonstruktion*. Frankfurt a.M.: Suhrkamp.
Lorenzer, Alfred (1981), *Das Konzil der Buchhalter. Die Zerstörung der Sinnlichkeit. Eine Religionskritik*. Frankfurt a.M.: EVA.
Lorenzer, Alfred (2002), *Sprache, Sinn und das Unbewusste. Psychoanalytisches Grundverständnis und Neurowissenschaften*. Stuttgart: Klett Cotta.
Lorenzer, Alfred (2006), "Psychoanalyse als kritische Theorie," in Alfred Lorenzer, *Szenisches Verstehen. Zur Erkenntnis des Unbewussten*, herausgegeben von Ulrike Prokop und Bernard Görlich. Marburg: Tectum Verlag, pp. 89–114.
Lorenzer, Alfred (ed.) (1986), *Kultur-Analysen*. Frankfurt a.M.: Fischer.
McLaren, Peter (2015), *Pedagogy of Insurrection. From Resurrection to Revolution*. New York et al. Peter Lang.
Mead, George Herbert (1934/1967), *Mind, Self & Society from the Standpoint of a Social Behaviorist*. Works of George Herbert Mead Volume 1. Edited and with an Introduction by Charles W. Morris. Chicago/London: University of Chicago Press. Paperback Edition.
Merleau-Ponty, Maurice (1962), *Phenomenology of Perception*. London: Routledge & Kegan Paul.
Oevermann, Ulrich (1983), "Zur Sache. Die Bedeutung von Adornos methodologischem Selbstverständnis für die Begründung einer materiellen soziologischen Strukturanalyse," in Ludwig Von Friedeburg and Jürgen Habermas (eds.), *Adorno-Konferenz 1983*. Frankfurt a.M.: Suhrkamp, pp. 234–89.
Straub, Jürgen (1999), *Handlung, Interpretation, Kritik. Grundzüge einer textwissenschaftlichen Handlungs- und Kulturpsychologie*. Berlin/New York: Walter de Gruyter.
Winter, Rainer (1986), *Rahmen-Analyse der Therapeut/Klient-Interaktion. Erving Goffmans Beitrag zur Analyse der therapeutischen Beziehung*. Unveröffentlichte Diplomarbeit im Fach Psychologie, Universität Trier.
Winter, Rainer (2014), "Ein Plädoyer für kritische Perspektiven in der qualitativen Forschung," in Günter Mey and Katja Mruck (eds.), *Qualitative Forschung. Analysen und Diskussionen—10 Jahre Berliner Methodentreffen*. Wiesbaden: Springer VS, pp. 117–32.
Winter, Rainer (2001/2017), *Die Kunst des Eigensinns. Cultural Studies als Kritik der Macht*. Zweite Auflage. Weilerswist: Velbrück Wissenschaft.
Wollenhaupt, Jonas (2018), *Die Entfremdung des Subjekts. Zur kritischen Theorie des Subjekts nach Pierre Bourdieu und Alfred Lorenzer*. Bielefeld: transcript.

Zima, Peter V. (2007), *What is Theory? Cultural Theory as Discourse and Dialogue*. London: Continuum.
Zima, Peter V. (2020), *Soziologische Theoriebildung. Ein Handbuch auf dialogischer Basis*. Tübingen: Narr Francke Attempto Verlag.

3

Naturalizing Kögler

Stephen Turner

Bert Kögler has been an advocate of a hermeneutic approach to intercultural understanding in such texts as: *The Power of Dialogue* (1999), Hermeneutic Cosmopolitanism, or: Toward a Cosmopolitan Public Sphere (2011), "Hermeneutics, Phenomenology, and Philosophical Anthropology" (2006), "Recognition and Difference" (2005), "Agency and the Other" (2012). In what follows I would like to conduct a kind of philosophical experiment: to translate the basic ideas of this approach into the language and concerns, and also the findings, of cognitive science. My strategy will be to replace some key ideas from the basics of his account with cognitive science concepts dealing with the same or similar phenomena, and ask whether the same kinds of conclusions Kögler draws about social theory and normative matters could be made to follow from these substitute starting points, and what other conclusions might be drawn. My goal is to create a kind of dialogue, indeed a dialogue that invites reflexivity of the kind to which he aspires in his work.

Why It Is a Problem

Kögler's work represents the confluence of multiple traditions of thinking about understanding and dialogue, but for the most part they represent variations on the rich tradition of German idealism. These operate with a more or less shared view of the autonomy of the realm of ideation, formulated, however, in different ways. In some sense, his work has been an attempt to synthesize these variants in such a way as to account for the core problems of cultural difference and to create the possibility of constructive engagement across cultures.

A radical approach, which one could develop historically, would contrast this entire tradition to its arch-enemy of empiricism and the solutions it has offered to the same set of problems.[1] A somewhat different approach would be to try to translate the concerns Kögler has articulated into the most contemporary form of this tradition, namely cognitive science. This is what I will do, in little more than an outline form, in this chapter. But to prepare for doing so, I will explain what I take to be the historically rooted issues with this strategy, which arise primarily from one source: the idea that the human and ideational is a special realm, irreducible and fundamentally unlike the processes one can ascribe to brains and "natural" cognitive processes.

The difficulties here are old as well as new: mind-body, scheme-content, ideas-impressions, the problem of consciousness itself, and much more are entangled with it. They are apparent in a topic Kögler has worked on, the problem of empathy. Empathy, to make a bad pun, brings these problems to a head: it is simultaneously mental and physical. In a naïve sense, the issue is this: people need a theory of mind to understand other people. Theories are semantic and explicit. But understanding, and acting on understanding, is physical, tacit, and associated with known brain processes, such as the activation of mirror neurons.

Defining the issues is difficult on its own, but a simplified view of the problem might go like this. There is a long tradition of taking the conceptual as a mark of the non-natural, in order to argue that the conceptual is presupposed by such natural phenomenon as causal relations: to have cause means to have a concept of cause. Thus a "theory" is conceptual and therefore can't be explained empirically. But psychologists routinely regard theories as natural facts, and possessions of natural minds. Thus Alison Gopnik gives an account of the theory of mind as a theory *in* the mind (Gopnik and Wellman 1992) rather than as an external model of cognitive processes. And there is another naturalistic response: that empathy is not theoretical in the first place, and, therefore, neither is understanding, at least the understanding of other people. Texts and explicit theories are another matter, though they need to be "understood" as well. But they are objects, part of the objective world, in a way that intentions and other mental entities are not.

For the naturalist, either the "theory" can be given a naturalistic explanation or is actually unnecessary to account for understanding other people. And here these claims intrude into the domain of interpersonal and even intercultural hermeneutics. The question it raises is this: Do the categories of cognitive science exhaust the category of understanding? Is there a different order of understanding that hermeneutics captures and naturalistic cognitive science cannot? What is fundamentally different between the famous episode of the chimp whose action-producing nerves fire for eating a bowl of gelato when he observes the experimenter doing it, and a human seeing where someone is going and what they are doing, or what they mean by saying or even writing something?

The philosophical task of naturalism is to make philosophical problems into empirical questions, usually by re-describing problems in an empirically equivalent way. The relevant empirical domain is plausibly thought to be cognitive science. And this produces another problem, especially in relation to culture. Cognitive Science (or at least its theoretical form, which is the philosophy of cognitive science) has a tradition of working on "hard problems," such as perception, and puzzles, such as the problem of qualia or the problem of consciousness, and typically has concerned itself with mental processes that are either shared with, or can be exemplified with, non-human models, either animals or computers. You can think of these as "disencultured." So, with a few exceptions, such as Dan Sperber, and, in a formal way, the theorists of cultural evolution, there is not a standard bridge to Kögler's cultural concerns. But there are elements of cognitive science that match elements of his project, including the problem of empathy, and it is worth matching the concepts to see whether a difference in description makes a difference.

Kögler's Project

The project Kögler has developed over many writings is determinedly non-naturalist. He seeks "a dialogical notion of self-consciousness, an inter-subjectivist model of self-identity, and a social source for ethical recognition," and says that these can constitute "major premises for critical social inquiry in the human and social sciences" (2012: 49). This model is based on the assumption "that intersubjective understanding, as it is oriented toward another intentional agent, is different in kind from the explanation of non-intentional natural events" (Kögler 2006: 209). Understanding is defined as "the adequate reconstruction of the other's intended meaning, the meaning which the interpreter or agent is encountering in the objectification of a text, artwork, speech act, or social act" (2006: 209).

Reconstruction, in this sense, is idealist: it is "(a) based on some mediating interpretive scheme; and (b) nonetheless bound by the presupposition that we are dealing with an intentional expression" (Kögler 2006: 209). The question, in this account, is "how intersubjective understanding is affected by the fact that all understanding is mediated by some symbolic pre-construction of the object, or, inversely, what the general pre-schematization of experience means if we are dealing with another agent's symbolically mediated acts" (Kögler 2006: 209). This points to the problem of culture, which is the source of these pre-schematizations. This is a problematic familiar from neo-Kantianism, and its distinction between logic and psychology: "logical" categories are in some obscure sense built into experience, and experience is impossible without the categories; but if this is the case, how is it that categories or schema vary between people and between cultures, and why are they not, therefore, psychological facts rather than "logical" ones?

Part of his answer to such traditional questions involves the notion of agency, which he takes to link the world of ideas and the real world. Thus: "First, a subject with agency has to have the capacity to affect real change in the world. Concretely, this means that a self which is situated in an objective order must have at its disposal the means to transform the status quo of its existent context, regardless of whether this context is conceived in terms of holistic discursive relations, social–institutional arrangements and practices, or natural or biological preconditions for existence" (Kögler 2012: 48). For "a pure mind deprived of any causal powers, or in an epistemologically conceived observer's attitude without any connection toward the observed context, talk about agency would fail to make sense." He adds that agency also requires "a realistic understanding of one's own place, i.e., that one has to be able to distinguish which actions or events are caused by oneself and which ones are not, i.e., which ones are instead attributable to external causes beyond one's influence" (2012: 48).

Are there cognitive science resources to account for the development of such capacities? They are, it turns out, part of the infant's earliest development, and they come along with the basic capacity to recognize others, which Andrew Meltzhoff illustrated with his famous photographs of newborn babies imitating the facial expressions of an adult. This is the early stage of a complex process, but it is striking that the recognition of others as being like one's self, and in addition the capacity to interact with facial expressions without learning them, is fundamental to social interaction, and enables a developmental path through interaction that eventuates in moral recognition. As Meltzhoff explains:

> We think that infants' ability to detect that something out there in the world is like me and can do what I do, has cascading developmental effects. The reciprocal imitation games between parents and infants serve a didactic function prompting infants to elaborate a sense of self and self-other correspondences beyond the neonatal level. The developmental progression would be from seeing another as an entity who behaves like me, to someone who shares other deeper equivalences as well as a being who has goals, desires and intentions just like the self, and, farther along the developmental pathway, moral rights equivalent to one's own.
>
> Meltzoff and Moore 1999: 30; see also Meltzoff 1995

Along this developmental pathway, an awareness of intentionality occurs. Infants at 8 months can distinguish intentional and non-intentional actions. So can animals.

Is this primary intersubjective understanding? The intersubjectivity of learning about the world and oneself and others seems to be pre-linguistic, and concerns the key elements of "understanding." When children learn about themselves, they also learn about others, and learn the two in parallel. But what they do tacitly and what they do explicitly or discursively turn out to be two different things. "Children as young as 18 months could sense others' desires when they made faces" (Repacholi and Gopnik 1997: 12). Before three, they learn about love, perception, desire, but can't answer questions about false beliefs and issues about belief (Repacholi and Gopnik 1997: 12).

The test of the development of a theory of mind, including in the Critical Theory literature (see Nunner-Winkler 1992), is the ability of the child to solve the false belief problem, which involves experimental situations in which the child must infer the existence of a false belief in a person enacting a scene involving a hidden object which has been moved to location the child knows but which the person has seen in a different, original location. The traditional test is to ask the child where the person will look for the object. It was thought that this capacity developed around 30 months of age, when they began to give the correct answers, and this was taken as evidence that they had a "theory of mind" which enabled them to make the correct inferences. Newer research, based on attention studies that do not require a high level of linguistic competence suggests that infants at 18 months may be able to detect false belief situations, but not articulate them (Onishi and Baillargeon 2005; Baillargeon et al 2010; Choi and Luo 2015). This appears to involve

> at least three processes: (i) a *false-belief-representation* process, carried out by SS2 in the psychological-reasoning system (children must represent the agent's false belief); (ii) a *response-selection* process (when asked the test question, children must access their representation of the agent's false belief to select a response) and

(iii) a *response-inhibition* process (when selecting a response, children must inhibit any prepotent tendency to answer the test question based on their own knowledge).
Baillargeon et al 2010: 113–15; emphasis in original

Distinguishing these processes raises a number of important questions, which bear on the problem of interpersonal understanding, and also on culture.

When does enculturation start? The usual argument is that it starts with expectations: "human agents are constantly (deliberately or automatically) adjusting what they are doing to what relevant others (e.g., role models or anti-role models, specific or generalized) expect, and expect them to expect, and so on. Much of this is accomplished implicitly (Tomasello et al. 2005)" (quoted in Veissière et al. 2019: 6–7). But they acquire these culture specific expectations, "the doxa of backstage behavior" which "is itself already culturally patterned, despite the immediate absence of others' enforcing gaze (and the foregrounding of inferences we make about what others know and expect in context)" (Veissière et al. 2019: 6). But how? "A first hint is the fact that usually through nonverbal communication with gesture, facial expression, posture, and pantomime, but also through language when necessary" (Veissière et al. 2019: 7). And this is the kind of pre-linguistic interactive knowledge found in the experiments cited above. The capacities for understanding others are not innate, though they are based on innate capacities, but are a matter of social learning. But "the main role of others in this kind of social learning is to direct attention rather than to convey specific semantic content (Tomasello 2014)" (quoted in Veissière et al. 2019: 8). Immersion in particular social contexts in which attention is directed produces "*regimes of attention* and imitation that direct human agents to engage differentially in forms of shared intentionality" (Veissière et al. 2019: 8; emphasis in original). These are taken to "play a central role in the enculturation of human agents (Ramstead et al. 2016)" (Veissière et al. 2019: 8), and "human beings seem particularly specialized for such forms of social learning (Sterelny 2012)" (Veissière et al. 2019: 8).

How does this fit with Kögler's argument? He rejects accounts which make understanding pre-linguistic, because they imply that "language makes the expressed and articulated self-understanding of the other a second-best: the true intersubjectivity must be seen as existing in a pre-articulated dimension prior to the linguistic-grammatical crust, prior to those lifeless crystallizations that exist in the form of documented linguistic facts." He reasons that

this reading would, I suggest, falsely assume that to escape a structuralist (and one-sided) conception of language, we have to suggest a pre-linguistic, inner expressive medium. It would make us believe that to bring agency, process, and creativity into language; we have to introduce an ethical-metaphysical dimension deeper than language.
Kögler 2005, 258–9

His aim is not simply to make interpretation dependent on language, however, but to avoid what he takes to be an unsatisfactory dilemma, indeed the dilemma that motivated *Lebensphilosophie*: between languages as a set of rigid forms that constrains expression and a pre-linguistic form of expression that is more vital. He suggests an alternative view:

> ... that the expressive self exists truly in and through the linguistic cultural medium by articulating multiple perspectives, by engaging in reinterpretation and novel accounts, by disclosing the world through constructing its own relation to it. What agents are is given not prior to language, but only in language, after the event of language—which must not mean that the form dominates, not, in the words of Humboldt, the "ergon," but rather suggests the power of an interpretive "energeia."
>
> 2005: 258–9

On the surface, this is an irreconcilable conflict. But with a little help from Russian psychology we can bring the two a little closer.

Materialism and Children

Russian psychology referred to language as the second signal system; the first being the pre-linguistic system of expression that corresponds to such things as love, perception, and desire, mentioned above, or, in Wittgenstein's private language discussion, pain, which he thought of being associated with, along with many other things, "natural reactions" (Rubinstein 2004). The basic idea is that children acquire this second system and doing so reorganizes their brains. But the Russian approach to acquisition, which especially interested such thinkers as Vytgosky and Luria (Luria and Yudovich [1956] 1971; Vytgosky and Luria [1930/1993] 2009), is also of interest here, because it was directly aimed at providing a materialist alternative to "idealism" of the kind derived from the German traditions.

Because the traditions they rejected assumed abstract thought as constitutive, the "materialist'" focus was on the problem of explaining abstract thinking from the ground up. They observed what has been observed many times since: that children become able to describe their own and others' activities at the same time. They also learn mental terms for themselves and others at the same time, and in association with activities. This was the beginning of abstraction, but there was a much more powerful step: elementary symbol construction, which they could observe in children's play, which involved a simple step, which they called conditional dependence, which allowed them to designate an object as another object—to say this stick is my horse, for example. This basic cognitive skill shows up at an early stage. And it fits well with current research which shows that children can easily assign properties of one object to another.

Is this "symbolic" thinking? It is not pre-linguistic, but pre-abstract—it shows up at the stage of describing activities, the first language phase, and as part of mastering the second symbol system. It requires language. And it involves intersubjective understanding, of the conditional designation of the object as another object, and the intention of the designator, which is linguistically mediated. Is this form of intersubjective understanding through symbols, via the second signal system, the kind of understanding Kögler has in mind? He describes the interpretive situation as one that

> ... does not overcome the interpretive predicament that to make sense of another shall always involve some projective attribution, a "hermeneutic circle" where I assign the most plausible and rational meanings to the other's symbolic expression on the basis of my own background assumptions. What is now gained is the focus on the *adequacy of the cultural interpretation*, the assessment of what defines the concrete meaning expressed by the symbolic act of another subject.
>
> Kögler 2006: 209; emphasis in the original

The simple child's act of making a stick into a horse seems to do exactly this: the meaning of the object becomes detached from the original act of interpretation, so that it can become intersubjective. I can tell another child "that is his horse." And it can become known as his horse without any interaction with the child who originally said it was his horse. All that is needed is the linguistic framework for doing so: the capacity to understand the meaning of the next child's statement "that is his horse."

Is "that is his horse" a "theory," or an "assumption"? Is it constitutive? Does it amount to creating what Kögler calls a "mediating interpretive scheme" (Kögler 2006: 209)? Gopnik's criteria for calling something a theory is that it is some sort of mental content that is revisable through experience, which assumes in advance that mental content takes the form of a theory. This, and all of these uses, is analogical. The "theory," scheme, assumptions and so forth are attributed, not formulated by the speakers. They may not be able to be articulated. Attributing them trades on the similarity between something explicit, like Euclid's elements, which for two millennia and beyond was the paradigm of rationality, and something tacit. The topic of triangles loomed large for the neo-Kantians, such as Friedrich Trendelenburg, precisely because space was constituted by categories, ideal triangles were regulative rather than real, concepts of space were abstract, but also in some sense empirical, and because all of this seemed to follow from a difficult to locate a priori place.

The Russian account has answers to these questions, which can be illustrated by Kögler's own problem, the intentional/causal distinction. Is the intentional/causal distinction something that happens early in cognitive development, or is there something there that is different from our distinction—a secondary development of intention detection/recognition that arrives along with language and overlays the original "natural signs" distinction? And is there something in between? The Russian view is that the acquisition of the second signal system reorganizes the brain. So the distinctions, expectations, linkages, and so forth that are part of the second signal system, or language, becomes part of the brain, through its reorganization. The system becomes second nature—habitual—and no longer directly accessible to consciousness. We can reflect on our thoughts and actions, but this is not the same as access. The deep structure of our linguistic habits is not something we can simply recall, because they have never been present to us in a recallable way in the first place.

We make the intentional/causal distinction in action. But do we do it in our linguistically structured theory of the world in the same way? This question tells us something about the notion of theory. We, as modern scientific people, do not think that plants have souls, or emotions. What is the status of this thought and when does it arrive in the developmental process? I can give an odd personal illustration of this issue. I was asked to speak to my son's class of ten year old children on what a philosopher does. I went online to look for children's philosophy resources, and came across something like the following prompt. "My aunt went away for a trip, and we had to check her plants. When we saw them, they were sad." This was to be followed by a discussion of whether plants could be sad. I asked the students what they thought about this question. They could not see the problem: they agreed that of course plants can be sad.

The plants they probably visualized were droopy, and thus "sad." They needed water. They were easily anthropomorphized, and indeed it would decimate children's literature if plants, houses, not to mention animals, could not have emotions. Children's play would be very different if they could not treat a stick as a horse. And it is far from clear that we outgrow this kind of response to the physical, non-intentional world. What we learn instead, and the children had not learned, is something that is like a theory: materialism. And we learn a vocabulary for making distinctions that amount to a kind of affirmation of materialism. In terms of this theory-like doctrine, or truth, the linguistic practices of children and children's literature do not make sense.

This allows us to pose some questions, and wade into the morass of distinctions alluded to above. There is something between the first signal system, natural signs, and the second, language, namely, a great deal of learning that is tacit. Learning about love and desire, to take the examples already mentioned, precedes its linguistic formulation. Gopnik would think of this learning as empirically based refinements of the child's innate or near-innate theory of mind. Without judging this claim, an observation is in order. The idea that being amendable to empirical input means that one has a theory is just odd. Tacit knowledge, obviously, is a response to empirical input: one learns to ride a bike by the feedback of balance, for example. Odd as this may sound, children's play produces feedback and therefore empirical input, on such things as social roles, for example, in playing house, which teaches appropriate acts, responses, and so forth. But play does this not by rote, but by joint improvisation between playmates who have observed what they are enacting, or have heard about it. This open-ended learning is more like learning to ride a bicycle than mastering a theory by rote. But even if we regard the child as a scientist in the crib, as Gopnik does, and attribute theories to the child, the empirical feedback will differ from child to child, and cultural situation to cultural situation, even if both theory and tacit knowledge converge in a common direction with more experience.

Once a child enters into full social interaction, which occurs even before birth and expands afterwards, experience individuates, and also directs, through interaction, toward the kind of convergence that enables mutual understanding about more and more things. Play is a mechanism of convergence, for example, in understandings of social roles—one of the things children routinely play at. Some of this occurs before language, though this stage is often described as "parallel play." With language a large range of possibility for joint improvisation opens up. Designating a stick as a horse, and having others accept this designation, allows for new roles to be enacted through joint improvisation. This is where social skills develop. Play involving them is a matter of assigning properties: "you are the mommy."

This is also a place where taking the role of the other, and learning the game of justification, interdiction, explanation, judging actions, and so forth takes place, based at least in part with their experiences with, and imitation of, adult behavior, as well as their engagement with adults who are playing the games of forbidding, justifying, explaining, and question-asking themselves: the "why, mommy?" stage. This is important in innumerable ways, but has a special relation to the explanation and meaning of actions. The older reasons and causes literature was focused on the impossibility of a person taking an "action" without having a concept of the action: such an "action" would be a behavior or reflex, but not an action (Winch 1958; Melden 1961; MacIntyre 1962). This distinction seemed to imply that action was a conceptual phenomenon governed by conceptual rather than causal relations. This tight link between action and concepts has been challenged by cognitive science—from the time of Herbert Spencer to the present—by arguments that separate the cognitive processes that go into action from the social phenomenon of justification.

The most recent and most detailed formulation of this argument has been given by Mercier and Sperber, in a book (2017) and a major review article (2011). They argue that justification and persuasion are social strategies that are learned and are situation specific and culturally specific, and do not represent cognitive processes, which they take to be modular; though in their case modularity is understood not as the fixed and evolutionarily dependent product of life in the ancient African savannah, but as the cognitive short-cuts that the brain develops in response to the environment, including the social environment. Fast cognition, problem-solving, recognition, and the rest of what goes on under the level of consciousness is, presumably, modular in this sense. But we need not accept this idea of modularity to accept their point about justification: it is part of a social activity directed at producing a response in other people rather than a record or depiction of the mental processes involved in action.

A curious proof of this separation between justification and cognition is found in the case of hypnotized subjects, who, when asked for an explanation of the actions they undertook under the influence of hypnotic suggestion, were capable of immediately inventing creative answers, and a variety of them, without feeling they were fabricating any of them (Wegner 2002). But we can reestablish the tight link, at least partially, by noting that the reorganization of the brain through the second signal system *includes* the habitual, or second-nature, resorts to these justifications and explanations of action which become part of the set of expectations associated with a given action. We learn, in short, that an action "means" that responses involving particular justifications, sets of questions, along with other consequences will predictably result from an act, and anticipating this, and anticipating our own response to demands for explanations and justifications, becomes second nature to us. Thus justification gets incorporated into cognitive processing, without representing the cognitive processes themselves.

Where does this Leave Us?

My goal in this little conceptual experiment has been to substitute cognitive science concepts for the concepts Kögler relies on, some of which come from hermeneutics, others from critical theory. This is enough material to raise some questions for Kögler's argument. Gopnik describes the scientist in the crib, formulating theories and testing hypotheses. Does Kögler's account require a hermeneutic analyst in the crib? If so, where do the interpretive schemes come from, and how do they get revised? Kögler typically deals with a regulative ideal, the idea of "a true and authentic encounter with the other." He claims that "the face-to-face encounter is culturally mediated; it is no primordial experience as such, but is embedded and "disclosed" through interpretive schemes, which themselves are always related to linguistically articulated beliefs and assumptions (Kögler 2005: 258).

The classic papers on play and pretending are by Leslie and Nichols and Stich (Leslie 1987; Nichols and Stich 2000: 2003), and are designed to argue that a certain kind of representation is necessary to account for pretending.

> As summarized by Varga (2011), Leslie's account explains the following aspects of pretense: *object substitution* (using an object as if it is something else, e.g., using a banana as a phone); *attribution of false properties* (ascribing a pretend property to something, e.g., pretending that the doll's dry hair is wet); and *making a reference to an absent object* (the invention of an imaginary object, e.g., feeding the doll invisible cake, and referring to it as if it were present).
>
> Rucińska 2016: 145; emphasis in original; see also Rucińska 2019a, 2019b

There are alternative approaches—representational (as in Leslie and Nichols and Stich), enactive, and behavioral—to account for pretending. And they shed a certain light on the issue of the cognitive basis and nature of hermeneutics and where it starts, which tells us something about what hermeneutics is. The core issue is between two general approaches to cognitive development.

The first is represented by Leslie and Nichols and Stich: for them cognitive development is an internal process, in which cognitive elements are built on top of one another and presuppose earlier elements. Thus, it becomes plausible to think of the three "aspects" listed above as sequential cognitive achievements which together make pretense possible. To simplify only slightly, cognition follows the path of explicit justification, in which one consideration depends on a prior one, which is developmentally as well as logically prior. These can be depicted as operating on representations, and indeed depending on them. It is natural to say that making reference to an absent object requires having a representation of it, and being able to make logical operations over that object.

The alternative to this way of thinking is less well defined, but can be sketched out. Critics of some of the standard forms of cognitive science analysis have pointed out that its main variants, such as predictive processing, make it difficult to account for divergent cultures and values, and for such things as the fact that people can and do put values above survival, and above epistemic gain, i.e., the benefits that are supposed to flow from fundamental cognitive processes such as predictive processing. The alternative to the internal development approach takes the following line: Children are never pre-social: they are immersed always in a world of social interactions and distinctive usable objects and things with apparent uses, so-called "affordances."

This account fits nicely with an account of cultural difference that relies on the notion of scaffolding.

> According to some anthropologists, "the underpinnings of scaffolding are human niches [that] comprise affordances that can be figured out, rediscovered, or rebuilt by human individuals in each generation without the 'transmission' of a purportedly separate realm of 'cultural representations'" (Ingold 2001). Although Ingold's critics argue that "what humans learn over their life spans in order to become proficient at functioning in their local worlds, is learned *socially*— that is to say, learned primarily from other humans, and not just from what things or situations themselves afford." Ingold responds that "many aspects of human life are simply emulated (Hamilton 2008), "shown," or "pointed to," and left to be explored, "figured out," and experimented with by individual learners (for example, in play).
>
> Veissière et al. 2019: 8; emphasis in original

Emulation is a good place to start on getting to an alternative, and one that provides us with a way of thinking about culture and enculturation. In the first place, emulation is by definition social and interactive: one emulates something one sees someone else doing. But emulation also is a learning device: one emulates and discovers for oneself how to do something, what the consequences are, what it feels like, and so forth. The neonate's face-making in response to a facial expression is a form of emulation, but it also produces feedback and thus learning. And it is so early in the developmental process that it is implausible to treat it as the outcome of a series of presupposed cognitive achievements in a logical sequence. And this gives us a clue about how to think of the beginning points of cultural hermeneutics.

Consider the game of peek-a-boo. It is usually interpreted as having to do with object permanence, with the thought that very young infants do not have a grasp of object permanence, but that at six months they have expectations for the identity and location of a returning person, and they enjoy conformity to these expectations, and that by 8 or 9 months they enjoy surprises in the form of mild deviations from these expectations. In a few more months, the baby can play the game herself: hiding and showing her face to produce a response (see Stafford 2014). This is regarded by some as proto-linguistic, in that it involves turn-taking.

But peekaboo is not *just* about expectations. Covering a face is not the same as removing the person with the face—it is removing a property, facial visibility, and returning it. Otherwise there is continuity. So the game teaches something abstract about the possibility of removing properties and returning them, i.e., the detachability of properties from things. It does not assume a presupposition. Moreover it seems to be learned: the child initially responds as though the mother is gone; later responds as though the mother is expected to return; still later as though the baby expects the mother to be in the same state of expectation and to respond in the same way, producing joint emulation.

Detaching properties from things—in this case visibility from the person—can be thought of on the model of presuppositions, as a step toward the higher game of assigning properties to things—making a banana a phone, or a stick into a horse. But this can be thought of much more simply: the act of using a banana as a phone is a kind of emulation. So is the use of a stick for a horse. The emulation is in the activity: that the banana does not speak and the stick does not go to the stable is our adult response. For the child, the act of emulation with these odd objects does something that is sufficient for them. Odd as the objects used as a substitute seem to us, they are close enough to emulate recognizable aspects, properties, of the activity. And to be "social" in a pragmatic sense is to be able to convey something recognizable by this emulation.

Language, of course, substantially expands our capacity for doing this. One may see a child riding a stick like a horse and grasp that they are pretending, or that they are playing with an imaginary friend. While it is possible to imagine cases in which one understands pretending without language or affirmations, such as saying "this stick is my horse," this kind of affirmation does seem to take us to a new level: the symbolic. When one announces that we are "playing house," and that "I am the mother," one is appealing to linguistic categories—the second signal system. And doing so both disciplines—because we are now limited in our play to the plausible enactment of social roles—and expands our capacity to play. This is the beginning, in some sense, of culture. These roles are affordances, as are the habits and expectations of others, that allow us to act, not just in rote forms, but by improvising, in ways that can be understood by others.

What is play? What is pretending? We are inclined to think of play and pretending as the anomalies, and to regard the serious business of mutual understanding to involve something more basic—real intentions, real meanings, and real understanding. But we can invert this relationship, as it is in fact inverted in the experience of the child. Play, in the form of peekaboo or later playing house, is foundational. It is where reciprocity is established in more complex forms. The relations are not mechanical, as the neonate's response to facial expressions is, though they may depend on the capacity to recognize and feel empathically in response to these expressions. They involve something like "as if" thinking. It is as if the mother is gone when she is hiding her face, and as if the child playing house is the mother. But in these cases the "as if" is the condition of play, and of understanding. For them the social roles are also play—just as the stick as horse is.

Developmentally, we go from play to "reality." But from the point of view of cognitive development, play is not an inferior form of dealing with reality, but the reverse: dealing with reality is a circumscribed, and in many respects impoverished, form of play. To be a real Mother requires meeting conditions that a play mother need not meet. But paradoxically, these conditions are also empowering. To enter into the linguistically rich world of the language of motherhood is to gain the power to evoke responses in strangers, in symbolic forms, in print, and to avail oneself of the affordances supplied by people's habits of mind, mental associations, sentiments, emotions, and so forth, and to do so much more reliably because these things are linguistically ordered. This is the important truth in Kögler's argument.

But there is something more than language. Language builds on and transforms things that are already there. The enculturation involved in learning the mother role is emulative. Not only does one receive this emulative experience in play, one sees mothers behaving as mothers. And much of this emulation is unconscious, though mixed with verbal signals. This was the point of Nancy Friday's book *My Mother, My Self* (1977), which dealt with mother daughter relations and the powerful unconscious effects of modelling on one's mother.

The sheer complexity of the process of transforming oneself—reorganizing the brain—to cope with and function within a cultural niche, to use its affordances, to adapt to the expectations of others and unconsciously rely on their patterns of behavior, patterns, and so forth, has profound consequences nevertheless. In adapting to complex structure, a niche, we become unadapted to other structures, other ways of thinking. This is the source of the problem of intercultural communication. The phenomenon of justification is central to this, because justification is socially specific, local, and cultural. And the differences are the obstacle to intercultural understanding.

We do not lose our capacity to play, to emulate, and to perform acts of substitution such as making a stick into a horse. Indeed, we become practiced in combining properties to make new things. If this is the basis for abstract and symbolic thought we have already achieved it, through play, at a young age. Nevertheless the gains we receive through mastery of the second symbol system, and its more complex variants, gains in the power to persuade, to influence others, and to extend our influence through impersonal communication, are offset by losses. There is a famous quotation from J. Robert Oppenheimer that

> there are children playing in the streets who could solve some of my top problems in physics, because they have modes of sensory perception that I lost long ago.
>
> quoted in McLuhan 1967: 93

This is, if anything, more true for cultural differences: we lose emotional responses, connections, modes of empathy, as we gain mastery of the affordances of our cultural niche. And we lose the capacity to comprehend others who have made the same transition in mastering their own cultural niches.

Kögler's strategy for cultural hermeneutics, which seeks a "dialogical conception of cultural identity that productively mediates between the Scylla of social holism and the Charybdis of atomistic individualism" (2007: 359), fits this basic picture, when he says that

> Selves are shown to be dialogical identities, which means that they are (a) essentially shaped by the recognition of other agents, with whom they are engaged in social interaction in mutually shared cultural contexts, and (b) agents are essentially open, internally diverse, and never fully accomplished structures, which follows from the derivation of their identity from dialogical processes of perspective-taking.
>
> 2007: 354

For Kögler, this diversity and openness, and our capacity to transcend our cultural limitations, is the condition for the possibility of authentic intercultural communication. And this leads to a final observation: it is not in the merging of fixed horizons, of different culturally constructed "realities," that understanding becomes possible, but rather in the area of open and improvisational interactions that more closely resemble play. It is in the recapturing of this mode, rather than the appeal to universal standards of validity, that authentic dialogue becomes possible. On this Kögler and the developmentalists can agree.

Note

1 I have provided something like this in "The Cognitive Dimension" (2021).

References

Baillargeon, R., R.M. Scott, and Z. He (2010), 'False-Belief Understanding in Infants," *Trends in Cognitive Sciences*, 14 (3): 110–18. https://doi.org/10.1016/j.tics.2009.12.006.

Choi, You-jung and Yuyan Luo (2015), '13-Month-Old's Understanding of Social Interactions," Psychological Science, 26 (3): 274–83.

Friday, Nancy (1977), *My Mother, My Self: The Daughter's Search for Identity*, New York: Bantam.

Gopnik, Alison and Henry M. Wellman (1992), 'Why the Child's Theory of Mind Really Is a Theory," *Mind and Language*, 7 (1–2): 145–71.

Hamilton, A.F. de C. (2008), 'Emulation and Mimicry for Social Interaction: A Theoretical Approach to Imitation in Autism," *Quarterly Journal of Experimental Psychology*, 61 (1): 101–15. https://doi.org/10.1080/17470210701508798.

Ingold, T. (2001), 'From the Transmission of Representations to the Education of Attention," in H. Whitehouse (ed.), *Debated Mind: Evolutionary Psychology versus Ethnography*, 113–53, New York: Berg.

Kögler, H. (1999), *The Power of Dialogue: Critical Hermeneutics after Gadamer and Foucault*, Cambridge, MA: MIT Press.

Kögler, H. (2005), 'Recognition and Difference: The Power of Perspectives in Interpretive Dialogue," *Social Identities*, 11 (3): 247–69. DOI: 10.1080/13504630500257082.

Kögler, H. (2006), 'Hermeneutics, Phenomenology, and Philosophical Anthropology," in Gerard Delanty (ed.), *Handbook of Contemporary European Social Theory*, 203–17, London/New York: Routledge.

Kögler, H. (2007), 'Roots of Recognition: Cultural Identity and the Ethos of Hermeneutic Dialogue," *Proceedings of the International Wittgenstein Symposium*, 353–71, Kirchberg, Austria: Ontos Publishing House. https://ebooks.mpdl.mpg.de/ebooks/Record/EB001123174.

Kögler, H. (2011), 'Hermeneutic Cosmopolitanism, or: Toward a Cosmopolitan Public Sphere," in M. Rovisco and M. Nowicka (eds.), *The Ashgate Research Companion to Cosmopolitanism*, 225–41, UK: Ashgate Publishers.

Kögler, H. (2012), 'Agency and the Other: On the Intersubjective Roots of Self-Identity," *New Ideas in Psychology*, 30: 47–64.

Leslie, A. (1987), 'Pretense and Representation: The Origins of "Theory of Mind,"' *Psychological Review* 94: 412–26.
Luria, A.R. and F. Ia. Yudovich ([1956] 1971), *Speech and the Development of Mental Processes in the Child*, ed. Joan Simon, Middlesex, UK: Penguin Books.
MacIntyre, A. (1962), 'A Mistake about Causality in Social Science,' in P. Laslett and W, G. Runciman (eds.), *Philosophy, Politics, and Society*, 48–70, Oxford: Blackwell.
McLuhan, M. (1967), The Medium is the Massage: *An Inventory of Effects*, New York: Bantam Books.
Melden, A.I. (1961), Free Action, London: Routledge & Kegan Paul.
Meltzoff, A.N. and M.K. Moore (1999), 'Persons and Representation: Why Infant Imitation is Important for Theories of Human Development,' in J. Nadel and G. Butterworth (eds.), *Cambridge Studies in Cognitive Perceptual Development. Imitation in Infancy*, 9–35. Cambridge: Cambridge University Press.
Meltzoff, A.N. (1995), 'Understanding the Intentions of Others: Re-Enactment of Intended Acts by 18-Month-Old Children,' *Developmental Psychology*, 31 (5): 838–850.
Mercier, H. and D. Sperber (2011), 'Why Do Humans Reason? Arguments for an Argumentative Theory,' *Behavioral and Brain Sciences*, 34: 57–111. doi: 10.1017/S0140525X10000968.
Mercier, H., and D. Sperber (2017), *The Enigma of Reason*. Cambridge, MA: Harvard University Press.
Nichols, S. and S. Stich (2000), 'A Cognitive Theory of Pretense,' *Cognition* 74: 115–47.
Nichols, S. and S. Stich (2003), *Mindreading: An Integrated Account of Pretence, Self-Awareness and Understanding of Other Minds*. Oxford: Oxford University Press.
Nunner-Winkler, G. (1992), 'Knowing and Wanting: On Moral Development in Early Childhood,' in A. Honneth, T. McCarthy, A. Wellmer, C. Offe (eds.), *Cultural-Political Interventions in the Unfinished Project of Enlightenment*, 218–43, Cambridge, MA: The MIT Press.
Onishi, K. H., and R. Baillargeon (2005), 'Do 15-Month-Old Infants Understand False Beliefs?,' *Science*, 308 (5719): 255–8. https://doi.org/10.1126/science.1107621.
Ramstead, M.J.D., S.P.L. Veissière, and L.J. Kirmayer (2016), 'Cultural Affordances: Scaffolding Local Worlds through Shared Intentionality and Regimes of Attention,' *Frontiers in Psychology* 7: 1090. https://doi.org/10.3389/fpsyg.2016.01090.
Repacholi, B.M. and A. Gopnik (1997), '*Early Reasoning about Desires*: Evidence from 14- and 18-Month-Olds,' *Developmental Psychology*, 33 (1): 12–21.
Rubinstein, D. (2004), 'Language Games and Natural Reactions,' *Journal for the Theory of Social Behaviour*, 34 (1): 55–71. https://doi.org/10.1111/j.1468-5914.2004.00234.x.
Rucińska, Z. (2016), 'Enactive Mechanism of Make-Belief Games,' in P. Turner and J.T. Harviainen (eds.), *Digital Make-Believe*, 141–60, Switzerland: Springer International Publishing.
Rucińska, Z. (2019a), 'Social and Enactive Perspectives on Pretending,' *AVANT*, X(3): 1–26. DOI: 10.26913/avant.2019.03.15. http://avant.edu.pl/en/2019-03-15.
Rucińska, Z. (2019b), 'Pretense and the Enactivist Explanatory Reversal,' in A. Kind (ed.), *The Junkyard: A Scholarly Blog Devoted to the Study Of Imagination*, 27 November, n.p. https://junkyardofthemind.com/blog/2019/11/23/pretense-and-the-enactivist-explanatory-reversal (accessed February 15, 2021).
Stafford, T. (2014), 'Peekaboo Is a Game Played Over the World, Crossing Language and Cultural Barriers. Why Is It So Universal? Perhaps Because It's Such a Powerful Learning Tool,' *BBC Future*, April 17. https://www.bbc.com/future/article/20140417-

why-all-babies-love-peekaboo?referer=https%3A%2F%2Fen.wikipedia.org%2F (accessed February 15, 2021).
Sterelny, K. (2012), *The Evolved Apprentice*, Cambridge, MA: The MIT Press.
Tomasello, M., M. Carpenter, J. Call, T. Behne, and H. Moll (2005), 'Understanding and Sharing Intentions: The Origins of Cultural Cognition," *Behavioral and Brain Sciences*, 28 (5): 675–91; discussion: 691–735.
Tomasello, M. (2014), *A Natural History of Human Thinking*. Cambridge: Harvard University Press.
Turner, S. (2021), 'The Cognitive Dimension," in S. Abrutyn and O. Lizardo (eds.) *Handbook of Classical Sociological Theory*, 693–725, Cham, Switzerland: Springer Publishing.
Veissière, S.P.L., A. Constant, M.J.D. Ramstead, K.J. Friston, and L.J. Kirmayer (2019), 'Thinking through Other Minds: A Variational Approach to Cognition and Culture," *Behavioral and Brain Sciences* 43 (e90): 1–75. doi: 10.1017/S0140525X19001213.
Vygotsky, L.S. and A.R. Luria ([1930/1993] 2009), *Studies on the History of Behavior: Ape, Primitive, and Child*, ed. and trans. V. Golod and J. E. Knox, New York/London: Routledge.
Wegner, D.M. (2002), *The Illusion of Conscious Will*, Cambridge, MA: The MIT Press.
Winch, P. (1958), *The Idea of a Social Science and its Relation to Philosophy*, London: Routledge & Kegan Paul.

Part Two

Recognition, Cosmopolitanism, Religion

4

The Moral Stance, Our Moralizing Nature, and the Hermeneutic and Empathic Dimension of Human Relations

Karsten R. Stueber

Introduction

The nature of morality—what it consists in, why we care about it, and, most importantly, why we should care about it—has been one of the central preoccupations of philosophy since morality constitutes a normative domain that humans always have been deeply interested in or at least claim to be interested in. Yet, despite the fact that morality has been so dear to our hearts, the focus of countless treatises of philosophical reflection, of essays addressed to the general public, and myriad works of the literary imagination throughout the ages, nothing seems to fully satisfy our urge to find answers to the above questions as each generation regards the answers provided by its predecessors as somewhat lacking.

Moreover, in thinking about morality researchers differ in how broadly they think about the proper domain of morality, whether it has to do only with issues of justice and harm avoidance or also with sexual matters and questions of loyalty to one's group. To get a clearer grasp on what exactly is at issue here, it is best to distinguish between the idea of the *moral stance* and what I refer to in this chapter as the domain of our ordinary *moralizing attitudes*. Moralizing is what we humans are "born" to do. It is part of our nature as fundamentally social creatures to endow some of our normative expectations that we have of each other within a particular culture with an exalted status, that is, as norms that we regard as particularly important for us to follow. Accordingly, we tend to be particularly sensitized to violations of such norms and respond emotionally at times rather strongly by clearly expressing our contempt, disgust, or anger directed at violators of such norms.

When philosophers talk nowadays about morality they are not merely talking about the moralizing attitudes of a specific and culturally contingent group of people. Moral judgments in their sense do not address us merely as members of a particular group, as either Germans, Americans, or Chinese. Rather, they address us from a perspective where we leave behind the framework of personal relations, of distinguishing between friend and foe, and move, as David Hume expresses it, to "some universal principle of the human frame, and touch a string, to which all mankind have accord and symphony" (Hume 1987: 75). Similarly, Jay Wallace defines morality in the contemporary context as "a cosmopolitan normative structure" and the moral community as "a maximally inclusive group of individuals whose interests are taking to matter equally" (Wallace 2019: 37). Since for Wallace "moral requirements and claims constitute a self-standing normative domain, one that is not grounded in any antecedent relation or connection between parties that fall under its manifold," the moral community is a "notional community," a community, that we are never concretely integrated in but to which we are nevertheless in some sense committed. Wallace's characterization of the moral community, as that of so many other writers in the contemporary context (see particularly Korsgaard 1996 and Darwall 2006), reflects ultimately deeply held Kantian convictions about human beings as members of a possible kingdom of ends. Such kingdom is conceived of as a realm where we respect each other's personal dignity, encounter each other on equal footing, and regard ourselves to be equidistant from each other. Here it seems we are neither separated from or bound to each other by merely historically contingent circumstances such as family relations, social class, or biologically but morally irrelevant distinctions such as gender and race. I therefore take genuinely moral judgments to be judgments that address us from the perspective of the moral stance or the perspective of the moral community thusly conceived. A fortiori, it is also the perspective within which our historically contingent moralizing attitudes are validated.

These considerations do however raise an obvious question: Why is it that judgments that are grounded in or address me from the perspective of the moral stance place normative demands on me, if they address me only as a member of a "*notional community*" rather than a member of a concrete social group that I am actually a part of as an American or German, as a professor, a husband or as a father? There certainly are a number of philosophers, Nietzsche most prominently among them, who would deny that this question can be answered in a philosophically persuasive manner. A fortiori they claim that the above conception of the moral stance that drives us to ask the question in the first place should be rejected and that moral judgments should be understood as nothing more than sophisticated and rhetorically embellished strategies of imposing one's own values on others, as an expression of our will to power. From that perspective morality is always defined by the moralizing attitudes of the victorious social group.

In this chapter, I will do three things. First, I will briefly talk about how to think about the most plausible philosophical strategies for validating the moral stance within the framework of philosophical naturalism. Second, I will programmatically outline my favored strategy for such validation by taking my cues from Adam Smith, for whom humans are essentially social creatures whose very sociality rests on the psychological capacity for mutual and reciprocal empathy. The normative authority of the moral stance will be revealed as a commitment to the impartial spectator perspective, a commitment that is implicit in our folk psychological practice of making sense of each other by reenacting our reasons for acting through empathic perspective-taking. Since such practice is not only epistemically central for making sense of people within a specific culture but has to be applied cross-culturally the scope of the moral stance transcends cultural contingency.

To fully understand the above argument we need to remind ourselves of the almost forgotten aesthetic—or what one could also call the appreciative—dimension of our empathic grasp of other minds. Grasping another person's reasons through empathic reenactments allows us to become more sensitive to the full range of possibilities for human existence and human agency and the full range of potential reasons for acting. I will refer to such sensitivity as the *sensus communis*, a notion that Kant emphasized in his *Third Critique* and a notion that has also been important to Gadamer's hermeneutics (Gadamer 1989), so central to Kögler's work.

In the last part of my chapter, I will turn to Kögler's hermeneutic conception of the ethical dimension of interpersonal understanding. Ultimately, Kögler grounds the authority of what I call the moral stance ontologically following G.H. Mead in thinking that a self can constitute itself only in light of another person's agency. The self therefore seems to owe a normative debt to the other. Interestingly, Kögler's suggestions have also been used by Samuel Fleischacker (2019) for a similar reading of Smith. As I will respectfully suggest, even if one agrees with the fact that human selves are socially constituted such social constitution ultimately happens only within a rather limited domain of a particular group or culture. From a naturalistic perspective, our social constitution is biased toward the in-group and it is difficult to understand how exactly we could validate the perspective of the impartial moral stance in this manner. Yet I do think that a hermeneutic conception of interpersonal understanding should also be open to my Smithean analysis of the working of empathy in the social context.

Naturalism and Strategies for Validating the Normative Authority of the Moral Stance

To philosophically explicate the validity of the moral stance means to show that the moral stance has genuine normative authority over me because from its perspective I am judged according to standards that belong intrinsically to me, standards that I have to regard as standards that I own, irrespective of the particular group that I concretely belong to. A fortiori it means to explain why it is that the verdicts, judgments, or exhortations from the moral stance possess normative authority over creatures like us; creatures who are social and who are emotionally tied to one another; creatures who are also rational in that we can be responsive to reasons; and creatures, who possess, compared to other species, impressive cognitive powers, even if those cognitive powers are limited and prone to well-known inferential shortcomings. My exploration of the normative authority of the moral stance will thus proceed within the framework of philosophical naturalism, a framework that minimally commits philosophers to be constrained in their epistemic and metaphysical explorations by what the sciences tell us about the world (See also DeCaro and Macathur 2010). Generally, that is understood as implying that philosophers cannot appeal to supernatural entities or properties that cannot be accounted for in terms of the natural properties that scientists postulate when making sense of the world. More concretely, I take it also as implying that any philosophical exploration of the normative authority of the moral stance has to be compatible with what the empirical sciences tell us about the structure of human sociality and our psychological and cognitive capacities.

Yet, in order to explicate the normative authority of the moral stance, we also have to explain how it is that judgments from its perspective constitute reasons that are understood as being of central importance from the first-person perspective where we deliberate about how to proceed in our interaction with the world and each other. Only in satisfying these two demands—what I also call the naturalism and the normativity constraints—are we ultimately able to explicate the normative authority of the moral stance for us vulnerable and fallible creatures with our psychological and cognitive structure, that is, us humans rather than perfect "dear little angels."[1]

Nevertheless, how exactly do we go about trying to explicate the normative authority of the moral stance in a manner that can satisfy both of the above constraints? It is often claimed that the empirical sciences ultimately can only address causal questions and that they never can address questions of *quid iuris*, that is, questions regarding normative validity. The sciences, one often hears, at most can tell us why we care about morality but not why we *should* care about it. What the sciences tell us about human nature thus does not seem to constitute immediately a reason for acting from the first-person perspective.

Moreover, is asking for an explication of the normative authority of the moral stance even a sensible endeavor? The question seems to look for an answer that would provide a rational agent with a reason for being moral. It assumes that our moral practices are optional choices for us, that is, we could rationally opt out of them in the same manner that we could choose not to eat vanilla ice cream. As already H.A. Pritchard (1912) argued, a satisfactory reason for explicating the normative authority of the moral stance has to point to something like a normatively obligatory reason. But in that case, one seems to presuppose want needs explaining. Merely pointing to a mere desire, however, would reduce the normative authority to the same level as the pull that my desire for eating vanilla ice-cream has on my will.

Kant most explicitly favored two venues for validating the moral stance. On the one hand, he argues in the Grundlegung (part III) for the normative authority of the moral stance by tying it to the notion of freedom of will and the fact that we are allowed to conceive of ourselves as being free since we can think of ourselves as also belonging to a noumenal realm. On the other hand, in his *Critique of Practical Reason*, he appeals to an unanalyzable fact of reason (Faktum der Vernunft), which reveals itself in our acknowledging, for instance, that it is plainly wrong to provide false testimony against an honest man, even if refusing to do so would cost us our life. Both accounts of the normative authority of the moral law are deeply unsatisfying. The first explication clearly violates the commitment of naturalism by pointing to a noumenal realm. And appealing to the phenomenal consciousness of our moral obligations and designating it as a fact of reason ultimately presupposes what needs explaining, that is, why the moral law and the moral stance possess categorical normative authority.

There is, however a very different way of thinking about the perspective from which we ask for a validation of the moral stance. Here I am not asking for a yet another justifying reason for having moral reasons from a perspective outside of any social practice where morality appears to be merely optional. Rather I presuppose that I already feel the pull of such reasons that we call moral reasons insofar as I am a social animal. The question of why we should care about morality is then primarily understood as asking why moral demands do not constitute merely demands that are imposed on us from an external perspective, such as the rules imposed on a country conquered by a foreign power. Take the following analogy. I might certainly ask why my behavior should be evaluated by the rules of soccer. If I am not playing soccer, there seems to be no satisfactory answer that would force me to recognize the normative authority of the rules of soccer. All one could do is to try to motivate me to play soccer by showing me what a great game soccer really is. Yet if I am already playing soccer, the only answer possible consists in pointing out that these are the rules of the game. Ordinarily these questions do not arise as we tend to know whether or not we are involved in playing soccer or not. As far as morality however is concerned—and more particularly morality tied to what we have called the moral stance—our situation is more analogous to knowing that we play some kind of game and that there are certain rules that we are supposed to follow without knowing what kind of game it is and what its point is for us humans living our life. Being able to situate the structure of the game that we are playing in living a human life then seems to be going a long way of explicating the normative authority of the moral stance if the moral stance indeed can be shown to be in some sense part of that game.

Some of the most interesting attempts in contemporary metaethics can be seen as implicitly adopting this strategy in a variety of ways. Prominently among them is Korsgaard's so-called Kantian constructivism arguing that the categorical imperative and its equivalent—the principle of humanity to never treat another only as a means but always also as an end-in-itself—are constitutive principles of practical rationality (Korsgaard 1996). Violating moral principles is for her the same as acting practically irrational since moral principles are the condition of the possibility for being able to choose something for a reason. Not only does Korsgaard meet the normativity constraint in this manner, note also that the Kantian constructivist strategy meets the naturalism constraint by default without having to engage directly with the empirical sciences, or so Korsgaard would be inclined to argue. After all, however we think about our psychological capacities, we have to take it for a given that we are agents who are ultimately able to act for reasons. Indeed denying that ability seems to be repudiating the very framework within which it would make sense to have the debate about the normative authority of the moral stance in the first place.

Here is certainly not the space to engage in an extensive critique of Korsgaard. I, like others, ultimately find her argument for the claim that immorality is a form of irrationality to be unpersuasive (for my critique see Stueber 2017a). Smith provides a more plausible alternative since it is grounded in an empirically more credible conception of human psychology and sociality. Accordingly, in following Smith I understand myself also as explicating the status of the moral stance by more precisely situating it within the game that we as humans play.[2] Yet I do not think of morality as a transcendental principle or constitutive principle of practical rationality. Rather I take a contingent yet naturalistically unassailable starting point, that is the structure of human sociality and the underlying psychological processes and causal mechanisms that are contingently necessary for maintaining that very structure. In recognizing empathy as one of the central processes for maintaining social cohesion and in conceiving of empathy as involving imaginary perspective-taking, Smith acknowledges the involvement of the first-person deliberative perspective for understanding and appreciating other minds. Simultaneously, he recognizes that another person's understanding and appreciation provides me with a mirror allowing me to see and evaluate my own way of looking at the world. A Smithean explication of human sociality will also enable us to meet the normativity constraint as such naturalistic analysis also resonates with our deliberative first-person perspective. In understanding the psychological basis of human sociality we reflect on what is going on in our mutual involvement of our first-person perspectives in encountering each other, thereby reimagining such encounters.[3] And in that process, I submit, we reflectively recognize that we are committed to the impartial spectator perspective or the moral stance as a *regulative ideal* for thinking about ourselves and each other.

Empathy, Human Sociality, and the Moral Stance: Adam Smith and Kant's *Sensus Communis*

Before outlining the argument in more detail, let me explicate my understanding of the structure of the social realm based on the result of empirical research drawing from evolutionary anthropology and various subfields of psychology. As it is often noted, humans are not merely social animals. They are an ultrasocial and extraordinarily cooperative specie whose ability to form social bonds extends to extremely large groups of genetically unrelated individuals (Richerson and Boyd 2005). Such intensive and extensive cooperation is commonly seen as being causally related to the fact that we are also passionately normative animals, whose social interactions are structured, guided, and constrained by an intricate web of norms, rules, and guidelines to which we feel obliged to conform and which we also enforce on others. Such web of norms is maintained and is constituted by humans having acquired dispositions and capacities that make them highly sensitive toward the emotions and attitudes that others have toward them and the world (For a survey see Roughley and Bayertz 2019). Moreover, they have (innate and acquired) expectations about how others are to behave and are highly sensitive to monitoring, protesting, and sanctioning violations of what is to be expected of others. Importantly, humans do not only monitor others according to such normative expectations. They also monitor and regulate their own behavior accordingly.

Some of these norms are regarded to be particularly important for members of the group. Already children from the middle of their third year are able to distinguish between so-called moral and conventional norms, a distinction that possesses also cross-cultural validity (See Smentana, Jambon, and Ball 2014). Yet we have to be careful in assuming that such distinction already commits all humans to the perspective of the moral stance from which we all regard ourselves as having equal value. From an empirical point of view accepting this distinction only means that moral norms are prima facie like other social norms except that they are in addition characterized by unique "signature response patterns" (Kelly et. al. 2007). They are distinguished from conventional ones in that they are in some sense regarded to be "unconditionally obligatory, generalizable, and impersonal" (Turiel, Killen, and Helwig 1987: 169-70). That does indeed mean that they are thought to be independent of social authority or specific social practices and agreements, their scope is also judged to be much broader—they are thought of to be valid in other countries, for example—, and the violation of moral norms is generally understood to be a more serious offense than the violation of other norms.

Despite these universalizing features of our ordinary concept of morality, empirical research also suggests that for humans the arch of their moral universe does not bend toward universal justice but toward the in-group. Groups, as some more recent research indicates, constitute the boundaries of natural morality. Children, for instance, understand moral obligations as applying most directly only toward members of their in-group, whereas they seem to understand their obligations toward members of the outgroup analogous to conventional rules (for a summary of this research, see Chalik and Rhodes 2020). Human beings as social creatures are particularly concerned with the cohesion of their group with which they identify and endow certain of their mutual expectation about each other through what I would like to call their moralizing impulse with an exalted status. For that very reason, we should also conceive of the domain of what one could call natural morality, or what I would like to call more appropriately the domain of our moralizing attitudes, in a broad sense. That is I would suggest we should not think of it as being merely defined by concerns of harm, fairness, or welfare (as social domain theorists like Turiel think) but as also including normative expectations about the loyalty toward the group, consideration about its purity or sanctity, and obedience to its leaders, as Jonathan Haidt in his moral foundation theory suggests.[4]

As such moralizing animals, humans constantly evaluate each other, particularly in regard to norms we care deeply about. Knowing this, we are also very sensitive to how others think about us. Moreover, human beings are not merely interested in the conformity of behavior, our normative and moralizing impulse is also very much concerned with the internal states of our minds that lead to such behavior. Already infants have certain expectations not only about how people behave but, equally important, they expect others to express their emotions, take those emotions as cues for risk assessment of their environment, and do pay attention to the intention and the mental engagement of others, particularly in collaborative contexts (for a survey, see Tomasello 2019). As it is well known, infants and children do acquire over time a rather sophisticated way of thinking of others as intentional and mental agents. Recently there has been quite an extensive debate of how exactly we should understand the underlying mechanisms of such capacities, whether it depends mainly on an implicit theory or whether we use our own mind in simulating and reenacting the emotions and psychological states of others (see Stueber 2006). Smith in emphasizing empathy generally is understood to be on the side of simulation theory. Yet, in contrast to contemporary simulation theorists, for Smith empathy is not merely a means for gaining knowledge of other minds. Rather it is Smith's great contribution—building here on insights by David Hume—to understand empathy as the primary psychological mechanism that allows us to become embedded in a social context within which human beings constantly judge each other. In empathizing with the other person we bring his of her thoughts and sentiments home to ourselves and reveal in this manner our common humanity, as beings that are like each other (See also Fleischacker 2019). Empathy is something human beings crave of each other since it is in this manner that their existence as a human being is recognized and acknowledged. Moreover, it is also the manner in which a certain conformity of our psychological attunement toward the world and each other is established, since we ourselves regulate our own emotional responses so that others can empathize with them. Such attunement does not only concern our emotions, but also concerns the whole range of our mental life including beliefs and normative expectations.

As it is well known, empathy, or what Smith calls sympathy, has a variety of psychological dimensions and researchers tended either to lump them together or tended to focus on only one of those dimensions to the exclusion of others (See Stueber 2019). Even Smith does not always sufficiently distinguish among different aspects of these empathy-related phenomena. Yet insofar Smith's ethical considerations are concerned, the notion of empathy that is at the center of his attention comes close to what I have referred to in my own work as reenactive empathy understood as a resonance phenomenon involving imaginative perspective-taking allowing us to reenact the thoughts and emotional sentiments of another in our own mind (Stueber 2006). More importantly, taking another person's perspective means to imaginatively reenact the outlook that that person has onto the world, "it does not arise from the view of the passions, but from the situation that excites it" (Smith 1759: 12). Consistent with my conception of reenactive empathy, I read Smith as suggesting that it is through empathic reenactment that we are able to grasp an agent's state of minds—covering the whole range of his mental states including beliefs, desires, emotions, and also his normative commitments—as his reasons for acting and deliberating. In reenacting his states of minds as being oriented toward the situation he confronts, we understand his response as a rational or reasonable one. His fear or his resentment become, for instance, intelligible since we understand them as responses to seeing a snake or being insulted by another person. Accordingly, we also would understand them as his reasons for running away or asking for an apology because that is the way we would react for those very same reasons.

Smith's analysis of empathy is particularly astute because he reflects on the effects that mutual practices of empathy have on the empathizer and the target of empathy. As far as the empathizer is concerned, for Smith, our ability to reenact another person's sentiment is closely related to approving or disapproving of such thoughts or actions based on those thoughts. Being able to empathize with the sentiments of another leads to our approval while being unable to do so leads supposedly to disapproval. Based on these empathic reactions the target of empathy is provided with a mirror to see the quality of his own sentiments. Indeed, for Smith it is only in this manner and only in a social context that we ourselves become aware of our own character and start recognizing the "propriety and impropriety" of our own passion and the "beauty and deformity" of our own mind (Smith 1759: 110).[5] Accordingly, Smith conceives of notion of the intelligibility of our actions right from the start as an intersubjective one. We as humans acting for reasons feel diminished in our own apprehension of reasons if those reasons cannot be empathized with by others. Our own existence as rational agents would become doubtful to ourselves if an uptake of our reasons by others is impossible.

I will talk a bit more about the effect of empathy on the target of empathy in the next section when I will discuss Kögler's position. Here I want to understand the process leading to approval and disapproval in a bit more detail. In particular, I want to understand its normative significance or normative authority in making demands on the other person. Let us grant that reenacting another person's thoughts and sentiments leads to a subjective form of approval if perspective-taking would just mean that I put myself in another person's perspective assuming that we share most of our attitudes. In that sense, I understand your grief imagining how I would feel if a loved one had died, and I grasp your reasons for it. Since an agent's reasons for acting are also reasons in light of which he would attempt to justify and provide an account of his action to another, we can agree with Smith that such reenactment in some very minimal sense constitutes an approval of the action in that we agree with an agent's outlook of the world from which the agents act. Given that human beings are in need of such empathic uptake we also could think of such mutual empathy within the social context as the underlying psychological process that leads us to conform generally to the normative expectations of the group we identify with.

Yet how exactly should we think about the normative authority that the judgments of others have based on their ability of empathic uptake? Given that we like to be liked and like to belong to a group it seems we ought to conform to those judgements for merely instrumental reasons. Those judgments have normative validity for me only insofar as I recognize myself as a member of the group in the same manner that I recognize the rules of soccer when playing soccer (ultimately because I like playing soccer). Why should I otherwise listen to what you say? I am happy if you agree with me but why do you have the normative authority to tell me to change my ways merely because you cannot reenact my reasons. Nothing so far said seems to come close to explicating the normative authority of the moral stance that we are interested in. Smith, as it is well known, answers these questions by appealing to the impartial spectator perspective, a perspective that is neither yours nor mine but a third perspective that judges us impartially from a stance from which "we are but one of the multitude, in no respect better than any other in it" (Smith 1759: 137). Approval or disapproval that is based on empathy from the impartial spectator perspective is then understood as having the normative authority of the moral stance that everybody has to accept.

In Smith one finds a diversity of cues of how to think about the emergence of the appeal to the impartial spectator perspective and its ultimate normative authority.[6] The best way to understand the normative authority of the impartial spectator perspective is to think more carefully about the case where we first seem to be unable to reenact another person's sentiments and thoughts because our outlook toward the world is culturally so different. Most often we just assume that the other person shares most of our attitudes and if that is not the case it becomes difficult to see how exactly he deliberates about a particular situation. While it is certainly true that some people might in this case just disapprove of the other person, it seems to constitute first and foremost an epistemic puzzlement.[7] It means that we do not find another person's actions intelligible because we cannot grasp his thoughts as reasons. Moral culpability however seems to presuppose exactly that, that an agent acted for a reason and that we fundamentally disapprove of those reasons. A disapproval merely based on us finding somebody unintelligible also does not have be taken very seriously from the perspective of the target of empathy, if it is based on not fully understanding the relevant differences between the empathizer and her target. To use one of Smith's example, I might merely grasp that the other person is angry (based on her facial expression) but not what her reasons for her anger are.

What is required in such cases is to take into account differences between me and the target of my empathy. We have to imaginatively adopt the attitudes that we do not share with the other person and quarantining our own attitudes that the other person does not share with us in order for our reenactment to provide us with reliable insight into the other person's mind. Let us assume that in taking into account those relevant differences, we are able to bring the other person's sentiments and thoughts home to ourselves and recognize them as reasons.

Yet finding the other person intelligible in this manner does not in automatically constitute approval or disapproval either since we did not fully bring his case home to ourselves. Rather in recreating his perspective we are at the same time aware of the fact that our perspective on the world differ in relevant respects from the other person's. His reasons in this sense would not be our reasons if we were put with our unchanged attitudes in his situation. We recognize them only as reasons by imagining how he would feel in that situation, that is, we recognize them as potential reasons if our own perspective would undergo relevant changes. It is exactly in this situation, however, that our reenactment of another person's reasons addresses us as a critical, reflective, and therefore self-critical reasoner. Reenacting another person's perspective and his reasons makes a demand on us that requires a rational response that answers the question of why it is that we do not make his perspective our perspective, given the fact that his reasons are perfectly intelligible to us. And it is exactly in this context that we appeal implicitly to the perspective of the impartial spectator within which we conceive of ourselves as equal reasoners, or so I would like to argue. The impartial spectator perspective then is to be conceived of as the "highest tribunal" (see in this respect Smith 1759: 128–30) to which we appeal in order to adjudicate between our reasons for acting.

To fully understand the demand that the reenactment of another person's reasons makes on us, it is important to grasp that in reenacting another person's perspective we reenact a holistic web of attitudes within which a person's thoughts constitutes a reason. Moreover, as already Aristotle understood our reasons tend to be hierarchical organized. Not only do we have first-order reasons, we also have reasons for having those reasons. We do not only recognize that somebody likes a neat office and therefore keeps his office neat. Such recognition would indeed not put much pressure on our own messy way of keeping our office. Additionally, we recognize that the person has a reason for keeping his office neat such as that cleanliness is next to godliness. In imaginatively taking up another person's point of view, we ultimately reenact a differently structured framework of reasons. I would suggest that in this manner we enlarge our own possibilities of conceiving of rational agency and of considerations that could count as reasons for acting. In reenacting them in our own mind, even if an "incapsulated" manner as Collingwood might call it,[8] we imagine them in some way as reasons we can "live" by, that we might feel at home with. Such reenactment ultimately sharpens our sensitivity to our common humanity as rational agents in our local distinctiveness. It is a sensitivity that does not yet constitute full approval. It constitutes a somewhat appreciative engagement with the "vitality" and "life potentiality" (Lipps 1903) that lies in the reenacted perspective, an appreciation that can be felt as something positive when trying to reenact a Buddhist perspective with its emphasis on sympathy or as something negative and almost scary such as when trying to reenact the perspective of a Holocaust perpetrator. Such sensitivity to the full range of humanly possible ways of reasoning about one's actions and agency I refer to with Kant as *sensus communis*, that is the "idea of a communal sense" mediated by our capacity for empathy that takes reflectively into account "everyone else's way of representing in thought" (Kant, 2000, § 40, 173). Kant's idea of the sensus communis seems also to include what Smith calls the dimension of the impartial spectator within which we adjudicate between reasons and rank them as better, worse, or even as equally reasonable. I, in contrast, distinguish between our appreciative sensitivity (i.e., *sensus communis*) and the ideal spectator perspective. It is in light of our sensitivity that we are challenged to reflect and reevaluate our own reasons and in this way implicitly appeal to a dimension of thinking about reasons that is neither yours nor mine but is impartial.

One final consideration is needed to recognize the idea of the impartial spectator perspective as the moral stance within which we as rational agents—inclusive of our emotional life—have equal importance. We need to recognize that it is only in light of our empathic and reenactive abilities that we can find the actions of another person intelligible, even if that person belongs to a very different culture. I have argued for this claim elsewhere quite extensively (Stueber 2006 and 2018). If this is so, then the perspective of the impartial spectator is potentially an open-ended one. It is dimension within which attention is paid to a potentially infinite number of agents from a vast array of cultural backgrounds who like me act for reasons and whose reasons for acting I attempt to reenact in order to find their behavior intelligible (see Sen 2002). Consequently, the recognition of the normative authority of the moral stance is ultimately a reflective achievement and not something that is directly part of our natural attitude toward each other. Yet it is a reflective achievement that is based on reflecting on a naturalistically unassailable fact, that is the central and constitutive involvement of our empathic activities within the social realm.[9] Having outlined my explication of the normative authority of the moral stance, it is now time to turn, as promised, to Kögler's reconstruction of the moral or ethical dimension human life within the context of his position of critical hermeneutics.

Kögler's Hermeneutic Conception of Morality

Kögler's position combines intriguingly and imaginatively central insights of Gadamerian hermeneutics, Habermasian critical theory, and a Foucaultian sensitivity to social power relations. For that very reason and in contrast to Gadamer's own position, the notion of agency stands at the very center of Kögler's reflection of the interpretive process. Similarly, Kögler emphasizes the importance of empathy and perspective-taking in his analysis of the interpretive process and highlights the reflective and self-critical dimension of interpretation in the interpretive encounter with others. At the same time, he rejects a mere psychologistic conception of interpretation (as proposed by some simulation theorists) since it does not do justice to the social constitution of meaning (Kögler 2000). A fortiori he always emphasizes the mediating role of language and culture in his conception of the nature of understanding.

Accordingly, there already exists a partial fusion of horizons in regard to some of my assumptions about the interpretative process. Yet while I agree that interpretation is always mediated by cultural context and differences between those contexts, I ultimately view our capacity for empathy (what I call basic and reenactive empathy)[10] as pre-linguistic capacities that already young children possess and that allow them to be initiated into a common language and normative social structure in the first place. Autistic children who seem to lack such capacities and the ability to engage in joint attention have indeed difficulties in this respect. Having said that, I agree that after becoming initiated into such structure our thoughts and emotional sensitivities are very much couched and conceptually structured in a certain manner. For that reason, I agree also with so-called narrativists (Gallagher and Hutto 2008) and Kögler that taking the perspective of another person, particularly a person from a very different culture, requires additional information about our differences in cultural, biographical, or social backgrounds. I insist though that all of this additional information does not make the use of our empathic capacities epistemically superfluous (Stueber 2012 and 2018). There is no other way to fully understand somebody else's thoughts as his reasons. Finally, when I am talking about the impartial spectator perspective, I am talking about a *regulative ideal* to which we are normatively committed. The claim that we occupy such a stance is always a fallible and at times a very contested assertion. In order to resolve such conflicts, theoretical insights about features—such as cognitive limitations or detrimental social influences—that are responsible for us deviating from true impartiality could indeed constitute important means for helping us to see more clearly in this respect.

Kögler and I however most importantly agree that the interpretive stance implicitly commits us to universalist moral assumptions. In contrast to some cultural theorists, Kögler takes the Kantian idea of human subjects as ends in themselves and thus the idea that we are all bound to a universal moral community seriously. Moreover he intends to "dialogically reconstruct" that idea as an ethical imperative to respect each other's claims within the contours of his critical hermeneutics (Kögler 2015) as he regards intercultural dialogue to be normatively grounded in "egalitarian intuitions" (Kögler 2018: 367). Yet one wonders why that is so. Remember if we take a Smithian starting point, the basis for judging and evaluating another person and his sentiments is our ability to bring another person's sentiments home to ourselves. Ultimately, from a naturalistic point of view we cannot give up our perspective for the very reason that it is our perspective. Why then should we treat the other perspective as being of equal importance? That we owe the other respect, that we are normatively committed to the moral stance, I have argued is only a reflective achievement recognizing the implicit commitment in our ordinary interpretive practices within which the involvement of our reenactive and empathic capacities is an epistemic necessity.

Kögler's own answer does not proceed merely epistemically. On the one hand, he recognizes that the concrete interpretive encounter with the other—an encounter that at times mediates between very different cultural contexts—epistemically requires empathic perspective-taking skills within which we also experience another person's assertions as making normative demands on us. Yet he is also very much aware of the fact that such an encounter is always a socially embedded one, an encounter that is distorted by the contingency of social power relations. Accordingly, the structure of real existing dialogues disguises and obstructs its implicit dependence on the configuration of an open and "true dialogue" that would also require the recognition of the other as an end in itself. It is exactly at this stage that Kögler's considerations take an ontological turn via Mead's considerations about the intersubjective, social, and dialogical constitution of the self and self-consciousness in order to reveal the normative source of this very presupposition of any concrete interpretive encounter (see particularly Kögler 2015). As he explains it, the "other's irreducible agency is constitutive of the self's capacity to establish an identity" (Kögler 2012: 47) and "lies at the center of the interpreting self" (Kögler 2015). It is because of this ontological debt toward the other that we are also ethically obliged toward him or her in our interpretive endeavors, or so Kögler claims, if I understand him correctly. It is, however, exactly at this stage, that I would like to hear a bit more as I am not sure how exactly one should think about the relationship between ontological and ethical debts or why the intersubjective constitution of the self implies a normative claim. After all, teenagers do not seem to be much obliged toward their parents in recognizing that their parents are their creators. As far as I understand it, the case about the ontological conception of the self is different because, as Kögler argues, this ontological fact about ourselves is grasped from the first-person perspective in the dialogical encounter with the other so that the same normative attitude we have toward ourselves as persons is extended to the other (Kögler 2012: 60–1). Kögler's Meadean reflections certainly resonate with some of the things that Smith has said about the self, a fact corroborated by Fleischacker's (2019) use of Kögler (2000) and his claim that for Smith, like for Kögler, the self is fully constituted in an intersubjective and dialogical manner.

Ultimately, I am a bit doubtful that these ontological considerations alone can sufficiently carry the normative weight of the moral stance. I suspect that might be one of the reasons why I do not read Smith as suggesting that all aspects of our self-consciousness are socially constituted. Rather he insinuates only that those aspects for which we are held normatively accountable by others around us are constituted in this manner. The self is socially constituted only insofar as it evaluates itself. Such self-evaluative stance however presupposes a non-reflective apprehension of the self. It presupposes, for instance, that we are able to distinguish our bodies from other objects in the environment, and certainly from the bodies of other persons. It also presupposes that the infant as an embodied self is able to recognize that the emotional attitudes of the other are directed toward itself. After all, to recognize oneself in a mirror presupposes that one is able to distinguish oneself from one's image in the mirror. Through such mirroring our conception of the self certainly becomes more sophisticated. Yet it is a mistake to think of all dimensions of our self to be socially constituted (see in this respect also Frank 1991 and Zahavi 2015).

Most importantly, from a naturalistic perspective that I have adopted in this chapter, it seems that the social constitution of the self-evaluative dimension of our self tends to be bound by the concrete encounters with others, and those others tend to be normally people in our in-group. My self is thus constituted by me having grown up in Germany and so on. Granted, the borders of such identity remain fluid. In moving to America, I admit, I have changed in that now I seem to occupy something of an in-between position, at home neither fully in America nor in Germany, but at the same time a citizen of both countries. So while I agree that in some sense the other is an irreducible part of myself, that other is always a concrete other and never seems to be the other of the all-encompassing dimension of the moral stance where all human beings are equidistant of each other. To respect the other in that sense I would submit requires that we put the epistemic considerations that I have outlined in this chapter rather than ontological reflections at the center of our hermeneutic reflections, even within the context of a critical hermeneutics.

Notes

1 See in this respect Frazer's critique of Kant (Frazer 2017) from the perspective of moral sentimentalism. The expression "dear little angel" originates from Schopenhauer's characterization of Kant's approach to moral philosophy.
2 Within the framework of contemporary philosophical metaethics, positions inspired by Strawson's emphasis on our reactive attitudes like resentment and indignation provide other important examples of this approach (See Wallace 1994 and Darwall 2006). I would also count Axel Honneth (1995) among this group although coming from a very different philosophical tradition taking the Hegelian notion of recognition as basic. From the perspective of evolutionary anthropology and child development, Michael Tomasello's position also stands out (Tomasello 2016, 2019, 2020). I will discuss these positions extensively in my next book *The Moralizing Animal: Empathy and the Foundation of Morality*. Suffice it here to say that I do not think these positions allow us to sufficiently ground the moral stance naturalistically.
3 Interpreters have noticed Smith's literary style that always backs up his philosophical claims with an analysis of concrete examples of interpersonal understanding. See in this respect also Griswold 1998.
4 In mentioning the work of Jonathan Haidt (2012), I am not committed to accepting the limited range of categories, what he refers to as foundations, as comprehensively delineating the moralizing domain. Indeed I think that humans are rather promiscuous moralizers. Whatever feature of the social realm human beings regard as centrally important for their group identity is a feature toward which they can take a moralizing attitude. As a result they become emotionally very attuned to violations of those features. For interesting and illuminating research in this area and how it relates to the potential of political violence, see particularly the work of Linda Skitka (Skitka et. al. 2021 and Skitka and Morgan 2014).
5 Here I do not have the space to textually validate my interpretation of Smith in greater detail. Smith also distinguishes between the propriety and the merit of an action as

forms of approval of slightly different features of an action, that is in terms of its cause and its effects on others (Smith 1759: 18.) I will abstract from these complications here, since my purpose in this chapter is a systematic one. For a textually closer reading of Smith, see Stueber 2017a.
6 See in this Smith Part III, chap. i-iii. Smith also appeals to two different kind of desires, the desire to be praised and the desire for praiseworthiness. It is however difficult to understand how an appeal to a mere desire can ground the normative authority of the impartial spectator perspective.
7 Admittedly though this might be the situation that factually describes the colonial attitude. However, in addition, the colonial attitude is characterized by the further claim that the Western attitude already represents the position of the impartial perspective. One therefore lacked sufficient motivation to empathize with the perspective of the other, that is, it led to what I would call epistemically lazy empathizing. Such distortion of the empathic practice is obviously always possible, and it is an interesting question of how to avoid this kind of situation. This practical question is beyond the scope of this chapter. Here we are mainly concerned with the question of how to validate the idea of the moral stance in the first place.
8 More precisely Collingwood talks about historical knowledge as the "reenactment of a past thought incapsulated within a context of present thoughts, which by contradicting it, confines it to a place different from theirs" (Collingwood 1939: 114).
9 Historically speaking, this claim fits also well with Lynn Hunt's account of the invention of human rights as being closely tight to the encouragement of empathy in eighteenth-century literature (Hunt 2007).
10 For simplicity sake, this distinction does not play a role in my explication of the normative authority of the moral stance. I focus here only on reenactive empathy. Basic empathy, which in all likelihood involves so-called mirror neurons on the neurobiological level, is our non-conceptual ability to grasp the bodily motions of another as skilled and goal-directed movements and also as being expressive of certain emotions.

References

Chalik, L. and M. Rhodes (2020), "Groups as Moral Boundaries: A Developmental Perspective," in J.B. Benson (ed.), *Advances in Child Development and Behavior*, vol. 58, 63–93. Cambridge, MA: Academic Press.
Collingwood, R.G. (1939/2002), *An Autobiography*. Oxford: Clarendon.
Darwall, S. (2006), *The Second Person Standpoint: Morality, Respect, and Accountability*. Cambridge, MA: Harvard University Press.
DeCaro, M. and D. Macathur (2010), *Naturalism and Normativity*. New York: Columbia University Press.
Fleischacker, S. (2019), *Being Me, Being You: Adam Smith and Empathy*. Chicago: Chicago University Press.
Frank, M. (1991), *Selbstbewußtsein und Selbsterkenntnis: Essays zur Analytischen Philosophie der Subjektivität*. Stuttgart: Reclam.
Frazer, M. (2017), "Interdisciplinary before the Disciplines: Sentimentalism and the Science of Man," in R. Debes and K.R. Stueber (eds.), *Ethical Sentimentalism*, 15–31. Cambridge: Cambridge University Press.

Gallagher, S., and D. Hutto (2008), "Understanding Others Through Primary Interaction and Narrative Practice," in J. Zlatev, T. Racine, C. Sinha, and E. Itkonen (eds.), *The Shared Mind: Perspectives on Intersubjectivity*, 17–38. Amsterdam/Philadelphia: John Benjamins Publishing.
Gadamer, H.-G. (1989), *Truth and Method*. New York: Crossroad.
Griswold, C. (1998), *Adam Smith and the Virtues of Enlightenment*. New York: Cambridge University Press.
Haidt, J. (2012), *The Righteous Mind: Why Good People are Divided by Politics and Religion*. New York: Vintage Books.
Honneth, A. (1995), *The Struggle for Recognition: The Moral Grammar of Social Conflicts*. Cambridge, MA: MIT Press.
Hume, D. (1987), An Enquiry Concerning the Principles of Morals. Indianapolis: Hackett Publishing.
Hunt, L. (2007), *Inventing Human Rights: A History*. New York/London: Norton.
Kant, I. (2000), *Critique of the Power of Judgment*. Transl. By P. Guyer and E. Matthews. Cambridge: Cambridge University Press.
Kelly, D., S. Stich, K. Haley, S. Eng, and D. Fessler (2007), "Harm, Affect, and the Moral/Conventional Distinction." Mind and Language 22: 117–31.
Kögler, H-H. (2000), "Empathy, Dialogical Self, and Reflexive Interpretation: The Symbolic Source of Simulation, in *Empathy and Agency: The Problem of Understanding in the Human Sciences*," ed. by H.-H. Kögler and K. Stueber, 194–221. Boulder: Westview Press.
Kögler, H-H. (2010), "Recognition and the Resurgence of Intentional Agency," Inquiry 53: 450–69.
Kögler, H-H. (2012), "Agency and the Other: On the Intersubjective Roots of Self-Identity," *New Ideas in Psychology* 30: 47–64.
Kögler, H-H. (2014), "Empathy, Dialogue, Critique: How should we understand (inter-cultural violence?" in Ming Xie (ed.), The Agon of Interpretations: Towards a Critical Intercultural Hermeneutics, 275–301. Toronto: University of Toronto Press.
Kögler, H-H. (2015), "Ethics and Community," in J. Malpas and H.-H. Gander (eds.), *Routledge Companion to Hermeneutics*, 310–23. London/New York: Routledge.
Kögler, H-H. (2018), "The Hermeneutic Foundations of a Cosmopolitan Public Sphere," in A.K. Giri (ed.), *Beyond Cosmopolitanism: Towards Planetary Transformations*, 357–75. Singapore: Palgrave Macmillan.
Lipps, Th. (1903/1979), "Empathy, Inner Imitation and Sense-Feelings," in Melvin Rader (ed.), *A Modern Book of Esthetics*, 374–82. New York: Holt, Rinehart and Winston.
Korsgaard, C. (1996), *The Sources of Normativity*. Cambridge: Cambridge University Press.
Pritchard, H.A. (1912), "Does Moral Philosophy Rest on a Mistake?," *Mind*, 21: 21–37.
Richerson, P.J. and R. Boyd (2005), *Not by Genes Alone: How Culture Transformed Human Evolution*, Chicago: Chicago University Press.
Roughley, N. and K. Bayertz (2019), *The Normative Animal?: On the Anthropological Significance of Social, Moral and Linguistic Norms*. Oxford: Oxford University Press.
Sen, A. (2002), "Open and Closed Impartiality," *The Journal of Philosophy* 99: 445–69.
Skitka, L.J. and G.S. Morgan (2014), "The Social and Political Implications of Moral Conviction," *Advances in Political Psychology* 34: 95–110.
Skitka, L.J., B.E. Hanson, G.S. Morgan, and D.C. Wisneski (2021), "The Psychology of Moral Conviction," *Annual Review of Psychology*, 72: 347–66.

Smetana, J.G., M. Jambon, and C. Bell (2014), "The Social Domain Approach to Children's Moral and Social Judgments," in M. Killen and J.G. Smetana (eds.), *Handbook of Moral Development* (2nd edition), 23–45. New York/London: Psychology Press.

Smith, A. (1759/1982), *The Theory of Moral Sentiments*, ed. D.D. Raphael and A.L. Macfie. The Glasgow Edition of the Works and Correspondence of Adam Smith. Indianapolis, IN: Liberty Fund Press.

Stueber, K. (2006), *Rediscovering Empathy: Agency, Folk-Psychology and the Human Sciences*. Cambridge, MA: MIT Press.

Stueber, K. (2012), "Social Cognition and the Allure of the Second Person Perspective: In Defense of Empathy and Simulation," in A. Seemann (ed.), *Joint Attention: New Developments*, Cambridge, MA: MIT Press, 265–92.

Stueber, K. (2017a), "Smithian Constructivism: Elucidating the Reality of the Normative Domain," in *Moral Sentimentalism*, co-edited by R. Debes and K. Stueber, 192–209. Cambridge: Cambridge University Press.

Stueber, K. (2017b), "Empathy and Understanding Reasons," in H. Maibom (ed.), *The Routledge Handbook of the Philosophy of Empathy*, 137–47. London/New York: Routledge.

Stueber, K. (2018), "Understanding Individual Agency: How Empathy and Narrative Competence Cooperate," in A. Waldow and D. Matravers (eds.), *Philosophical Perspectives on Empathy: Theoretical Approaches and Emerging Challenges*, 129–43. London/New York: Routledge.

Stueber, K. (2019), "Empathy," *The Stanford Encyclopedia of Philosophy* (Fall 2019 Edition), Edward N. Zalta (ed.), URL https://plato.stanford.edu/archives/fall2019/entries/empathy.

Tomasello, M. (2016), *A Natural History of Human Morality*. Cambridge, MA: Harvard University Press.

Tomasello, M. (2019), *Becoming Human: A Theory of Ontogeny*. Cambridge, MA: Harvard University Press.

Tomasello, M. (2020), "The Moral Psychology of Obligation." *Behavioral and Brain Sciences* 43: 1–58.

Turiel, E., M. Killen, and C.C. Helwig (1987), "Morality: Its Structure, Functions, and Vagaries," in J. Kagan and S. Lamb (eds.), *The Emergence of Morality in Young Children*, 155–243. Chicago: University of Chicago Press.

Wallace, R.J. (1994), *Responsibility and the Moral Sentiments*. Cambridge, MA: Harvard University Press.

Wallace, R.J. (2019), *The Moral Nexus*. Princeton: Princeton University Press.

Zahavi, D. (2015), *Self and Other: Exploring Subjectivity, Empathy, and Shame*. Cambridge, MA: MIT Press.

5

Dialogue, Cosmopolitanism, and Language Education

Werner Delanoy

Introduction

My main field of research is language education, which aims for integrating language learning concepts and socio-cultural approaches. In other words, language learning is not treated as an end in itself, but as a medium for furthering democratic, ecological, transnational, and (self)-critical life-perspectives. For this educational project, a post-Gadamerian hermeneutic concept of dialogue has been at the heart of my theory building. Here, Hans-Herbert Kögler's critical hermeneutics has proven particularly useful because of its combination of Gadamerian principles and power-critical approaches. As a result, bridges have been built between a hermeneutic intercultural-learning pedagogy and schools of ideology critique (Delanoy 2002, 2007a, 2017).

In the past decades, language education has become increasingly global in orientation, moving from national to transnational perspectives. In these debates, cosmopolitanism has received little attention so far. Cosmopolitanism is a broad church with a variety of concepts, cutting across different academic disciplines. Cosmopolitanism's rich body of thought and its focus on global issues can benefit language education in its global orientation. In the following, therefore, a dialogic concept of cosmopolitanism will be presented as a perspective for language education. First, a post-Gadamerian concept of dialogue will be outlined. Secondly, different concepts of cosmopolitanism will be linked dialogically, and, thirdly, their implications for language education will be discussed.

Dialogue

The notion of dialogue suggested in this article is hermeneutic in orientation. Its main influences are a critical hermeneutics after Gadamer as developed by Hans-Herbert Kögler (1992), Peter Zima's (2000) discourse-analytical approach, Mikhael Bakhtin's (1981) writings, Seyla Benhabib's (2002: 8, 40) definition of a "complex dialogue," and Lothar Bredella's (2002) hermeneutic concept of language education. The key ideas underlying this notion can be listed as follows:

(a) Following Gadamer (1990: 280–1) and Kögler (1992: 79, 301; 2014: 49), dialogue is based on the conviction that all human understanding is subject to basic limitations. For this hermeneutics, human understanding is tied to the pre-understanding of concrete people with finite lives, who are only partly aware of the forces shaping them, and who are situated in specific and developing socio-cultural contexts. Moreover, the world(s) in which they live their lives are perceived as so complex that they can only be grasped in parts (Gadamer 1990: 298, 456; Kögler 1992: 37, 398). Finally, for this school, there is no transcendent perspective permitting recourse to absolute truth (Kögler 1992: 289). Hermeneutics, therefore, cannot offer definitive reference points for judging human action and reflection; it can only hope that constructive person-, situation-, and context-specific solutions can be found through dialogue itself (Bredella 2002: 59).

(b) These limitations can be partly overcome through (self)-critical engagement with other positions (Bredella 2002: 124; Kögler 1992: 25). Although these positions are also limited, they may be limited in different ways, thus offering insight beyond one's existing knowledge base and structures of feeling. For example, through confrontation with other viewpoints humans can better understand what constitutes their pre-understanding; they can discover new perspectives and become aware of (still) irreconcilable differences between different life-approaches.

(c) Such a concept rests on the belief in a partly autonomous, (self)-critical subject capable of initiating and further developing dialogic relationships. Such a notion of agency is suggested by Kögler (1992: 86) and Zima (2000: 193–5). Within hermeneutics this understanding of individual agency calls into question Gadamer's belief in an overwhelming tradition that ultimately swallows up individual initiative. Such a belief in agency also clashes with post- or anti-humanist approaches (e.g., Rosi Braidotti's [2012] notion of *zoé*), where humans are at the mercy of an all-encompassing life-force. Finally, the belief in a partly autonomous subject runs counter to poststructuralist concepts, where the subject is only considered as a fragmented, split, and incoherent entity. Kögler's hermeneutics does not deny such fragmentation. However, it stresses the importance of a partly coherent subject for critical agency, and it considers establishing coherence as an ongoing and arduous dialogical process (Kögler 1992: 86). For Kögler (2011: 143, 237), this subject remains an *individual* because of its specific "Erfahrungs- und Erlebnishorizont," its unique horizon of lived experience. In in a similar vein, Seyla Benhabib (2002: 16) views "individuality as the unique and fragile achievement of selves weaving together conflicting narratives and allegiances into a unique life history."

(d) Simultaneously, this individual is a social being because of its embeddedness in socio-historical contexts and its growth through social interaction. Following Terry Eagleton (2016: 43), the fact that humans are born "prematurely," that is, as totally dependent on the care of others, makes sociality a universal condition for human development. Contrary to Gadamer, such sociality, however, cannot be grounded in *one* commonly shared tradition, because such a belief would ignore socio-cultural differences (Kögler 1992: 111). As will be shown in the following section, acknowledgement of different socio-cultural perspectives is indispensable in the context of cosmopolitan debates, where different traditions—a European and a post-colonial one—both stand in opposition to and are nested in each other.

(e) Moreover, a case is made for respectful engagement with other people and their viewpoints (Delanoy 2007b: 50), where respect does not stop when other perspectives conflict with or call into question one's own convictions. In Kögler's (2017: 378) words, the other person is treated as "an invaluable subject in her own right." In line with its different dictionary meanings, the term *respect* here includes both appreciation of, care for and a certain caution about otherness. While appreciation increases the motivation to learn from other viewpoints, care implies the responsibility to support others in their development plus a high dose of self-criticism to help prevent imposition of one's own values and beliefs on other people. What I mean by caution is a questioning of other viewpoints to avoid their uncritical acceptance.

(f) Respect and openness, however, do not suffice to better understand other people and their positions. What is also needed are suitable perspectives and analytical tools (Kögler 1992: 90). On the one hand, existing tools and perspectives provide a starting point. On the other hand, they may prove insufficient in the light of new challenges. Therefore, dialogue incudes the continuous search for new solutions, which may work in some but not in other contexts.

(g) Dialogue, therefore, is an open-ended and creative process. To quote Bakhtin (1981: 30), "there is no first word (no ideal word) and the final word has not yet been spoken." Without a master narrative and a pre-given toolkit, dialogue is a creative act, where person-, situation-, and problem-specific solutions need to be found and redefined in the light of changing demands. This notion of dialogue, therefore, interlinks with concepts of education, where the focus is on preparing learners to engage with challenges going beyond the tried and tested. In pedagogy, such an approach is suggested by Hans Christoph Koller (2012).

(h) Ideally, dialogue is a meeting of equal partners with equal opportunities to bring in and further develop their interests. In real-life contexts such encounter is the exception rather than the rule. In real life, people's place in the world is shaped by power divisions, particular social roles, uneven discursive capabilities, and unequal access to material and educational resources (Kögler 2014: 57). Moreover, the participants in dialogue are often entangled in a problematic history, which makes trust in and respect for other people difficult. Any attempts at dialogue, therefore, must (self)-critically address existing power imbalances and antagonisms to help transform them into more egalitarian and convivial structures.

(i) Following Peter Zima (1991: 402) a distinction needs to be made between "intersubjective" and "interdiscursive" forms of dialogue. In the case of "intersubjective" dialogue the dialogue partners share important convictions, while in the latter case basic beliefs and values are at odds. It goes without saying that the latter poses more serious obstacles. A good example, here, is the clash between the late-capitalist belief in continuous economic growth and the degrowth-position suggested by William Gaudelli (2016: 24–5).

(j) Dialogue is inclusive of different logical systems. One major force-field concerns the co-existence of a constructive logic, permitting coherent reflection and action, and a deconstructive one drawing attention to inconsistencies and inviting a reworking of existing practices. Similarly, Bakhtin (1981: 272) distinguishes between "centrifugal" and "centripetal" forces, the former bringing elements together, the latter driving them apart. Along these lines, another distinction has been made between a logic of equivalence and a logic of difference (Laclau 2000: 303), the first one shifting the focus to similarities and overlaps, while the latter gives preference to divisions and specificities. For Kögler (1992: 86) and Zima (2000: 414 ff.) these different logics should inter-animate and contest each other in a continuing and open-ended debate. Within this debate, one of the two may prove more important at times. Whether one is temporarily preferred over the other is not a matter of principle, but a decision reached through dialogue itself. Furthermore, all these logics can prove conducive to dialogue, that is, all can lead to creating dialogic connections. Indeed, "connection ... *despite* difference" can prove particularly important for cosmopolitan dialogue (Appiah 2007: 132). Here, mutual respect and growing awareness of the other person's perspective remain possible despite (still) unbridgeable differences.

(k) Another clash between logics emphasizes the fragility of dialogue, drawing attention to the tension between idealistic concepts and real-life practices. As stated above, dialogue is an idealistic concept, which only works when its participants play by its rules. When Gaudelli (2016: 50) points out that "human history has witnessed more war than peace, more intercultural discord than accord, more environmental degradation than preservation," a belief in dialogue may seem an unrealistic pie-in-the-sky, which may even divert attention away from pressing issues. To my mind, hope for dialogue has a right to exist even in the darkest of times. Moreover, ideals serve an important purpose; they suggest directions for further development. On the other hand, concrete reality always provides a critical perspective on the limitations, presuppositions, and implications of idealistic suggestions.

(l) Finally, dialogue is created in and through language and other symbolic systems. In other words, dialogue represents a specific form of language use informed by the criteria listed in this section. A dialogic concept of language education, as will be further discussed in section 3, therefore, implies development of certain symbolic capabilities.

Let me conclude this section by adding that the notion of dialogue advocated in this article is located in a specific socio-historical context. First, a liberal-humanist tradition is continued with its belief in a deliberative and secular democracy, critical thinking, and a partly autonomous subject. Secondly, it marks a response to concepts emphasizing the end of metanarratives, plus the fragmentation and commodification of the self in a late-capitalist modernity. While being aware of such development, while even welcoming the loss of overwhelming tradition, the concept also implies a cross-cultural "normative horizon," that is, a shared belief in dialogic principles (Kögler 2011: 240). Moreover, there is hope for a deep-going understanding of others plus for creating deep and lasting relationships with other people, despite the shallowness and indifference written into a market-driven ideology. Finally, this notion of dialogue is not blind to late capitalism's exploitation of people and the environment. Therefore, a case is made for establishing more egalitarian and ecological socio-economic structures and practices.

However, there is no denying that this perspective remains implicated in a Western and European scholarly tradition. Moreover, as in my case, it is suggested by a professionally and socio-economically privileged subject, that is, a tenured professor living in a country (Austria) benefitting from worldwide unequal wealth distribution. In other words, it is not my intention to present this approach as *the* way forward. Instead, by laying bare underlying assumptions colleagues are invited to engage in a dialogic debate of interdiscursive proportions.

Cosmopolitanism

In recent debates cosmopolitanism is discussed in the plural as a variety of different approaches. Therefore, whenever I speak of cosmopolitanism in general terms, I have in mind its manifold and different manifestations. What unites most of the concepts is their focus on issues of global relevance and a shared concern for global conviviality. Moreover, there is agreement on the importance of an outward-looking perspective permitting wider-reaching reflection and action. On the other hand, differences abound, and they can be fundamental in orientation. A good example, here, are the different genealogies brought into play by scholars arguing from European and post-colonial perspectives. Another major difference lies in the level of abstraction chosen to discuss cosmopolitan issues. At one end of the spectrum, one can find general comments, while at the other end the focus is on concrete cases. From a dialogic perspective such variety is highly welcome to invite a controversial and differentiated discussion of cosmopolitan projects.

Different Genealogies

In my discussion of different cosmopolitan concepts, I will focus on two approaches where different genealogies have been invoked.

A Western/European Genealogy

This genealogy traces cosmopolitanism back to the Greek word *kosmopolites* and to Greek philosophy, that is, to the Cynics and Neo-Stoics (Delanty 2009: 20 ff.).[1] The term is attributed to Diogenes the Cynic, who, living in exile, stated that he was a citizen of the world and not of a *polis*. The other reference is to the Stoic philosopher Hierocles, who "describes each of us being surrounded by an extending series of concentric circles beginning with our innermost self, family, relatives, neighbors, and so on, and ending with a final circle embracing humanity as a whole" (Mitsis 2017: 176). In recent cosmopolitan debates Hierocles's idea has been taken up by Kwame Appiah (1998) and Martha Nussbaum (2010) in their attempts to demonstrate that local affiliation can go hand in hand with wider-reaching solidarities.

Within this genealogy, cosmopolitanism is then linked to Renaissance humanism and the Enlightenment with a special focus on Immanuel Kant's contributions. In *Idea for a Universal History* (2010), Kant claims that "the greatest problem for the human species … is that of attaining a civil society which can administer justice universally" (ibid.: 20) in the interest of a "perfect civil union of mankind" (ibid.: 25). In the twentieth century, another milestone in this tradition is Hannah Arendt's (1961: 220–1) notion of an "enlarged mentality," which in a Kantian sense implies a universalistic morality. Arendt's concept is a response to the holocaust, which she discusses as a crime against humanity. Such thinking interlinks with the post-World War Two development of a human-rights agenda to be respected globally. In recent cosmopolitan debates, Kwame Appiah (2007: 144) strongly advocates such a position by naming the principle of "everybody matters" as the central idea of his cosmopolitanism.

In recent decades, debates have centered around the idea of globalization as a "rapidly developing … network of interconnections and interdependencies" (Tomlinson 1999: 2). For example, Ulrich Beck (2011) argues that global cooperation can no longer be viewed just as an option but as a must, when considering threats like climate change, ecological devastation, gross global power imbalances or mass migration. Moreover, the Kantian notion of a just world order still plays an important role in these debates (Fine 2011; Nussbaum 2004). Other concepts, however, have become more difficult to maintain, the concentric circles model being a good example. Its distinction between separable circles, starting with self and family and then reaching out to bigger social entities, is too static and mono-directional to capture the ramifications and dynamics of identity construction in a globalized modernity. Here, a more appropriate model is to focus on people's situatedness in complex, interconnected and open-ended networks.

A Post-Colonial Genealogy

A different genealogy is suggested by post-colonial scholars. For Walter Mignolo (2011: 330–1), the starting point is not Greek philosophy but the sixteenth century with "the emergence of the Atlantic commercial circuit, the genocide of the Indians, the massive appropriation and expropriation of land by European monarchies and the massive slave trade and exploitation of labour." Such critique goes hand in hand with laying bare the underbelly of the European Enlightenment project. Nick Stevenson (2011: 246), for example, states that "racism is not an aberration of Enlightenment thinking but actually integral to its foundation." Concomitantly, a case is made for delinking cosmopolitanism from Kant and his legacy. For Mignolo (2011: 331), this legacy still helps uphold colonial practices by "hid[ing] the logic of coloniality." In similar terms, Bruce Robbins (2017: 42) emphasizes that Kant failed to address economic inequalities, thus disregarding a major obstacle to universal justice. This criticism is also levelled at the cosmopolitan concepts suggested by Appiah or Beck for their neglect of "a more equitable distribution of resources" (Robbins 2017: 43).

Moreover, post-colonial cosmopolitan approaches have questioned the central position of European modernity. People in the west often claim to have a monopoly on modernity and enlightened thinking. From a post-colonial perspective, this claim is part of a hegemonic program justifying the West's right to intellectual and economic domination and exploitation. Enrique Dussel (2013: 14) argues that this myth of superiority makes Western modernity appear in a highly favorable light, while simultaneously masking its will to dominate, exploit and silence others. Dipesh Chakrabarty (2011), therefore, stresses the need to provincialize Europe, that is, to replace Eurocentrism with a polycentric concept, where non-European notions of cosmopolitanism and democracy are given a voice. Gerard Delanty (2009: 20), for example, refers to ancient Chinese civilization with its cosmopolitan concept of *Tian Zia*, while Amartya Sen (1999: 232–42) highlights Buddhist and Islamic traditions of freedom and tolerance of diversity. Following Gillian Brock (2011: 187), "respect for human rights and ideas of democracy are not simply Western values, ... substantial elements of these ideas can be found in all major cultures, religions and traditions."

General Concepts and Cosmopolitanism as a Grounded Category

In their introduction to the *Ashgate Research Companion to Cosmopolitanism*, Maria Rovisco and Magdalena Novicka (2011: 2) refer to recent shifts of direction in cosmopolitan debates. As for older approaches, there is a body of literature engaged with defining central characteristics of cosmopolitanism. Moreover, when concrete practices are studied the focus is on institutions "of supranational and transnational governance" (ibid.: 3). In recent debates, research has shifted attention to the micro-level of cosmopolitan practices. Here, the focus lies on how concrete people live their lives in socio-culturally diverse and hybrid settings, where personal and local interests interlink with issues of global import. One central aim of such research is to make accessible "ordinary ways of thinking and acting of those agents that are active at the grassroots level in a range of transnational networks" (ibid.: 3). Such networks go far beyond the institutional, they include trans-local family links and grassroots initiatives like *Fridays for Future* or *Human Lives Matter*.

General concepts

Here, definitions of cosmopolitanism are a key concern. According to Delanty (2012: 2), cosmopolitanism "in the broadest sense possible ... is about the extension of the moral and political horizons of people, societies, organizations and institutions." Moreover, cosmopolitanism implies "an attitude of openness as opposed to closure." This definition stresses the importance of being outward-looking and open to new ideas. It draws attention to "moral and political horizons," which to my mind is too narrow in conception, since, for example, technological, environmental, economic, or cultural dimensions are not explicitly mentioned. I would, therefore, opt for a more extensive concept, while retaining its attitudinal direction.

Moreover, all general definitions require some contextual grounding to situate them in a specific socio-historical problematic. Here, Miriam Sobré-Denton and Nilanjana Bardhan (2013: 5) offer a specification that—to my mind—can act as a complement to Delanty's definition. For them, cosmopolitanism is a concept discussed by different disciplines (e.g., philosophy, sociology, law, anthropology, pedagogy) "that promises hope for a world increasingly connected through technology, media and travel, and yet plagued by continuing neo-colonial and post-colonial inequities, social and global injustices, terrorism, poverty, ethnic conflicts and wars." Like Beck, Sobré-Denton and Bardhan (2013: 5) argue that "there is a growing realization that we live in a world where we must find ways to address problems that are global in scope and *cannot be solved by any one country or group of people alone*, e.g., environmental degradation, global warming, world hunger, arms proliferation, terrorism and so on." In line with my notion of dialogue, Sobré-Denton and Bardhan make *hope* an important constituent of their concept. Despite an imperfect world, they make a case for global cooperation in the interest of a peaceful world and a more equitable distribution of resources.

Cosmopolitan debates have also focused on the general applicability of universal suggestions. On the one hand, there are positions like Martha Nussbaum's (2000: 78–80) capabilities approach, where a set of basic conditions for a dignified life is formulated as a general pre-given for humans all over the globe. On the other hand, such an approach has been critiqued for neither addressing its context of emergence nor paying sufficient attention to how people differ in their life worlds (cf. Levy and Sznaider 2011: 201). Hence, according to Levy and Sznaider (ibid.: 201) Eurocentric interests can be masked as universal and "respect for what makes others different" is bracketed out. Therefore, a different approach to universals has been suggested. Sobré-Denton and Bardhan (2014: 12) speak of a "diversity of universals" to emphasize that all universal concepts are rooted in specific contexts. In line with a dialogic agenda, none of them can claim universal validity per se. Instead, they are all treated as suggestions to be discussed in an open-ended dialogue.

Cosmopolitanism as a Grounded Category

In recent debates, bottom-up approaches have been advocated, where everyday interaction becomes the center of cosmopolitan research. A key proponent, here, is Hans-Herbert Kögler (2011, 2017). His focus is on how structural changes in a globalized modernity "… are reflected at the level of the individual agents' self-understanding, how they impact on their concrete beliefs and practices, and how they redefine their lives and values within their situated settings" (Kögler 2017: 375). Kögler, however, not only looks at how structural conditions affect individual lives; he is also focused on how people in turn can act on these structures. In his research, Kögler (2011: 231–2) gives priority to forms of agency beyond settings such as the state or official organizations, thus drawing attention to grassroots practices. Like Nussbaum, Kögler also links the study of concrete cases to a discussion of general capabilities. Other than Nussbaum, he stresses their tentativeness and contextual embeddedness, thus speaking of a "possible normative horizon" open to redefinition (Kögler 2011:

240). As stated above, this normative horizon results from dialogic principles. For Kögler, basic dialogic capabilities comprise "[the recognition of] situated validity claims, [engagement] in empathetic perspective-taking," and the critical analysis of power-related issues (ibid.: 240).

Cosmopolitanism and Dialogue

In this section, I have discussed cosmopolitanism as an ensemble of complementary and conflicting approaches, where a European tradition is confronted with post-colonial concepts, and where perspectives vary in their level of generality, ranging from suggestions for general, universal principles to case studies focused on everyday interactions. In my dialogic approach, these different orientations can be graphically interlinked as follows:

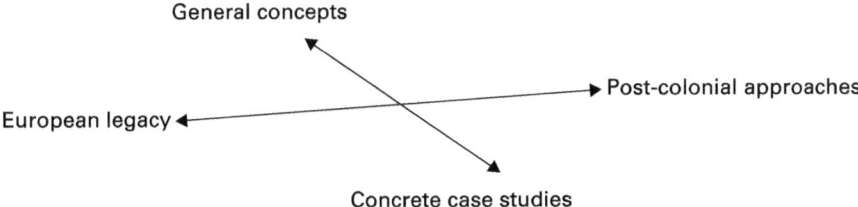

In this model, cosmopolitanism is shown as a crossroads with two intersecting axes, one focused on the contextual embeddedness of cosmopolitan theory-building, while the other refers to different levels of generality. In this model, the four starting positions are all partners in a dialogue, where they can critically question, complement, and inter-animate each other. None of them is privileged over the others per se, all of them are subject to limitations, and the outcome of their meetings cannot be pre-determined. Dialogue may lead to awareness of (still) irreconcilable differences and the discovery of unexpected similarities. It may lead to mutual transformation and joint projects. Dialogue may also result in significant socio-economic change if dominant practices prove inappropriate and counterproductive to tackle topical issues. To my mind, late-capitalism's belief in continuous growth is a dead end, which will further aggravate ecological devastation and socio-economic power imbalances. Here, the degrowth perspective advocated by Gaudelli (2016) can provide a useful starting point for alternative concept-building.

None of these orientations is treated as a monolith, but each as a diverse set of practices which may be entangled in manifold ways with oppositional concepts. Following Benhabib (2002: 24), for example, the European Enlightenment legacy is not a uniform body of thought. The Kantian legacy is not only racist resonances and blindness to unequal economic power divisions. For example, Kant's understanding of hospitality also includes awareness of colonial violence. Following Fine (2011: 154), the Kantian right of the host to turn the 'visitor' away is a response to abuses of hospitality "unleashed on non-European people by European states and trading companies" (Fine 2011: 154). At the other end, post-colonial approaches also include a variety of different concepts. While Enrique Dussel (2013: 181), for example, argues against Western participation in the post-colonial project, Edward Said (2004), on the other hand, does not reject Western humanism despite his criticism of the Enlightenment's complicity in colonial suppression and exploitation.

Of course, establishing and strengthening dialogic links between a European legacy and post-colonial programs can be a formidable task. According to Zima, such dialogue may well turn out to be interdiscursive in orientation, thus including a clash between different values, aims and power positions. However, the two programs must not be seen as radically opposed. They have also cross-fertilized each other. Scholars in the West have critically questioned a European genealogy with the help of post-colonial writings (Calhoun 2017; Gaudelli 2017), and post-colonial critics have stressed the importance of liberal-humanist ideas (cf. Dussel 2013; Said 2004). As for the latter, Dussel (ibid.: 167), for example, despite his wish to keep Western scholarship at a distance, still acknowledges the importance of Western critical thinking. Indeed, in recent debates the two perspectives have been integrated, as is the case in Sobré-Denton's and Bardhan's (2013) approach to cosmopolitanism.

As for the other axis, the hermeneutic circle necessitates the integration of general concepts and concrete experience. While the concrete can only be understood with reference to the general, the latter can undergo modification and change in the light of the concrete. The recent shift toward a grounded cosmopolitanism certainly makes sense in the light of a dialogic program. Following Bakhtin (1981: 39), dialogue happens "in the zone of direct contact with inconclusive present-day reality." In other words, dialogue is lived in developing, diverse, contradictory, and incomplete everyday settings. Indeed, engagement with the dialogic potential of everyday interaction is indispensable to firmly root dialogue in everyday experience. Such a focus aligns with a democratic agenda aiming for the inclusion of as many people as possible in concrete dialogue-building.

Language Education

As stated above, language education interlinks language and socio-cultural learning. The aim of such education is to develop symbolic and socio-cultural capabilities permitting the creation of dialogic relationships in local and trans-local contexts. Such a perspective builds on Lothar Bredella's (2002: 198–214) intercultural language learning approach, which already includes engagement with cosmopolitan perspectives.[2] Other important influences are concepts of task-based humanistic language learning (Legutke and Thomas 1991; Müller-Hartmann and Schocker-v. Ditfurth 2004), the multiliteracies movement (Kalantzis and al. 2016), and Claire Kramsch's (2009) notion of symbolic competence.

Such an approach has specific implications for (foreign) language learning and teaching:

(a) Dialogue is created through language. Hence, language and content should not be separated. Instead, forms of language use are promoted which can foster dialogue building in the context of complex and controversial issues. This includes trust-building activities, the avoidance of hurtful language use, engagement in joint projects, a careful study of different perspectives, their discussion despite language limitations, and the development of critical abilities.

(b) As for developing language competencies, such an approach, for example, stands in opposition to a narrow definition of language skills stripped of content and emotions. From a dialogic perspective, learning to speak, write, read, and listen goes hand in hand with widening one's knowledge base plus questioning and reorienting one's attitudinal disposition. Another example is learning to ask questions. Here, the focus is not only on the mastery of certain question forms but also on the epistemological value of question types. In their critique of traditional humanism, Harry Kunnemann and Caroline Suransky (2011: 391–2) argue in favor of "slow questions," which can raise awareness of the limitations of fast solutions and draw attention to human interdependencies. In the light of such a concept, developing communicative competence, therefore, is linked to conversation about issues of existential significance.

(c) Dialogue implies relationship-building. While in a test-driven language pedagogy a language skill like listening is reduced to comprehending the pre-given, dialogue requires a radically different approach. Here, the outcome is uncertain, and the listener engages in empathetic perspective taking. In Kramsch's (2006: 251) words, all partners in dialogue are treated as "whole persons with hearts, bodies and minds, with memories, fantasies, loyalties, identities," which rules out merely functional and instrumental uses of language.

(d) In a globalized modernity, dialogic language use requires multimodal and multi-media capabilities, thus inviting exploration of and experimentation with different semiotic systems and media.

(e) In language education a shift has been suggested from inter- to trans-cultural learning, the latter being focused more strongly on transnational issues and hybridization practices. While some trans-culturalists see their approach as the way forward and interculturalism as an outmoded concept still mired in nationalism, closer inspection reveals that this does not do justice to intercultural learning debates (Bredella 2010; Delanoy 2014). Indeed, both schools share transnational concerns, and pooling their resources can help broaden, deepen, and question educational concepts and practices. Cosmopolitanism can further enrich concepts of language-and-culture learning since its global reach goes beyond that of the other two schools.

(f) This global orientation also invites critical reflection upon English as the medium for international communication, which of course also reflects global power divisions. Here, a central question is whether language education should give priority to English or opt for multilingual education (Delanoy 2007b). For dialogue, widespread proficiency in English can facilitate communication on global levels considerably. Different languages, however, offer a wealth of linguistic and socio-cultural possibilities going beyond that of a single language. An English-only approach, therefore, risks losing this rich potential for new insight. Moreover, the dominance of English gives those a head-start who have learned it as a first language, thus leaving speakers of other languages at a disadvantage. To my mind, context-specific solutions need to be found which can constructively combine the two perspectives (Delanoy 2007b).

(g) Since dialogue is an open and ongoing process, its participants cannot rely on the tried and tested. Creativity is of central importance to such an approach. On the level of language, creativity implies language practices going beyond the pre-given, which may be negatively loaded and stereotypical in character. On the level of content, priority is given to input challenging the learners' views and convictions.

(h) In cosmopolitan debates, Thomas Bender (2017: 117) argues that "new experience for the cosmopolitan is moderately unsettling." He is taken to task for this comment by Paulo Lemos Horta (2017: 158). Horta claims that moderate discomfort does not lead to transformation but to a cosmopolitanism, where existing comfort zones can stay intact, and the status quo is reaffirmed. From an educational perspective, discomforting learners without placing excessive demands is a major challenge, which in case of going too far may block the way for further learning. In this context, therefore, Bender's approach makes sense, and if coupled with self-reflexivity the comfort zone itself can become a topic for introspection and discussion.

(i) A cosmopolitanism grounded in the everyday world is highly pertinent to dialogic concepts of language education. On one level, everyday interaction can be studied, for example, through literary texts, films, documentaries, or blogs. On another level, the study of everyday interactions between learners in and beyond classroom contexts, whether they happen face-to-face or in virtual settings, can shift attention to forms of grassroots agency. That way, cosmopolitanism can be grounded in educational practice, and educational practice can become a workshop for experimenting with ideas and language in the interest of cosmopolitan dialogue.

(j) Following Cameron (2004: 1–2), dialogue is both learner- and learning-centered. Learner-centeredness refers to the inclusion of learner needs and interests, plus to active learner participation in co-shaping learning processes. Learning-centeredness implies a well-defined learning program giving teachers and learners a direction for structuring learning processes. In my own work, the main challenge has been to make dialogue more plannable without curtailing its open-endedness. On the one hand, models have been suggested for scaffolding emotional, cognitive, and linguistic complexity (Delanoy 2007c). On the other hand, the learners need to be given as much space as possible to act as dialogue builders.

(k) Developing such a program for a cosmopolitan approach to language education is still a research desideratum. Such a project requires cooperation between scholars, teachers and learners from different educational backgrounds and different parts of the planet. To my mind, a grounded approach as suggested by Hans-Herbert Kögler can provide a useful starting position. In other words, multiple case studies could be conducted to better understand teacher and learner perspectives. In a second step, the results can be pooled and discussed in the interest of a trans-local learning program. Such a project is time- and cost-intensive; yet, it is worth the investment judging by the challenges which humans face in a globalized modernity.

Summing up, a timely concept of language education cannot but address issues of globalization. Cosmopolitanism can enrich such a program because of its global focus, its diversity of concepts, its critical dimension, and its hope for a more just, ecological, and equitable future of humankind. A dialogic approach can draw attention to the different cosmopolitanisms in circulation. It can also provide a basis for building relationships across socio-cultural divisions. Moreover, it can make language education a workshop for developing new ideas and bonds between people, thus enabling learners to address complex issues through cooperation in local and trans-local contexts. Finally, further research is needed to help cosmopolitanism take root in language education.

Notes

1 In this article, despite their different implications, the terms "Western" and "European" are used interchangeably.
2 Bredella opposes cosmopolitanism to pluralism and aims for linking some of their concerns dialogically. However, his understanding of cosmopolitanism does not address the diversity of cosmopolitan concepts as is discussed in more recent debates.

References

Appiah, Kwame A. (1998), 'Cosmopolitan Patriots,' in Cheah Pheng and Bruce Robbins (eds.), *Cosmopolitics: Thinking and Feeling Beyond the Nation*, Minneapolis: University of Minnesota Press, 91–116.
Appiah, Kwame A. (2007), *Cosmopolitanism: Ethics in a World of Strangers*, London: Penguin.
Beck, Ulrich (2011), 'Cosmopolitan Sociology: Outline of a Paradigm Shift,' in Maria Rovisco and Magdalena Nowicka (eds.), *The Ashgate Research Companion to Cosmopolitanism*, Farnham and Burlington: Ashgate, 17–32.
Arendt, Hannah (1961), *Between Past and Future: Six Exercises in Political Thought*, New York: Meridian Books.
Bakhtin, Mikhael M. (1981), *The Dialogic Imagination: Four Essays. Edited by Michael Holquist*, Austin: University of Texas Press.
Bender, Thomas (2017), 'The Cosmopolitan Experience and Its Uses,' in Bruce Robbins and Paolo Lemos Horta (eds.), *Cosmopolitanisms*, New York: New York University Press, 116–26.
Benhabib, Seyla (2002), *The Claims of Culture: Equality and Diversity in the Global Era*, Princeton and Oxford: Princeton University Press.
Braidotti, Rosi (2013), *The Posthuman*, Cambridge and Malden: Polity.
Bredella, Lothar (2002), *Literarisches und interkulturelles Verstehen*, Tübingen: Gunter Narr.

Bredella, Lothar (2010), *Das Verstehen des Anderen: Kulturwissenschaftliche und literaturdidaktische Studien*, Tübingen: Gunter Narr.

Brock, Gillian (2011) 'Cosmopolitanism and the Struggle for Global Justice," in Maria Rovisco and Magdalena Nowicka (eds.), *The Ashgate Research Companion to Cosmopolitanism*, Farnham and Burlington: Ashgate, 179–94.

Calhoun, Craig (2017), 'A Cosmopolitanism of Connections," in Bruce Robbins and Paolo Lemos Horta (eds.), *Cosmopolitanisms*, New York: New York University Press, 189–200.

Cameron, Lynne (2004), *Teaching Languages to Young Learners*, Cambridge: Cambridge University Press.

Chakrabarty, Dipesh (2008), *Provincializing Europe: Postcolonial Thought and Historical Difference*, Princeton and Oxford: Princeton University Press.

Delanoy, Werner (2002), *Fremdsprachlicher Literaturunterricht: Theorie und Praxis als Dialog*, Tübingen: Gunter Narr.

Delanoy, Werner (2007a), 'Gender and Literature Didactics," in Helene Decke-Cornill and Laurenz Volkmann (eds.), *Gender Studies and Foreign Language Teaching*, Tübingen: Gunter Narr, 185–207.

Delanoy, Werner (2007b), 'Dialogue as a Perspective for English Language Learning," in Wolf Kindermann (ed.), *Transcending Boundaries: Essays in Honor of Gisela Hermann-Brennecke*, Berlin: LIT, 49–69.

Delanoy, Werner (2007c), 'Structuring Cultural Learning Processes," in Eva-Maria Graf and Allan James (eds.), *English Studies in Flux: New Peaks, New Shores, New Crossings*, Tübingen: Gunter Narr, 103–16.

Delanoy, Werner (2014), 'Transkulturalität als begriffliche und konzeptuelle Herausforderung an Fremdsprachendidaktik," in Frauke Matz, Michael Rogge, and Philipp Siepmann (eds.), *Transkulturelles Lernen im Fremdsprachenunterricht: Theorie und Praxis*, Frankfurt/M.: Peter Lang, 19–35.

Delanoy, Werner (2017), 'The Case of Gloria Anzaldúa: Translating a Postcolonial Perspective into (English) Language Education," in Christiane Lütge and Mark Stein (eds.), *Crossovers: Postcolonial Studies and Transcultural Learning*, Wien and Zürich: LIT, 121–37.

Delanty, Gerard (2009), *The Cosmopolitan Imagination: The Renewal of Critical Social Theory*, Cambridge: Cambridge University Press.

Delanty, Gerard (2012). 'Introduction," in Gerard Delanty (ed.), *Routledge Handbook of Cosmopolitan Studies*, Abingdon, Oxon: Routledge, 1–8.

Eagleton, Terry (2016), *Culture*, New Haven and London: Yale University Press.

Fine, Robert (2011), 'Cosmopolitanism and Natural Law: Rethinking Kant," in Maria Rovisco and Magdalena Nowicka (eds.), *The Ashgate Research Companion to Cosmopolitanism*, Farnham and Burlington: Ashgate, 147–62.

Dussel, Enrique (2013), *Der Gegendiskurs der Moderne: Kölner Vorlesungen*, Wien and Berlin: Turia + Kant.

Gadamer, Hans Georg (1990). *Wahrheit und Methode: Grundzüge einer philosophischen Hermeneutik*. Sixth Edition, Tübingen: J.C.B. Mohr.

Gaudelli, William (2016), *Global Citizenship Education: Everyday Transcendence*, New York and London: Routledge.

Kalantzis, Mary, Cope, Bill, Chan, Eveline and Dalley-Trim, Leanne (2016), *Literacies: Second Edition*, Cambridge and New York: Cambridge University Press.

Kant, Immanuel (2010), 'Idea of a Universal History with a Cosmopolitan Purpose," in Garrett Wallace Brown and David Held (eds.), *The Cosmopolitanism Reader*, Cambridge and Malden: Polity, 17–26.

Kögler, Hans-Herbert (1992), *Die Macht des Dialogs. Kritische Hermeneutik nach Gadamer, Foucault und Rorty*, Stuttgart: J.B. Metzler.
Kögler, Hans-Herbert (2011), 'Hermeneutic Cosmopolitanism, or: Toward a Cosmopolitan Public Sphere," in Maria Rovisco and Magdalena Nowicka (eds.), *The Ashgate Research Companion to Cosmopolitanism*, Farnham and Burlington: Ashgate, 225–42.
Kögler, Hans-Herbert (2014), 'A Critique of Dialogue in Philosophical Hermeneutics," *Journal of Dialogue Studies*, 2/1, 47–67.
Kögler, Hans-Herbert (2017), 'Reflexivity and Globalization: Conditions and Capabilities for a Dialogic Cosmopolitanism," *Human Affairs*, 27, 374–88.
Koller, Hans Christoph (2012), *Bildung anders denken: Einführung in die Theorie transformatorischer Bildungsprozesse*, Stuttgart: Kohlhammer.
Kramsch, Claire (2006), 'From Communicative Competence to Symbolic Competence," *The Modern Language Journal*, 90, 249–52.
Kramsch, Claire (2009), *The Multilingual Subject*, Oxford and New York: Oxford University Press.
Kunnemann, Harry and Suransky, Caroline (2011), 'Cosmopolitanism and the Humanist Myopia," in Maria Rovisco and Magdalena Nowicka (eds.), *The Ashgate Research Companion to Cosmopolitanism*, Farnham and Burlington: Ashgate, 387–402.
Laclau, Ernesto (2000), 'Constructing Universality," in Judith Butler, Ernesto Laclau and Slavoj Zizek (eds.), *Contingency, Hegemony, Universality: Contemporary Dialogues on the Left*, London: Verso, 281–307.
Legutke, Michael and Thomas, Howard (1991), *Process and Experience in the Language Classroom*, London & New York: Longman.
Lemos Horta, Paulo (2017), 'Cosmopolitan Prejudice," in Bruce Robbins and Paolo Lemos Horta (eds.), *Cosmopolitanisms*, New York: New York University Press, 153–68.
Levy, Daniel and Sznaider, Natan (2011), 'Cosmopolitan Memory and Human Rights," in Maria Rovisco and Magdalena Nowicka (eds.), *The Ashgate Research Companion to Cosmopolitanism*, Farnham and Burlington: Ashgate, 195–210.
Mignolo, Walter D. (2011), 'Border Thinking, Decolonial Cosmopolitanism and Dialogues Among Civilizations," in Maria Rovisco and Magdalena Nowicka (eds.), *The Ashgate Research Companion to Cosmopolitanism*, Farnham and Burlington: Ashgate, 329–48.
Mitsis, Phillip (2017), 'A Stoic Critique of Cosmopolitanism," in Bruce Robbins and Paolo Lemos Horta (eds.), *Cosmopolitanisms*, New York: New York University Press, 171–86.
Müller-Hartmann, Andreas and Schocker-von Ditfurth, Marita (2004), *Introduction to English Language Teaching*, Stuttgart: Klett.
Nussbaum, Martha C. (2000), *Women and Human Development: The Capabilities Approach*, Cambridge: Cambridge University Press.
Nussbaum, Martha C. (2010), 'Patriotism and Cosmopolitanism," in Garrett Wallace Brown and David Held (eds.), *The Cosmopolitanism Reader*, Cambridge and Malden; Polity, 155–62.
Robbins, Bruce (2017), 'George Orwell, Cosmopolitanism, and Global Justice," in Bruce Robbins and Paolo Lemos Horta (eds.), *Cosmopolitanisms*, New York: New York University Press, 40–58.
Rovisco, Maria and Magdalena Nowicka (2011), 'Introduction," in Maria Rovisco and Magdalena Nowicka (eds.), *The Ashgate Research Companion to Cosmopolitanism*, Farnham and Burlington: Ashgate, 1–14.
Said, Edward (2004), *Humanism and Democratic Criticism*, Basingstoke: Palgrave.
Sen, Amartya (1999), *Development as Freedom*, Oxford: Oxford University Press.

Sobré-Denton, Miriam and Bardhan, Nilanjana (2014), *Cultivating Cosmopolitanism for Intercultural Communication*, London and New York: Routledge.
Tomlinson, John (1999), *Globalization and Culture*, Chicago: Chicago University Press.
Zima, Peter V. (1991), Literarische Ästhetik, Tübingen: Francke.
Zima, Peter V. (2000), Theorie des Subjekts, Tübingen and Basel: Francke.

6

Secularity, Religion, and Dialogue

Rethinking the Conditions of the Possibility for Genuine Complementary Learning

Paul Healy

Introduction

While Habermas's recent writings on post-secularism have been welcomed by many as opening up new possibilities for secular-religious interaction, it has drawn significant criticism from others for falling short of delivering the rapprochement between the religious and the secular it seemed to promise. In particular, Habermas's controversial translation proviso has attracted a great deal of critical commentary, centering largely on the question of whether it places "asymmetrical," and correspondingly untenable "burdens" on religious citizens. But the critical prominence accorded this theme has deflected attention away from another very pressing consideration, namely, whether the Habermasian discursive framework is actually well-suited to delivering on its purported aim of promoting mutual understanding and complementary learning between the secular and the religious as a corrective for the growing social fragmentation and generalized awareness of semantic deficits in contemporary liberal democracies recently diagnosed by Habermas himself. To redress this imbalance, the present chapter seeks to critically appraise the Habermasian proposal regarding its ability to promote genuine complementary learning between the religious and the secular with a view to vindicating the comparative merits of a hermeneutico-dialogical alternative, informed by the work of Hans-Herbert Kögler amongst others.[1] From this perspective, Habermas's controversial translation proviso can be seen as just one manifestation of a significantly more extensive problem deriving from his implicit characterization of religion as subservient to the secular, while simultaneously valorizing mutual reciprocity and complementary learning between these domains.

In response, the present chapter contends that only a more equitable and inclusive process of complementary learning between the secular and the religious can succeed in delivering the outcomes that Habermas envisages. To this end, it focuses on rethinking the conditions of the possibility for mutual learning such that the strengths of one position can compensate for the weaknesses of the other and vice versa, in a manner conducive to advancing the common good through forging an enhanced "situation definition" that can to justice to the complexities at issue. To this end, we begin by briefly reviewing the parameters of the Habermasian framework within which the need for complementary learning arises as a propaedeutic to its critical appraisal.[2]

Habermasian Complementary Learning: Scope and Limits

Not surprisingly in an era characterized by a widespread perception that religion has become outmoded and supplanted by scientific naturalism, Habermas's vocal defense of the ongoing significance, if not indispensability, of the religious contribution has evoked considerable interest, especially in light of his professed "methodological atheism" (Harrington 2007: 52). Whether viewed as continuity or as break with his earlier thinking (see further Mendieta 2013, Portier 2011, Vander Schel 2016), there can be no doubt that Habermas's recent writings on post-secularism express a more direct appreciation of religious discourse as a potential force for social good, most notably in terms of enhancing social solidarity and assuaging an "awareness of what is missing" in contemporary society, as epitomized in his contention that "religious traditions have a special power to articulate moral intuitions, especially with regard to vulnerable forms of communal life" (Habermas 2008: 131). They likewise seem to signal awareness of a heretofore untapped potential for complementary learning between the religious and the secular and, more generally, for an enhanced reciprocal relationship between the two domains (e.g., Habermas 2008: 119, 140, 144; 2010: 19, 21), capable of correcting for the deficiencies of "a modernization spinning out of control" (2008, 211). But while the extent of Habermas's recent contribution or its positive potential should not be underestimated, on closer analysis it transpires that there are significant shortcomings in its potential to underwrite a robust process of complementary learning between the secular and the religious. Moreover, as we shall see in critiquing his cognitive preconditions, there is good reason to conclude that, although widely interpreted in a significantly broader and more inclusive sense,[3] Habermas himself always conceived this concept in a considerably more restricted sense. At any rate, it becomes clear that, initial perceptions notwithstanding, the Habermasian framework is highly circumscribed in its ability to underwrite the kind of complementary learning between the secular and the religious that would be needed to enhance social solidarity and restore meaning along the lines prefigured by Habermas himself. It thus seems appropriate to speak of its unfulfilled potential in this regard. A brief appraisal of some of the main ways in which the Habermasian framework constrains the prospects for "a cooperative and constructive dialogue between religious faith and secular reason" (Vander Schel 2016: 52, cf. Schmidt 2010) of a sort conducive to complementary learning will pave the way for foregrounding the comparative merits of a hermeneutic template as an alternative.

Post-Secular Context

What is striking about Habermas's characterization of our post-secular status is not so much his acknowledgment of the ongoing persistence of religion despite his earlier more tentative assessments, but rather his valorization of religious discourse as a potential antidote for a purely secular conception of reason which "no longer has sufficient strength to awaken, and to keep awake, in the minds of secular subjects, an awareness of the violations of solidarity throughout the world, an awareness of what is missing, of what cries out to heaven" (Habermas 2010: 19, cf. Brieskorn 2010: 29–31). It is on this basis that he valorizes the prospects for a "constructive dialogue" (Reder and Schmidt 2010: 7) between "a self-critical reason which is willing to learn and contemporary religious convictions," while repudiating the excesses of a strident secularism "founded on a naïve faith in science" (Habermas 2010: 18) which altogether denies religion a role in secular democracies. But the prospects for genuine complementary learning between the religious and secular that this appears to hold open are counterbalanced by other features of the Habermasian framework deriving from his postmetaphysical philosophy, coupled with his insistence on the primacy of the secular in the institutional public sphere and his related "translation proviso" and cognitive preconditions. Taken together, there significantly circumscribe the potential for complementary learning of the sort that could enhance social solidarity and restore lost meaning.

Postmetaphysical Thinking

Given that postmetaphysical thinking not only constitutes "the orienting center" of Habermas's thought (Wolterstorff 2013: 95), but is also deemed philosophically well-attuned to our post-secular status (Habermas 2008: 140), it significantly conditions Habermas's stance in this debate.[4] As it concerns relations between the secular and the religious, postmetaphysical thinking is "an agnostic, but non-reductionist philosophical position" which while refraining from "passing judgment on religious truths," nonetheless insists "on drawing a strict line between faith and knowledge" (Habermas 2006a: 16). Notwithstanding its benign intent, this uncompromising demarcation gives rise to some problematic tensions in its construal of secular-religious relations. Thus, while it aspires to constituting a "dialogical approach" which is open to "learning from" religious traditions (Habermas 2008: 245) and which recognizes the genealogical intertwinement of the secular and the religious, it "remain[s] agnostic in the process" (Habermas 2006a: 17); and while exhorting secular citizens "not to treat religious expressions as simply irrational" (Habermas 2010: 220), it not only posits "a sharp distinction" between the secular and the religious but simultaneously asserts the primacy of the secular. Moreover, while it does not aspire "to launch a 'hostile takeover,'" it remains "solely concerned to salvage cognitive contents from religious traditions" which can be "translated" into a secular form of discourse "decoupled" from their religious origin (Habermas 2008: 245). As detailed below, this "ambivalent attitude of postmetaphysical thinking to religion" (Habermas 2008: 143, cf. Vander Schell 2016: 52) significantly restricts the potential for complementary learning between the secular and the religious that it seems to promise.

Postmetaphysical thinking also remains ambivalent about whether this process of learning from religion will need to continue indefinitely or whether it will, after all, be rendered redundant by an ongoing process of societal rationalization (Areshidze 2017:

726–7). Furthermore, notwithstanding its other strengths, the related Habermasian discourse model is not well suited to underwriting robust dialogical interaction of a sort conducive to advancing genuine complementary learning through learning from difference. In this regard, its core limitations include its circumscribed focus on the critical appraisal of validity claims, its heavily consensual orientation, its homogenizing tendencies, and its effectively monological conception of argumentation (Healy 2017: ch. 1; cf. Healy 2011: 306–9). Of more immediate concern, however, are the ways in which the potential for genuine complementary learning is further restricted by the "cognitive preconditions" and related "translation proviso" which Habermas stipulates as conditions for the religious voice engaging in serious dialogue in the institutional public sphere.

Cognitive Preconditions and Translation Proviso

The foregoing impediments to genuine complementary learning deriving from Habermas's philosophical commitments are significantly reinforced by the "cognitive preconditions" he stipulates as prerequisites for the religious contribution to gain a hearing in the public sphere.[5] Specifically, religious citizens are required to accept the reality of worldview pluralism, the authority of scientific knowledge in deciding contested empirical issues, and the priority of secular reasons in the "political arena" (Habermas 2008: 137). While seemingly innocuous,[6] they impede genuine complementarity in several respects. In particular, on Habermas's own telling, they "demand that religious citizens make an effort to learn and adapt that secular citizens are spared" (2008, 136). But this demand seems unjustified as well as undesirable on several counts.

Thus, firstly, the preconditions imposed on religious discourse seem to conflict with Habermas's longstanding commitment to free, open, and inclusive debate such that not only is every competent subject "allowed to take part in a discourse" but also *"to introduce any assertion whatever into the discourse"* (Habermas 1990: 89, emphasis added). They also reinforce the primacy of secular reasoning in the public sphere in ways that effectively delimit, if not preclude, the distinctiveness of the religious voice (Arishedze 2017: 729–30), and hence its potential to contribute to a robust process of complementary learning capable of enhancing social solidarity and restoring meaning as envisaged by Habermas himself. Similarly, they implicitly, if inadvertently, stereotype religious (and by default, secular) citizens as wedded to a narrow set of predefined attitudes and beliefs notwithstanding the wide diversity of views actually entertained by citizens of both categories along with the overlaps and intertwinements between them (cf. Dillon 2012: 265–7). Such a narrow and fixed specification of presuppositions is unlikely to be endorsed by religious citizens of diverse persuasions and hence is more likely to pose a barrier rather than provide a stimulus to meaningful and productive dialogue (cf. McCarthy 2013: 116–17, 120–1).

The Habermasian preconditions likewise implicitly, if inadvertently,[7] threaten to characterize religious citizens as comparatively unenlightened, if not "backward" (cf. Brieskorn 2010: 33), in their "epistemic attitudes" and correspondingly ill-equipped to engage in serious dialogue in the public sphere (Dillon 2012: 258–9). In so doing, they contribute to dichotomizing the relationship between the secular and the religious to the unjustified exclusion of more productive and judicious ways of conceptualizing it. Indeed, despite earlier intimations of a significantly more extensive, interactive, and productive form of dialogical engagement, Habermas's commentary on the preconditions indicates that he does not actually intend the envisaged "complementary learning" to extend beyond a two-track process of revising their epistemic attitudes undertaken separately by religious and secular citizens respectively (see especially Habermas 2008: 140, cf. Habermas 2006b: 23, Cooke 2011: 481–2). But although commensurate with his post-secularist agenda as "solely concerned to salvage cognitive content from religious traditions" (Habermas 2008: 245) in the service of the secular, this clearly falls far short of the type of conjoint and interactive learning process needed to enhance solidarity and mutual understanding, and correspondingly fails to fulfil the potential for genuinely reciprocal relations between the secular and the religious anticipated by many commentators (as epitomised by Schmidt 2010). After all, as Habermas himself puts it, "it makes a difference whether we speak with one another or merely about one another" (Habermas 2010: 16). The foregoing limitations are significantly compounded by Habermas's controversial "translation proviso" whose intent is to ensure that in parliaments and other institutional settings religious discourse must be "translated" into secular language so that its "cognitive content" can be appropriated in the service of the secular, although this is not required of proponents of other worldviews.

Essentially, the controversial translation proviso derives from Habermas's contention that the principle of neutrality, which enjoins that the state must be neutral toward diverse worldviews, requires that every citizen must accept that "only secular reasons count beyond the institutional threshold" separating the informal from the formal (or institutional) public sphere. Although Habermas recognizes that this places a special "epistemic burden" on religious citizens, he maintains that it can be counterbalanced by a symmetrical burden accrued by secular citizens to seriously and respectfully attend to the "cognitive content" embedded in the religious contribution when this has been duly "translated" into a secular idiom (Habermas 2008: 130–8, see further Holst and Molander 2015: 551–2). While the translation proviso has already evoked widespread critical attention from a diversity of perspectives, in keeping with the core thrust of the present chapter, the concern here is with the barriers it poses to genuine complementary learning between the religious and secular in conjunction with the restrictive cognitive preconditions. From a dialogical perspective a primary objection is that these limitations cannot be corrected, as Habermas proposes (Habermas 2008: 130ff), by the postulated sharing of "epistemic burdens" such that, to counterbalance the imposition on religious citizens, secular citizens assume the burden not only of taking religious claims seriously but also of assisting with their secular translation. Instead, as contended below, genuine complementarity presupposes a form of conjoint interaction and inquiry whereby citizens of both persuasions are prepared to listen to and learn from one another on a basis of comparable validity and dialogical equality such that claims emanating from either perspective can be addressed and evaluated of their merits irrespective of their origin.

Given the foregoing limitations, Habermasian post-secularism turns out to be more of a mixed blessing in its receptiveness to the religious voice than at first sight appears to be the case. In effect, it constitutes "a highly attenuated conception of learning from religion" (Areshidze 2017: 724). As we shall now consider, a hermeneutico-dialogical approach is altogether better suited to underwriting a process of genuine complementary learning given its inherent capacity to accommodate real difference, equal partnership, and conjoint inquiry.

Rethinking the Conditions of the Possibility for Genuine Complementary Learning: Toward a Hermeneutically Informed Dialogical Alternative

As epitomized by Gadamer (1989), a hermeneutically informed approach is committed to the equal partnership of the parties to the dialogue in a manner conducive to promoting complementary learning through attentively listening to and learning from one another regarding the subject matter under consideration.[8] Accordingly, it avoids imposing preconditions that restrict the scope and limits of the dialogue in advance, especially those that disadvantage one of the dialogue partners, in favor of endorsing ground rules that enable problematic issues to be attended to as they arise in the course of the dialogue itself. Moreover, while similar to the Habermasian in promoting equality and inclusiveness, these ground rules include a commitment to treating the encounter with difference as a resource for stimulating mutual understanding and learning rather than as a barrier to consensus and to relating to the other on a basis of comparable validity and dialogical equality. As we shall see, these features are central to its ability to provide a viable alternative to the Habermasian model.[9]

Overcoming Barriers to Complementarity

With a view to vindicating the comparative merits of the hermeneutic template in facilitating complementary learning on a more equitable basis, we now need to revisit the more restrictive aspects of the Habermasian framework.

Overcoming Dichotomous Thinking

As prefigured above, the Habermasian approach to complementary learning is marred by some untenable dichotomies, most notably, between the religious and the secular, the cognitive status of the religious versus the secular, and the dichotomous divide between the formal and informal public spheres. In each case, these polarized characterizations overlook the multiple meanings these concepts may legitimately embody and the potential crossovers between them, although much of significance is lost when "these important points of difference" are suppressed "through the imposition of singular understandings" (May et al. 2014, 331). From a dialogical perspective, then, these dichotomies need to be deconstructed both in the interests of clarifying the complexities involved and of paving the way for finding and building on common ground. Here we focus briefly on the core secular/religious dichotomy, deferring related issues for consideration below.

Thus firstly, despite valorizing the genealogical intertwinement of the religious and secular, Habermas construes their relationship as dichotomous and hierarchical, postulating a "sharp distinction" (Habermas 2008: 245), or unbreachable "cleavage" (Habermas 2010: 17), between them with the former subordinate to the latter. In effect, then, "religion is thematized as the other of reason" (Reder 2010: 41). Moreover, he crystallizes the dichotomy by deeming the religious a special case compared to other worldviews because of its allegedly extra-rational foundations (e.g., Habermas 2008: 140, 143, 242, 245; Habermas 2010: 17), contending that "religious convictions are *uniquely* insulated from discursive rationality due to their dogmatic core as revealed truth claims" (Arishedze 2017: 729).[10] But in so doing, Habermas sidelines a long tradition of philosophical and theological debate which posits a more reciprocal and complementary relationship between the domains of reason and faith along with conceptions of reason more attuned to the interconnections between the two domains (Reder 2010: 43–8; Ratzinger 2006: 77–9; cf. Harrington 2007: 48) as well as to the phenomenological experience of religious citizens who "fully participate in a secular society while simultaneously holding religious beliefs and highly rational beliefs" (Dillon 2012: 265–6). Equally problematically, Habermas treats these domains as internally homogeneous and uniform, thereby neglecting the wide spectrum of "epistemic attitudes" exhibited by both religious and secular citizens ranging from the fundamentalist through the moderate to the liberal/progressive (cf. Chambers 2010: 16; Dillon 2012: 250, 252). He thereby overlooks the multiple potential crossovers between these allegedly dichotomous categories such that, for example, the moderates of each category may share more in common, in terms of "epistemic attitude" and otherwise, than either does with adherents of the more extreme positions within their own secular or religious demarcation in ways that would confound any dichotomous ascription of "cognitive attitudes." Moreover, as we have seen, in stipulating preconditions which religious citizens must fulfil to gain a hearing in the institutional public sphere, Habermas likewise portrays the religious citizen as burdened by "epistemic attitudes" which, unlike those of her secular counterpart, impede her ability to participate constructively in serious public debate (cf. Dillion 2012: 258). But in so doing, he implicitly construes the contemporary religious believer in a narrow and atypical way, overlooking the numerous ways in which religious citizens routinely and effectively participate in "secular" public life, as well as the ease with which they typically navigate between the two domains, with only the most fundamentalist or conservative, whether religious or secular, perceiving an inherent incompatibility. Indeed, as Dillon points out, "for mainstream religious adherents ... being religious and being secular are mutually reinforcing orientations" (Dillon 2012: 266). As elaborated below, these problems are compounded in that Habermas also affirms the primacy of secular over religious justifications in ways that minimize, or exclude, the possibility of a distinctively religious contribution. In thus positing a dichotomous and hierarchical relationship between the secular and religious, Habermas effectively precludes the possibility of genuine complementary learning by negating the opportunity for treating the encounter with difference as a resource rather than as a barrier to a secular consensus.

In contrast, a hermeneutico-dialogical approach facilitates recognition of the religious and secular as equal partners and co-participants in a discursive process of advancing the common good through contributing to forging an enlarged and enriched understanding of the issues under consideration (cf. Healy 2011: 303–6). Given its dialogical underpinnings, a hermeneutically informed approach is well equipped to underwrite a dual process of deconstructing dichotomies through finding and building on common ground while at the same time promoting "contrastive foil" learning through preserving differences which can challenge entrenched presuppositions and alert participants to new possibilities of which they were hitherto incognizant (cf. Kögler 1996: ch. 5). Thus, on the one hand, the hermeneutic commitment to conceptualizing boundaries as mobile, fluid, and inherently open to one another (Gadamer 1989: 447; cf. Bernstein 2010; Healy 2013: 270) better enables it to encapsulate the cross-overs and intertwinements between the religious and secular. Correlatively, its commitment to non-invidious comparison and to respecting the holistic integrity of the other worldview enables it to preserve difference to the extent that it can pose a challenge to established ways of thinking (Healy 2013; cf. Kögler 1996: ch. 5). Hence, in contrast to an approach which posits dichotomies and fosters assimilation, it treats the encounter with difference as a resource for promoting an enlarged understanding of the contested issues through conjoint complementary learning. Indeed, in thus treating difference as a resource rather than a barrier to consensus, it can give rise to a potentially transformative fusion of horizons, resulting in an enhanced situation definition capable of doing justice to the contested issues in their multifaceted complexity (Healy 2011: 307–8). This is all the more the case given its commitment to investigative openness, fuelled by recognition that neither party can claim to have an adequate understanding of what is at issue at the outset but are conjointly investigating with a view to finding out.

Overcoming Barriers to Reciprocity

While reciprocity is likewise integral to complementary learning, as prefigured above, Habermas's effort to address this in terms of counterbalancing "epistemic burdens" deriving from his controversial translation proviso is not tantamount to reciprocity in a sense that would facilitate genuine complementary learning, notwithstanding its merits in according greater recognition than heretofore to the religious contribution. Rather, here again, the Habermasian stance falls far short of delivering on its initial promise in terms of enhancing dialogical engagement, in that it fails to promote a form of conjoint inquiry whereby citizens of both persuasions are committed to listening to and learning from one another on a basis of equality such that claims emanating from either perspective can be evaluated on their merits irrespective of their origin. Instead, the Habermasian proposal threatens to assimilate the religious to the secular. For one thing, the Habermasian injunction requiring religious citizens to align their thinking more closely with the secular worldview is not matched by a corresponding requirement in the opposite direction on the part of secular citizens. In addition, the Habermasian injunction enjoining secular citizens to take religion seriously effectively amounts to the requirement that secular citizens help "salvage" whatever "cognitive content" can be readily assimilated to the secular worldview with a view to enriching the latter. Hence, Habermasian reciprocity threatens to be purely unidirectional, in the service of advancing the secular. In short, Habermas "stacks the deck in favour of secularism" (Allen 2013: 149). Likewise, notwithstanding his explicit recognition that "religion can neither be reduced to morality nor be assimilated to ethical value orientations" (Habermas 2011: 27–8), Habermas's persistent tendency to assimilate the religious to the secular through translation inherently restricts the extent to which the religious, in its distinctiveness, is allowed to pose a challenge to the secular. Far from rectifying this deficit of reciprocity, the stipulation of a post-facto translation procedure, whereby "secular citizens" assist "religious citizens" with the translation of religiously motivated claims into secular language, could be said to exacerbate the problem by implicitly, if inadvertently, representing the religious citizen as dependent on the comparatively enlightened cognitive disposition of the secular citizen as a precondition for engaging in serious public debate.[11]

In contrast, on a hermeneutico-dialogical analysis, reciprocity entails a conjoint process of listening to and learning from one another with a view to enhancing mutual understanding concerning the issues under consideration, along the lines prefigured above. Hence, a more equitable conception of reciprocity and mutual learning is needed "than merely unidirectional translation," a conception which allows each perspective to "challenge, correct, or enlarge" the other (cf. Arishedze 2017: 733). In this regard, the Habermasian concern with perspective-taking (e.g., Habermas 1993: 52) shows greater promise as a template for the requisite kind of reciprocity than a preoccupation with the sharing of reciprocal burdens deriving from the imposition of a translation proviso. But to qualify as appropriately dialogical, it needs to transcend a conception of perspective taking construed as either symmetrical or asymmetrical reciprocity. Thus, in contrast to symmetrical reciprocity, dialogical reciprocity enjoins that while the attempt to place oneself in the shoes of the other has its merits, neither party should assume that their attempt to imaginatively recreate the perspective of the other can do justice to the original party's experience of it. In contrast to asymmetrical reciprocity, it reminds us that while differences in standpoint may be significant, they are not so great as to preclude the possibility of the secular citizen attaining a judicious understanding of the religious worldview provided that appropriate care is taken to ensure that this is the case. To this end, dialogical reciprocity enjoins that truly to take the other's perspective seriously we must listen to and learn from the account they themselves give of it in appropriately structured dialogical exchanges. While potentially beneficial as a component, mutual perspective taking alone cannot adequately replace this (Healy 2011: 299–302, cf. Kögler 2011: especially 236–7).[12] Hence, contra Habermas, "the burden" accrued by the secular citizen is not appropriately construed as that of assisting with the translation of the religious voice into a secular idiom on the assumption that the former has already adequately understood it, but rather, as elaborated below, that of undertaking to listen to and learn from it on a basis of comparable validity and dialogical equality, once she has adequately understood it through appropriately structured dialogical interaction.

Rethinking Secularism

The possibility of genuine complementary learning is further diminished by Habermas's insistence on the priority of the secular over the religious. For postmetaphysical thinking, this primarily entails the priority of secular reason or justification, but it extends by implication to the related *worldviews*. Not only is this stance incompatible with genuine complementarity, it also seems to conflict with core Habermasian tenets. Thus, firstly, Habermas's contention that "only secular reasons count beyond the institutional threshold" (Habermas 2008: 130) seems to conflict with his (immediately preceding) reiterated contention that the state "must be neutral toward competing worldviews," as the former clearly implies the priority of secular over religious justification in this domain. While Habermas maintains that he can justify this exception by deeming religion a "special case," as contended below this is by no means self-evident. It likewise challenges his contention that postmetaphysical thinking is more accommodating to religion than is Rawls's public reason, given that Habermas denies a hearing to the religious voice, in its distinctiveness, at the institutional level where the serious legislative and political decision making takes place. At this crucial stage, it thus risks draining "religion of the very strength and meaning of the 'moral intuitions' that Habermas thinks can be beneficial to democracy" (Arishedze 2017: 729).

Moreover, notwithstanding his valorization of the potential religious contribution, Habermas's emphasis on the primacy of secular reason—on "self-sufficient reason," as Taylor terms it (Taylor 2011: 56; cf. Habermas and Taylor 2011: 64)—is more indicative of a view that construes secularism in terms of the absence of religion,[13] a reading that is reinforced by his lingering endorsement of the possibility that the religious could yet be replaced by the secular in its ongoing evolutionary trajectory. Although commensurate with common usage, this construal of secularism does not do justice to the conceptual or historical complexities at issue nor to our post-secular situation, nor does it seem consistent with Habermas's explicit acknowledgment of the genealogical intertwinement of the religious and secular as "two complementary intellectual formations" (Habermas 2010: 18). These internal conflicts aside, it is clear that Habermas's emphatic defence of the priority of secular reason is not conducive to complementary learning construed dialogically as entailing equal partnership, conjoint inquiry, and open-minded engagement with the other. For, thus construed, "'taking religion seriously' entails being open to its insights not only when they agree with the conclusions of secular reason, but even and especially when they challenge them" (Arishedze 2017: 725).

As prefigured above, Habermas's prioritization of secular justifications in the institutional public sphere is grounded in his assumption that there is an in principle difference between secular and religious worldviews such that the latter warrant special treatment in the form of a translation proviso not applicable to the former. This implies that while there is no in principle postmetaphysical barrier preventing, say, Marxists, utilitarians, feminists, or Kantians defending their discursive contributions in the public sphere with direct reference to the fundamental presuppositions and assumptions underwriting these various worldviews, contributors from a religious perspective are precluded from so doing. The proffered justification is that religion's "opaque core" renders it immune to the kind of rigorous "discursive examination" to which secular worldviews can be exposed (Habermas 2008,129, 143). Hence, although Habermas does not wish to deny religious discourse its rationality, "religious traditions" are nonetheless characterized "as the opaque other of reason" (Habermas 2008: 142). But this assessment highlights further significant tensions in Habermas's stance. Thus firstly, it appears to conflict not only with his explicit affirmation of the genealogical intertwinement of the religious and the secular, but also with his valorization of postmetaphysical thinking as not assuming the a priori validity of a particular worldview, but rather as committed to facilitating dialogue between worldviews while remaining agnostic about them. Accordingly, it engenders the kinds of dichotomous tensions canvassed earlier such as the assumption that faith and reason are mutually exclusive so that a grounding in faith necessarily precludes the possibility of a rational grounding notwithstanding the fact that, within theological circles, these have frequently, even typically, been treated as mutually complementary stances.

Moreover, as elaborated below, the attempt to resolve these conflicts by the imposition of a translation proviso threatens to rob the religious voice of its distinctive character, in the absence of which it would lack the ability to enhance social solidarity and revitalize democracy as Habermas envisages. After all, if this function could adequately be fulfilled by secular alternatives, Habermas could simply have appealed to communitarian or socialist worldviews to enhance solidarity and compensate for the "awareness of what is missing" in contemporary post-secular democracies.[14] Equally problematically, it fails to recognize not only that all worldviews are ultimately grounded in fundamental presuppositions that cannot be justified without circularity within that worldview itself (precisely because of their constitutive status), but also that this does not impugn their ability to rationally and cogently contribute to policy debate in the public sphere. It also unjustifiably assumes that rational justification of one's stance on a legislative or policy issue necessarily entails reference to one's foundational presuppositions and self-transparency about the connecting links whereas, as Chambers observes: "Most people would be very hard put to estimate just how far their sets of beliefs are rationally grounded, and those who can do so confidently are probably deluding themselves" (2010, 18). In sum, then, embracing secularism should not entail according priority to the non-religious over the religious, but should rather seek to ensure that, along with other reasonable contributions to the public sphere, the religious and the secular are afforded an equal voice and given an impartial hearing on a basis of comparable validity and dialogical equality as elaborated below.

Here again, a hermeneutically informed dialogical approach can provide a corrective for the Habermasian proclivity to assimilate the religious to the secular since, from this perspective, the religious and the secular constitute two irreducibly distinct, but potentially complementary and mutually enriching, worldviews, a conceptualisation which, as already noted, accords more readily with traditional theological reflections about the relationship between faith and reason as well as with the everyday phenomenological experiences of religious citizens. From this perspective, secularism is recognized as a presence and not just an absence (Calhoun 2010: 35). Thus construed, "the secular" is not a presuppositionless view from nowhere, nor can its epistemic superiority be assumed a priori; rather, it is itself a worldview amongst others (e.g., Taylor 2011; cf. Spohn 2015: 127) which inevitably embodies its own possibilities and limitations, strengths and weaknesses as well as foundational presuppositions. Hence, instead of subscribing to a translation proviso which threatens to homogenize the religious contribution through assimilating it to the secular, a hermeneutico-dialogical approach endorses the need for each position to retain its distinctiveness, while seeking to understand the other and remain open to the challenge it poses (cf. Arishedze 2017: e.g., 725, 735),[15] in the interests of reaching an enlarged understanding of the issues under consideration and facilitating the emergence of a new, more comprehensive situation definition (cf. Warnke 1992: 130–2).

On this view, then, it is important that no voice tries "to limit in advance what we might learn from others" (Warnke 1992: 157), because no worldview can claim a monopoly on understanding the problematic issues in their multifaceted complexity and, hence, stands in need of learning from others so as "to develop a richer, more differentiated understanding" (Warnke 1992: 162, cf. Kögler 2005: 312). To this end, a hermeneutico-dialogical approach embraces comparable validity and dialogical equality as a corrective, a stance which enjoins that all well-grounded positions are accorded a hearing on a basis comparable to other such positions and in a manner which accurately reflects the self-understanding of proponents of that worldview even when articulated in a common language (Healy 2011: 302–3). As elaborated below, this enables diverse positions to engage on an equal footing in a well-structured debate regarding the common good in both institutional and informal settings in a manner which, while not privileging the one over the other, remains subject to dialogical ground rules (akin to the Habermasian discourse ethic though with an emphasis on equal partnership and conjoint inquiry) operative in the particular contextual setting in question. Notably, however, comparable validity does not entail equal validity regarding the issues under consideration as the comparative merits of each contribution can only be ascertained in the course of the ensuing critical debate, subject to the dialogical ground rules applicable in the context in question, on the understanding that neither position is inherently superior but that each has specific strengths and weaknesses from which participants are well advised to learn. For as Habermas elsewhere aptly puts it, "no participant has a monopoly on correct interpretation" (Habermas 1984: 100).

Deconstructing the Informal/Formal Divide

As prefigured above, the putative need for an "institutional translation proviso" is a direct outcome not just of the assumed primacy of a secular worldview, but also of the postulated divide between the informal and formal public spheres beyond which only secular reasons count, a divide which not only further distances the prospects for complementary learning but also conflicts with core tenets of Habermas's discourse ethics. Thus, while the latter enjoins that no voice is denied entry to the public sphere and that every voice is accorded an equal hearing, the postulation of an informal/formal divide beyond which only secular reasons count effectively precludes the possibility that the religious contribution is preserved and assessed on its merits on a basis of comparable validity and dialogical equality. Rather, it serves to ensure that the religious voice is appropriated in the service of the secular, so as to render the latter "more powerful and persuasive" (Chambers 2010: 19). The postulated divide also clearly conflicts with the discourse model's purported aim of advancing participatory democracy in that it effectively confers on the "Babel of voices" in the "wild" (informal) public sphere (Habermas 2008: 131) the status of a mere epiphenomenon in comparison to the formal public sphere where serious debate regarding legislative and policy issues is deemed to take place. A genuinely participatory approach could not support such a division. Significantly too, in that it shears the religious voice of its distinctiveness and effectively assimilates it to the secular, the Habermasian divide robs it of its potential to underwrite the kind of complementary learning between the secular and the religious needed to enhance social solidarity and restore meaning as Habermas himself intends.[16] In calling for the deconstruction of the informal/formal divide, or "firewall," as Chambers (2010) terms it, a hermeneutic approach deems it not only undesirable but also unnecessary to ensure the judicious and rational adjudication of legislative or policy proposals.

As a corrective, a hermeneutic approach can provide an alternative which ensures that the religious contribution can gain a judicious hearing and is assessed on its merits in terms of its contribution to the common good without the need for postulating a formal/informal divide and related translation proviso. From this perspective, the primary commitment, accrued by all participants, becomes that of assisting others in rendering their viewpoint and supporting rationale accessible to all so that these can be assessed on their merits; and doing so in such a way that each party's contribution is assessed on its best interpretation rather than criticised for its presumed deficiencies (cf. Warnke 1992: 157), with a view to enhancing mutual understanding and learning regarding the issue under consideration. Accordingly, a hermeneutic approach postulates a direct continuity between the informal and formal public spheres with the emphasis throughout on facilitating the possibility of mutual understanding and learning in a manner conducive to promoting the common good in accordance with democratic principles.[17] Hence, in place of the postulated divide it appeals instead to the common awareness that different styles of discourse and modes of argumentation befit different institutional contexts, such as the academic, scientific, parliamentary, and judicial, since this already suffices to ensure that contributions are articulated in a language appropriate to the context in question without the need for additional, potentially discriminatory, distinctions affecting designated worldviews such as the religious.[18] Thus, as Chambers contends (2010, 18–19), the appropriate criteria for inclusion in public debate in whatever forum, formal or informal, should be that contributions are "reasonable, respectful, civil, open, non-dogmatic" and so on, without the need for further restrictions that would "exclude large classes of people or types of reasons from the start." On this basis, specific contributions that are considered problematic can be identified and addressed in the normal course of debate regulated by dialogical ground rules akin to Habermas's own discourse ethics, without the postulation of additional thresholds and provisos. This would include religious contributions that violate the operative ground rules for reasons other than that they are religiously informed.[19]

This is all the more the case since, as Chambers also points out (2010, 18), it is by no means as easy to differentiate a priori between religious and non-religious reasoning as the Habermasian dichotomy suggests; rather, such distinctions will often only emerge in the course of further inquiry and debate. Accordingly, on a hermeneutic analysis, the dialogical "burden" accrued by secular citizens vis-a-vis the religious contribution is not that of facilitating its translation into a secular idiom, but rather that of ensuring that not only is its distinctiveness preserved when articulated in a "language accessible to all," but also that it is assessed on its merits, alongside contributions from other perspectives, on a basis of comparable validity and dialogical equality. Hence, to the extent that some form of "translation" (or "transformative assimilation," as Habermas also comes to characterise it (2013, 353)) is needed to facilitate the religious (or other) perspective with articulating its contribution to the best advantage in the public sphere, the intent must be to preserve the meaning and impact of the original formulation to the extent possible, rather than requiring its homogenization or assimilation to a language that neutralizes its distinctiveness (cf. Ricken 2010: 57). Accordingly, as prefigured above, the primary reciprocal obligation accrued by all parties to such debates consists in ensuring that they, themselves, have correctly understood and seriously attended to the other's stance in its implications for the common good. In effect, then, the hermeneutic alternative is the reverse of the Habermasian translation proviso, with the secular citizen instead seeking assistance from the religious to ensure he has appropriately understood the intended contribution in its distinctiveness so that it can be judiciously assessed on its merits. It is on this basis that a hermeneutic approach can claim to underwrite a genuine process of complementary learning between the religious and the secular of the sort conducive to enhancing social solidarity and revitalizing democracy as valorized by Habermas himself.

Conclusion

Although the present chapter has been critical of the way in which Habermas frames the issues, it is undeniable that his recent intervention has done much not only to reignite interest in this challenging topic but also to foreground the ongoing significance of the religious contribution to the contemporary democratic public sphere. Nonetheless, as contended throughout, in an increasingly cosmopolitan public sphere, it is crucial that the issues are framed in ways that acknowledge the equal status of the religious voice on a basis comparable to that of other worldviews. Accordingly, as the foregoing analysis has sought to establish, if the religious voice is to succeed in enhancing social solidarity and compensating for "an awareness of what is missing" along the lines that Habermas himself envisages, it is crucial that it retains its distinctiveness to an extent beyond what Habermas's controversial translation proviso and related institutional divide can allow for. In foregrounding the merits of comparable validity and dialogical equality in this regard, the intent is to ensure not that the religious voice will prevail, but that it will be judiciously assessed on its merits in terms of its contribution to the common good in the democratic public sphere. On this basis it can contribute to the development of a more textured and judicious understanding of complex legislative and policy issues than was initially available to any of the parties to the debate in formal as well as informal contexts.

In developing these themes, several convergences with the work of Hans-Herbert Kögler have been noted, most notably, his vigorous defence of a diversely constituted cosmopolitan public sphere, his ongoing emphasis on the indispensability of carefully attending to and factoring in the perspective of the other, the importance of "contrastive foil" learning in developing an enlarged and potentially transformative understanding of the issues under consideration, and likewise the importance of relating to the other on the basis of, what I have termed, comparable validity and dialogical equality. While Kögler and myself may approach these issues from somewhat different perspectives, in somewhat different language, and with somewhat different concerns to the foreground, in my view our approaches are productively complementary[20] and, accordingly, Kögler's work has contributed to my development of the present chapter in ways beyond what my specific citations may indicate.

Notes

1 Unfortunately, I only became acquainted with Kögler's recent writings on religion (specifically, Kögler 2017, 2020a, 2020b) when making final revisions to this paper. Hence, the present chapter does not adequately reflect this dimension of Kögler's work but derives its inspiration rather from his earlier writings on cultural rationality and cosmopolitan hermeneutics. Fortunately, however, this limitation does not greatly impact the core thrust of the present chapter as the dialogical approach it espouses, which valorizes the possibility of finding and building on common ground between diverse cultural traditions or worldviews (here, the secular and the religious), seems to me to have greater affinities with Kögler's earlier work (cf. note 7 below). In contrast, in foregrounding structural and procedural differences between these two domains, Kögler's recent writings on religion and religious discourse are indicative of a potential divergence in our approaches which does not, however, preclude their complementarity. Since it would require another chapter to begin to do justice to Kögler's writings on religion and to the affinities and difference between our approaches, I confine myself here to a couple of other last-minute endnote insertions (see further notes 8, 17).
2 I would like to thank the editors for their helpful feedback on the original version, and I regret that I was unable to incorporate all of it in my final revisions. Many thanks too to Dr. Ľubomir Dunaj for his assistance and support throughout.
3 Thus, for example, Ungureanu and Thomassen observe that: "Habermas, for one, speaks of a new "post-secular society" in which religious and nonreligious citizens engage, predominantly in the social-public sphere, in a process of mutual learning and reconciliation through dialogue and the exchange of reasons" (2015, 103).
4 For an incisive introduction to Habermasian postmetaphysical thinking, see Yates 2011.
5 As readers familiar with this topic will know, the themes broached in this short section have been at the center of an extended critical debate about Habermas' stance on this issue, in which a diversity of views have been proffered both pro and con the Habermasian proposal. Notably too, in contrast to the approach defended here, some

prominent commentators contend that Habermas goes too far in accommodating the religious voice in the contemporary post-secular public sphere. Against this background, the present contribution aspires to outline the case for a significantly more robust conception of *complementary learning* than that proposed by Habermas himself. The diversity of critical stances on the translation proviso and related cognitive preconditions is well represented in Calhoun, Mendieta, and VanAntwerpen 2013. The Editor's Introduction provides a succinct overview of these critical perspectives, while Mendieta's Appendix provides an insightful outline of the progression of Habermas's thinking about the role of religion in the contemporary public sphere.

6   Like Habermas himself, many would regard these factors as taken-for-granted, if not non-negotiable, features of the contemporary (post-secular) public sphere. In what follows, I do not intend to cast doubt on the cogency of the first two principles in particular. My concern is rather with their status as preconditions for religious citizens as such. Moreover, a great deal depends on how they are interpreted in the context of specific, situated dialogues. If anything, a commitment to openness on the part of *all* participants would be more defensible. To accept unquestioningly the third Habermasian precondition would, I think, be to beg the question regarding the issues raised below.

7   It is quite clear that Habermas does not actually intend this outcome as, for example, when he points out that: "A public practice of secularism would amount to secular citizens not taking their fellow citizens seriously as modern contemporaries because of their religious outlook" (Habermas 2011: 32, n. 22).

8   Bubner (1994, 72–3) succinctly characterizes the core Gadamerian template as follows:

> Here, partners, with their different points of view, come together in a conversation governed by a subject matter of common interest. It is this orientation to a subject matter that leads both sides into a dialogical context and binds them for the course of the dialogue. The process is not motivated by the chance of success of a single, one-sided viewpoint, for its limits are already set by the resistance of the partner. What is much more definitive is that both sides are bound by the task of the actual elucidation of the subject matter. The process of dialogue, however provisional its outcome may be, consists in... coming-to-an-agreement-with-another, [a process that] always occurs in reference to a subject matter in terms of which we produce unity through dialogue.

9   For a detailed account of the background to the development of this approach, see Healy 2017. For its application to rethinking deliberative democracy, see Healy 2011. In developing it, I was significantly influenced by the early work of Hans-Herbert Kögler, especially Kögler 1996. Several of the main crossovers with Kögler's critical hermeneutics as they bear on the present topic are noted in what follows. For convenience, I also refer to the present approach as the hermeneutico-dialogical approach or simply the dialogical approach. This approach also shares much in common with the idea of a cosmopolitan hermeneutics as developed in Kögler 2005, 2011 and Delanty 2009, and in particular a strong commitment to learning from otherness, or difference, on a basis of equality in a diversely constituted public sphere.

10 Kögler's contention that "[d]ominant features of religious world-disclosure are *diametrically opposed* to such a modern post-metaphysical construction of meaning"

(2017, 31, emphasis added) would seem to be indicative of a similarly polarized conception of relations between the secular and the religious, though it would require a separate chapter to do justice to the texture of Kögler's stance (which includes an explicit defense of religious discourse's potential for openness when construed in hermeneutic terms (see especially Kögler 2020b)). Briefly stated, however, as contended regarding Habermas, my concern is that such a stark characterization tends to minimize, if not eliminate, the middle ground crucial for dialogue, while failing to accommodate the varied phenomenological experiences of contemporary religious believers or the diversity of contemporary theorizing about the transcendent. Moreover, while it is clearly important to be appraised of, and to remain alert to, the potentially polarizing "dangers" and totalizing excesses inherent in all worldviews, the religious included, to which Foucault, for one, has alerted us, it remains equally important to reinforce the prospects for finding and building on common ground in all domains of the Habermasian public sphere with a view to advancing the common good, while preserving the diverse contributing worldviews in their distinctiveness.

11 Cf. Holst and Molander 2015: "Surely, it must be burdensome for religious citizens to be positioned as an essentially dependent group in need of translation support from the secular side. Habermas ends up treating religious citizens as a category of people who in the end—and in contrast to secular citizens—cannot represent themselves, but need help from benevolent, hermeneutically minded secular citizens. This is arguably a case of adding insult to injury. In addition to the burdensome requirement of having to argue on secular premises beyond the institutional threshold, religious citizens find themselves treated as dependent on secular benevolence" (554–5).

12 Perspective-taking is, of course, a prominent theme in Kögler's work. But while Kögler's analysis focuses primarily on its elucidation as a "reflexive capability" constitutive of a cosmopolitan public sphere, the hermeneutico-dialogical approach focuses primarily on elucidating the dynamics and logic of the requisite dialogical interaction. In my view, the two approaches are thus productively complementary.

13 Cf. also Habermas 2006b, where Habermas equates "a secular justification of political rule" with "a justification that is *nonreligious* or postmetaphysical" (22, emphasis added).

14 These tensions could justifiably be regarded as manifestations of the "ambivalent attitude of postmetaphysical thinking to religion" (Habermas 2008: 143). For while it is clear that Habermas does not wish to impugn the rationality of religious belief and while he is not insensitive to the complexities and subtleties of the historical interaction between reason and faith, it is nonetheless the case that, for postmetaphysical thinking, the religious voice enjoys a lesser, more "dubious" (cf. Taylor 2011: 53), status in the institutional public sphere.

15 Cf. also Kögler 1996: 174: "it is crucial to frame and pursue historical or cultural understanding in such a way that it can engender an illuminating contrast to one's own symbolic assumptions."

16 Cf. Kögler 1996: 138: "If the hermeneutic distance between symbolic orders is not emphasized and rigorously analyzed, the other may be all too easily assimilated to one's own premises."

17 The hermeneutico-dialogical approach thus concurs with Taylor that what is important "is that citizens relate their arguments to the [relevant] democratic values ... regardless of whether they explain their support of these in terms of Kantianism, Utilitarianism, Christianity, or any other comprehensive doctrine" (Spohn 2015: 125). Spohn's article provides an excellent basis for exploring the similarities and differences

between Habermas and Taylor in their approaches to religious discourse in the public sphere.

18 After all, as Yates notes, "In many ways, human embeddedness in specific linguistic background cultures is the starting point for Habermas' philosophical project ... Our claims can only be understood, or rationally redeemed, against the backdrop of a wide range of pretheoretical assumptions about our shared world" (2011, 38–9). Surely these "pretheoretical assumptions" can be presumed to include an awareness of the dialogical ground rules operative in the particular (institutional) context in question.

19 It is worth emphasizing that, as dialogical theorists have long maintained, such a possibility presupposes a significant degree of openness on all sides. Indeed, openness is perhaps the primary precondition for productive dialogue. In this connection, Kögler (2020) performs an important service in clarifying what openness in the context of religious belief might entail. While some may equate this hermeneutic emphasis on openness with Habermas's insistence on pluralism as a precondition for dialogue, I consider the former to be primary.

20 As indicated at the outset, I only became appraised of Kögler's recent writings on religion and religious discourse at the last minute and hence am unable to do them justice here. While some differences in orientation are clearly evident between us in this domain (as instanced in note 8 above), in my view, this reinforces rather than detracts from the potential complementary of our hermeneutic stances.

References

Allen, Amy (2013), "Having One's Cake and Eating It too: Habermas's Genealogy of Postsecular Reason." In *Habermas and Religion*, edited by Craig Calhoun, Eduardo Mendieta and Jonathan VanAntwerpen, 132–53. Cambridge: Polity.

Areshidze, Giorgi (2017), "Taking Religion Seriously? Habermas on Religious Translation and Cooperative Learning in Post-secular Society." *American Political Science Review* 111 (4): 724–37.

Bernstein, Richard J. (2010), "Naturalism, Secularism, and Religion: Habermas's Via Media." *Constellations* 17 (1): 155–66.

Brieskorn, S.J., Norbert (2010), "On the Attempt to Recall a Relationship." In *An Awareness of What is Missing*, edited by Jürgen Habermas et al., 24–35. Cambridge: Polity.

Bubner, Rudiger (1994), "On the Ground of Understanding." In *Hermeneutics and Truth*, edited by Brice Wachterhauser, 68–82. Evanston, IL: Northwestern University Press.

Calhoun, Craig (2010), "Rethinking Secularism." *The Hedgehog Review* 12 (3): 35–48.

Calhoun, Craig, Eduardo Mendieta, and Jonathan VanAntwerpen (2013), *Habermas and Religion*. Cambridge, UK: Polity Press.

Chambers, Simone (2010), "Secularism Minus Exclusion: Developing a Religious-Friendly Idea of Public Reason." *Good Society Journal* 19 (2): 16–21.

Cooke, Maeve (2011), "Translating Truth." *Philosophy and Social Criticism* 37 (4): 479–91.

Delanty, Gerard (2009), *The Cosmopolitan Imagination: The Renewal of Critical Social Theory*. Cambridge: Cambridge University Press.

Dillon, Michele (2012), "Jürgen Habermas and the Post-Secular Appropriation of Religion: A Sociological Critique." In *The Post-Secular in Question: Religion in Contemporary Society*, edited by Philip S. Gorski, 249–78. New York: NYU Press.

Gadamer, Hans-Georg (1989), *Truth and Method*. Translated by Joel Weinsheimer and Donald Marshall. 2nd ed. New York: Continuum.
Habermas, Jürgen (1984), *The Theory of Communicative Action, vol. 1: Reason and The Rationalization of Society*. Translated by Thomas McCarthy. Boston: Beacon press.
Habermas, Jürgen (1990), "Discourse Ethics." In *Moral Consciousness and Communicative Action*, 43–115. Cambridge, MA: MIT Press.
Habermas, Jürgen (1993), *Justification and Application: Remarks on Discourse Ethics*. Translated by Ciaran Cronin. Cambridge, UK: Polity.
Habermas, Jürgen (2006a), "Religion in the Public Sphere." *European Journal of Philosophy* 14 (1): 1–25.
Habermas, Jürgen (2006b), "Pre-political Foundations of the Democratic Constitutional State?" In *Dialectics of Secularization: On Reason and Religion*, edited by Florian Schuller, 21–52. San Francisco: Ignatius Press.
Habermas, Jürgen (2008), *Between Naturalism and Religion: Philosophical Essays*. Cambridge, UK: Polity.
Habermas, Jürgen (2010), "An Awareness of What is Missing." In *An Awareness of What is Missing: Faith and Reason in a Post-Secular Age*, edited by Jürgen Habermas et al., 15–23. Cambridge: Polity Press.
Habermas, Jürgen (2011), "'The Political': Rational Meaning of a Questionable Inheritance of Political Theology." In *The Power of Religion in the Public Sphere*, edited by Eduardo Mendieta and Jonathan VanAntwerpen, 15–33. New York: Columbia University Press.
Habermas, Jürgen and Charles Taylor (2011), "Dialogue: Jurgen Habermas and Charles Taylor." In *The Power of Religion in the Public Sphere*, edited by Eduardo Mendieta and Jonathan VanAntwerpen, 60–9. New York: Columbia University Press.
Habermas., Jürgen (2013), "Reply to My Critics." In *Habermas and Religion*, edited by Craig Calhoun, Eduardo Mendieta and Jonathan VanAntwerpen, 347–90. Cambridge: Polity.
Harrington, Austin (2007), "Habermas's Theological Turn?" *Journal for the Theory of Social Behaviour* 37 (1): 45–61.
Healy, Paul (2011), "Rethinking Deliberative Democracy: From Deliberative Discourse to Transformative Dialogue." *Philosophy and Social Criticism* 37 (3): 295–311.
Healy, Paul (2013), "Overcoming Incommensurability through Intercultural Dialogue." *Cosmos & History* 9: 265–81.
Healy, Paul (2017), *Rationality, Hermeneutics and Dialogue*. London: Routledge. Original edition, 2005. Reprint, 2017.
Holst, Cathrine and Anders Molander (2015), "Jürgen Habermas on public reason and religion: do religious citizens suffer an asymmetrical cognitive burden, and should they be compensated?" *Critical Review of International Social and Political Philosophy* 18 (5): 547–63.
Kögler, Hans-Herbert (1996), *The Power of Dialogue: Critical Hermeneutics after Gadamer and Foucault*. Cambridge, MA: MIT Press.
Kögler, Hans-Herbert (2005), "Constructing a Cosmopolitan Public Sphere: Hermeneutic Capabilities and Universal Values." *European Journal of Social Theory* 8 (3): 297–320.
Kögler, Hans-Herbert (2011), "Hermeneutic Cosmopolitanism, or: Toward a Cosmopolitan Public Sphere." In *The Ashgate Reserach Companion to Cosmopolitanism*, edited by Maria Rovisco and Magdalena Nowick, 225–42. Farnham, Surrey: Ashgate.
Kögler, Hans-Herbert (2017), "The Religious Face of Evil." *Berlin Journal of Critical Theory (BJCT)* 1 (2): 21–46.

Kögler, Hans-Herbert (2020a), "Introduction: Challenges of a Postsecular Public Sphere." *Berlin Journal of Critical Theory (BJCT)* 4 (2): 5–16.

Kögler, Hans-Herbert (2020b), "Tradition, Transcendence, and the Public Sphere: A Hermeneutic Critique of Religion." *Berlin Journal of Critical Theory (BJCT)* 4 (2): 107–46.

May, Samantha, Erin K. Wilson, Claudia Baumgart-Ochse, and Faiz Sheikh (2014), "The Religious as Political and the Political as Religious: Globalisation, Post-Secularism and the Shifting Boundaries of the Sacred." *Politics, Religion & Ideology* 15 (3): 331–46.

McCarthy, Thomas (2013), "The Burdens of Modernized Faith and Postmetaphysical Reason in Habermas's 'Unfinished Project of Enlightenment." In *Habermas and Religion*, edited by Craig Calhoun, Eduardo Mendieta and Jonathan VanAntwerpen, 115–31. Cambridge: Polity.

Mendieta, Eduardo (2013), "Appendix: Religion in Habermas's Work." In *Habermas and Religion*, edited by Craig Calhoun, Eduardo Mendieta and Jonathan VanAntwerpen, 391–407. Cambridge: Polity.

Portier, Philippe (2011), "Religion and Democracy in the Thought of Jurgen Habermas." *Society* 48 (5): 426–32.

Ratzinger, Joseph Cardinal (2006), "That Which Holds the World Together: The Pre-political Moral Foundations of a Free State." In *Dialectics of Secularization: On Reason and Religion*, edited by Florian Schuller, 55–80. San Francisco: Ignatius Press.

Reder, Michael. 2010), "How Far Can Faith and Reason be Distinguished?" In *An Awareness of What is Missing*, edited by Jürgen Habermas et al., 36–50. Cambridge: Polity.

Reder, Michael and Josef Schmidt (2010), "Habermas and Religion." In *An Awareness of What is Missing*, edited by Jürgen Habermas et al., 1–14. Cambridge: Polity.

Ricken, S.J., Friedo (2010), "Postmetaphysical Reason and Religion." In *An Awareness of What is Missing*, edited by Jürgen Habermas et al., 51–8. Cambridge: Polity.

Schmidt, S.J., Josef (2010), "A Dialogue in Which There Can Only Be Winners." In *An Awareness of What is Missing*, edited by Jürgen Habermas et al., 59–71. Cambridge: Polity.

Spohn, Ulrike (2015), "A Difference in Kind? Jürgen Habermas and Charles Taylor on Post-secularism." *The European Legacy* 20 (2): 120–35.

Taylor, Charles (2011), "Why We Need a Radical Redefinition of Secularism." In *The Power of Religion in the Public Sphere*, edited by Eduardo Mendieta and Jonathan VanAntwerpen, 34–59. New York: Columbia University Press.

Ungureanu, Camil, and Lasse Thomassen (2015), "The Post-secular Debate: Introductory Remarks." *The European Legacy: Post-secularism: Between Public Reason and Transcendence* 20 (2): 103–8.

Vander Schel, Kevin (2016), "Jürgen Habermas on the (Non-)Translatability of Religious Meaning." *Theological Research* 4: 35–58.

Warnke, Georgia (1992), *Justice and Interpretation*. Cambridge: Polity.

Wolterstorff, Nicholas (2013), "An Engagement with Jurgen Habermas on Postmetaphysical Philosophy, Religion, and Political Dialogue." In *Habermas and Religion*, edited by Craig Calhoun, Eduardo Mendieta and Jonathan VanAntwerpen, 92–111. Cambridge: Polity.

Yates, Melissa (2011), "Postmetaphysical thinking." In *Jürgen Habermas: Key Concepts*, edited by Barbara Fultner, 35–53. Acumen Publishing.

7

The Limits of Interreligious Hermeneutics and the Need for Alternative Understanding

John C. Maraldo

The work of Hans-Herbert Kögler has moved hermeneutics into a dialogue with critical theory and thus transformed both, giving dialogue a cutting edge in challenging power relations, and opening social critique to empathetic understanding. The present chapter, encouraged by Kögler's pathbreaking work, examines the limits of traditional hermeneutics from another direction: its application to interreligious dialogue. A critique of these limits points to a dimension of religions that is not expressed in the form of beliefs or propositional claims and convictions and, in turn, this dimension of embodied, non-instrumental practice compels an alternative notion of understanding.

The Strictures of *Interreligious Hermeneutics*

At first sight, the prospects for an interreligious hermeneutics seem bleak. Its possibilities seem bounded on all sides by assumptions that are as restrictive of its presumed aims (mutual understanding among religions) as they are invisible to its advocates. The assumptions lie behind the very words: interreligious, hermeneutics. The word *hermeneutics* refers historically to a discipline focused on texts, and on language under the guise of texts. The word *interreligious* refers foremost to interaction between so-called world religions. But when religion is confined to the aspects of traditions that are globally represented, when the interaction between them is restricted to linguistic understanding, and when hermeneutics is supposed to guide this understanding of language as it becomes focused in texts, then a lot is left out. There are notable aspects of religion that have nothing to do with texts and little to do with language, and there are religious interactions between people who do not represent world religions or their various sects. If reflection on possible mutual understanding between identifiably different religions is the aim of interreligious hermeneutics, then an alternative sense of understanding is called for.

The Bounds of Religion in *Interreligious* Dialogue

The standard understanding in much interreligious dialogue takes religion to be primarily a matter of teachings and belief in teachings. It presupposes that teachings are formulated and handed down in texts, or at least that they can be so formulated. It often assumes that belief means belief that the teachings are true. Although belief is not necessarily restricted to a set of propositions that can be true or false, it does, in the prevailing assumption, primarily concern linguistic expression. The question of the truth of the teachings vis-à-vis those of another religious tradition, in some sense of truth, is frequently a topic of discussion. To be sure, the mode of believing, often called faith, is also a topic. The standard understanding does not confine religious faith to believing that a set of linguistically expressible teachings is true, and the notion of faith may include trust and *believing in* some reality, as opposed to *believing that* a teaching is true; it may consider faith a mode of belief that is not properly understood epistemologically, in distinction from knowledge. Nevertheless, the usual emphasis is on what adherents of the religion believe, on expressible content. When the standard understanding attends to what adherents do, it more often than not assumes that what is going on is *worship*, the veneration of the object of belief, an expression of faith that arises from religious belief. These assumptions are particularly evident whenever religions are called *faiths* and adherents are called *believers*. The *sacred scriptures* of the believers become a privileged target of investigation.

Many scholars in Religious Studies today, particularly those who do research from a socio-scientific perspective, consider the traditional focus on teachings and scriptures as limited to the subjective self-understanding of religious people and oblivious of social, economic, and political factors that enter into the formation and practice of religions. They call into question the validity of the very notions of faith, scripture, and even religion.[1] Many scholars regard the traditional focus as a study of the elite, of the theological expression of literate authorities. They turn their attention to everyday rituals and practices (and sometimes texts) that are describable from a third-person point of view. Their shift has influenced interreligious dialogue and the practice of theology as well, so that theological dialogue now also frequently includes discussion about ritual and practice. Phrases such as "teachings and practices" "beliefs and practices," and "teachings, practices and rituals," are now common paraphrases of religion. Yet the predominant position goes to the first-mentioned, to teachings or beliefs, and a central concern in interreligious dialogue is their truth, even where truth is not explicitly defined in logical or epistemological terms, even when *truth* is left relatively undefined.

The Boundaries of *World Religions* and the Limitation of *Interreligious*

I will not try to define what *religion* is or what makes something *religious*. My call for an alternative sense of understanding would not limit that understanding to specifically religious matters, and it allows for these terms to be used as they commonly are in interreligious dialogue—up to a point. That point is reached when the *inter* of interreligious serves to designate interactions solely between world religions. The focus on world religions carries with it the assumption that adherence to the religion entails some degree of consistent commitment over time, primarily to a set of globalized teachings, even where participants in the dialogue avow the possibility of belonging to more than one religion at the same time. The standard understanding presumes the central *role of teachings* in different religions as a major part of their common denominator, if not their only point of interconnection; and it tends to assume that the teachings of a religion are both what distinguish it from other religions and what explain its geographical spread in the world.

World religions, it is presumed, come in a variety of sects or denominations, which are nevertheless distinguished from those of other world religions by an embracing set of basic beliefs and a history that the sects share. Interactions between sects of the same religion, between Lutherans and Roman Catholics, for example, count more often as "ecumenical" than as interreligious. And standard interreligious dialogue has scarcely if at all included discussions between representatives of a world religion and those of a regional religion, much less a "folk religion," or between representatives of two or more regional religions. To be sure, the interactions within the scope of standard interreligious dialogue typically engage people who represent only one part of a religious tradition. As Catherine Cornille points out, the dialogue occurs for the most part "not between Islam and Christianity, but between Shi'ites and Methodists, or between member of a particular Sufi order and those of an order with the Roman Catholic Church."[2] Standard interreligious dialogue presumes, nevertheless, that the particular sect or order counts as a cross-section of the world religion.

Scholars who would eliminate *religion* as useful category have taken the category of *world religion* as a specific target of their critique. They too have stressed the text-orientation of that category. Richard King summarizes the link between textualism and the modern concept of "world religions":

> The universalizing aspects of literacy therefore provide a means of idealizing religions and locating it within the abstract world of the text. It is in this sense that we can understand [Walter] Ong's reference to the "imperialist" tendency of writing. [Jack] Goody argues that it is the development of literature that effectively allows certain religious worldviews to spread beyond their particular and local context and become "world religions".... The "world-religions" approach to the study of religion, which focuses upon a few globalized religious entities as expressive of the religious experience of humankind, shows clear evidence of this texualist bias.... In effect, an exclusive focus upon the so-called "world religions" concentrates attention upon those religious ideologies that remain directly comparable with the universalistic and proselytizing elements of Christian theology, with its emphasis upon universal human salvation.[3]

Insofar as these scholars intend to expose not only the textual bias of the category *world religions*, but also—as they see it—its Christian, theological, and colonialist presuppositions, their intention differs from mine. I do not seek to subvert the discipline of hermeneutics or eliminate the category of religion. The alternative notion of understanding I seek would serve, among other things, to make interreligious hermeneutics better prepared to guide the interpretation of religious phenomena, and to make it more responsible in representing religions. If standard interreligious hermeneutics takes its clues from examples of interreligious dialogue that represent the norm—text-based dialogue between so-called world religions—then the alternative will need to explore religious interactions that are not focused on understanding texts and not cast as differences (and similarities) between globally represented religions.[4]

The Textual Binding of Hermeneutics

What Do I Mean by Text and Textual?

Before documenting the ways that hermeneutics has been bound to texts, even in and after Heidegger, a clarification of the terms *text* and *textual* is in order. By *text* I wish to designate an enclosure of language in sequences of sentences that build up a body of writing presumed to make sense. (The terms I use to define *text* are just as indefinite as that word itself.) Because of its relative unity, a text can be printed on pages that are bound together, or digitally reproduced as a unit with definite boundaries that once again make it possible to reproduce the electronic text in a physical book.[5]

By *textual* I mean linear discourse embodied in sentences, one following after another in a sequence defined by the effort to make sense. Sentences may come in the form of statements, questions, and commands, and also in the form of grammatically incomplete sentences and even single words, but the presumption is that any of these can all be transformed into precisely written, punctuated sentences.[6] That kind of sentence—even if logically a mere shadow of an atemporal "proposition" cast in one temporary, natural language among others—serves as the primary unit of meaning whose parts are referential words that have their own interdependent meanings. (Dictionaries pretend they have their own quasi-independent meanings.) The text may serve as the context of the sentences whose meanings emerge in a hermeneutical circle or interplay between part and whole, between "parts of speech" and whole sentence, sentence and whole text. Precisely where hermeneutical theory problematizes the relations between part and whole, word and sentence, sentence and text, text and context, it reaffirms its binding to language as textual. Each of these relations is conceived as an ordering, a sequencing of parts made to make sense. Of course, this sequencing is of a specific kind, not merely temporal but also referential. We makers of sense take these parts to lead us beyond them to their "meanings." The referential character of most language is already familiar to us in the talk of signifier and signified. Something functions properly as a signifier when we see straight through it to what it signifies. The more transparent a sign is, the better it functions. In textual language, however, we look for a whole that does not immediately make sense, and to compensate, we try to capture meanings in the form of sentences. Sentences function as the units of meaning, and all "meanings" come to be transcribable into sentences.

The sentential structure of textual language makes it suitable for expressing religious doctrines, and perhaps makes religious doctrines possible in the first place. A doctrine is meant (by an authoritative body if not by an author) to refer to a whole that does not (yet) make sense, that is never completely at our disposal, yet is condensed into a statement. A religious "teaching" is perhaps more ambiguous than a "doctrine," but the common presumption is that teachings too can be transcribed into sentences.

I use the word *textual* also to describe the practice of understanding language, and of using language to render meaning into the form of sentences arranged to refer to a whole that does not make immediate sense. Texts need to be interpreted. Of course, many things besides written texts need to be interpreted. Things like a pet dog's notably non-linguistic response, a person's behavior or utterance or facial expression, the typical patterns of behavior of a group or its entire culture. Human be-ing itself. But when we seek to make sense of these things we often coax them into isolatable units that can theoretically be put in written sentences. They become texts we understand by "reading" them.

The Figurative Text

A text becomes a figure for any whole supposed to make sense. No matter how unbounded and contextual the whole, no matter how indeterminate the text or limitless the endeavor to make sense of it, the text comes to stand for any phenomenon temporarily taken as a whole that can eventually make sense to a reader. The whole may be truly a comprehensive horizon, the world so to speak, that along with consciousness allows meaning to take place; the *world* becomes a text. An author becomes a text, or a collection of texts (This is the way I use the names Heidegger, Gadamer, Ricoeur, etc.) A culture becomes a text. My speech acts and antics in any given situation are *read* as a text. They are taken to communicate culturally shared meanings that can be interpreted by any competent, acculturated interlocutor or observer. I may *misread* the meaning of another person's gesture because of cultural difference; the Japanese gesture for "come here" (to put it in sentence form) is easily mistaken by Americans to mean "go away." The figurative uses of *text* and *reading* do not disguise the presumption that the understanding of any phenomenon can be articulated in sentential, textual form. This presumption is also at work in the metaphoric uses of "message," "information" and "communication" in computer science and brain research, even where they tend to forget that messages and information require a conscious reader, and communication requires conscious, intersubjective beings.

What is Non-textual Language?

Not all language use is textual. In actual situations in which focus on language is central, such as a philosophical symposium or meeting of speakers, communication is facilitated by usages of language that are not sentential, not amenable to formulation in sentences building up a text, spoken or written. Communication also flows through gesture, posture, intonation, tone of voice, sighs, the rolling of eyes—all aspects of non-textual language that need not be "read" to be understood. Much of this is meant to be captured in the expression "body language," but what I wish to point out is not so much the language conveyed by the human body as the body of language.

The body of language encompasses the enormous range of lived language not encoded in grammar or vocabulary, syntax or semantics, that includes non-referential as well as referential elements, and that overlaps with the culture in which one lives.[7] Linguists increasingly recognize that the study of language cannot be confined to analyses of structures and signs but must include the study of situations in which languages are learned and performed.[8] Language in its fully embodied form is learned through personal interaction with others in live situations, usually situations in which one is bodily present with others. In fact, to gain communicative competence in a language requires personal interaction well beyond the exchange of linguistic signs. Interaction in person provides a shared context, crucial to language learning and distinct from any form of "distant learning," including learning by listening to audio and video devices. Distant learning or learning via devices takes place by bridging two "places," two or more initially unshared contexts, the situation of the learner and that of the distant source. This is where a "fusion of horizons" comes into play. Although the minds of learner and teacher who are not equally competent in the language might constitute two different "mental horizons" that need to be fused, the presence of co-speakers opens a horizon that is shared from the beginning. That context may be marked by differences in culture, gender, class, and power; but its initially shared nature makes it singular.

I will return to the implications of this view of language for an alternative sense of understanding. But first let us consider the ways that hermeneutics has been bound to texts, not only among classical philologists, jurists, and biblical commentators, but more surprisingly in the theories of Schleiermacher, Dilthey, and their later heirs who are known for expanding its scope and deepening its significance.[9] Here space permits only some indication in the three most important representatives of twentieth-century philosophical hermeneutics, Heidegger, Gadamer, and Ricouer.[10]

How Heidegger Binds Understanding to Texts

Heidegger is known for definitively releasing hermeneutics from its binding to texts, and for placing understanding at the roots of everyday human comportment in the world. But when the Heidegger of *Being and Time* existentialized understanding, he unintentionally textualized it as well.

Heidegger is after the "meaning of Being" [*Sinn des Seins*]. He uses *meaning* here to indicate the intention or projection of what we seek to understand [*das Erfragte*].[11] *Hermeneutics* names the kind of analysis that fulfills this inquiry. Ostensibly *the meaning of Being* is not a sentence, and *hermeneutics* is not a text that supplies its ultimate meaning. Yet Heidegger's own text exhibits an unmistakable drive to state "the meaning of Being is time" or "is temporality," or (later) "is presencing" [*Anwesenheit*]— however tentative and groping these sentences are. Hermeneutics is a way of reading the meaning of Being wherever it is disclosed, in its being there. Dasein becomes a text that discloses the meaning of Being. But Dasein is also the reader. Dasein reads itself, discloses itself. It (we) can do so because we already always exist as a form of disclosedness—as *understanding*. The main thing (or sentence) that is disclosed is that we exist as beings inseparable from our world. *World* names the context in which we live, that within which we seek and project meanings. The world is structured as a "relational totality of signification," something with significance [*Bedeutsamkeit*]. Usually this referential totality goes unnoticed, but it can show up sometimes when our projections of meaning are interrupted, as when a tool we are using breaks. The tool exists in a whole matrix of relations in which we use this for that, in the same way that we say X to refer to Y within a particular, unarticulated situation. *Understanding* [*Verstehen*] uncovers the "for the sake of which" [*worumwillen*] we inevitably do things; *understanding* is the name for this kind of disclosure.[12] And Heidegger made this *understanding* an "Existential," a fundamental way of being—not a way we sometimes could choose to be at will, but a way we inevitably are.

The alternative sense of practice I propose undercuts any "for the sake of which," and calls for an alternative sense of understanding. Heidegger's treatment of *understanding* pretends a fundamental expansion if not reversal of the term, but implicitly betrays a textual model. Heidegger would expand *Verstehen* beyond understanding language, even beyond any thematic cognitive grasp, to mean know-how [*können*]. I understand a hammer when I know how to hammer. Thus, understanding for Heidegger includes (to use my words) bodily interacting with things; it suggests the body's practiced know-how (a suggestion that will feature in my alternative notion). But Heidegger comes to know of this know-how by reading Dasein's comportment with *things* in the world (not primarily with other Dasein, other people, but with things "ready to hand" [*zuhanden*]), and he implicitly treats this know-how as a capacity we gain in the same way we learn to read automatically through words and sentences to their significations. We take a hammer in hand and, paying little heed to it, with our eye on the goal, see through the hammer to what it's for—just as we take a book in hand and see through the print to the meaning of the words. Our engagement with tools is directed away from them toward the goal or purpose of the activity, to its *Worumwillen*, just as our engagement with texts is directed to the matter they discuss. Heidegger's analysis brilliantly elucidates the working of everyday human activities, but it does not take into account *the kind of practice that is not aimed at a goal separable from the activity of performing it*, much less the kind of activities that have no goal. I will suggest how this kind of practice is at the heart of much religious activity, and calls for another sense of understanding.

Heidegger's later work more explicitly challenged that notion that language is a tool, and even in *Being and Time* he anticipates his later emphasis on language as " world disclosure." Later he also framed language as " the house of Being." He began to pay attention to poetic language and other possibilities of "using" language in a way that does not objectify.[13] But by modeling the notion of understanding after the usage and referential system of tools, in *Being and Time* he cast understanding in the framework of textual referentiality, a house constructed of sentences.

One might think that two of those who followed Heidegger's expansive interpretation most closely, Gadamer and Ricoeur, would have freed hermeneutics from its binding to textuality. They shifted the focus from *texts* in some literal sense, but remained within the same textual horizon.

How Gadamer Restricts Understanding to Language, and Language to Textualized Dialogue

Some indications of the implicit textual horizon of Gadamer's hermeneutics are evident in his model of dialogue or conversation, which itself counts explicitly as the model of understanding. Other indications appear in his broader notion of language.

Gadamer's focus on the back and forth, question and answer dialectic of conversation [*Gespräch*] is rightly celebrated as a major advance in theories of interpretation. What goes unnoticed, however, is the limited kind of conversation he seems to have in mind. Perhaps as a scholar of Plato as well as a hermeneutical philosopher, Gadamer envisions Plato's Socratic dialogues as an ideal, just as Plato in writing these dialogues may have aimed for an ideal form of what he encountered in actual, everyday conversations in the polis. Be that as it may, Gadamer's model of dialogue is a far cry from ordinary, everyday conversations, and betrays a noticeable tendency to the textual guise of language. Gadamer's model is the sort of conversation that takes place in situations like a philosophical symposium. Philosophical conversations are often based on pre-written texts and proceed with participants speaking coherently, in more or less complete and sequential sentences. To be sure, a good deal of back and forth, questioning and responding, enliven such conversations, but in a style more self-conscious and linguistically aware than the conversations of people on the streets in the workaday world are likely to be. A number of distinct language games are probably evident in what goes by the names of dialogue and conversation; certainly the back and forth of question and answer is not the sole factor. Gadamer's model of dialogue, even in its dialectical structure, depends on sentential semantics and syntax. Non-textual factors that constitute actual conversations, one's tone of voice and gestures, for example, as well as the non-referential aspects of the body of language, go unnoticed in Gadamer's hermeneutics.

A surprising orientation to the text is also indicated in the role assigned to language. For Gadamer language is not first and foremost the object to be understood; it is rather the horizon within which all understanding takes place. The sentence, "*Sein, das verstanden werden kann, ist Sprache*" ("Being that can be understood is language")[14] means, phenomenologically: if something is to be understood, it must manifest in the form of language. Gadamer explicitly criticizes the theory that takes words as signs and language as a tool. We misunderstand "the life of language," language as it lives in speech, when we reduce it to signs as instruments with more or less univocal designations.[15] As does Heidegger, Gadamer defines (or unbinds) language as *world-disclosure*. What his discussion implies, however, is that the form of language that best reveals its life and discloses world is the dialogical form of an exchange of sentences.

This reading seems at first sight at odds with what Gadamer writes: *Authentic language is found first in conversation, not in the statement*, as the early Greeks thought. Making oneself understood is not another matter of acting purposefully, for example by producing signs, in order to communicate to others. Communicating is not in need of tools at all; it is a process of living that a community lives out. Language becomes real only in the realization of communication. The statement [*Aussage*] covers up, with the exactness of some method, the horizon of meaning of what there is to say. What is left over is the supposedly "purified" meaning of the stated. This is what goes on record. But meaning reduced to what is stated is always a distorted meaning.[16] This is clearly Gadamer's contention. What could disqualify more strongly than these statements do, a hermeneutics that takes its cues from statements and texts?

Ironically, the limits of Gadamer's understanding of language are apparent in a series of statements that emphasize the power of spoken words to render the totality of being. Gadamer writes:

> to say what one means, to make oneself understood, is to embrace in one meaning both what is said and an infinity of what is not, and in this way to offer what is said for understanding. One who speaks in this manner may use only the most ordinary and most commonplace words and yet precisely because of that is able *to put into language [zur Sprache zu bringen] what is unsaid and to be said*. The one who speaks does so by surmising or speculating, insofar as his words are not copies of things but rather *express a relation to the whole of Being and let it be put into language*. Connected to this is the fact that one who repeats what is said, *just as one who reports statements, need not consciously distort anything at all and yet will change the meaning of what is said*."[17]

One might ask whether, by reporting Gadamer's statements, I have changed the meaning of what he has written; indeed whether he himself has changed the meaning of what language can say by putting it into—not just any kind of language but—a series of statements. After all, Gadamer does not present his theory in the form of dialogue, much less of living speech. In the "infinity of what is not [said]" lie features of the body of language that social linguists point out as parts of every embodied instance of language, features that escape not only the semantics and syntax of the statement but the expressive range of the spoken word, that for this reason escape the words that can be rendered in sentences and texts.

More than the terms of his theory, it is Gadamer's hermeneutical practice that veils his pre-disposition toward textual understanding. Gadamer discusses phenomena like living speech that at first sight cannot be equated with textual language, and he reflects on the conditions for the possibility of their appearance (i.e., world, human be-ing, language). But he evidently intends to capture the significance of non-textual language and phenomena, and to describe the disclosive power of language, in the form of sentences building up a text. Gadamer fashions his understanding in the form of a text; and he presumes that textual writing is adequate to disclose this understanding.

How Ricoeur Textualizes Self and World

The hermeneutical theory of Paul Ricoeur follows the trajectory of expanding classical hermeneutics but ultimately returns it to its *locus classicus* in the text. In the end, it is the meaning and scope of *text* that undergoes expansion—to the point of understanding both self and world in terms of the text. Here I can offer only two examples of how this expansion occurs, namely, in the 1960s and 70s, when Ricoeur was explicitly concerned with hermeneutics. His critique of the Romanticist hermeneutics of Schleiermacher and Dilthey aimed to break the bondage of interpretation theory to the understanding of texts as exemplary forms of dialogue between an author with particular intentions in mind and a reader who is the anticipated audience. It placed interpretation theory in a broader theory of discourse in its double role, as self-understanding and as world-disclosure.

This theory harks back to Heidegger, but with a correction. In one essay Ricoeur writes that "Language itself, as a signifying milieu, must be referred to existence."[18] Because Heidegger's existential analysis or hermeneutic can fall prisoner to language, however, it needs to surpass the linguistic level. For Ricoeur, we need a further step that links the understanding of signs to self-understanding.

> In proposing to relate symbolic language to self-understanding, I think I fulfill the deepest wish of hermeneutics. The purpose of all interpretation is to conquer a remoteness, a distance between the past cultural epoch *to which the text belongs* and the interpreter himself. By overcoming this distance, by making himself contemporary with *the text*, the exegete can appropriate its meaning to himself: foreign, he makes it familiar, that is, he makes it his own. It is thus the growth of his own understanding of himself that he pursues through his understanding of the other. Every hermeneutics is thus, explicitly or implicitly, self-understanding by means of understanding others.[19]

Yet, to complete this last thought in line with the previous sentences, we would need to write, "understanding others by means of their texts." Or more precisely, "self-understanding by means of understanding other texts." While self and other are not exactly reduced to text here, the text functions as the means to understanding self via understanding other, as the means to the telos of hermeneutics in its expanded sense. In stressing the disclosive power of the text, Ricoeur not only intentionally grafts hermeneutics onto phenomenology; he unwittingly grafts it onto textual understanding. Again and again he slips from talk of language to talk of text. "Let us in fact reflect upon what the self of self-understanding signifies, whether we appropriate the sense of a psychoanalytic interpretation or that of a textual exegesis." As textual interpretations that take place through language, psychoanalytic interpretation and textual exegesis are evidently equivalent. The language Ricoeur writes of here, moreover, is not the living *parole* but the abstract *la langage*.[20]

In the conclusion to lectures given in 1973–5, Ricoeur notes the shift that took place in early twentieth-century hermeneutics from historicist to logicist views; from understanding a text as a historical object confined to its time, its author's intentions, and its particular addressees, to explaining a text as a kind of atemporal object that refers to ideal meanings beyond the confines of psychological intention and immediate historical context. Ricoeur's guiding interest here lies not only in maintaining objectivity in interpretation but also in exposing the dialectical nature of relations in the hermeneutical endeavor: the dialectics of understanding and explanation, of alternately distancing and appropriating the object of understanding/explanation, of event and meaning within discourse, and of sense and reference within meaning. All the while, the consistent referent of Ricoeur's analysis of hermeneutics remains the text as *the* form of fixing discourse. Every general statement about appropriation or distanciation, understanding or explanation, etc. is exemplified in terms of "a text." Exceeding propositional logic, what hermeneutics has to do is to disclose "a possible way of looking at things," a possible world never merely referred to ostensively, but rather disclosed—through the text. Such world disclosure "constitutes the [ultimate] reference of the text."[21] It is the text that opens a possible mode of being in the world, a project of the world. Another dialectic is at work here, but only by implication, an ineluctable dialectic of world and text. Moreover, the ideality of meaning that Ricoeur welcomes as assurance of the objectivity of hermeneutics is traced by him back to Frege's and early Husserl's notion of the ideal meaning—not of a text per se, but of a sentence.

To be sure, if the text is enclosed within sentences that have meanings beyond the intentions of the author and the egoistic reader whose mind is made up, the act of appropriating these meanings requires the opening of the self, indeed the creation of a new self. The last sentences of Ricoeur's lectures read:

> Only the interpretation that complies with the injunction of the text, that follows the "arrow" of the sense and that tries to think accordingly, initiates a new self-understanding... It is the text, with its universal power of world disclosure, which gives a self to the ego [that is, which replaces ego with self].[22]

In this manner Ricoeur's hermeneutics is clearly fixated on the text; and the text, however disclosive of world and creative of self, is still fixed in sentences.

Toward an Alternative Sense of Understanding

If the textual language inscribed in philosophical hermeneutics and invoked in much interreligious dialogue does not reach all there is to be understood in religions, what then is the alternative? In proposing an alternative sense of understanding, I am not suggesting that we have a choice between two or more incompatible approaches. Rather, the alternative I propose is complementary. Language in textual form does enable understanding and experiencing. But not all of it.[23]

What goes by the name of interreligious dialogue itself provides examples of understanding that is facilitated by non-textual, even extra-linguistic practice. Complementing the textual interpretations and the conversations that exemplify much dialogue between representatives of distinct religions are shared activities such as prayer, meditation, chanting, or participating in other religious rituals.[24] Inter-monastic exchange is an exemplary arena for illustrating an approach to non-textual understanding, not because monastics are religiously superior to other people but simply because their lives, on the margins of "world religions," are more focused on religious practices. The exchange between European Benedictine monks and Japanese

Zen monks, for example, has required a suspension of judgment about truth claims formulated or implicit in the texts of the other's religion. Instead of debating truth or interpreting a text, monks learned how to do something, an activity that is distinct from believing in or believing that something is the case—distinct from textual matters, in other words.[25] The understanding that takes place in such "inter-monastic dialogue" is first and foremost an understanding of the religious life of the other, and this understanding comes about by living that life as fully as possible during the prescribed period of time. It involves mindful bodily engagement in addition to linguistic comprehension. Understanding via bodily engagement does not obviate the apparent need for and actuality of textual understanding in the encounter between religions. It offers a complement that adds an indispensable dimension to interreligious hermeneutics. It would be possible to give many other examples of understanding among religions as it is sought and achieved through mutual practice. All would call us to the hermeneutical task of clarifying further an alternative sense both of understanding and of practice. For now, the following contrasts may serve as pointers.

An Alternative Notion of Practice

Activities such as prayer, meditation, chanting, or participating in other religious rituals engage the body and mind differently than do observation, reading, analyzing, and translating. They engage the body more consciously and disengage discursive thought. We cannot employ such embodied practices as we do concepts or judgments that form beliefs about the world. In the case of concepts and judgments, we may merely mention them while standing back and remaining detached, or we may assent to them and direct our beliefs accordingly while still remaining bodily disengaged. In contrast, practices in the alternative sense require coordinated bodily action and mental attention.

What makes this sense of practice more specifically an alternative to the dominant sense in much philosophical literature is its relation to an objective or end. The word practice predominantly implies an activity that is geared toward an objective or purpose separate from the activity. Religious activities too may well be regarded as practices in the dominant sense and given soteriological significance: they may be aimed ultimately at salvation, for example, or at liberation or enlightenment. Seen in a different light, however, activities, whether explicitly religious or not, can be exercised and experienced as an end in themselves, not a means to an end different in kind from the activity. Such activities may indeed have an objective, but the objective is not external to the activity that achieves it. The activity embodies the objective in incipient form. To refer to the previous example of inter-monastic practice, the intention of Benedictine chanting may ultimately be to glorify God, and that of Zen chanting may be to concentrate the mind and embody the Dharma, but the intention is repeatedly fulfilled in the very act of chanting. If monks engage in a particular activity to partially fulfill the intention of their entire religious life, the performance of each activity in itself can function as an expression of the totality of that life. Chanting for example can function as a kind of hologram of the monks' entire religious life when practiced whole-heartedly. The activity expresses a whole that may transcend it.

Practice in the alternative sense, then, includes activities performed for their own sake or for the sake of an objective inseparable from their very performance, with the whole person, "body and soul," engaged. Whole-hearted engagement in such activities allows each performance to express a whole life of practice.[26]

The Alternative Notion of Understanding

Practices in the alternative sense generate a form of understanding distinct from understandings that are merely intellectual, textual, or empathetic. The alternative to textual understanding, however, does not entail an attempt to abandon all language, since not all language use is textual. Language no more than religion can be bound to logos, to worded reasoning. Understanding the non-sentential aspects of the body of language mentioned earlier provided some examples of non-textual understanding. The practice of learning a language offers a related set of examples. Non-linguistic practices provide examples of another sort that are equally relevant to interreligious hermeneutics.

Learning a language is a practice that involves understanding that language, of course, but understanding in this case is not a prerequisite. Rather it is achieved in the process of learning the language. Understanding the language here means the ability to use it, to live in it, rather than to take it as an object of an act of interpretation. Reminiscent of Gadamer, we may say that understanding a language is coming to understand the world through that language. But linguistic understanding is not the only way to an understanding of the world, and it is not confined to textual understanding.

The bond of traditional hermeneutics to textual language actually veils an opening to the alternative notion of understanding—by reminding us of the incompleteness of textual language. When one learns a language, one learns more than what words mean, what their references are, and also more than how they are linked together. Of course, one learns vocabulary and grammar (or, in the view of Cartesian linguists, one activates universal structures of a pre-existent grammar). More significantly, however, one learns how language is used in concrete situations, and that usage involves situationally dependent elements that are not coded in grammar or vocabulary—elements like tone of voice, gesture, and facial expression, as mentioned earlier. Acquiring language and becoming a competent speaker and writer takes practice, and that practice involves more than understanding what words refer to. In particular, learning non-referential aspects of the body of language is different from, perhaps even prior to, studying the semantics and structures of a language.[27] The relevant difference appears in the stance of the learner: when she is engaged in using the language competently, in living or embodying the language, she makes it her own and ceases to examine it from an outsider's perspective.

It might be thought that the practice of learning a language involves an objective separate from that activity. One learns a language in order to communicate; one usually learns a foreign language for one purpose or another, but not simply as an end in itself. We might look at it differently, however. In practice, the end or goal can be inherent in the very activity of using the language. I may practice Japanese to get better at speaking and reading Japanese, but being good or better at it is still speaking and reading Japanese. I may want to learn Japanese in order to read Japanese Buddhist texts, and that in order to pursue a certain line of research; but reading the texts is already an end or goal in the practice of learning. Learning a language by using it exemplifies an alternative kind of understanding.

Non-linguistic practices, that is, practices that do not depend on the employment of language, are particularly exemplary of the alternative sense of understanding. The descriptions of inter-monastic exchange intimate their relevance for the alternative sense, but barely hint at the full range of such practices in the wider domain of religion. A more detailed account must await another occasion.

The alternative form of understanding, I have suggested, is at work in practices done for their own sake or for the sake of a goal inseparable from their very performance. What then is the role of intention in achieving such understanding? The hermeneutical theories of Heidegger and Gadamer stress that no understanding occurs without a pre-understanding, whereby a person has a particular intention in mind, anticipates a particular outcome, or is guided by a pre-formed set of beliefs, however subject to revision they are. The alternative sense of understanding would seem to call for a total suspension not only of one's own background beliefs but also of any intent to understand the beliefs of the other. I do not think such a double suspension is possible, and doubt that it would be necessary. One is not likely to leap blindly, without anticipation, into the activity practiced by another, although one might be called upon gradually to limit one's intention to imitating the activity of the other or simply following instructions. The crucial point is that the practice can induce a radical alteration of such anticipations, and even of intentional consciousness. There is nothing necessarily mystical or exceptional about such alteration; it occurs regularly in learning and appropriating an initially foreign language. One stumbles in speaking a language when one has to try to speak it; one speaks it competently when the intention of learning it dissolves.

Intentions may also initiate religious practices known for their suspension of intentionality, such as the *zazen* or seated meditation practiced in Zen Buddhism, and the *vipassanā* or insight meditation of modern Theravāda Buddhism. The practitioner is likely to begin the exercise with a certain goal in mind. She may intend to achieve a peaceful state of "no-mind," an awareness that does not clings to its objects; she may wish to gain insight through mindful breathing, or even to gain enlightenment or have a *satori* experience. Typically, this kind of intention will only get in the way, as would a pianist's conscious focus on her hands while performing a piece. In short, the practice dissolves initial intentions and anticipations; it concentrates one's attention on the performance, until the performance can occur by second nature, by bare attention alone.[28]

Practice not only enhances, but also transforms understanding in the alternative sense. Engaging in practices may not only increase the amount of content understood; it can change the very way that one understands. One can learn anew, often tacitly, *how* to understand.[29] We could in fact call this transformation a kind of conversion—not a switch to another set of beliefs but a turn in the way one does things. Insofar as hermeneutics in a broad sense arises from reflection on how understanding takes place, it necessarily refers back to the experience of understanding (or, as hermeneutical philosophers might put it, to experiencing *as* understanding). In the alternative notion of understanding, this experiencing occurs in the process of practicing. In the context of interreligious hermeneutics, it can occur in the course of practicing what members of the other religion practice, as distinct from coming to believe what others believe. As is the case with the learning of a language, the alternative sense of understanding aims at competence, not at adherence to a set of beliefs. While this kind of learning and practicing may not come easily, may involve frustration or even "lead nowhere," its difficulties are nevertheless distinct from those of teaching the other to understand what seems self-evident to oneself.

Understanding in any sense removes barriers, not distinctions. Distinctions remain, but they can be viewed from two or more sides. Coming to understand a foreign language removes the barrier between one's own tongue and the previously alien tongue, but not the distinction between them. It lets things be seen from the perspective of the other language. Becoming competent in another language does not require that one abandon one's mother tongue or any other acquired language, although at times it may require disengaging them. Similarly, coming to understand the religion of others by engaging in their practices does not eliminate the differences between them. It may call for a temporary disengagement with one's religious beliefs, but it does not require that one abandon them. It dissolves barriers, not differences, and this is one reason the alternative can still be considered a form of *understanding*. It lets one experience in a different way, along the way to seeing how others experience the world.

Insofar as religions include non-textual practices, understanding religions requires an approach quite different from the kind of understanding usually conceived in hermeneutics. That approach is through a bodily (re)enactment of the practices rather than a discursive reading of texts and teachings. If interreligious hermeneutics is to account for the full range of religious life, it must articulate an alternative notion of understanding that gives access to religious practices as they are lived. This chapter is meant as a step in that direction.

Notes

An earlier but longer version of this chapter was published as "A Call for Alternative Understanding in Interreligious Hermeneutics," in Cornille and Conway 2010: 89–115. Reprinted with permission of Wipf and Stock Publishers, www.wipfandstock.com.

1   For critical examinations of the category *religion*, see Fitzgerald (1997), McCutcheon (2003), and Josephson (2012). For critical discussions of the notions of *scripture*, see Levering (1988). Kögler (2017) advances a hermeneutical way to overcome the authoritarian aspect of the concept of religion and to re-integrate religious discourse into the public sphere in post-secular society.
2   Cornille (2008, 68) notes further that "[g]eneral religious categories such as 'Christian' or 'Buddhist' have often obscured the reality of internal diversity and dissonance

within religions, while at the times setting unnecessary limits on our understanding of 'sameness' and 'difference' across religious traditions."

3   King (1999), 65–7.

4   The alternative I propose thus supplements and stands in tension with Kögler's (2020) hermeneutic critique of religion that focuses on the doxological (or belief) dimension of global religions, especially as they seek to root their authority in vertical and transcendental sources. The religious interactions I explore are by nature horizontally rooted in certain practices that are intersubjectively grounded and neither private nor directed toward reception by a public sphere. Their critical import is their potential to challenge common-place notions of religion and hermeneutical understanding, and thus to broaden the scope of tradition and of dialogue.

5   Does the postmodern internet disrupt the relative unity of the text and fragment it into an undefined and unbound intertext? To a degree, perhaps, but my use of the internet in doing research for this article suggests that its fragments easily lend themselves to inclusion into a new or another text.

6   In *Philosophical Investigations* #23, Wittgenstein (1968) notes that there are *countless* kinds of sentences [*Sätze*], and in #8, 19 and 20 he gives examples of single words functioning as sentences. When the house builder calls out to his assistant, points, and says "Brick" he is using the word to mean "Hand me a brick!" (That is, "hand me a brick" is what we say when we transcribe this particular usage of that word into a complete sentence.) "To understand a sentence," Wittgenstein writes, "means to understand a language" (#199).

7   For a treatment of the overlap between language and culture, see Agar (1994).

8   Recent social linguistics has elucidated numerous aspects of language not encoded either in its semantics or in its structure. *Prosodics* for example studies the vocal elements of language that are not encoded in grammar or vocabulary. This shift from text-oriented explanations of grammar and vocabulary and from structural analyses of language, was anticipated some seventy years ago by the empirical research of Lev Vygotsky. Vygotsky's work suggested that all levels of language learning and all aspects of language (what I call "the body of language") originate as actual person-to-person relationships between individuals, in more or less flexible "zones of proximal development." Infants learn language through interaction with care-givers in their immediate presence. Language is not externalized thought; thought is internalized language that first appeared on a social level, in social interactions.

9   For a more detailed treatment of philosophical hermeneutics, see Maraldo (1974 and 1984). Here I focus on an aspect of hermeneutics, its text-orientation, that went unnoticed in that dissertation, which itself was an epitome of textuality so different from the German I was using in everyday life.

10 Equally relevant, if space permitted, would be an examination of the extent to which non-Western hermeneutics, the theories of interpretation found for example in Asian religions, are not bound to textual understanding. To give but one example, Carpenter (1992, 28) writes: "one does not 'understand' the Veda, one enacts it; and ideally one *becomes* it."

11 In this context it is important to note what sorts of things are thought to have "meaning." Words do, of course, and discourse (and perhaps by extension even life and love). But phenomenology had by this time already expanded meaning far beyond a feature of linguistic entities. Each and every phenomenon is imbued with meaning by virtue of its being intended by acts of consciousness. Husserl's notion of the constitution of phenomena by consciousness refers to the construction of their

meanings for consciousness. Heidegger's attribution of meaning to Being itself—to "*the* phenomenon of phenomenology" that is not really a phenomenon at all but more like the very appearing (and concealing) of phenomena—expands the reach of meaning even further. When Heidegger seeks the meaning of Being he is not looking for what the word *Being* (and its Indo-European cognates) means. He is seeking the ways that things (phenomena) have come to be manifest; and these ways are by no means necessarily linguistic. Yet at the same time (it may be said) the attribution of meaning to Being imbues it with a language-like character: in *Being and Time* (1996, 81), the ways things come to be manifest or concealed are read out of the texts of the philosophical tradition and the comportment of Dasein. Dasein is both something to be understood and that which understands. "In its familiarity with these [referential] relations, Da-sein 'signifies' to itself. It primordially gives itself to understand its being and potentiality-of-being with regard to its being-in-the-world.... Da-sein gives itself to understand its being-in-the-world beforehand."

12 Heidegger (1963), 85–143.
13 Heidegger (1976), 22–31.
14 Gadamer 1965: 451. Kögler's (1996: ch. 2) elucidation of this famous statement shows how and why, for Gadamer, *experience* and the constitution of being are inseparable from language, but Kögler also critiques the structural ideality of Gadamer's notions of preunderstanding and understanding. Kögler's argument that all experiencing involves a complex of interpretive acts remains consonant with my view that understanding can occur through non-linguistic, non-textualized, interaction.
15 Gadamer 1965: 410 and 382.
16 Ibid.: 442 and 445.
17 Ibid., 444–5, my translation with italics.
18 Ricoeur (1974), 16.
19 Ibid., 16–17, my italics.
20 Ibid., 16–17.
21 Paul Ricoeur (1976), 91–5.
22 Ibid., 95. Even after his turn to narrativity and story-telling, Ricoeur (1983, 191–4) continued to insist that self-understanding is ineluctably mediated by language in the form of texts; that the text and the (real) world relate dialectically, with the text transfiguring the world; and that textual understanding forms the heart of hermeneutics. "Writing tears itself free of the limits of face-to-face dialogue and becomes the condition for discourse itself becoming-text." The task of hermeneutics is to explore "the implications of this becoming-text for the work of interpretation." Moyaert (2010) indicates how Ricoeur's later philosophy of self and other, while still language-oriented, is no longer bound to textual understanding.
23 I am acutely aware of the ironies of this article, itself a sequence of sentences that requires textual understanding, even as it calls for a non-textual hermeneutic.
24 The recent rise of ritual studies as a subfield of religious studies indicates a renewed recognition that religions do not reduce to textually formulated beliefs. But insofar as the scholar of rituals remains an objective or "outside" observer, the practice of this scholarship differs from the engaged practice at the heart of the alternative mode of understanding I call for. Anthropologists like Barbara Tedlock try to negotiate this difference in modes of understanding by practicing a kind of observant participation, described in Tedlock (1992, xiii). Wright (2008) articulates the limits of the observers' understanding of how rituals function internally for practitioners. I present an

alternative to the opposition between outsider and insider, between "objective understanding" and the stance of the believer, in Maraldo (2003).
25 The expanded version of this chapter, in Cornille and Conway (2010: 106–10) gives details of this exchange.
26 I elaborate on the alternative notion of practice in Maraldo (2009).
27 The linguist Sandra J. Savignon (1997, 35) writes, "*C'est en forgeant que l'on devient forgeron.* Just as one learns to be a blacksmith by being a blacksmith, one learns to communicate by communicating. Or, to put it differently, one develops skills by using skills. It is only when we have an incentive to communicate and the experience of communication that structures are acquired. In this sense, then, one might speak of going *from communicative competence to grammatical competence.*"
28 Insofar as this mode of practice begins with embodied attentiveness, the "second nature" it induces essentially differs from that induced by Pierre Bourdieu's sense of *habitus* or interiorized social dispositions and structures, as well as from Alfred Lorenzer's sense of "unconscious forms of interaction anchored in the body." See the chapter by Rainer Winter in this volume, pp. 71–86.
29 There are notable similarities between this alternative understanding and Michael Polyani's notion of tacit knowledge, which he developed as the core of an alternative epistemology.

References

Agar, Michael (1994), *Language Shock: Understanding the Culture of Conversation*. New York: William Morrow.
Carpenter, David (1992), "Bhartrihari and the Veda," in Jeffrey R. Timm (ed.), *Texts in Context: Traditional Hermeneutics in South Asia*. Albany, NY: State University of New York Press, 16–32.
Cornille, Catherine (2008), *The Im-possibility of Interreligious Dialogue*. New York: Crossroad Publishing Company.
Cornille, Catherine and Christopher Conway (eds.) (2010), *Interreligious Hermeneutics*. Eugene, OR: Cascade Books.
Fitzgerald, Timothy (1997), "A Critique of 'Religion' as a Cross-cultural Category," *Method & Theory in the Study of Religion* 9/2, 91–110.
Hans-Georg Gadamer, Hans-Georg (1965), *Wahrheit und Methode*. Tübingen: J.C.B. Mohr, 2nd edition.
Heidegger, Martin (1963), *Sein und Zeit* (Tübingen: Max Niemeyer Verlag. Trans. By Joan Stambaugh (1996), *Being and Time*. Albany NY: State University of New York Press.
Heidegger, Martin (1976), *The Piety of Thinking*, trans., notes, and commentary by James G. Hart and John C. Maraldo. Bloomington, IN: Indiana University Press.
Josephson, Jason Ananda (2012), *The Invention of Religion in Japan*. Chicago: University of Chicago Press.
King, Richard (1999). *Orientalism and Religion: Post-Colonial Theory, Indian, and the 'Mystic East.'* London: Routledge.
Kögler, Hans-Herbert (1996), *The Power of Dialogue: Critical Hermeneutics after Gadamer and Foucault*. Cambridge, MS: The MIT Press.
Kögler, Hans-Herbert (2017), "The Religious Face of Evil. Ethics and the Critique of Religion," *Berlin Journal of Critical Theory* 1/2, 21–46.

Kögler, Hans-Herbert (2020), "Tradition, Transcendence, and the Public Sphere: A Hermeneutic Critique of Religion," *Berlin Journal of Critical Theory* 4/2 (July 2020), 107–46.
Levering, Miriam (ed.) (1988), *Rethinking Scripture: Essays from a Comparative Perspective*. Albany NY: State University of New York Press.=
Maraldo, John C. (1974 and 1984), *Der hermeneutische Zirkel: Untersuchungen zu Schleiermacher, Dilthey und Heidegger*. Freiburg: Karl Alber Verlag.
Maraldo, John C. (2003), "Can Scholars Understand Zen? A Re-examination of the Opposition between Objective Scholarship and Religious Practice," in H. Eisenhofer-Halim (ed.), *Wandel zwischen den Welten: Festschrift für Johannes Laube*. Frankfurt, Berlin, New York, and Oxford: Peter Lang, 439–50.
Maraldo, John C. (2009), "An Alternative Notion of Practice in the Promise of Japanese Philosophy," in Lam Wing-keung and Cheng Ching-yuen (eds.), *Facing the 21st Century: Frontiers in Japanese Philosophy 4*. Nagoya: Nanzan Institute for Religion and Culture, 7–21.
McCutcheon, Russell T. (2001), *Manufacturing Religion: The Discourse on Sui Generis Religion and the Politics of Nostalgia*. Oxford and New York: Oxford University Press.
Moyaert, Marianne (2010), "Absorption or Hospitality: Two Approaches to the Tension between Identity and Alterity," in Catherine Cornille and Christopher Conway (eds.), *Interreligious Hermeneutics*. Eugene, OR: Cascade Books, 61–88.
Ricoeur, Paul (1974), *The Conflict of Interpretations: Essays in Hermeneutics*. Evanston IL: Northwestern University Press.
Ricoeur, Paul (1976), *Interpretation Theory: Discourse and the Surplus of Meaning*. Fort Worth: the Texas Christian University Press.
Ricoeur, Paul (1983), "On Interpretation," trans. Kathleen McLaughlin, in Alan Montefiore (ed.), *Philosophy in France Today*. Cambridge: Cambridge University Press.
Savignon, Sandra (1997). *Communicative Competence: Theory and Classroom Practice*, 2nd ed. New York: McGraw-Hill.
Tedlock, Barbara (1992), *The Beautiful and the Dangerous: Dialogues with the Zuni Indians*. New York: Penguin Books.
Wittgenstein, Ludwig (1968), *Philosophical Investigations*, trans. G.E.M. Anscombe. Oxford: Basil Blackwell.
Wright, Dale (2008), "Introduction: Rethinking Ritual Practice in Zen Buddhism," in Steven Heine and Dale S. Wright (eds.), *Zen Ritual: Studies of Zen Buddhist Theory in Practice*. New York: Oxford University Press, 3–19.

Part Three

Toward a Critical Hermeneutics of the Present

8

The Ontology of the Present and the Tasks of a Future Sociology

Frédéric Vandenberghe

No one knows whether a new Parsons, Habermas or Luhmann will appear. The fact is that, in sociology, we no longer have a general theory of society capable of integrating the philosophical foundations (metatheory), the elaboration of a system of fundamental concepts (social theory) and a reflection on the structural transformations of modernity (sociological theory) into a single theory that would be at once general, systematic and historical. The time of Grand Theories seems to be over. Philosophers like Hans-Herbert Kögler continue to work out the foundations of a critical hermeneutics that would be capable of objectivating the social constraints that structure social practices without derogation of the lay actors' reflexive capabilities, but in sociology, at least in French and American sociology, theoretical work is hardly encouraged. It is enough to venture off the field to indulge in the pleasures of speculation, systematization or axiomatization to exclude oneself from the language game of sociology and to jeopardize one's career prospects.

While this chapter is written in homage to a German scholar who has worked at the intersection of critical theory and hermeneutics, I will mainly focus here on the discipline of sociology.[1] In the following pages, I would like to suggest a double shift. First, from the discipline of sociology to a new synthesis of the social sciences, philosophy and the new humanities and, second, from sociology's glorious past to the analysis of the present. What is important now is no longer to know what sociology is or does, but rather to try to interpret the events that are destroying societies around the world and pushing them toward the abyss, catastrophe and death. As Karl Mannheim, Theodor W. Adorno, and Talcott Parsons did in the interwar period, today, we must urgently revise and update our research agendas. Foreign colleagues (Russians, Indians, Turks, etc.) who, like me, live under an authoritarian regime (I live in Brazil) did not wait for the coronavirus pandemic to give lectures on current events. Against the background of a triple crisis—the crises of society, modernity and sociology (Macé 2020), I will propose the ontology of the present as an undisciplined reflection on the second postmodernity. In dialogue with Hans-Herbert Kögler, I will foreground questions of communication between disciplines, but also occasionally between the metropolis and former colonies.

Landscapes of Sociology

A new alliance between philosophy, the social sciences and the humanities is needed (Caillé and Vandenberghe 2021). As sociologists are not really interested in philosophy or in the human sciences, the latter two should perhaps take up the lead and propose a theoretically informed diagnosis of the age.[2] It is time again to join the analysis of the conjuncture to a critical analysis of social pathologies in a totalizing interpretation of the epoch. In sociology, theory no longer has a good press, though. It is considered too airy and too abstract. For sociologists, theory refers to a kind of synthetic reorganization of the themes that transcends the different points of view on a certain field of research (culture, class, consumption, social movements, etc.) one finds in the specialized literature of the various sub-disciplines of sociology (sociology of education, work, stratification, etc.). What is missing, it seems to me, is a rise to generality that does not so much try to reorganize the materials of research in a sociological theory of the middle range, but rather reorganizes and synthesizes these in a general theory of society.

The variation of scales of generality and the extension of the range of theorizing are important, because by varying the resolution of the different approaches to reality—moving from Google Street View to Google Earth, and back—we can not only maintain continuity between the transcendental and the empirical, the abstract and the concrete, the conceptual and the observational, but we can also more easily continue the dialogue between the sub-specialists and the generalists who are the guarantors of the unity of the discipline.[3] The unity of the discipline also involves the rational reconstruction and ritual reinterpretation of the classics. In fact, this is their main function. If we return obsessively to Karl Marx, Max Weber and Emile Durkheim, it is not because they have aged well, but because the obligatory references to their work makes it possible to put new wine in old bottles and old wine in new ones. It is thus by canonization and incorporation into the disciplinary corpus that sociology maintains its coherence and closes in on itself—like an autopoetic, self-referentially closed system of sorts.

The advantage of a general theory of society is that it is "overarching"—to reclaim a term that is used to disparage totalizing approaches. Like the belvedere, it allows to widen the horizon and to see the landscape in all its extent: the mountain ranges, the valleys, the rivers that are invisible from the lower observatories only become visible from the top. Of course, the lower lookouts also allow one to see part of the landscape, including from the upper observatory that observes them. I conceive of the theorist not as the creator of the universe, but rather as the painter who can move from one belvedere to another. The beautiful metaphor of the "landscapes of truth" (Löwy 1985) is convenient, but misleading, because social reality is not static, but dynamic. Nature is not dead, but alive. History has been set in motion again. Societies are in turmoil. Culture is contested. Individuals are politicized, polarized and hyperactive, even in lockdown.

What we need is a new dynamic synthesis, like the one Karl Mannheim (1936) proposed as an alternative to the philosophy of Marxist history. In this vision of a dynamic and synthetic sociology, the painter is an unattached intellectual who floats freely between disciplines to try to understand what is happening in the world, with nature, with culture and with societies when there is no longer (or not yet) a philosophy of history. Mannheim is good example of a synthetic theorist. Coming from philosophy, his sociologies of culture, knowledge and education have incorporated the intellectual currents of his time, notably the hermeneutics of Dilthey, the phenomenology of Heidegger, the Marxism of Lukács, the sociologies of Weber and Simmel and the psychoanalysis of Freud, in a dynamic, open reflection on the existential determination of encompassing worldviews of the various social strata.

Contemporary sociology feels uncomfortable not only with theory and philosophy, but also with the spectacle of world politics and national news. Indeed, until recently, essays on the *Zeitgeist* and situational analyses were rather frowned upon—well received and welcomed as expressions of engaged citizenship, but not read as professional contributions in their own right. Interpretations of the "signature of the time" are best left, according to sociologists, to media philosophers, investigative journalists and other essayists who can speak out on a wide variety of subjects (terrorism, populism, epidemics) without discipline, data or fieldwork.

The success of "public sociology" (Burawoy 2005) does not contradict this observation, but confirms it. Successor to the critical Marxist sociology of the 1970s, it is indeed a heterodox and militant sociology, rooted in everyday life, that finds in sociology its conceptual resources to engage in the struggles of active minorities against domination, discrimination and exclusion. We see it at work in new journals, discussion forums, working groups, petitions and manifestos on a multiplicity of themes—from migrants' rights to animal rights, from identity politics to police violence, from the critique of nanotechnologies to climate change (Durand 2019). Although public and critical sociology cannot and should not occupy the entire field of the discipline, I nevertheless believe that the critical situation of society transforms every professional into an intellectual, which does not mean an activist. Maintaining standards of academic rigor is essential for a sociology that seeks to interpret and explain current events. As Bourdieu (2002) once said, scholarship and commitment are not exclusive, but inclusive. While opening up sociology to neighboring disciplines and engaging in the public sphere, sociology must maintain its autonomy as a science to defend the values that are its own—communism, universalism, disinterestedness and organized skepticism (Merton 1973)—which are threatened both by the privatization of knowledge (markets) and the return of authoritarian regimes (states).

Sociology's double malaise in relation to theory and the diagnosis of the age, its tense relationship with philosophy and journalism as "poles that should disappear from the field of a more scientifically demanding discipline" (Lahire 2002: 46, note 6) partly explain why the discipline finds itself overtaken on its borders. Nowadays, social theory is produced outside sociology. One finds it among post-Marxist philosophies ("critical theory" not so much in the municipal (Frankfurt) sense as in the ecumenical sense of the term) and also in Cultural Studies, including here specialties such as gender, media, and post-colonial studies, which break open the perspectives of old Europe by giving voice to the dominated minorities and the subaltern majorities.

Given the circumstances (the pandemic), the fluid conjuncture (populism), the geopolitical turbulence (the new cold war) and the planetary upheavals (climate change) that we are going through, one can think that, as in the 1960s and 1970s, sociology will be more historical and political, more preoccupied with an analysis of the present than with an investigation of its philosophical presuppositions and conceptual coherence. It is doubtful that it will be in the vanguard of thought in the years to come. Not that it cannot contribute to the reflection on the ontology of the present, but less than ever, it will be able to do so by turning in on itself. Only if it sees itself as an integral part of the social sciences and opens itself toward its edges, only if it succeeds in resuming the dialogue with critical theory and the Studies, as well as with philosophy, will it be up to the task. It does not matter whether this reflection on the ontology of the present is done by sociologists, anthropologists, politicians, economists or philosophers; neither does it matter whether it is science or high-level journalism. In order to make sense of the present, one must open all the registers, transcend the disciplines and read widely.

Ontology of the Present

Sociology may well go the way of metaphysics, arts and social democracy. Its end has already been announced (Vandenberghe and Fuchs 2019). It may well be more productive, though, to redefine its ends and to reconceptualize its tasks within a larger interdisciplinary compound that takes the present as its object. To launch the debate, I propose the notion of ontology of the present and conceive it as a successor (*Aufhebung*) to the sociology of late modernity. I speak of ontology of the present not by presumption, but simply to indicate with Hegel the need for a collective, interdisciplinary and unattached reflection that tries to "seize its time in thought" (Hegel 1970: 26). This is not easy to do when history is in turmoil and no one knows what the future will bring.

We are confronted with a typical "Minerva problem." As long as we are caught in the whirlwind of the present, we cannot interpret it. With the pandemic, we are finally coming out of the twentieth century. We know that an era has just ended. With the sudden resumption of events that puncture the continuum of history, epochal thought has also reached its limits. One might even think that any sociology of the future will necessarily be event-driven, which will not prevent it from analyzing historical trends, proposing diagnostic concepts (like "risk society") or projecting the present into future social change (the digitalization of work and education). To the contrary. As a science of the present, anticipating future change in times of contingency, sociology will self-consciously continue its analytic, diagnostic, and therapeutic function. In its interpretation of current events, it will use social theory to extrapolate from the present and reorganize the data in a larger conceptual framework that tries to make sense of historical disjunctures.

Henceforth, sociology will have to give more attention to local events that directly attain the structure and have systemic significance. The problem of social order: "How is society possible?—or, equally Kantian: "What are the conditions of possibility for a relatively stable social order?"—is no longer on the agenda. The question as to "what keeps society together" has been displaced by the timely question "what drives it apart" (Heitmeyer 1997). We move from the problem of integration to that of social disintegration with its spectacle of economic precarity, political polarization, cultural fragmentation, normative anomie and physical violence. Perhaps we should invert the reflection and start from the hypothesis of an original chaos that spreads throughout the world with ubiquitous pockets of relative order in an ocean of contingencies.

It may seem counter-intuitive to invoke the ontology of the present to indicate the instability and non-permanence of the world. Is ontology not the study of Being (*das Seyn*) rather than of beings (*das Seiende*) that are part of the ontic? On this point Portuguese and Spanish are more instructive than Heidegger's German. It has two verbs to designate two modalities of being: *ser,* which refers to what is permanent and intransitive, and *estar,* which refers to what is transitory, fugitive and transitive. The ontology of the present tense, as I understand it with Foucault (1984a, b), is an ontology of *estar,* of states of things that are in motion, that escape our control and befall us. In the Global South, the ontological difference is a situational and existential difference. The state of the world is never completely stable. Crisis is not the exception, but the rule. Society is not a thing, but an unstable correlation of moving forces. Institutions are not beings, but dynamic processes in a continuous process of reconstruction and destruction. Actors know that nothing is stable and that it is necessary to continually adapt and invent to survive. The force of the real finds its counterpoint in a nominalist vision of the world as a scatter of events that are not governed by God, reason or nature.

If I take the liberty of speaking, following Foucault, of an ontology of the present as a critical reflection on our "historical mode of being"—understanding "the events that have led us to become what we have become" so as open up "the possibility of no longer being, doing or thinking what we what we are, do or think" (Foucault, 1984a: 574)—it is to recall that, in the end, it is indeed the social actors who make history, even if they do not make it in the circumstances they have chosen and even if it inevitably escapes them. Together, the order of things (truth), the analytics of power (norms) and the practices of the self (subject) configure a "historical ontology of ourselves in modernity" (Kögler 1994: 9) that is susceptible to change. We need a little optimism to think that underneath the rubble there are living forces just waiting to get history back on track.

The Studies

With the emergence of disciplines in the nineteenth century, the division of labor enters into thinking. While history continues to deal with the past without fragmenting as a discipline, anthropology and sociology divide time in much the same way that colonial powers divide space (Connell 2007). Anthropology will deal with peoples without history in the colonies, while sociology will study modern societies in the metropolis. As a reflexive "self-description" (Luhmann 1994: vol. II, chap. 5) of modern societies, sociology is coextensive with modernity. The reflexivity of the sociological discourse of modernity comes from the fact that this discourse, which takes over from the philosophical discourse of modernity, is itself modern, including in its critique of modernity. Normatively, sociology presupposes and pursues the philosophical project of the Enlightenment with its entangled notions of authenticity, justice and progress. If it occasionally introduces the hermeneutics of suspicion into the philosophical discourse of modernity, it does it to better realize its ends. Conceived of from the onset as a normative and political project, its critique of society is immanent to society, which does not impede philosophers to seek to found the normative principles of critique in reason and to give them a transcendental foundation. From this hermeneutic perspective, sociology is indeed a science of reality, but it is also a science of the objective spirit that investigates the dynamic interconnection between the worldviews, the institutions and practices of an epoch that constitute society. The explanation of social structures that condition and, at times, limit the realization of the basic principles that define an age is thereby subordinated to the interpretation of the collective meaning structures that form the background of the interpretative practices of the social actors.

If I've learned anything from Kögler's critical hermeneutics and its incursions into Bourdieu's sociology (Kögler, 1997a and b) and Foucault's genealogy (Kögler, 1992 and 1996), it is that a critical theory of society needs to carefully parse its conceptual articulations between the social structure, culture and subjectivity, with culture being the mediator that connects the social conditions to the social practices. Without a solid concept of structure and social systems, social theory becomes idealistic and looses its critical edge (as is the case with the philosophical hermeneutics of Heidegger and Gadamer); without an adequate conception of culture and symbolism, it becomes mechanistic and deterministic (as is the case with Althusser, Bourdieu and Foucault); without a convincing theory of practices, social and cultural structures are reified into anonymous processes without subjects (as is the case with Horkheimer and Adorno).

Sociology is born with modernity and we can assume that it will disappear with it. It bears the marks of its origins in European societies shaken by the religious revolutions of the sixteenth century (Germany), the scientific revolutions of the seventeenth century (England), the political revolutions of the eighteenth century (France) and the industrial revolutions of the nineteenth century (England). Even though the first modernity developed on the Iberian Peninsula with the opening of the Atlantic Ocean and the discovery of the New World (Dussel 1993), sociology was not born in the sixteenth century in southern Europe, but in the nineteenth century in northern Europe.

Looking back at the history of sociology, we can distinguish at least five generations that have succeeded one another. Each generation was deeply marked by the events of its time: i) the "precursors" (Auguste Comte, Herbert Spencer and Karl Marx, who can also be seen as the first of the classics) who positioned themselves in relation to the revolutions of 1789 and 1848; ii) the "classics" (Max Weber, Emile Durkheim and Georg Simmel) who lived through the fin-de-siècle and were shattered by the brutality of the First World War; iii) the "successors" (Talcott Parsons, Norbert Elias and Karl Mannheim) who experienced the rise of totalitarianism and the return to democracy in Europe; iv) the "contemporaries" (Pierre Bourdieu, Jürgen Habermas, Niklas Luhmann and Anthony Giddens) of the world revolution of 1968, and then us, the "post-moderns" who are emerging from the twentieth century.

We did not become postmodern out of principle, but out of necessity. It is because we have quite suddenly shifted into a new epoch that we have come to accept the post-modernism(s) and poststructuralism(s) of yesteryear. Even though we may have opposed at first the dissemination of French Theory (Foucault, Derrida, Deleuze) and the proliferation of the Studies that were inspired by them, it must be said that with their insolent youth they have succeeded in capturing the *Zeitgeist* better than sociology, with which they share sensitivity for domination, exclusion and discrimination. For, in fact, although they are themselves symptoms of the crisis, the Studies have succeeded in introducing the crisis into philosophy, anthropology and the humanities. Where sociology was looking for society, they were directly linked to the new social movements and analyzed the production of culture and identities from the perspective of the interrelation of knowledge, power and resistance. In doing so, they forced the older disciplines to open up to current events and to renew critique beyond Marxism.

By pulling the rug from under the epistemic foundations of the disciplines, by showing their complicity with domination, by following new technological developments, by directly attacking societal problems and by speaking on behalf of active minorities, the new humanities have surpassed critical theory in their analyses and diagnoses of the ontology of the present (Kögler 2017). By deconstructing all the fundamental concepts of the old disciplines—the reason of the philosophers, the culture of the anthropologists, the text of the humanists, the society of the sociologists—the in(ter)disciplines have introduced plurality, fracture and disjunction into the discussion and put thought under tension. The Studies have entered the fields of philosophy (the critique of reason), anthropology (the study of cultures and communities) and sociology (the study of class and mass societies), and they've done so coming from the humanities. Thanks to a poststructuralist sensibility, they have been able to generalize the Marxist critique of exploitation to all forms of domination and broadened the spectrum of cultural analysis beyond class to race, caste, gender and sexuality. They have invaded the spaces of sociology and anthropology, criticizing their approaches, capturing their themes, but often without reciprocating. The result is the emergence of the in(ter)disciplines of the Studies with their own authors and their own journals that generally escape the eye of the sociologist and the philosopher. One need only look at the new journals and bibliographies of cultural, feminist and post-colonial studies to realize that they do not need sociology to speak about social and societal issues.

Why should sociologists accompany debates on gender, race, caste, sex, colonialism, etc.? Because students demand it and activists too? Yes, that is a good reason, especially when one is on the left and identifies with the critical and civic part of sociology. To answer this question satisfactorily, it would also be necessary to reverse the question and to show how the Studies could also benefit and learn from sociology. Here, as elsewhere, there is only one solution: listen, learn, read and teach, all this in the dialogical spirit that characterizes the hermeneutic encounter with the other that is at the very heart of all of Hans-Herbert Kögler's writings, from his first book on Gadamer, Foucault and Rorty to his later reflections on intercultural dialogue and self-identity. If we transpose the "ethos of hermeneutic dialogue" (Kögler 2007) from intercultural understanding to interdisciplinary communication, there's no reason to assume that understanding across and between the disciplines will necessarily fail. It is only by opening up our own understanding to the self-understanding of the other, that learning can occur through discussion, reading and writing. The self-understanding of the self thanks to the other transforms the self. Reciprocity is a mutual process of learning and discovery that expands the limits of one's world and of one's self. One cannot read everything, of course, but neither can one close oneself off to everything and limit oneself to one's own discipline by claiming that the Studies don't do science, but radical politics; that in the name of the struggle against racism and patriarchy, they bring back essentialist conceptions of race and gender; that they proclaim an inverted anti-white, anti-Western racism and that victimhood, vindication and resentment should have no place in academia.[4] So where does all this fear of the Studies come from? Why this violent rejection and all these diatribes against feminism, anti-racism and post-colonialism that one can see as the Studies are now arriving at last in France? Have we really learned nothing from Stuart Hall, Judith Butler or Achille Mbembe?

Take *Brutalism*, the latest book by the Cameroonian philosopher Achille Mbembe (2020). He proposes a theory of the reification, demolition and carbonization of human bodies and criticizes the convergence of the instrumental and utilitarian reason of neoliberal government technologies, the electronic and digital reason of information capitalism and the biological and neurological reason of biotechnology in a *mathesis universalis* that erases the ontological distinction between living beings and machines, humans and things. To support his thesis of the artificial future of humanity in the new era of brutalism, which he analyzes from the vantage point of Africa, he discusses drones, bombs, refugee camps, mining, biotechnology, governmentality, animism and African masks with a perfectly updated bibliography on capitalism, the Anthropocene, populism, migration flows, torture, big data, etc. coming from a multiplicity of disciplines (philosophy, sociology, anthropology, geography, law, literature) and hybrid fields (technology and literature, agnotology and algorithms, architecture and archives). This is very much critical theory at the edge, not coming from Frankfurt though, but from the suburbs of Johannesburg.

As the Studies proliferated, their development was accelerated by a rapid succession of anti-paradigmatic "turns" (Bachmann-Medick 2016) that at first radicalized the linguistic and interpretative turns, but then increasingly opposed themselves to the linguistic turn, trying to revert to a pre-Kantian universe in which one would be able to access the "things in themselves" without any symbolic mediation. Whereas the Studies seek to go beyond the straitjacket of disciplines, the turns follow an artistic logic—it is necessary to be "absolutely modern," to innovate and to introduce each time a new revolution in the sciences that captures the attention and radicalizes the previous turn. In general, the turns take a theme (language, culture, practice, affects, etc.) and transform it into a perspective that transforms and transfigures reality. Since Richard Rorty's announcement of the linguistic turn in 1969, some sixty turns (and counting) have been proclaimed. We can distinguish four "moments" and as many "intellectual movements" that have attempted to disarticulate and revolutionize philosophy, anthropology and the human sciences: the linguistic and cultural turns (1960–70), the postmodern and poststructuralist turns (1970–80), the global and post-colonial turns (1990–2000) and, finally, the practical, ontological and speculative turns (2000–20).

As in the case of the Studies, it would be just as wrong to ignore them as to follow them all. The drift of the turns, twists, and returns is not uninteresting, however. Let us take as an example the "affective turn" (Vandenberghe 2017). Coming after the practice turn in contemporary theory, the affective turn is one more turn within the poststructuralist movement that opposes the constructivism of cultural studies (all tendencies included) and challenges all forms of representation. Unlike emotions, which are culturally constructed, affects are visceral, infinitesimal and molecular. They are sensations and vital pulsations that pass through the body, yet escape consciousness. They are flows that are at once infraindividual, intimate and transpersonal. Like viruses, they are contagious, pass from one organism to another and, like fear and excitement, affect them collectively, making them act as a single super-organism. With its vitalism, panpsychism and animism, the affective turn joins the sensitivity of the new anthropologies and its descriptive metaphysics (Latour, Descola, Viveiros de Castro, etc.). The question for a hermeneutically inspired theory of practices is whether the affects can really be disconnected from all processes of representation and signification? Affects may be pre-conscious and infra-linguistic, but as we've learned from Heidegger, Scheler and Merleau-Ponty that does not mean that as intentional states of the body and pre-predicative moments of consciousness they cannot be brought into language or that they are not always already pre-formed at a deeper level by a practical (*Vorhabe*), visual (*Vorsicht*) and preconceptual (*Vorgriff*) background of interpretation (Kögler 1991: 70–8 and Kögler 2000). The relation between the body and the mind, the intention and the execution, the pre-predicative and the linguistic is not disjunctive. It is not a broken arc, but a dynamic circle that interrelates the elements of the continuum into living chiasm.

While anthropology has been hard hit by cultural studies and post-colonial critiques, it has emerged renewed and resourced (Comaroff 2010). Sociology for its part has not experienced any notable crisis since the 1970s. Certainly, it has gone through its chapel wars, and for a brief moment, it had some doubts about its "methodological nationalism," but otherwise it has continued to professionalize while positioning itself more clearly on the left, not only on questions of class, gender, and race, but also on other themes such as the definition of populism, social welfare, animal rights, new forms of family, police violence, etc. (Durand 2019). Now the crisis is also affecting sociology; however, it is not an endogenous crisis. It is because societies worldwide have gone off the rails and are facing deep crises that sociology is also panicking. The upheavals of recent years are so radical; societies are in such a bad way and social change is so rapid that sociology is overwhelmed by current events and struggles to grasp the present with its concepts of the recent past. The gap between the experiences of the past that are crystallized into its concepts and theories on the one hand and the horizon of expectations that open up a future on the other has become a gaping chasm. To bridge it, sociology will need the assistance of the Studies. With their poststructuralist insistence on discontinuity, they are more sensitive to epochal ruptures.

The Second Postmodernity

It is true that as early as the 1980s, sociologists had taken the measure of the structural, cultural and technological transformations of their societies. They were well aware that their theories of the 1960s were no longer useful for thinking adequately about the societies at the turn of the century. In response to the theories of postmodernity, they called for the development of a sociological theory of "late modernity" that would analyze in a more sober way the effects of the cultural, structural and societal changes that took place after 1968 and that tipped Western societies into a new phase of modernity, if not into a new type of civilization (Bonny 2004). With the crisis of 1973 and the election of Thatcher and Reagan, the conjunction of Fordism and Keynesianism of the post-war was slowly undone. The state began to retract in favor of the markets. The new information and communication technologies made their appearance. Henceforth, economies would be liberal, societies post-industrial, cultures post-modern and subjects highly individualized.

In the 1990s, following the fall of the Berlin Wall, the controversy about postmodernism and postmodernity was relayed by the Great Globalization Debate (Held et al., 1999). Initially, the debate centered on the economy (the deregulation of markets, the rise of transnational corporations, financialization), politics (the decline of the state, transnational connections, cosmopolitanism) and technology (information technology, the network society). Soon it expanded to encompass all dimensions of existence (law, culture, identity, subjectivity). The rise of emerging countries (the so-called Brics) subsequently challenged Eurocentrism and the evolutionism of inherited theories. Global Studies emerged as a specialized field of study with its own constantly updated bibliographies.[5]

In order to understand the state of the world, one must not only decenter and "deprovincialize," one must also "undiscipline" oneself and open all disciplinary windows at the same time. Moreover, in the Global South, it is not so much a question of "deprovincializing" Euro-American metropolitan theories as of "reprovincializing" them. Reprovincialization implies that one tests them on terrains they could not foresee, confronts them with life worlds that reveal their limits, dismounts and remounts them in order to reterritorialize them. Let's take just two examples to illustrate the conceptual challenges the social theorist faces in the postcolony. Foucault's analysis of surveillance and prisons does not work in a context of violence that remains scarred by the experience of slavery. It's true that unlike Habermas, Foucault has a few texts on colonization, but they are not sufficient to think through the colonization of the life-world in the strict sense of the term. Moreover, the problem of reification in developing countries is often compounded by the reverse problem of patrimonialism whereby the domestic sphere corrupts and corrodes the administrative and economic systems from within. And when a sanitary crisis comes on top of a political, economic and military crisis, the legitimation crisis of late fascism transforms the life world into a biopolitical world of death and denial (Vandenberghe 2020).

The critique of globalization and the emergence of a global civil society that contests the neoliberal hegemony suggested that another world would be possible. It was the time of the World Social Forum, the anti-globalization movement and a renewal of cosmopolitanism. Then, suddenly, in 2001, with the spectacular Al Qaeda attack in New York, the world tipped into violence. The Middle East (Iraq, Syria, Libya, Yemen) was set ablaze as the Balkans had once been, unleashing a global civil war. In 2008, the subprime crisis exposed the fragility of the world economy. Neo-liberalism was ideologically delegitimized, but by imposing a policy of austerity, it became all the more operational. The election of Trump in 2016 came like a meteor that destabilized the course of the world. National-populism progressed and the extreme right gradually established itself on every continent. Just as the urgency of an ecological transition imposed itself on everyone in the developed countries, the pandemic spread through the world, heralding new, more sober and darker times.

Our great theories of late modernity, post-Fordism and post-industrialism are valid only until 2000, at most until 2007. Not that they are false, but the analyses of Wallerstein, Habermas, Giddens, Beck, Castells, Boltanski et al. need to be updated, if not completely reformulated. To sharpen the mind, I propose to call the present era the "second postmodernity." It emerges in the ruins of the first postmodernity. The latter was characterized by the radical questioning of the culture of modernity. Now it is the structures of the system that are collapsing in real time. With hindsight, we now understand that postmodernism was a swan song of the West and that the cracking of the cultural code of modernity was only the opening phase of a prolonged process of global systemic drift. This time the change is "real." It is not only the culture of modernity that is fragmenting and diffracting. The second postmodernity means that the very structures of the global system are unraveling. Chaos can spread from the center to the periphery of the world-system, reorganizing geopolitics and unfolding from the economic and political subsystems to all spheres of social, cultural, and personal life. "The old is dying, the new cannot be born: during this interregnum we observe the most varied morbid phenomena" (Gramsci 1996: 283).

To this well-known quotation from Gramsci, we can add another equally classic one concerning the need to combine "the pessimism of the intellect" with "the optimism of the will" (the motto of the magazine *Ordine Nuovo* echoes the more romantic and mystical motto of Romain Rolland from whom Gramsci borrowed it). It is understood that it is necessary to keep the optimism of the intellect while avoiding the pessimism of the will. A lucid diagnosis of the ontology of the present is only possible if one allows oneself to think "without hope" and to act "with love." It is because we know that there is a local solution that we can confront the global situation, which does not have one. As Bruno Latour (2015: 22) says about the ecological crisis, "we are not in a crisis. It's not going to 'pass'. We're going to have to get used to it. It is definitive."

In order to grasp the ontology of the present, we must try to build a system of relatively stable and interconnected concepts that come from different disciplines and thematize, each in their own way, a critical problematic of the present at a level of generality that transcends the more specialized discussions of political economy, political science and ecology. The concepts chosen are neoliberalism, populism, and Anthropocene.[6] These are not really concepts or analytical categories, but rather politically charged and expressively colored notions on which leftist intellectuals project, as in a Rorschach test, their anxieties and phantasms. One must take the three notions together and explore how the permutations can vary and form a system. The point of the exercise is twofold: on the one hand, to explore in conjunction the "great transformation" of neoliberalism (Polanyi 1957), the "great regression" of populism (Geiselberger 2017) and the "great acceleration" of the Anthropocene (Steffen et al., 2015) and, on the other hand, to analyze their interrelationships which, initially, are contingent, but which have ended up converging into a morbid syndrome.

It is therefore necessary to take them together without reductionism and without giving oneself the facilities of a Marxism that solves the equation (neoliberalism-capitalocene-fascism), but does not question itself. Neoliberalism and populism are interconnected. The anti-democratic liberalism of markets provokes the rejection of globalization and the adherence to illiberal democracy. Together, the markets and the populists who oppose them reinforce the entropic tendencies that lead to ecological catastrophe, the former by stimulating growth, consumption and international travel; the latter by denying the problem and supporting heavy industry and economic growth at any price.

For three centuries, societies have been trying to solve an equation with two terms: capitalism and democracy. We know that there is a tension, if not a real contradiction, between the two. The historical link between democracy and capitalism is contingent. It has been tied and untied many times before. Now, as in the interwar period, it is unraveling again, probably for the same reasons that Polanyi indicated in his analysis of the collapse of nineteenth-century civilization. It seems that capitalism can do without democracy, just as democracy can do without liberalism. The good news is that, officially, we are still in the Holocene. But the theme of the Anthropocene indicates that from now on there will no longer be two terms, but three: capitalism, democracy and sustainability (Jaïz 2020). One would like to believe that humanity only ever poses itself the problems it can solve, but when it is humanity itself that poses the problem, one must step back and reflect how one could possibly rebuild the social sciences, societies and technology with the help of the humanities and philosophy.

Notes

1   Some of the ideas of this chapter find their origin in a doctoral seminar "Ontology of the Present: Neoliberalism, Anthropocene, Populism" which I taught at the Federal University of Rio de Janeiro in 2019. The collapse of Brazil under the extreme right government of Jair Messias Bolsonaro forms the background of my reflections on the past, present and future of sociology. An earlier version of this text was written in French and published in the *Revue du Mauss*, 2020, no. 56. I thank Ľubomír Dunaj and Kurt Mertel for their encouragement and insistence.
2   *Zeitdiagnose* is a typically German genre at the intersection of the social sciences and the humanities that addresses itself to the general public to critically interpret the signature of the epoch. See Lichtblau, 2017 for a general overview of the genre, from Georg Simmel and Hans Freyer to Ulrich Beck. For a more systemic approach that brilliantly theorizes the reflexive relation between sociology and the diagnostic self-descriptions of society, see Nassehi 2001.
3   The notion of the "variations of generality" has been obtained through a fusion of the "variations of scale" of the micro-historians (Revel 1996) with the rise to generality of the French pragmatists (Boltanski and Thévenot 1991).
4   Post-colonial studies may have arrived in France with a delay of quarter of a century, its rejection has been rather swift, visceral and irrational. For a coordinated attack by leftwing republicans on the identity politics of race, see the Observatory of decolonialism and identitarian ideologies (http://decolonialisme.fr) and the spirited reply by Mbembe (2020).

5   Global Studies are not part of Cultural Studies, although research on pop and post culture in different parts of the world may be included. Global Studies is concerned with "world governance" at the transnational level and is situated at the intersection of international relations, international political economy, international law and area studies. Critical Global Studies deals with the same issues, but from a Third World perspective that explores the contradictions of global capitalism and the alternatives that come from the South.
6   They are not concepts, but folders in which a large quantity of texts on the main current topics are arranged to guide the discussion. The approach should be further broadened to include geopolitics, international relations and the new technologies of warfare, the new information and communication technologies of digital capitalism and the political psychology of the new "authoritarian personality."

References

Bachmann-Medick, B. (2016), *Cultural Turns. New Orientations in the Study of Culture*. Berlin: De Gruyter.
Boltanski, L. and Thévenot, L. (1991), *De la justification. Les économies de la grandeur*, Paris: Gallimard.
Bonny, Y. (2004), *Sociologie du temps présent. Modernité avancée ou postmodernité?*, Paris: A. Colin.
Bourdieu, P. (2002), "Pour un savoir engagé," *Le Monde diplomatique*, n° 575, février: 3.
Burawoy, M. (2005), "For Public Sociology," *American Sociological Review*, 70 (1): 4–28.
Caillé, A. and Vandenberghe, F. (2021), *For a New Classical Sociology. A Proposition, followed by a Debate*, London: Routledge.
Comaroff, J. (2010), "The End of Anthropology, Again: On the Future of an In/Discipline," *American Anthropologist*, 12 (4): 524–38.
Connell, R. (2007), *Southern Theory. The Global Dynamics of Knowledge in Social Science*, Cambridge: Polity Press.
Djaiz, D. (2020), "Capitalisme, démocratie, soutenabilité: L'impossible équation?," *Le Débat*, 209 (2): 143–54.
Durand, J.-M. (2019), *Homo intellectus. Une enquête (hexagonale) sur une espèce en voie de réinvention*, Paris: La Découverte.
Dussel, E. (1993), "Europa, modernidad y eurocentrismo," pp. 41–53 in E. Lander (ed.): *La colonialidad del saber: eurocentrismo y ciencias sociales. Perspectivas latinoamericanas*, Buenos Aires: Clacso.
Foucault, M. (1984a), "Qu'est-ce que les Lumières?," in *Dits et Ecrits*, Tome IV (texte n°339): 562–78, Paris: Gallimard.
Foucault, M. (1984b), "Qu'est-ce que les Lumières?," in *Dits et Ecrits* Tome IV (texte n°351): 679–88, Paris: Gallimard.
Geiselberger, H. (2017), *Die große Regression. Eine internationale Debatte über die geistige Situation der Zeit*, Berlin: Suhrkamp.
Gramsci, A. (1971), *Selections from the Prison Notebooks*, New York: International Publishers.
Heitmeyer, W. (ed.) (1997), *Was treibt die Gesellschaft auseinander?*, Frankfurt am Main: Suhrkamp.
Held, D. et al. (1999), *Global Transformations. Politics, Economics, and Culture*, Cambridge: Polity Press.

Kögler, H.-H. (1991), *Die Macht des Dialogs. Kritische Hermeneutik nach Gadamer, Foucault und Rorty*, Stuttgart: J.B. Metzler.
Kögler, H.-H. (1994), *Michel Foucault*, Stuttgart: Metzler.
Kögler, H.-H. (1996), "The Self-Empowered Subject. Habermas, Foucault and Hermeneutic Reflexivity," *Philosophy and Social Criticism*, 22 (4): 13–44.
Kögler, H.-H. (1997a), "Alienation as Epistemological Source: Reflexivity and Social Background after Mannheim and Bourdieu," *Social Epistemology*, 11 (2): 141–64.
Kögler, H.-H. (1997b), "Reconceptualizing Reflexive Sociology: A Reply," *Social Epistemology*, 11 (2): 223–50.
Kögler, H.-H. (2000), "Empathy, Dialogical Self, and Reflexive Interpretation: The Symbolic Source of Simulation," pp. 194–221 in H.-H. Kögler and K. Stueber (eds.): *Empathy and Agency. The Problem of Understanding in the Human Sciences*, Boulder: Westview Press.
Kögler, H.-H. (2007), "Roots of Recognition: Cultural Identity and the Ethos of Hermeneutic Dialogue," pp. 353–71 in *Proceedings of the International Wittgenstein Symposium*, Kirchberg: Ontos Publishing House.
Kögler, H.-H. (2017), "A Critical Hermeneutics of Agency: Cultural Studies as Critical Social Theory," in B. Babich (ed.): *Philosophical Approaches to Social Science*, Berlin: de Gruyter.
Lahire, B. (2002), "Utilité. Entre sociologie expérimentale et sociologie sociale," pp. 43–66 in B. Lahire (dir.), *À quoi sert la sociologie?*, Paris: La Découverte.
Latour, B. (2015), *Face à Gaïa. Huit conférences sur le nouveau régime climatique*, Paris: La Découverte.
Lichtblau, K. (2017), *Zwischen Klassik und Moderne. Die Modernität der klassiken deutschen Soziologie*, Wiesbaden: Springer.
Luhmann, N. (1994), *Die Gesellschaft der Gesellschaft*, Frankfurt am Main: Suhrkamp.
Macé, É. (2020), *Après la société. Manuel de sociologie augmentée*, Lormont: Le bord de l'eau.
Mannheim, K. (1936), *Ideology and Utopia: An Introduction to the Sociology of Knowledge*. London: Routledge & Kegan.
Mbembe, A. (2020), *Brutalisme*, Paris: La Découverte.
Mbembe, A. (2020), "Pourquoi ont-ils tous peur du postcolonial?," *AOC Média*, 21 janvier.
Merton, R.K. (1973), "The Normative Structure of Science," pp. 267–78 in *The Sociology of Science, Theoretical and Empirical Investigations*, Chicago: University of Chicago Press.
Nassehi, A. (2001), "Gesellschaftstheorie und Zeitdiagnose. Soziologie als gesellschaftliche Selbstbeschreibung," pp. 551–71 in C. Bohn and H. Willems (eds.): *Sinngeneratoren. Fremd und Selbstthematisierungen in soziologisch-historischer Perspektive*, Konstanz: UvK.
Polanyi, K. (1957), *The Great Transformation*, Boston: Beacon Press.
Revel, J. ed. (1996), *Jeux d'échelles: La micro-analyse de l'expérience*, Paris: Gallimard.
Steffen, W. et al. (2015), "The Trajectory of the Anthropocene: The Great Acceleration," *The Anthropocene Review*, 2 (1): 81–98.
Vandenberghe, F. (2017), "To be or not to be affected," Newsletter *Society and Emotions* (TG8/ISA), (2) August: 10–17.
Vandenberghe, F. and Fuchs, S. (2019), "On the Coming End of Sociology," *Canadian Review of Sociology*, 56 (1): 138–43.
Vandenberghe, F. (2020), "Demokratur in Brasilien. Versuch einer Lehre vom Systemzusammenbruch," *Leviathan. Berliner Zeitschrift für Sozialwissenschaft*, 48 (4): 637–65.

9

Cherche pas à Comprendre

Cosmopolitan Hermeneutics in Difficult Times

William Outhwaite

"Freilich unsere Gegenwart macht es uns nicht leicht, sie zu lieben..." (It is admittedly hard to feel affection for our present time)—Stefan Zweig, "Geschichte als Dichterin," summer 1939.[1]

Introduction

Hans-Herbert Kögler's unique place in the recent history of critical hermeneutics is based, I think, on two related aspects of his work: his mediation between German and French traditions and his emphasis on dialogue. To begin with the first aspect, he is one of a surprisingly small number of scholars who took seriously the need to relate what we might call the "German interface" between hermeneutics and critical theory, marked by the work of Karl-Otto Apel and Jürgen Habermas in the 1960s and the 1971 exchange between Habermas and Gadamer, to the contemporaneous intellectual scene in France, shaped in particular by Michel Foucault both before and after his tragically early death in 1984.

Jürgen Habermas's exchange with Hans-Georg Gadamer in the late 1960s and early 1970s (Apel et al., 1971) is one of his more substantial, along with those with Niklas Luhmann (who had been Adorno's temporary replacement) (Habermas and Luhmann 1971), and later, in the 1990s, with John Rawls (Finlayson and Freyenhagen 2011). These contrast with the largely missed opportunities to engage with Michel Foucault, Jean-François Lyotard, Jacques Derrida (until close to the end of his life), and Pierre Bourdieu. Even in the exchange with Gadamer, although they were personally friendly and Gadamer had encouraged Habermas's career in a variety of ways and played an important part in his conception of interpretative social science (Müller-Doohm 2016: 95–100), they tend to exaggerate aspects of each other's positions, with Gadamer stressing Habermas's "leftism" and Habermas Gadamer's "conservatism."

It is worth remembering that Habermas's initial discussion, in *Zur Logik der Sozialwissenschaften* (1967), formed part of an argument about interpretive sociology which moved from Alfred Schütz's "phenomenological sociology" through Peter Winch's Wittgensteinian reworking of idealist hermeneutics, and invoked Gadamer in the service of what Habermas presented more fully in *Erkenntnis und Interesse*: a critique of the "latent positivism" of Wilhelm Dilthey's hermeneutics (Harrington 2001). The phenomenological and linguistic variants of interpretive sociology are, however, Habermas argued, vulnerable to a broadly based hermeneutic critique which argues, in essence, that their conception of meaning is too restricted and that they do not do justice to the hermeneutic basis of social theory. Symbolic interactionism, for example, focuses, as the term implies, on interaction; consequently, structural aspects of social life are overlooked. In the "phenomenological" tradition, the focus is on interpretations of reality, the relation between different typifications, with the result that the whole enterprise comes to resemble a sociology of knowledge and, in Peter Berger and Thomas Luckmann's *Social Construction of Reality* (1966), is explicitly presented as such. The approach recommended by Winch and following Wittgenstein brings out more sharply one of the problems which arise here: a "form of life" with its associated view of the world is not a cab which one can get in and out of at will. The hermeneutic process is not the replacement of the interpreter's "horizon" by that of the object of study, but a dialogical process in which the two horizons are fused.

So far so good, from Gadamer's point of view; where they diverge is with Habermas's critique of what he called "the hermeneutic claim to universality." The upshot of the hermeneutic critique of interpretive sociology is that it must broaden its concept of meaning and recognize the importance of interactively constructed frameworks of meaning. In other words, hermeneutic theorists object to an exclusively subject–object-focused conception of science. Yet even a broadened hermeneutic approach is not enough on its own. "Hermeneutic consciousness remains incomplete as long as it does not include a reflection upon the limits of hermeneutic understanding" (Habermas 1988: 302). These limits are of two related kinds. First, there is the general problem of "linguistic idealism" (Idealismus der Sprachlichkeit) built into hermeneutics, which neglects the fact that language is not just a means of communication which mediates our experience of the world, but "also a medium of domination and social power" (Habermas 1985: 172). "Sociology may therefore not be reduced to interpretive sociology" (Habermas 1985: 174). This limit to hermeneutic interpretation manifests itself at a more specific level in relation to what Habermas calls "systematically distorted communication," exemplified in the psychoanalytic concept of repressed motives. "In deciphering repressed intentions as unconscious motives, linguistic analysis transcends the dimension of subjectively intended meaning and cultural tradition" (Habermas 1985: 186). Habermas believes that this specific problem of distortion can and must be generalized into an awareness of the dependence of language and language-use on broader social processes. "Hermeneutic experience, encountering this dependence of symbolic context on actual (faktisch) relations, becomes a critique of ideology" (Habermas 1985: 172).

This is the approach which Habermas put forward in *Knowledge and Human Interests*. The broader context, in terms of the history of philosophy, emerges retrospectively in Habermas's 1982 preface to *On the Logic of the Social Sciences*: his "appropriation" of hermeneutics and linguistic analysis had convinced him "that critical social theory had to break free from the conceptual apparatus of the philosophy of consciousness (Bewusstseinsphilosophie) flowing from Kant and Hegel" (Habermas 1991: xiii). In Gadamer's "metacritical comments," while welcoming the fact that Habermas had "made visible" the contribution of hermeneutics to the social sciences (Apel 1971: 79), he rejects the distinction between "culture" and "material factors" and closes with a dismissive reference to the idea of freedom from domination as an "anarchist utopia." This is not the place to trace Habermas's subsequent returns to these issues in his conception of "reconstructive science." What remained from the debates of the 1970s was the idea of some sort of mediation, variously weighted, between broadly Gadamerian hermeneutics and the critical theory of the postwar generation. It is this which Kögler presents in the English version of his first book, which locates his perspective in a broader context of European and North American thought.

Critical Hermeneutics in Dialogue

In 1986, two years after Foucault's death, Axel Honneth published his *Kritik der Macht*, translated in 1991. Honneth began from the widely shared view that the first generation of critical theorists, despite their astonishing cross-disciplinary and interdisciplinary range, lacked an adequate theory of social action. With one foot in neo-Marxist economics and the other in Freudian theories of personality and culture, they were well placed to analyse what capitalism *does* to human beings and their social and political contexts, but less focused on counter-currents of resistance, which were anyway rather thin on the ground in the interwar period. (Erich Fromm's prophetically gloomy study of the German working class provided empirical documentation of what was anyway evident.)

Habermas rejected the pessimism of post-war critical theory, of what had come to be called the "Frankfurt School," and his principal work, the *Theory of Communicative Action*, published in 1981, aimed to provide the missing theory of social action as well as a normative foundation for social criticism and what he came to call a discourse ethics. For Honneth, this was the starting point, but he felt that it needed to be complemented by Foucault's analysis of power and a more prominent *theoretical*, as opposed to merely political, focus on concrete social conflicts. Where Habermas had circled around Foucault, clearly fascinated by him[2] but without entering into direct dialogue until just before Foucault's death in 1984, Honneth, like Albrecht Wellmer in the earlier generation of critical theory, was happy to engage with post-modern and poststructuralist thought, establishing the intellectual basis for an exchange between these two perspectives.

This exchange however barely occurred in the following years, and Habermas's *Der Philosophische Diskurs der Moderne* (1985) hardly helped. A conference in Utrecht in 1986 which brought together representatives of the two approaches was described by one participant as the "Franco-Prussian war," though I remember my friend Geoffrey Bennington, in the Derridean camp, saying that he had found Albrecht Wellmer much more approachable than other Habermasians.[3] With some exceptions, such as the work of Manfred Frank, in Geneva in the 1980s, and an edited volume in the UK

(Ashenden and Owen 1999), scholars tended to divide between France and Germany, rather as international air passengers arriving at Geneva or Basel choose between exits to France or Switzerland.[4]

Enter Kögler, with a major book published in Germany in 1992[5] and in translation, in an expanded form including a chapter on "Critical Theory as Critical Hermeneutics," in 1996: *The Power of Dialogue. Critical Hermeneutics after Gadamer and Foucault*. The sub-title of the book points to the first aspect of Kögler's work; the title to the second aspect: his constant emphasis on dialogue between individuals as well as between intellectual traditions divided on national lines. He has developed over the years a powerful model of interpretive capacities at work in everyday political contexts, and the forms of identity which underpin and sustain them.[6]

Difficult Times?

This chapter explores a possible challenge posed to this model by the *highly polarized* and *evenly balanced* conflicts which we have recently experienced with the twin disasters (as I see them) of Brexit and Trump as well as in a wide variety of other situations worldwide.[7] The foreseeable consequences in the two Anglosphere cases were so outlandish as to recall Hume's jokey example that it was possible to choose the destruction of the world over the scratching of his finger. To take up two of the themes central to Kögler's work, identity and cosmopolitanism, we are confronted here with anti-cosmopolitan nativist conceptions of identity and nationalism. Among the differences between the two situations is the fact that many supporters of Trump believed that he would or, in 2020, that he had improved the country's economic prospects, whereas a large number of Brexit supporters accepted the prospect of economic dislocation for the sake of "taking back control" from the EU.[8]

> I flatter myself that I can understand political positions radically opposed to my own. What I find harder to understand are inferences of the form:
>
> There are many things wrong with the EU *therefore* I want my country to secede from it.
>
> There are many things wrong with Hillary Clinton *therefore* I am voting for Trump.

The persistence of attachments to these positions as this book goes into production, nearly six years since the Brexit referendum and Trump's election,[9] is perhaps the most striking feature of the present situation. As Oscarsson and Holmberg (2020: 4) write in the Introduction to their handbook: "In an era of polarization, overheated public discourse, denialism and the spread of fake news, partisanship can…be a predominantly bad thing for both individuals and democratic systems." Conflicts of this kind are, in Chantal Mouffe's terms, "antagonistic" rather than "agonistic." Mouffe distinguishes between two forms of political antagonism: agonistic, in which the other is seen as an adversary in a conflict around the interpretation of shared values, and antagonistic, where s/he is seen as an enemy.[10] As Colin Hay (2020: 197) puts it, in his brilliant recent discussion of Brexit, "In British politics, at least, it seems that the electorate is no longer capable of believing that something is in *their* interests if it is not directly opposed to the interests of someone else."[11] We are familiar with forms of political exclusion in which terrorists or, sometimes, extremists such as fascists, are denied the title of legitimate adversaries; the peculiar feature of the current conflicts with which I am concerned is that they are also normalized through *inclusion* in normal electoral politics. In the US there was a choice between presidential candidates from the two dominant parties; in the UK between two alternatives in a referendum called by a majority government. The analysis of "authoritarian populism" which I discuss below[12] runs some danger of stigmatizing the bulk of Leave/Conservative voters in the UK and probably, by extension, the US Republican Party. I am, as it happens, fairly relaxed about this attribution in the case of the UK, and too ignorant of US politics to say anything about whether this is a fair attribution. Both the Conservatives and the Republicans however seem to fit the pattern found also, for example, in Poland (PiS) and Hungary (FIDESZ), of the radicalization of mainstream right-wing parties (Minkenberg 2015).

On both sides of these highly polarized countries, the other half of the divide is demonized,[13] and changing sides seems apparently almost as difficult as doing so in a civil war. In the UK, the marginal shift which occurred soon after the referendum and was consistently sustained until recently (apart from a very marginal move in the opposite direction in November/December 2019), from a majority in favor of secession to one against it, was largely explained by the expansion of Remain support to include a younger age cohort and/or the previously undecided or indifferent. Genuine switchers in the four years after the vote were a small minority, with fewer than five percent of respondents in April 2019 unsure they voted the right way, to the extent that they would change their vote and fewer than ten percent in December 2020 regretting their vote.[14] Of these, repentant Leavers have tended to cite the emerging evidence of what Brexit will mean in practice, while ex-Remainers, a tiny minority, usually stress the need to "respect" the Referendum result and sometimes their irritation at the perceived unwillingness of the Union to accommodate UK demands. The conflict seems set to persist in something like the way in which that over the Dreyfus affair persisted well into the twentieth century, until it was overlaid by the Second World War and the choice between collaboration and resistance.[15]

As with the Dreyfus affair, the recruitment base of the respective camps was mixed, dividing families, perhaps for ever. Ruth Harris (2010) has documented the fact that many Dreyfusards (supporting the case for the Jewish officer Dreyfus's innocence) were rabidly antisemitic and many anti-Dreyfusards were motivated more by concern for the reputation of the army than by other considerations. Mounting evidence in Dreyfus's favor had surprisingly little impact. In the recent UK and US cases, however, choices were also heavily driven by age and education and, to a lesser extent, by geographical location. (In the mostly Remain-voting large cities of the UK, and smaller cities with substantial universities, these go together.) In Poland, electoral opposition to the right-wing PiS regime is substantially shaped by the historical East-West divide (where the "West" includes ex-German Gdansk). In the 2016 Referendum and the 2019 UK election, there was a sharp divide between younger and older voters. In the Referendum, sixty-nine percent of eighteen- to thirty-year-olds and seventy-six percent of those aged eighteen to twenty-one in Sloam and Henn's sample voted Remain, compared to thirty-six percent of over-sixty-fives. These millennials also drove the substantial support for Labour in the 2017 election. In the 2019 election nearly three quarters of the young (eighteen to twenty-nine) voted Labour, Liberal, Green, SNP or Plaid Cymru, while nearly two thirds of the seventy-plus cohort voted Conservative or a few for the Brexit Party. Sloam and Henn (2017) stress the political alienation of their "cosmopolitan millennials" but note that this did not translate, as it did for a less educated minority, into Leave support.

The bases of these conflicts have also modulated in striking ways. In the Brexit case, and perhaps with Trump as well, we have slipped into playing a game of supercilious elitists and naïve young cosmopolitans versus knuckle-dragging morons (with a few better-informed anti-capitalists in the UK on the latter ("Lexit") side). To quote David Graeber (2020):

> ... in Brexit the right had discovered an almost perfect political poison, not only dividing British society into two hostile camps, but bringing out the absolute worst in both of them. Each side ended up hurling bitter invective against each other, much of which was true. Remainers insisted that many Brexit campaigners were overt racists, and that the Leave campaign was—much like Trumpism—normalizing forms of racist expression that would have been considered outrageous only a few years before. They were right. Reports of racist hate crimes, for instance, increased dramatically after the vote. Leavers countered that many of the most vociferous Remainers were overt elitists, and were likewise normalizing expressions of contempt for small-town or working-class England that would have once been considered equally outrageous. They were right, too.

Expertise was vilified, notoriously by a British cabinet minister, Michael Gove,[16] and terms like "fake news" and "free speech" were weaponized and inverted to legitimate falsehood and racism.[17] Racism itself has increasingly become culturalistic and reflexive; the Islamophobia cultivated by hard right parties often plays on the conflict between "western" values and the patriarchy and homophobia attributed to Muslims.[18]

In such conflicts, *understanding* the worldview of the other may *strengthen* feelings of revulsion at the perceived wrongness of alternative perspectives. As David Dwan (2018: 6) writes, summarizing George Orwell, "If it is obscene to supply reasons for torturing Jews, it is equally repugnant to furnish reasons for *not* torturing them." The film director Billy Wilder recounted a story of one person coming out of an Anne Frank film saying how shocking, overwhelming and unforgettable it had been and another replying that they would have liked to hear the other side's point of view (Ciment 1983: 4). A BBC program in February 2020 on Holocaust denial by the comedian David Baddiel actually included an interview with a denier; Baddiel recorded his own misgivings, and the strong advice against showing the interview by Deborah Lipstadt and Anthony Julius, but felt he had to include this element.[19] Benjamin Moffitt (2018: 11) spells out the issue in relation to what he calls "the increasing deadlock between populism and anti-populism in Western Europe":

It encourages antagonism, and forces those who are otherwise agonistic...to move their chips entirely on one side of the frontier or the other. There is no room for the conciliatory centrist with this divide. Are you for "the people" or "Brussels"? Are you a "true" democrat or a liberal? Are you Leave or Remain? Are you on the side of good or evil?[20]

A Challenge to Hermeneutics?

Hermeneutic theory has traditionally been concerned with the *limits* of the understandable. If someone's speech becomes unintelligible, we may reach for causal explanations involving jet lag or neurological disorders. Less dramatically, Habermas and Apel pointed to the need to complement a hermeneutic approach with causal explanations; the rest is history—the history of critical hermeneutics conjoined, for some of us, with critical realism.[21] Where does this leave us in the present conjuncture? First, a momentary Austinian reference to ordinary language. When we describe a decision or outcome as incomprehensible, we often mean not that we *cannot* understand or explain how it came about but that there is no rationale for it, no conceivable circumstances that would justify it.

This may be a point at which the UK and US situations diverge. The Trump presidency may come to be seen as a step on the way to more positive outcomes in US politics. This was Gramsci's initial response to Italian fascism; it didn't turn out well for him or for Italy, but you never know. I find it hard to imagine a comparable scenario for Brexit, assuming it does not become merely a trial separation, rapidly reversed. I cannot imagine ever becoming reconciled to it, even if I believed that it was or had become in many ways beneficial for the UK and, more importantly, for Europe. Nor can I imagine ever again feeling relatively comfortable about being English; there will be a lasting parallel with the West Germans of my generation whom I met in the late 1960s, though they could at least self-identify confidently as Europeans. Understanding the motivations of the "other side" may be helpful in an interpersonal or practical-political context, but I doubt if it will yield anything more. It may even be harmful: In the rather specialized but important area of constitutional law, Renata Uitz (2015: 299) has argued that the international response by constitutional lawyers to recent Hungarian incursions into the rule of law has suffered not only from a focus on the *letter* of the legal texts and a neglect of the broader context but also, more particularly, from an assumption of an underlying consensus on fundamental principles and a desire to build on common ground: "...without careful and informed analysis of the political, social and historical context, it will be increasingly difficult to tell if an illiberal constitutional regime is in the making."[22]

This is disturbing for those of us who are committed in principle to the understanding of others and to dialogue, and Kögler is of course fully aware of these challenges. In a fairly recent critical discussion of Gadamer, for example, he points to a possible trap of more general relevance which he calls "the *hermeneutic violence of immediate judgement*—namely the symbolic violence of an interpretation that conflates the act of making sense with the act of understanding such that one oneself can accept the other's view as true." If I have understood this correctly, an example might be to interpret the views of a white supremacist as just an erroneous inference from the fact that white people often enjoy a privileged position to the belief that they simply *are* superior. This is surely a step too far, and this is I think what Kögler (2014: 61–2) means when he goes on to say that "we need to conceive of the dialogical process in more robust terms as a continuous process of perspective-taking that allows for a variety of results…including alternative views of understanding an issue or irreconcilable ways of making sense of X."

What is to be Done?

Looking on the bright side, we might consider some crumbs of comfort. An evenly balanced conflict may tip the other way. (The failure of the British political system to respond to the shift in the balance of opinion over the years since the Referendum is one of the most depressing elements of the whole ridiculous saga.) There are also constitutional checks on the more egregious violations (impeachment in the US, the Supreme Court judgements in the UK—though the UK Court may have signed its own death warrant or, at best, laid itself open to political packing, as seen in the US and incipiently in Poland, where judicial independence is protected to some extent by European law.)

More substantially, another promising development is the growing appeal of deliberative democracy and citizens' assemblies. The latter seem to have played a very positive part in the 2016–18 reform of Irish abortion law and continued to pronounce on other issues such as climate change; a further country-wide assembly was established in 2019 to consider gender equality and is currently deliberating. In France, too, a citizens' assembly of 150 people debated climate change and measures to mitigate it, though this has been criticized as a cosmetic exercise. "Not only does the group of citizens not respect any of the participation rules foreseen by the European treaty for public participation, as environment lawyer Arnaud Gossement has underlined, but the National Commission for Public Debate has not been involved in the process, and no judge has been named to guarantee the process and its results."[23] More promisingly, Guy Verhofstadt was due in early 2020 to initiate similar debates across the EU, delayed by the pandemic and now underway again,[24] and there were some more informal assemblies in the UK.[25]

An issue which has received some attention among political theorists is what should count as an acceptable contribution to, or structure for, deliberation. On the latter issue, as with the distinction between rule and act utilitarianism, the question is whether deliberation is expected to pervade every part of the political system in question or merely to play a role in some of its aspects. (In what Robert Goodin (2008: 202) provocatively called "deliberative Schumpeterianism," deliberation is reserved for elected representatives.)[26] Habermas focuses more on deliberation in civil society and the public sphere and less on the mechanics of representative assemblies, allowing for majority voting when this has obtained general agreement. On the former issue, however, the threshold of acceptability for deliberative contributions, Habermas has been accused of setting the bar too high and excluding too many of those who are less used to formal debate than university professors.[27] As Martin Saar (2019: 274–85) notes, however, "Habermas's complex vision of politics...identifies both the power *and* the fragility of the rational in politics."

In a rare empirical contribution to discussion of this issue, Holdo, Öberg, and Magnusson (2019) studied messages sent to the Swedish integration minister over a period of growing controversy over immigration (2011–16). They found that only eleven percent, fewer than they had expected on the basis of the study by Arlie Hochschild (2016)), contained "stories" as opposed to more substantial evidential support, and that where these did occur they formed part of a broader argument or were introduced to legitimate the writer's competence to pronounce on the issue. There was no significant difference between supporters and critics of current immigration policy in their recourse to such anecdotal evidence. It may be that the presumably rare situation of writing to a government minister led correspondents, especially those opposed to government policy, to adopt a more formal approach. There is, however, something of a parallel in the (to me) surprising finding that British Leavers were not significantly less informed about EU matters than Remainers. Again, since they were going against the advice from the government and a massive line-up of normally credible sources (including President Obama), they may have felt more pressure to inform themselves.

In institutional politics, however, there is also a clear tension between the quality of deliberation and democratic decision-making. In the UK, it is generally agreed that the unelected House of Lords displays a higher quality of debate than the Commons; something similar could be argued in European-level politics for the role of specialized committees. (We can only guess or rely on memoirs to assess how far this is also true of Council meetings.[28]) The EU's constitutional convention in 2003 was a serious, if imperfect, attempt at something like a deliberative assembly, but it was sabotaged in its final stages by the member-state politicians and produced no satisfactory outcome except, eventually, the rebadged Lisbon Treaty.

At a more informal level, there have been initiatives to promote exchange between opposed camps or to draw in and engage with extremists. In one which has attracted some attention, the director of Dresden's Albertinum art museum, Hilke Wagner, personally responded to hate mail from her right-wing critics in 2017 and organized discussion events in the museum attended by up to 600 participants. The result was positive, though the hard-right AfD continues to stress the cultural field and is successfully appealing to younger voters; its youth organization has been active since 2013, with xenophobic and anti-feminist campaigns. (Going a little further than the British Conservatives' opposition to the BBC, the AfD opposes state support for public broadcasting—the Rundfunkbeitrag—and is close to the CDU-CSU Werteunion, founded in 2017, which opposed what it saw as the leftward drift of the Merkel government.)[29] All this raises questions about the practical benefits of engagement as opposed to a strategy which excludes antidemocratic forces.[30] To quote Habermas: "I have no sympathy at all for handling *enraged citizens with kid gloves* [Wutbürger in Watte zu packen]."[31]

A Problem with "Belief"

A further, more ambiguous element worth considering is the changed status of "belief." The UK's Equality Act of 2010, based on the EU's Equal Treatment Directive of 2006, goes beyond it in including religious and other beliefs as "protected characteristics" even outside the workplace. A "philosophical belief" is distinguished from a mere "opinion" and must not be discriminatory against others; thus holocaust denial or a belief in white supremacy do not count. In the language of the act:

For a belief to qualify for protection it must be established that it:

- is genuinely held;
- is a belief, not just an opinion or viewpoint;
- applies to a weighty and substantial aspect of human life and behavior;
- is sufficiently cogent, serious, cohesive and important;
- is worthy of respect in a democratic society;
- is not incompatible with human dignity;
- and does not conflict with the fundamental rights of others.

A ruling in January 2020 held that "ethical veganism" counted as such a belief, and an earlier ruling had given a similar status to the belief in catastrophic climate change.[32] Lurking in the background to this developing body of case law there seems to be a demand for respect for "my belief right or wrong" which may be a cause for concern, especially if it is taken to extend to the right to protection from criticism. The requirement of "balance" which led the BBC to give equal time to Leave and Remain views, however marginal and ill-informed the former might be, also benefited an essentially mendacious and at best simplistic campaign.

Not content with its success, the Brexit government seems likely to act on its "genuinely held" belief in left-wing bias in the BBC, the universities, and elsewhere. It is perhaps worth recalling an episode in October 2017 in which a government whip chose (or was chosen—we still do not know which was the case) to write to university Vice-Chancellors and principals asking them to provide information on those of their colleagues who taught about contemporary Europe and particularly about Brexit. A government, knowing that an estimated three quarters of academics viewed it with suspicion, and that scarcely anyone who knew anything about the prospects of Brexit would be in favor of it, might reasonably worry that that the case in favor of the government and its policies was not being fully aired. To monitor and perhaps intervene discreetly in what was going on in lecture theatres and seminar rooms would not violate any constitutional protection of academic freedom, since none exists in the UK, unlike most other European countries.[33] The present UK government may also withdraw from the European human rights regime and curtail judicial review of political decisions.

The silo effect of both old and new media reinforces polarization.[34] (Reading the *Guardian* and occasionally the *Financial Times* or *New York Times*, my most Eurosceptic regular media source is *Le Monde diplomatique*. A look at the rest of the UK press is always a shock.) In the US, there seem to have been more initiatives to bridge the gap; Arlie Hochschild (2017: 422) cites in particular the Bridge Alliance, which aims at reconciliation and non-partisan efforts to improve governance.³⁵ A *New York Times* interviewer, Kate Murphy (2020) has published a book urging us to listen more to others. Murphy cites Jean Piaget (1923: 18) and his analysis of the "collective monologues" of young children, in which others present are merely a stimulus: "l'interlocuteur n'est qu'un excitant." Overall, however, Cass Sunstein's research seems to confirm a pattern of polarized choice, even in contexts where political opinions are irrelevant (Sunstein 2017; Marks et al. 2019). This also drives the (non-)reception of alternative beliefs.³⁶ Particularly prominent in social media, though by no means only here, is the coarsening of political language in polemical contexts (Wodak and Forchtner 2017; Wodak 2019). Relatedly, lying has become normalized. British civil servants used to warn ministers that if they lied they would be found out and disgraced. This rule now applies only in Parliament; politics is increasingly perceived as a sport in which "professional fouls" are standard.³⁷ Identity politics is of course part of this syndrome.

Populism

The current anxiety over populism is probably misdirected, not just because the term covers both left and right variants but, more fundamentally, because there is an sense in which "we are all populists now," linked by a common suspicion of the political class, "la casta,"³⁸ and constrained to receive and formulate political messages in easy soundbites, repeated ad nauseam. Reaching adulthood amid the rise of social movements, I never quite understood the persistence of established political structures. This was later illustrated by the aftermath of the 1989 revolutions, where western-style political families emerged from the ashes of Stalinism and eventually took their more or less appropriate place in the European Parliament, and most recently by the way the UK in 2019 abdicated a decision over the issue of secession from the EU to the vagaries of a ridiculous electoral system and the choice between two thoroughly discredited major parties. It is characteristic of populist politics that, invoking a discourse of authenticity and a close relationship between political leaders and the "people," it denatures and degrades the political systems where it takes root. As Christopher Thornhill (2021: 9–10) puts it:

> Populism discloses a deep paradox at the core of modern democracy...expressed, simply, in the fact that populist movements frequently assume influence in polities that are deeply defined by global-constitutional processes...However, where they react against the depleted patterns of democracy (allegedly) caused by such global-constitutional patterns of norm construction, populist movements normally weaken democracy further. In other words, populism appears as a constitutional form that reacts critically against the promulgation of constitutional norms at the global level to establish democracy. Yet, its reaction to such global norms leads to the erosion of democracy at the national level.

The critique of the political sphere running from Marx's essay on the "Jewish Question" through Régis Debray's *Critique of Political Reason* remains pertinent. Bourdieu's provocative slogan in 1973 that "public opinion does not exist" pointed to the class stratification of the sense of political efficacy preceding political choices: the right to have an opinion. Sloam and Henn's *Youthquake* sheds an interesting light on this model. Their "Young Millennials," especially in the UK, share the general disillusionment with electoral politics while demonstrating a high degree of interest in political *issues*. They are substantially what Amnå and Ekman (2014) called "stand-by citizens" (amounting in Sweden to nearly half of young adults), increasingly mobilized in the UK for the 2016 Referendum, as the threat of a negative result became more imminent, and again for Labour by Jeremy Corbyn in the 2017 general election.[39]

In a 2016 YouGov study of authoritarian populism, a cosmopolitan or "liberal left" orientation was only slightly better represented among eighteen- to twenty-nine-year-olds than in the UK population (forty-three percent to thirty-seven percent).[40] This study, conducted with David Sanders, found that forty-eight percent of British voters held "authoritarian populist" views, though this score put Britain well down the list of twelve EU countries. Romania and Poland scored highest, followed by France; Germany was much the lowest (apart from Lithuania).[41] These attitudes are deeply entrenched and therefore not to be compared in their political expression with the fluctuations in social democratic politics between more or less radical options. Young Britons were however, as we have seen, overwhelmingly in favor of remaining in the EU and may have been pushed toward Labour support by Theresa May's repellent attack, in a speech in the autumn after the referendum, on "citizens of nowhere."[42] Henn had earlier conducted two studies of young people in which over half expressed a lack of confidence in their understanding of politics, and this may explain their relatively slow response in 2016 to the impending Brexit referendum and a lower turnout than for the population as a whole. In the event, Sloam and Henn suggest, "the EU referendum, whilst acting as a lightning rod for resurgent nationalism among many older and less well-off citizens, also led to the crystallization of a common sense of political identity amongst Young Millennials in reaction to the negative impact of austerity upon their lives and what was perceived as an economically costly and inward-looking Brexit vote."[43] It remains to be seen how the inevitable dislocation of Brexit reinforces these attitudes, and how long it will take for this to affect overall attitudes. We may have to wait for demographic renewal to take its toll on authoritarian populism, always assuming that it does not take hold more strongly among younger generations.

Jacob Rees-Mogg, a leading Brexiteer cabinet minister and sometimes referred to as "the honourable member for the eighteenth century," suggested in an interview in 2018 that the economic benefits of Brexit would take fifty years to become obvious. Not surprisingly, a large proportion of the generation which will with luck survive to see this result felt that its vote in 2019 had been irrelevant (thirty-seven percent of those aged eighteen to twenty-four, as against twenty-nine percent for the population as a whole).[44] "Remain" was always a weak basis for a slogan; "rejoin" or "remain aligned" even less so. But the cost of Brexit, as of mid-January 2020, was estimated at more than a quarter of a trillion dollars, and although the UK may be rich enough to lose in the longer term, as Greece did in the crisis of the last decade, up to a third of its GDP, it is not clear that the political fabric would survive this. (The UK, unlike Greece, has among the *lowest* state pensions in Europe.)

As Marx saw nearly two centuries ago, the normalisation of situations which might otherwise seem abnormal or aberrant is a key effect of the political illusion, like the religious illusion. The "mainstreaming" of extreme right politics,[45] in which Eastern Europe has arguably shown the way to the West, looks like being the flavour of the new decade. There may be no attractive alternative to sticking with critical hermeneutics as a framework, and rational deliberation as a practice,[46] but we should perhaps beware of over-estimating their effectiveness.

Acknowledgment

I am grateful to Trevor Pateman for comments on an earlier version of this chapter.

Notes

1. Printed version Vienna: W. Verkauf, 1946.
2. See the two chapters devoted to him in *The Philosophical Discourse of Modernity*.
3. Some of the contributions were published in the recently founded UK journal *Theory, Culture and Society*, 3 (3) (November 1986). Some years later, when Geoff organized a conference on critique and deconstruction, he introduced me to Derrida as "un des chefs du commando habermasien en Angleterre."
4. In the Anglosphere, language may have had some role. Another Sussex colleague, the Lukácsian István Mészáros, once suggested that the vogue for Althusser and other French theorists in the British intellectual left could be explained by their childhood exposure to French au pairs.
5. He was one of the rare doctoral students whom Habermas agreed to supervise.
6. See in particular Kögler 2005a; 2005b.
7. On the concept of polarization, see Zimmer 2019. The long-suppressed report finally published in July 2020 by the UK Parliament's Intelligence and Security Committee on "The Russian threat to the UK" refers to Russia's "general poisoning of the political narrative in the West by fomenting political extremism and 'wedge issues'"... It defines these as "highly divisive subjects which bifurcate a country's population..." (p.10).
8. Habermas, in a characteristically insightful immediate response to the Brexit referendum result, commented that he had not expected that considerations of identity would trump interest to such an extent.
9. In Europe, unlike the US, this polarization coexists with dramatic electoral volatility ("partisan dealignment"). For a useful overview of polarization, see McNeil-Willson et al., 2019, and other material from the BRaVE project: www.brave-h2020.eu
10. See Mouffe 2000; 2018. Martin Nonhoff (2006) applied her model in his analysis of the "social market economy." See also Ruser and Machin 2017; Leslie 2021.
11. This, he suggests, is an important element in the explanation of the referendum result: Remainers saw it as what he calls a "valence" issue of the public good, whereas Leavers saw it as a "positional" issue of political preference rather than something to which expertise might be relevant. Hence the failure of the Remainer strategy (which had worked in Scotland two years earlier) of "expert paternalism" (Hay 2020: 199).

12 The term was first used by Stuart Hall (1979), who drew on Nicos Poulantzas's account of "authoritarian statism," at the beginning of the Thatcher era. See also Jessop et al. 1984; Hall 1984. For Crewe and Sanders (2020: 3), authoritarian populism is "a two-pronged phenomenon. On the one hand, it consists of leaders who are elected on simplistic, nationalistic electoral platforms who pursue illiberal and authoritarian policies once they achieve office. On the other hand, it also involves a mind set among mass publics that embraces resentment of immigrants and immigration, cynicism about human rights, support for robust foreign policies, ideological sympathy for the market and rolling back the state and, in Europe, opposition to the European Union."

13 To be fair, British Leavers are more understanding and less disapproving of Remainers than the reverse (https://blogs.lse.ac.uk/brexit/2018/05/04/leavers-have-a-better-understanding-of-remainers-motivations-than-vice-versa) and this is reflected in supporters of the respective parties: http://cdn.yougov.com/cumulus_uploads/document/cdtc7pcf75/TheTimesResults_141121_friends_party_support_Website.pdf (accessed February 17, 2021).

See also https://www.theguardian.com/world/ng-interactive/2019/may/02/leavers-v-remainers-how-britains-tribes-compare (accessed February 17, 2021).

14 See also https://whatukthinks.org/eu/questions/how-do-you-feel-today-about-how-you-voted-in-the-eu-referendum-back-in-2016 (accessed February 14, 2021).

15 The Spanish Civil War, when you were not necessarily sure which side of the front prospective foreign combatants were headed to, may have acted as a foretaste of such choices.

16 There is of course a genuine problem with the relation between expertise and democracy. As Stephen Turner (2003: 15) has written: "specialized technical discourse…presents a fundamental political problem for liberal democracy…: 'government by discussion', in which the discussion is largely intelligible and effectively subject to the political influence of the population generally… In the face of expertise, something has to give: either the idea of government by generally intelligible discussion, or the idea that there is a genuine knowledge that is known to a few, but not generally intelligible."

17 In an early critique of fake news (properly understood), Zweig suggested in a speech in 1932 (in, of all places, fascist Italy), the establishment of a Europe-wide commission made up of a small number of respected experts which could be invited by individuals or nations to pronounce on alleged political lies affecting them. ("Die moralische Entgiftung Europas," in Zweig (1981: 114–15).

18 See, for example, Kallis 2018.

19 https://www.bbc.co.uk/iplayer/episode/m000fjqk/confronting-holocaust-denial-with-david-baddiel (accessed February 14, 2021).

20 See also Carreira da Silva and Brita Vieira 2019.

21 See, for example, Outhwaite 1987.

22 See also Wodak 2019: 66; Grabbe and Lehne 2019.

23 https://www.euractiv.com/section/all/short_news/paris-could-a-random-citizen-group-save-the-environment/?utm_source=EURACTIV&utm_campaign=33934b0212-The_Capitals_COPY_11&utm_medium=email&utm_term=0_c59e2fd7a9-33934b0212-115017935 (accessed February 17, 2021).

24 For a less optimistic view of this, see Alemanno 2020: 36.

25 https://www.opendemocracy.net/en/can-europe-make-it/convening-citizens-panel-penzance-10-things-i-learned (accessed February 17, 2021).

26 See Owen and Smith 2015: 227.

27 Miranda Fricker (2007: 1) speaks of testimonial injustice, "when prejudice causes a hearer to give a deflated level of credibility to a speaker's word," and "hermeneutical injustice," "when a gap in collective interpretive resources puts someone at an unfair disadvantage when it comes to making sense of their social experiences. An example of the latter might be that you suffer sexual harassment in a culture that still lacks that critical concept." See also Kreide 2019: 517.
28 See https://www.investigate-europe.eu/en/2020/behind-closed-doors-secrets-in-the-council (accessed February 17, 2021).
29 https://werteunion.net. See Julian Göpffarth, "Germany's New Ultranationalist Intelligentsia," *FP* September 24, 2019. https://foreignpolicy.com/2019/09/24/germanys-new-neo-nazi-intelligentsia (accessed February 17, 2021).
30 See for instance Emily Schultheis 2018. https://www.theatlantic.com/international/archive/2018/08/how-to-discuss-the-far-right-without-empowering-it/567520 (accessed February 17, 2021).
31 "Moralischer Universalismus in Zeiten politischer Regression. Jürgen Habermas im Gespräch über die Gegenwart und sein Lebenswerk," *Leviathan*, 48 (1) (2020): 15. https://www.nomos-elibrary.de/10.5771/0340-0425-2020-1-7/moralischer-universalismus-in-zeiten-politischer-regression-juergen-habermas-im-gespraech-ueber-die-gegenwart-und-sein-lebenswerk-volume-48-2020-issue-1?page=1 (accessed February 17, 2021).
  English version translated by Frederik van Gelder. https://adorno.net.
32 There is a useful list of successful and unsuccessful cases on https://www.personneltoday.com/equality-diversity/discrimination/belief-discrimination/
33 See http://portal.unesco.org/en/ev.php-URL_ID=13144&URL_DO=DO_TOPIC&URL_SECTION=201.html. (accessed February 17, 2021). For a discussion of the challenges of teaching about Brexit see, for example, https://blogsmedia.lse.ac.uk/blogs.dir/116/files/2019/11/LeaveRemainTeach-podcast-transcript-v2.pdf (accessed February 17, 2021).
34 See, for example, Timothy Snyder's analysis of the Russian contribution to the 2016 US presidential election, "And we dream as electric sheep. On humanity, sexuality and digitality," *Eurozine*, May 6, 2019: https://www.eurozine.com/dream-electric-sheep/?pdf.
35 Hochschild 2017: 422; https://www.bridgealliance.us.
36 See Tappin et al. 2017.
37 Lying or "being economical with the truth" was to be left to senior civil servants in public contexts. (See https://www.theguardian.com/politics/2020/feb/09/how-whitehall-will-fend-off-dominic-cummings-culture-of-secrecy.) See also Anna-Karin Selberg, "The contemporary art of lying," *Eurozine*, May 20, 2019: https://www.eurozine.com/contemporary-art-lying/?pdf. I am grateful to Ruth Wodak for reminding me of these issues.
38 Two parties which play on this theme are the rather successful Slovak party with the name OĽaNO (Ordinary People and Independent Personalities) and the until recently dominant Czech party ANO (Action of Dissatisfied Citizens); on the latter, see Havlík 2019.
39 In Sweden itself, however, there is substantial youth support for the hard-right Swedish Democrats (Bentsen and Bevelander 2019: 229–57).
40 Joe Twyman, cited in Sloam and Henn 2019: 32.
41 Twyman concluded: "Whilst in each of the twelve countries some variation of the 'liberal left' currently constitutes the largest single political bloc, in seven countries the

combined AP voter groups represent a greater potential electoral force. Should a politician or party be able to find a way to unite significant numbers of AP voters under their banner, they will be able to issue a serious challenge to the established political order." https://yougov.co.uk/topics/politics/articles-reports/2016/11/16/trump-brexit-front-national-afd-branches-same-tree. This has arguably come to pass.
42 Sloam and Henn, *Youthquake 2017*, p. 33.
43 Sloam and Henn, *Youthquake 2017*, p. 73.
44 https://yougov.co.uk/topics/politics/articles-reports/2019/12/23/young-people-are-more-likely-feel-disenfranchized
45 See Pytlas 2018: 164–85; Feldman 2019: 23–48. Feldman (p. 23) introduces the useful concept of the "near right," straddling traditional conservatives and the more familiar far right. The de facto fusion of the British Conservatives and the Brexit Party (whose withdrawal from the contest in Conservative constituencies secured—or at least augmented—the Conservative success in the December 2019 election) is a striking instance.
46 Habermas, in the postscript to *Auch eine Geschichte der Philosophie* (2019), p. 778, refers to "den prekären Status einer vernünftigen Freiheit, die sich die kommunikativ vergesellschafteten Subjekte sowohl selber wie auch gegenseitig zumuten müssen" (the precarious status of a rational freedom which communicatively socialized subjects must ascribe both to themselves and one another). For a comprehensive summary and insightful discussion of this book, see Kögler 2020.

References

Alemanno, Alberto (2020), "Europe's Democracy Challenge: Citizen Participation in and Beyond Elections," *German Law Journal*, 21: 35–40.
Amnå, Erik and Joakim Ekman (2014), "Standby Citizens: Diverse Faces of Political Passivity," *European Political Science Review*, 6 (2) (May): 261–81.
Ashenden, Samantha and David Owen (eds.) (1999), *Foucault Contra Habermas: Recasting the Dialogue between Genealogy and Critical Theory*. London: SAGE.
Bentsen, Beint and Pieter Bevelander (2019), "The Determinants of (Right-wing) Political Engagement among Adolescents in Sweden," in Pieter Bevelander and Ruth Wodak (eds.) *Europe at the Crossroads*. Lund: Nordic Academic Press, pp. 229–57.
Bevelander, Pieter and Ruth Wodak (eds.) (2019), *Europe at the Crossroads. Confronting Populist, Nationalist, and Global Challenges*. Lund: Nordic Academic Press.
Bourdieu, Pierre (1973), "L'opinion publique n'existe pas," *Les temps modernes*, 318 (January): 1292–1309. "Public Opinion Does Not Exist," in Armand Mattelart and Seth Siegelaub (eds.), *Communication and Class Struggle 1*. New York: International General, 1979, pp. 124–30.
Carreira da Silva, Filipe and Mónica Brita Vieira (2019), "Populism as a Logic of Political Action," *European Journal of Social Theory* 22 (4): 497–512.
Ciment, Michel (1983), "Billy Wilder urbi et orbi," *Positif*, July/August.
Connolly, William E. (1991), *Identity/Difference: Democratic Negotiations of Political Paradox*. Ithaca; London: Cornell University Press.
Crewe, Ivor and David Sanders (eds.) (2020), *Authoritarian Populism and Liberal Democracy*. Cham: Springer.
Dwan, David (2018), *Liberty, Equality, and Humbug. Orwell's Political Ideas*. New York: Oxford University Press.

Engler, Sarah, Bartek Pytlas, and Kevin Deegan-Krause (2019), "Assessing the Diversity of Anti-establishment and Populist Politics in Central and Eastern Europe," *West European Politics*, 42 (6), Varieties of Populism in Europe in Times of Crises, pp. 1310–36.

Feldman, Matthew (2019), "On Radical Right Mainstreaming in Europe and the US," in Bevelander and Wodak, *Europe at the Crossroads*, pp. 23–48.

Fricker, Miranda (2007), *Epistemic Injustice: Power and the Ethics of Knowing*. New York: Oxford University Press.

Goodin, Robert (2008), *Innovating Democracy*. Oxford: Oxford University Press.

Grabbe, Heather and Stefan Lehne (2019), "The EU's Value Crisis. Past and Future Responses to Threats to the Rule of Law and Democratic Principles," in Pieter Bevelander and Ruth Wodak (eds.), *Europe at the Crossroads*. Lund: Nordic Academic Press, pp. 49–61.

Graeber, David (2020), "The Center Blows Itself Up: Care and Spite in the 'Brexit Election,'" *New York Review of Books*, January 16, 2020.

Habermas, Jürgen (1985), "The Hermeneutic Claim to Universality," in Kurt Mueller-Vollmer (ed.), *The Hermeneutics Reader*. London: Bloomsbury, pp. 294–319.

Habermas, Jürgen (2019), *Auch eine Geschichte der Philosophie*. Band 2. Berlin: Suhrkamp.

Hall, Stuart (1979), "The Great Moving Right Show," *Marxism Today*, January, pp. 14–20.

Hall, Stuart (1984), "Authoritarian Populism: A Reply," *New Left Review* I/147, Sept/Oct.

Harris, Ruth (2010), *The Man on Devil's Island: Alfred Dreyfus and the Affair that Divided France*. London: Allen Lane.

Havlík, Vlastimil (2019), "Technocratic Populism and Political Illiberalism in Central Europe," *Problems of Post-Communism*, 66 (6): 369–84.

Hay, Colin (2020), "Brexistential Angst and the Paradoxes of Populism: On the Contingency, Predictability and Intelligibility of Seismic Shifts," *Political Studies*, Vol. 68 (1), pp. 187–206.

Hochschild, Arlie (2016), *Strangers in Their Own Land. Anger and Mourning on the American right*. New York: New Press.

Hochschild, Arlie Russell (2017), "A Response to William Davies' 'A Review of Arlie Russell Hochschild's Strangers in Their Own Land: Anger and Mourning on the American Right,'" *International Journal of Politics, Culture, and Society*, 30 (4): 421–3.

Holdo, Markus, PerOla Öberg, and Simon Magnusson (2019), "Do citizens use storytelling or rational argumentation to lobby politicians?," *Policy & Politics*, 47 (4) (October): 543–59.

Jessop, Bob, Kevin Bonnett, Simon Bromley, and Tom Ling (1984), "Authoritarian Populism, Two Nations and Thatcherism," *New Left Review* I/147, Sept/Oct.

Kallis, Aristotle (2018), "The Radical Right and Islamophobia," in Jens Rydgren (ed.), *The Oxford Handbook of the Radical Right*. New York: Oxford University Press, pp. 42ff. (no page extent provided for some reason on the electronic copy)

Kögler, Hans-Herbert (1997), "Alienation as Epistemological Source: Reflexivity and Social Background after Mannheim and Bourdieu," *Social Epistemology* 11, 2, pp. 141–64.

Kögler, Hans-Herbert (2005), "Recognition and Difference: The Power of Perspectives in Interpretive Dialogue," *Social Identities* 11, 3, pp. 247–69.

Kögler, Hans-Herbert (2005), "Constructing a Cosmopolitan Public Sphere: Hermeneutic Capabilities and Universal Values," *European Journal of Social Theory* 8, 3, pp. 297–320.

Kögler, Hans-Herbert (2006), "Normalität als Normalisierung? Zur Theorie des Subjekts in Moderne und Postmoderne," in Normalität, Normalisierung, Normativität Heft 1.

Hrsg. von Ulrike Kadi und Gerhard Unterthurner. *Mitteilungen des Instituts für Wissenschaft und Kunst* 1–2/2006, pp. 11–20.

Kögler, Hans-Herbert (2014), "A Critique of Dialogue in Philosophical Hermeneutics," *Journal of Dialogue Studies* 2: 1, pp. 47–67.

Kögler, Hans-Herbert (2020), "A Genealogy of Faith and Freedom," *Theory, Culture and Society* 37 (7–8), pp. 37–46.

Kreide, Regina (2019), "Politik der kommunikativen Macht. Kommunikations- und Handlungsblockaden in einer globalisierten Welt," in Ulf Bohmann and Paul Sörensen (eds.), *Kritische Theorie der Politik*. Berlin: Suhrkamp, pp. 494–518.

Leslie, Ian (2021), *Conflicted: Why Arguments Are Tearing Us Apart and How They Can Bring Us Together*. London: Faber and Faber.

McNeil-Willson, Richard, Vivian Gerrand, Francesca Scrinzi, and Anna Triandafyllidou (2019), "Polarisation, Violent Extremism and Resilience in Europe Today: An Analytical Framework," www.brave-h2020.eu.

Marks, Joseph, Eloise Coplanda, Eleanor Loha, Cass R. Sunstein, and Tali Sharota (2019), "Epistemic Spillovers: Learning Others' Political Views Reduces the Ability to Assess and Use Their Expertise in Nonpolitical Domains," *Cognition*, 188 (July): 74–84.

Minkenberg, Michael (2015), *Transforming the Transformation? The East European Radical Right in the Political Process*. London: Routledge.

Moffitt, Benjamin (2018), "The Populism/Anti-Populism Divide in Western Europe," *Democratic Theory* 5, 2, Winter, pp. 1–16.

Mouffe, Chantal (2000), *The Democratic Paradox*. London: Verso.

Mouffe, Chantal (2018), "The Affects of Democracy," *Eurozine* 23.11.2018.

Murphy, Kate (2020), *You're Not Listening: What You're Missing and Why It Matters*. New York: Harvill Secker.

Nonhoff, Martin (2006), *Politischer Diskurs und Hegemonie. Das Projekt "Soziale Marktwirtschaft."* Bielefeld: Transcript.

Oscarsson, Henrik and Sören Holmberg (eds.) (2020), *Research Handbook on Political Partisanship*. Cheltenham: Edward Elgar.

Outhwaite, William (1987), *New Philosophies of Social Science. Realism, Hermeneutics and Critical Theory*. Basingstoke: Macmillan.

Owen, David and Graham Smith (2015), "Survey Article: Deliberation, Democracy, and the Systemic Turn," *The Journal of Political Philosophy*, 23 (2), pp. 213–44.

Piaget, Jean (1923), *Le langage et la pensée chez l'enfant*. Neuchâtel-Paris: Delachaux et Niestlé.

Pytlas, Bartek (2018), "Populist Radical Right Mainstreaming and Challenges to Democracy in an Enlarged Europe," in Lise Esther Herman and James Muldoon (eds.), *Trumping the Mainstream. The Conquest of Democratic Politics by the Populist Radical Right*. Abingdon: Routledge, pp. 164–85.

Ruser, Alexander and Amanda Machin (2017), *Against Political Compromise. Sustaining Democratic Debate*. Abingdon: Routledge.

Saar, Martin (2019), "Selbstverständigung und Verselbstständigung. Zum 90. Geburtstag von Jürgen Habermas," *Leviathan*, Jahrgang 47, Heft 3, pp. 274–85.

Schultheis, Emily (2018), "How to Discuss the Far Right Without Empowering It. A lesson from Germany," *The Atlantic*, August 14.

Sloam, James and Matt Henn (2019), *Youthquake 2017*. Basingstoke: Palgrave.

Sunstein, Cass R. (2017), *#Republic: Divided democracy in the Age of Social Media*. Princeton, NJ: Princeton University Press.

Tappin, Ben M., Leslie van der Leer, and Ryan T. McKay (2017), "The heart trumps the head: Desirability bias in political belief revision," *Journal of Experimental Psychology: General*, 146 (8), pp. 1143–9.

Thornhill, Christopher (2021), *Democratic Crisis and Global Constitutional Law*. Cambridge: Cambridge University Press.

Turner, Stephen P. (2003), *Liberal Democracy 3.0: Civil Society in an Age of Experts*. London: Sage.

Uitz, Renáta (2015), "Can You Tell When an Illiberal Democracy is in the Making? An Appeal to Comparative Constitutional Scholarship from Hungary," *International Journal of Constitutional Law*, 13 (1) (January): 279–300.

Wodak, Ruth, and Bernhard Forchtner (eds.) (2017), *The Routledge Handbook of Language and Politics*. London: Routledge.

Wodak, Ruth (2019a), "Entering the 'Post-shame Era': The Rise of Illiberal Democracy, Populism and Neo-authoritarianism in Europe," *Global Discourse: An Interdisciplinary Journal of Current Affairs*, 9 (1) (January): 195–213.

Wodak, Ruth (2919b), "Analysing the Micropolitics of the Populist Right in the 'Post-shame Era.'" In *Europe at the Crossroads*, edited by Pieter Bevelander and Ruth Wodak, 63–92. Lund: Nordic Academic Press.

Zimmer, Thomas (2019), "Reflections on the Challenges of Writing a (Pre-)History of the 'Polarized' Present," *Modern American History* 2, pp. 403–8.

10

Playing More Seriously

An Enactivist Critique of Kögler's Critical Reflexive Dialogue

Lauren Swayne Barthold

Introduction

I have learned much from Hans Herbert Kögler's scholarship over the years, specifically from his careful explication of Hans-Georg Gadamer's hermeneutics, his insightful challenges that helped illuminate the potential for a critical hermeneutics, and his important esteem of a dialogic ethic lying at the heart of hermeneutics. In spite of both of our interests in defending a hermeneutic account of dialogue, this chapter challenges the role he assigns to "hermeneutic empathy" in the development of his concept of critical reflexive agency. Previously, I have argued that dialogue aims not at empathy but at mutual understanding, which occurs when interlocutors are able to take up the existential claim the other makes in order to affirm their common, underlying humanity (Barthold 2020). The existential emphasis of mutual understanding, I maintained, is irreducible to an empathetic exchange requiring mind reading. I demonstrated how dialogue aimed at mutual understanding is fundamentally relational, characterized by a playful openness, and yields a connection with the other *qua* human. In this way, it is unlike standard forms of propositional discourse that utilize a representational theory of mind to explain how an exchange of beliefs occurs.

This chapter extends my previous work on dialogue by incorporating components of enactivist theory to challenge the empathetic nature of understanding advanced by Kögler. In describing the dialogue between the I and Thou as driven by the quest to think the thoughts of the other, his account of empathy requires a fundamentally dyadic (i.e., self-other) exchange of representational beliefs. I argue, however, that taking seriously the way in which understanding is a playful event (Gadamer 1992) requires conceiving of dialogic mutual understanding as that which is not primarily located in the individual minds of the I and Thou but in the entirety of the dialogic event.

One gloss of the Western enlightenment's impetus for critique highlights how the exigency to avoid the implicit and tacit oppressive forces of society and tradition requires access to a critical, i.e., distanced, stance that allows us to see what "is" in order to best determine the emancipatory path. When institutions of all sorts began crumbling in the fifteenth century, Descartes' move was to search for a foundation for truth far removed from, and thus unencumbered by, the alleged grounds of uncertainty. We are all familiar with his efforts to secure a truth that ultimately would be accessible only by an individual's purely rational cognition thus curtailing any forms of doubt and uncertainty stemming from the unruly power of institutions. While this rendition obviously is lacking in subtlety, I think we can recognize how it functions as the ancestor to many forms of critique today. In this chapter I challenge the way that Kögler's notion of hermeneutic empathy relies on a critical agency that privileges distanciation, and defend what I call "enactivist empathy," which privileges open and dynamic connection.

Kögler's laudatory efforts to bring a hermeneutic voice into discussions of critique in order to ensure that the emancipatory quest does not base itself on a "prejudice against prejudice" have served to defend hermeneutics as a central resource in sociopolitical ethics. His critically reflexive dialogical hermeneutics has much to offer, in particular the way it addresses the objection that once we insist on dialogically engaging the common ground of our humanity neither agency nor emancipatory understanding is possible. Like Kögler, I believe we should defend the emancipatory trajectory of hermeneutics.

Unlike, Kögler, however, I do not think we need to summon distanciation, which serves to obscure some of the richer notions within Gadamer's hermeneutics. I think that we hermeneuts should stop worrying about how to access a "critical reflexive" agency to gain freedom and truth. It is not simply a better and more nuanced sort of distance we need, as Kögler maintains; to assert as much prevents us from fully rejecting the Cartesian dream and consequently from finding an effective path to emancipation. I maintain that hermeneutics invites us to develop a richer and more robust conception of true dialogic connectedness, which gets us closer to emancipatory understanding. Emancipatory understanding occurs when all dialogic participants experience freedom as a result of their fully engaged playful connection with the whole dialogue event. The mutual acknowledgment of shared humanity is not a mere cognitive realization but a visceral experience stemming from a genuine dialogic encounter with the other *qua* human. Gadamer's account of play elucidates the freedom and buoyancy found in immersive, immanent engagement with the humanity of oneself and the other, something hindered by removing oneself to a more distanced, reflective stand point.

I will draw on enactivist theory to demonstrate why the Gadamerian account of play should be taken seriously and why our goal should be increased communion rather than increased distance. By bringing enactivist insights to a robust account of dialogue I am offering a new take on an old hermeneutic adage: we do not need to figure out how to get out of the circle, but how to be in it more playfully. I begin by first presenting a brief overview of the dimensions of Kögler's work I will address; I then describe some key tenets of enactivism that will challenge what I refer to as Kögler's latent "dyadism," demonstrating its inability to do the work he claims it does; finally, I defend an alternative way of thinking about dialogue that proves promising to the task of utilizing enactivist empathy to achieve emancipatory understanding.

Critical Hermeneutics and the Power of Dialogue

I will focus on that aspect of Kögler's critical hermeneutics that explicates a "reflexivity-in-interpretation" that affords the individual criticality without requiring an Archimedean point of objective distanciation. Kögler names the sort of distanciation required as "self-distanciation" and explains: "with the loss of the Cartesian and Hegelian subject, *the other* becomes the point of departure for critical insight into the self. In critical interpretation, the reconstruction of the other and of her symbolic background serves as a critical foil from which to become, as it were, one's own other" (1999: 252). Thus, the potential for critique lies not in the lone individual, but in an individual's dialogic engagement with the other.

Kögler utilizes the concept of dialogue to elucidate the dynamic nature of starting from within one's own (and thus limited) symbolic life world (what he terms the "epistemic" dimension) and then moving, dialogically, to the encounter with the other in their particularity and differences (what he terms the "ethical" dimension). Kögler's epistemically and ethically integrated account is sensitive to the nagging question that often persists, namely: "If individual perspectives and beliefs are based on symbolic forms, which in turn are embedded in social power practices, then are not interpretive truths and subjective self-realizations ultimately reducible to nothing other than expressions of underlying power structures?" (254) In other words, he realizes the need to consider the objection that his account of critically reflexive self-distanciation can never really go far enough to invite concrete social liberation. His response details how critical hermeneutics has the resources to remain attentive to power without reducing all interactions between self and other to power. Taking seriously the dialogic component, he argues, is sufficient to "reopen a space for critical reflection within which subjects can reconceptualize their identities by seeing their taken-for-granted selves as social constructions of power" (255).

By replacing a reductionistic theorist-agent dualism with the dialogical nature of intersubjective interactions whose processes entail articulations to the other, Kögler aims to insure that such a dialogic encounter eventually exposes and elevates hidden and previously unscrutinized power (257–8). He puts it this way: "instead of restricting the first-person attitude to the symbolic level and the third-person approach to the sociopractical dimension, a dialogic strategy attempts to combine the self-understanding of subjects with a reconstruction of hidden features of their contexts both with regard to hidden symbolic assumptions and with regard to unrecognized patterns of behavior and practices" (259). He reiterates that the symbolic order is never wholly separate from the subject's own self-understanding and that therefore one's need for the other never dissipates. His work to emphasize the role of the dialogic encounter in achieving emancipatory understanding is original and significant on many levels.

Kögler defends an account of the criticality that embraces both subjectivity and distanciation. In elucidating how the criticality plays itself out in the epistemic encounter between theorist and agent, he writes:

> when power practices are at issue, the dialectic between theorist and agent works itself out in the reciprocal recognition of their interdependence in 'defining' power:

thus while the theorist helps the agent to get a clearer understanding of *how* power works, the agent helps the theorist to recognize which structural constraints should count *as* power. In this way, critical hermeneutics conceives of the project of interpreting symbolic as well as practical presuppositions of situated subjects as a process that involves a distanciating learning experience both on the side of the theorist and on the side of the agent.

Kögler 1999: 262

According to Kögler, there is a built-in criticality to the dialogic event between the agent's articulation of their self-understanding and the theorist's articulation of their theory. The anti-power efficacy here resides in the way the symbolic forms and practical experiences are always brought together. He insists on the constant need for distanciation to encourage continual reconstruction of the symbolic order, albeit a wholly adequate and complete reconstruction can never be formed.

I believe that Kögler's epistemic account that both insists on the epistemic humility of the theorist yet rejects an incommensurability stemming from standpoint theory is particularly prescient for thinking about the ethical dimension of dialogues with marginalized voices. He maintains that the theorist's starting point must be the acceptance of the experience of the agent. This starting point of openness and curiosity enables the theorist to learn from the perspective of the other and arrive at a new, mutual understanding. Current anti-racist work reveals how white supremacy is perpetuated due to a lack of awareness of, humility toward, and openness to the actual experiences of Black, Indigenous, People of Color (BIPOC). I read Kögler as insisting that the theorist's initial starting point must be an admission that "I really don't know what you are experiencing." Such an acknowledgment on the part of a white person addressing a BIPOC functions as the impetus for, not the culmination of, understanding. It is a way to affirm the epistemic and existential importance of standpoints while avoiding incommensurability.

According to Kögler, the enactment of critical subjectivity is only made possible by a reflexivity born of a dialogic interaction with the other (268) and he goes on to describe the relation between subject and world:

> This subjective sphere does not consist in a separate dimension or 'object domain' over against the other two realms. This subjective sphere should not be reified into a distinct 'world' in and of itself; rather, it establishes its 'ontological' distinctness in the ongoing possibility of subjects' taking a reflexive and specific stance of distanciation toward the symbolic and practical forms and structure of their contexts. Subjectivity, as an emphatic mode of self-reflexivity, *exists as a relation to the background,* not as a specific space or domain of the background within which biographical events take place ... By reconstructing the shared patterns of the symbolic and practical aspects of social life, the subject creates a distancing relation to the background that at the same time creates the distance between society and self. *The subject is nothing that can be defined in itself; it exists only in its differentiation from the shared horizon of social meanings and practices, and only in so far as this relation is activated in reflexive interpretation.*
>
> 268–9, emphasis added

Kögler's description of the nature of the trans-subjective background aligns well with Gadamer's own critique of subjectivity. Kögler's further insight here is to demonstrate how it is through dialogic interaction that subjects see themselves as emerging out from, and always connected to, a greater, irreducible background/whole, while at the same time gaining criticality (272). Thus the "other is an essential factor in one's own becoming reflexive" (273) in so far as the dialogic process itself creates a critically reflexive self, which he goes on to clarify is distinct from a merely "socially situated self." We are not just separate, independent selves inhabiting a social situation; our selves are created within our dialogic interactions with others. For Kögler, critical perspective taking is possible, in Gadamerian terms, only as horizons fuse, which allows him to use hermeneutics to move beyond a merely socially situated self. Yet, while his own account seems a promising way to blend a Gadamerian fusion of horizons with critical theory, scrutinizing his detailed account, particularly in some of his later essays on agency, leads me to part ways with him. For, I worry that the critically reflexive self has not really gotten us sufficiently further than the socially situated self and that the critically reflexive self does not put us on the most efficacious path toward achieving a more emancipatory understanding.

To orient my challenge, I would like to pose a question whose answer might seem so obvious as to border on the banal—especially to critical theorists—but I will defend its import below. Given his Gadamerian bent, why does Kögler privilege differentiation over connection? I take his defense of differentiation to be motivated by the following worry that he articulates, one that has become normalized in our Western philosophical tradition: "By emphasizing processes or structure beyond the conscious insight or control of individual agents, envisioned in terms of being, language, dialogic event, *différance*, force fields of power, and so on, both philosophical hermeneutics and poststructuralism have thrown out the baby of critical reflexivity with the bathwater of an untenable philosophy of consciousness" (271). His fear, in other words, is that hermeneutics' anti-subjective bent has led it to reject all possibility of critique, which is the baby he wants to save. I contend, however, that if we want to achieve emancipatory goals, then our focus should be on promoting an increased playful connection with the other rather than trying to insist on the legitimacy of a critically distanced stance from the other (or oneself). In order to achieve emancipatory understanding, we need a deeper appreciation of the tacit work that goes on in dialogue and we need to create more space for dialogic interactions that free up participants to engage in more unself-conscious, playful connection.

Kögler on Agency and Empathy

One way Kögler attempts to recover critical reflexive agency is by offering a more robust account of hermeneutic empathy. While I am completely on board with his rejection of the naïve and reductionistic claims of a psychological account of empathy (2000: 196ff), I maintain that if we want to achieve emancipatory understanding, hermeneutic empathy is not adequate; we need to develop "enactivist empathy." The focus of enactivist empathy, as I detail below, is on the whole, dynamic dialogic situation as opposed to the mind of an individual subject. Enactivist theory helps me show how his defense of hermeneutic empathy remains problematic insofar as its emphasis on the dyadic model of subject and object/other relies too much on a representational theory of mind. Even where he summons Mead to discuss the situational factors that are more in line with a triadic model (subject, object, world), there is a problematic reductionism that not only conflicts with his hermeneutic commitments but prevents the maximal exposure of hidden ideologies.

Kögler's "hermeneutic empathy" relies on a mind dependent intentionality that summons a representational theory of mind that conflicts with hermeneutic assumptions. In a 2014 essay, Kögler describes the emergence of a critically reflective self in a dialogic situation:

> We need to cultivate an intersubjective experience that allows us to encounter the presence of an irreducible other ... The source for authentic dialogue with the other can be found in the core of the self ... I take the perspective of the other towards me, and thus become an object of self-understanding. Agents develop by means of taking the perspective of another, of assuming another's viewpoint through imaginary *role-taking* in play. *They come to understand themselves as agents because they are able to take the perspective of other towards themselves. Therefore, the self emerges as a self by taking the role of the other towards herself.*
> 320, emphasis added

On the one hand, I agree with Kögler's account of the dynamic and dialogic unfolding of the self. Rather than requiring a critical reflection stemming from a transcendent or self-less position, he describes how the dialogic interaction with the other makes understanding possible. As I have argued elsewhere, our conscious selfhood cannot emerge without intersubjective interactions and what makes an "I" possible at all is its primordial and tacit connection with the Thou, as well as subsequent distancing, followed by a more intentional dialogic interaction (Barthold 2020). And when Kögler relies on the pragmatism of Mead to defend a non-reified self that emerges from its interaction with the other in, to borrow Dewey's term, a "situation," his account finds many common points with my own, which draws on Buber, Merleau-Ponty and Dewey.[1]

On the other hand, in spite of our similarities, I find problematic his insistence on the nature of the self-as-agent that requires "role-taking" as its method. I think he over-reaches, demanding the impossible: namely, for an individual self-as-agent to emerge from a role-taking process. When we take a closer look at how he envisions the details of such an emergent unfolding, the importance of the fusion of horizons dissipates. The result seems to re-establish the very reductionistic subjectivity that not only Gadamer, but at times even Kögler himself, aims to avoid. For example, while Kögler describes the pre-reflective "role-taking" that occurs implicitly in a social situation, he follows Mead in advocating for an explicit and conscious act of "role taking." It is this latter I find problematic. Kögler explains:

> If agent A becomes capable of representing to herself what agent B is to do, and vice versa, both agents become involved in an intersubjective situation which is

shared. This is so because each agent is now, so to speak, able to leave their practically assigned role in the intersubjective action-circle and switch, in an imaginary act, his or her own perspective with that of the other. If both agents are doing this, they mutually exchange their perspectives, and thus begin to inhabit a shared world of different perspectives within which each of them is specifically positioned and yet capable of representing the perspective of the other.

In the move toward an explicit mode of role-taking, such that 'taking-the-attitude-of-the-other' now becomes an explicit cognitive act for the agent, another desideratum for a theory of self-consciousness can be provided.

2012: 52

The critical power of dialogue for Kögler lies not in one's ability to lose oneself in its play and emerge changed, which is the Gadamerian reading I defend elsewhere (Barthold 2010). Rather, by insisting that explicit role taking must be representational in nature, he places the subject's intentionality and volition as the key driver in achieving the "truly human form of interaction" (2012: 52) of understanding. His Goffman-esque requirement for "role-taking" belies the fact that he has not fully shed the Cartesian cloak, which is carefully draped over a tacit representational theory of mind. One of the strengths of Gadamer's hermeneutics is his down grading of the role of subjectivity in understanding. Yet when Kögler claims that hermeneutic empathy entails representational role-taking, he seems to jettison from his project any sense of the play at the heart of the fusion of horizons. His account ends up covering over the fact that hermeneutics (and, as I will show below, enactivism) insists that individual cognition is not the primary unit of analysis when it comes to conceptualizing dialogue aimed at mutual understanding. As a result, the richness and complexity of the tacit layers of understanding that hermeneutics defends is lost. When the focus is on dyadic empathetic exchanges, the deeper level wherein the latent prejudices and fears operate remains untouched, leaving ideologies of individual hearts and systemic structures to remain unchallenged.

We need to avoid speaking about how empathy requires an intentional and cognitive exchange between self and other and instead emphasize "mutual understanding" that entails allowing a new perspective to emerge through play, which is always a non-intentionally driven event for Gadamer. While Kögler speaks of the importance, and indeed is offering a phenomenology, of shared meaning, which may seem to dovetail with my emphasis on "mutual understanding," we mean very different things by this. That his account requires a full-blown intentionality can be seen in the following claim: "the possibility of shared meaning consists of the capability to understand an articulated symbolic act from the perspective of the other, which entails that the meaning of each agent's perspective becomes available to both subjects and is thus shared" (53).

Rather than emphasizing the individual's cognitive empathetic exchange, whereby one attempts to put oneself in the place of the other, enactivist theory supports a hermemeutic account of mutual understanding wherein dialogic participants work to put their ideas into the center, surrendering to and eliciting a free-play of ideas, and creating a new way of being (and not just knowing) for all. In other words, rather than dialogue's engine being a dyadic (or even triadic: e.g., I-Thou-situation) and intentionally driven exchange between I and Thou that aims at new beliefs, we should conceive of the true power of dialogue as the ability to put one's perceptions into the center—not for a critical examination where "critical" requires an autonomous agent taking on the views of the other, but that allows the ideas to come into dialogic coherence "themselves."[2] Enactivist empathy refers to the attitudes of the participants whereby their play is characterized by openness toward the dialogic situation; they open themselves to the way in which their individual steps unfold organically to create a whole "dance," so to speak. We could say that enactivist empathy is a way to "sense the whole field" (de Geuss 2020), inviting participants to listen and speak "to the center," rather than to any individual(s).[3]

What happens to the agents in this scenario? Far from passive spectators, agents attend to and engage in a central dance of perceptions that changes them as new meanings emerge. Recall how Gadamer insisted that we neither intentionally step into the other's horizon nor volitionally shift our own horizon. Instead, as we seek to meet the other in mutual understanding, horizons playfully shift and fuse on their own accord. Volitional efforts by an individual (whether on an epistemic or ethical level) to shift a horizon prevent true change. Mutual understanding is the game we enter into and only when we surrender ourselves and actively get caught up in its play can we claim its success. In other words, the dyadic form of intentionality directed toward another individual, which Kögler's account seems to rely on, is not the driver of the change required by understanding. Kögler needs to take a Gadamerian account of play more seriously in the dialogic engagements he describes. It is just this sort of playful dialogic exchange that enactivism can help elucidate. By elucidating the holistic and robust nature of connection, enactivism can aid us in questioning the assumption that some form of distanciated critique must be embedded in the dialogic process.

Enactivism

Of the variety of strains of enactivist theories of mind on offer, I take my point of departure from Shaun Gallagher who offers this definition:

> enactivist approaches are similar to the ideas of extended mind and distributed cognition insofar as all of these approaches argue that cognition is not entirely 'in the head' but rather is distributed across the brain, body, and environment (e.g. Clark and Chalmers 1998). However, in contrast to the extended mind hypothesis, which embraces functionalism and finds a role for minimal representations, enactivists reject functionalism and claim that the material specifics of bodily processes shape and contribute to the constitution of consciousness and cognition in a way that is irreducible to representations.
>
> Gallagher 2017: 6–7

Enactivism, in other words, rejects representationalism, and therefore forecloses accounts of empathy like Kögler's, which are based on an intentional and representational theory of mind. If there is no clear way to demarcate body from mind from situation, then empathy, whereby one mind thinks the thoughts of the other's mind, becomes impossible to make sense of.

When Gallagher writes that "brain, body, and environment are said to be dynamically coupled in a way that forms a system" (8), he is emphasizing how a change in one part effects change in the whole and that enactivism entails a diachronic, dynamical system that includes processes and not just material components. Components external to the mind are actually constitutive of cognition—they do not merely cause cognition. Gallagher rejects a synchronic relation of constitution, which signifies no difference over time between components and where causation and constitution are taken to be different and separate. From a synchronic point of view, to say an entity is constituted by x, is to say nothing about x being its cause; it is also to maintain a stable and non-changing relation between x and what constitutes x (8). Against the synchronic model, Gallagher advances a diachronic model, where a change in one component creates a change in another, and it describes how different relations are created and manifest over time. Accordingly, constitution and causality are not regarded as separate relations. As different parts and relations change, the whole will change, changing, in turn, the parts. He maintains: "In a dynamical gestalt composed of processes that unfold over time, and characterized by recursive reciprocal causality relations, changes in any processual part ... will lead to changes in the whole, and changes in the whole will imply changes in the processual parts" (10).

Enactivism has several forerunners including Merleau-Ponty, John Dewey and George Herbert Mead. For example, in a chapter on the pragmatist underpinnings of enactivism, Gallagher quotes Dewey to explain the robustness of an enactivist theory of mind: "An idea is not primarily an intellectual entity in the head, but 'an organic anticipation of what will happen when certain operations are executed under and with respect to observed conditions' (Dewey 1938a, 109)" (55). And in describing Dewey's notion of "situation" Gallagher notes its enactivist emphasis: "Organism and environment are not two self-sufficient or easily distinguishable items. Rather, they are always found together in a dynamical transactional relation ... the situation is not equivalent to the environment. That is, it is not that the organism is placed in a situation. Rather the situation is constituted by organism-environment, which means that the situation already includes the agent or experiencing subject" (54, 55–6).

Thus in a Deweyian vein, albeit with more neuroscientific precision and depth, enactivists define the mind as composed of body, society, and culture; cognition equals the "dynamic relation between brain and environment" (11). Neural activity, kinesiology, present circumstances, people, desires, affects, as well as one's past, social history, etc. all comprise the mind. The emphasis is on the fact that "the mind is relational. It's a way of being in relation to the world" (Thompson 2014: 1, quoted in 12). Shared meaning, in other words, refers to the entire, dynamic situation and not to the meaning that is merely shared by, or resides solely in, two different brains.

If, as enactivists maintain, cognition is not just "neuronal processes in the brain of an individual" (12), then it seems problematic to speak, as Kögler does, of an empathetic exchange whereby two distinct minds exchange representations. Gallagher summons Dewey and other pragmatists to maintain that "we are *in the world* in a way that is not reducible to occupying an objective position in the geography of surrounding space, and in a way such that the world is irreducible to an abstraction of itself represented in one's brain" (59). While Kögler's account, like Gallagher's, does reject a spatially, objective self, it nevertheless still utilizes representationalism to account for the critical component of the self. Enactivism helps us realize the limitations of representationalism and provides tools of analysis to elucidate a better way to conceptualize the sort of interpersonal understanding that occurs in dialogue. It builds on a hermeneutic analysis by giving us detailed insight into the underlying and holistic nature of thought and positions us to more aptly address the tacit prejudices that work to entrench oppression and thwart freedom.

In further support of an enactivist theory of mind, Gallagher turns to empirical studies on out-group behavior. For the purposes of this chapter, I will note how such studies challenge the efficacy of empathy when encountering the other in a particularly polarized atmosphere. In such a context, it seems doubtful to expect one to be able to put oneself in the shoes of the other one finds so insidious. Does a Black person really want to make the intellectual and emotional effort to put herself in the shoes of the white nationalist who defends the superiority of the "white race"? Even should she be willing to attempt as much, empirical studies show that: "We are simply less responsive to out-group members and we display significantly less motor cortex activity when observing out-group members (Molnar-Szakacs et al. 2007). Most strikingly, in-group members fail to understand out-group member actions, and this is particularly prominent for disliked and dehumanized out-groups. The more dehumanized the out-group is, the less intuitive the grasp of out-group member intentions and actions (Gutsell and Inzlicht 2010)" (122). In other words, even where one is whole-heartedly devoted to consciously willing to try to put oneself in the other's shoes, there are significant limitations to doing so. And what one comes away with will likely be a highly reductionistic viewpoint of the other, which is not conducive for mutual understanding. Other research concurs on the intractability of implicit biases of all sorts and reveals how tenacious and dominant implicit biases are—even when we wish they were not.[4] If beliefs, particularly identity-based and oriented beliefs, are often what divide us and fuel polarization, and if we want to change beliefs that obstruct the creation of a well-functioning, democratic society, then we need an approach to change that takes seriously that way that beliefs are irreducible to "functional states of the brain" and recognizes that beliefs "may be constituted in terms of disposition or action-tendencies that vary across different situations" (63).

While I have in no way offered a full-blown defense of enactivism here, my rehearsal of some of its highlights is meant to pose some challenges to Kögler's work and to question his reliance on concepts like "critical reflexive self" and "distanciation." In so doing, I am summoning enactivism in the aid of a hermeneutically motivated criticism targeting his desire to privilege distanciation over connection, a desire I find rooted in his failure to have adequately expunged all traces of subjectivism. Far from a quibble about pedantic terminology, the significance of my challenge lies in how we are to understand an operationalized account of dialogue. How we conceive of mutual understanding will prove essential for identifying the type of dialogic event most apt for countering polarizing and fragmenting tendencies that thwart the very possibility of pluralistic democratic communities.

What we need then, following the trajectories of both hermeneutics and enactivism, is to consider the holistic and dynamic dialogic environment, which the latent Cartesianism of Kögler's representationalism ignores. For understanding to occur, we need an environment of open and curious inquiry, which demands more than asking individuals to take up the role of the other and/or to restrict their implicit biases affecting their individual thought processes (e.g., like the stereotype effect). We need a structure that allows the entire dynamic system to self-regulate in a way that increases the playful activity of, and connection amongst, participants in order to achieve emancipatory understanding. No one side, or horizon, emerges as the dominant one. Emancipatory understanding occurs when, to use Gadamer's language, we experience a change as a result of moving to a newly formed horizon, *and* this change manifests as a more vibrant engagement in the whole dynamic process of the dialogic exchange. Freedom here correlates with one's ability to connect more robustly with others in a new whole. Retreating into a critically reflexive self that requires the explicit volition of a single individual occludes the organic, dynamic play of the whole dialogic process and prevents the buried layers of implicit biases that foment latent ideology from being exposed. As I detail below, the spontaneous and organic dialogic process central to emancipatory understanding replaces suspicion of a particular other with belief in a common humanity in order to allow insights to emerge—even those previously hidden from explicit consciousness. The clinical, distanced gaze can prevent truths lodged deeply in human experience from becoming explicit. In other words, losing oneself in the play of the dialogic event is necessary for finding oneself in freedom.

But, some may object, if we do away with a "critically reflexive agent," won't we be susceptible to mass hysteria and cult-like submission? This is an important objection and I acknowledge the need for a fuller account of connection that specifically addresses this worry. Unable to offer a fuller account here, however, this chapter's aim is to expose the falsity of the assumption that "*either* we bolster the individual *or* we succumb to despotism," an assumption that relies on an enlightenment and neurocentric model of human cognition that trades on the individual's autonomous and explicit rationality. Following the hermeneutic impetus to reject such a reductionistic account of subjectivity, I maintain we should take seriously our need for a dynamic connection with the whole, which is based on, ultimately, not a trust in this or that particular individual's beliefs but in a more generalized belief in a shared humanity. Privileging connection over distanciation, as I show below, does not mean rejecting dialogic constraint writ large in order to achieve emancipatory understanding but requires us to rethink the terms of that constraint. The particular approach to dialogue I describe clarifies that the criterion of a successful dialogue is the ability for all participants to contribute to and fully engage in it. Emancipatory understanding occurs when all participants are able to freely and fully engage (albeit a never completed task) in the play of dialogue. The play of dialogue is constrained not by intentional role-taking and an empathic gesture directed at a single individual but by the dynamic play of the dialogue itself, which entails an engaged belonging to the whole on the part of all participants. The goal is to keep the game going rather than for one side to win.

Enactivist Empathy in Dialogue

What does an account of dialogue look like that rejects a representational theory of mind and takes seriously the fact that "all kinds of affective processes, and even variations in circulation and heartbeat, can influence perception (Garfinkel et al. 2014)" (quoted in (Gallagher 2017: 118)? Such an account must acknowledge the holistic and enacted nature of organism and environment and reject describing the dialogic process solely in terms of the exchange of beliefs (defined as functional brain states). It must recognize and take seriously, the fact that, as Gallagher writes,

> such things as affects and the effects of respiration and heart rate are not *represented* as part of my perception; they are non-representational factors that have an effect on perceptual response ... On the enactivist view, the perceptual system is not just in in the brain; it includes the organism (brain-body) embedded in or engaged with the environment that is characterized by certain regularities and affordances and action possibilities.
>
> 118–19

In other words, an enactivist concept of "situation" means acknowledging that no amount of intersubjective back-and-forth can achieve the sort of hermeneutic empathy, much less a distanciated perspective on the situation, that Kögler defends. My call for enactivist empathy does not require the subject to obtain a critically distanced perception to gain agency but invites a deeper and more holistic engagement in the situation.[5] Enactivist empathy, then, is a way to achieve the coherence that a hermeneutic account of dialogue seeks, a coherence achieved by a playful engagement. Enactivist empathy rejects a representational discursive strategy that assumes a dyadic transference of fragments of beliefs, allegedly contained in individual minds. The coherence of mutual understanding addresses the fundamental fragmentation that produces broken and incapacitated organisms (both humans and institutions). If the "master's tools will never dismantle the master's house," we could say that it is futile to attempt, as Kögler's critical hermeneutics does, to attenuate polarized political discourse by developing a dialogic approach that utilizes individualistic cognition that further exacerbates fragmentation of thought. We need a better way to think together, a way that does not rely on upholding a *paean* to individuated and fragmented thought. The antidote for fragmentary thought is coherence, which accords with the biological underpinnings of enactivism described by Gallagher:

> The free-energy principle applies to any biological system that resists a tendency to disorder (Friston, Kilner, and Harrison 2006). It states that for an adaptive self-organizing (i.e., autopoietic) system to maintain itself it needs to minimize entropy or free-energy ... In theoretical biological terms, if we think of the living organism as a self-organizing system, it survives by anticipating sensory input or by taking action, which in turn changes its sensory input ... Living systems and cognitive systems share this same organizational principle.
>
> 127[6]

While an adequate development of the sort of discourse required for emancipatory understanding is not possible here given space limitations, I conclude with a brief description of several of its requirements.

Rejecting a traditional, dyadic account of empathy, enactivist empathy requires "listening to the whole field," which maximizes the amount of hidden beliefs that can be exposed and the number of marginalized voices that can be heard. The focus of understanding is not the set of beliefs inhering in a single individual mind (or several minds, for that matter), but the whole of the dialogic event, as it is unfolding in the wider, dialogic space. This requires participants to refrain from modes of persuasion or argument that privilege their own individual triumph and success at the expense of others. Enactivist empathy rejects the efforts of any individual to win and instead affirms that the success of the game is manifest in the on-going propensity to keep playing. Where only one side or individual wins, understanding has not occurred, and fragmentation remains. Fraught and competitive debate-style discourse is to be rejected. Akin to Gadamer's account of play, enactivist empathy means that dialogic "players" allow the dialogue to take over, eventually allowing the emergence of coherence. Unlike standard accounts of empathy, enactivist empathy does not require an individual to "think the thoughts" or "feel the feelings" of the other-as-separate-individual. Enactivist empathy refers to the ability to become attuned to and engaged in the whole dialogue playfully unfolding. It is a way of describing what goes on in the dialogic "zone," so to speak—akin to how athletes describe the experience of being caught up in play where the play itself takes over in a way that far from diminishing agency actually increases it. Similarly, enactivist empathy occurs when one is able to sense the whole of the dialogic activity that is unfolding and to experience oneself actively engaged and caught up in it. We could say, then, that an enacted *cogitamus* takes the place of a representing *cogito* as the core of emancipatory understanding.

In other words, dialogue entails listening, reflecting and observing rather than defending and asserting. Understood this way, dialogue is a practice of openness toward a particular other that is based on a belief in common humanity.[7] I use the term "belief" rather than "trust" to emphasize the importance of a generalized openness toward experiencing a connection with the other-qua-human as opposed to the requirement of having to "trust" a particular individual at the outset of the dialogue or trust in the particular views that the other may hold. Belief in a common humanity is not a blind or naïve feeling that denies difference and oppression. Rather, it entails a courageous openness toward the other that requires intentional cultivation. One way to foster courageous openness is to ask dialogue participants to abide by explicit communication guidelines that encourage people to speak from their own experiences in order disarm stereotypes and generalizations and expose implicit biases. Truth telling can be hard for all sides and so trained facilitators can be used to help participants spend time in silent reflection that slows down reactive responses that exacerbate defensiveness toward the other and shuts down further inquiry. Connecting across difference requires the hard work of more truth telling—not less—thus benefiting marginalized voices whose truths are often silenced. But truth telling must be offered in a way that maximizes listening and understanding. In order to minimize reactivity and avoid a fight-flight-freeze response, silent reflection is encouraged as is listening with curiosity. Participants are asked to observe and notice "the whole field," which includes not only one's own assumptions and beliefs, but one's body, emotions and the entire dialogic activity that is unfolding. Attending to what is actually unfolding in the present moment fosters an embodied, experiential means for uncovering implicit structures of dominance. Such a practice invites an openness to those who express that they do not feel a sense of belonging.

The effects of such a dialogue are twofold. First, through a holistic experience of a common endeavor individuals come away with not so much a new belief that "the other and I are part of a greater whole," but a visceral, enacted experience of such connection. The exchange amongst particular individuals gives rise to the lived experience of a shared humanity, one that transcends that of any individual, and where the whole that emerges is greater than the sum of its parts. In other words, the collective whole is one that emerges as a result of the process of curious questioning and honest speaking; it is not a uni-lateral effort on the part of a pre-established dominant group to colonize the marginalized. Furthermore, the experience of connecting via our humanity does not entail that we all agree or that justice and accountability are not required; neither is it an instantaneous and simple process. Rather, with effort, dialogue can be a first step that lays the foundation for subsequent discourse aimed at political and juridical outcomes. The problem with Kögler's critical hermeneutics is that his representationalism with its focus on cognitive exchange works only under ideal circumstances and cannot bring about change in highly polarized communities. As out-group studies referenced above attest, change results from holistic experience and engagement and not from cognition, much less volition, alone. Before law enforcement officers and members of marginalized communities sit down to hammer out a "use of force" policy, there must be some basic level of the acknowledgement of the shared humanity of the other. Civic dialogue is a form of discourse that lays this foundation.

Second, new meaning, ideas and thoughts do emerge, but they are not essentially attached to or derived from any single individual mind or side. There is no genius who is credited with solving or fixing the problem. Neither is the aim to declare one side the winner. The coherence that emerges from such a dialogue allows individuals, and groups or systems of individuals, to work together more productively and to break through impasses that already have given or might yet give rise to incommensurability, violence and oppression. What is gained are not more accurate representations, sharper fragments so to speak, but a more robust playful connection leading to increased freedom. For this reason, we can think of the sort of understanding achieved as a form of emancipatory understanding—where individuals experience increased freedom that results from belonging to and engaging with the whole. It is the constraint of inclusivity that prevents culturally dominant ideologies from being strengthened and thus further reigning in opposing viewpoints.

In conclusion, I propose we think of dialogue as aiming at deeper and more robust connection, one that utilizes enactivist empathy, rather than attempting a critical distanciation. The lenses of hermeneutics and enactivism help us discern the limitations of representationally reconstructing meaning for effecting change in so far as it leaves untouched the fragmentary thought that feeds polarization. Emancipatory understanding requires deepening our playful, dialogic connection with others.[8]

Notes

1. Even where he summons Mead to discuss the situational factors that are more in line with a triadic model (subject, object, world), there is a problematic reductionism that conflicts with his hermeneutic commitments: "As Mead and our previous analysis have shown, I become a conscious and interpreting self only by entering into dialogical practices. Those practices immerse me in a symbolic identity by taking the attitude of others toward me. The symbolic representations allow me to fix such meaning and represent it to myself as my meaning. Accordingly, in this primary process of symbolic self-constitution, I come to identify with symbolic acts as my own acts, and I thus develop a personal narrative, a symbolically and culturally rich self-understanding" (Kögler 2000: 214). Drawing on Gallagher (2017: chap. 3) I would argue that Mead's thought prioritizes the dynamic nature of the situation such that a separate self cannot be maintained.
2. This description is similar to the account of hermeneutic truth I have developed elsewhere, namely, that truth occurs in the dialogic event when both interlocutors find meaning and are changed, where change is indicated by the emergence of a new horizon (Barthold 2005). This account of truth clarifies how change itself is not a criterion for truth; truth requires that the individuals are brought to a deeper experience of meaning demonstrated by the creation of a new horizon. The shift of perspective connects one more deeply to one's own existence, as well as that of the other.
3. Willian Isaacs writes, "*Dialogue, as I define it, is a conversation with a center, not sides.* It is a way of taking the energy of our differences and channeling it toward something that has never been created before" (Isaacs 1999: 19).
4. See, for example, Brownstein and Saul 2016a, b.
5. Gallagher writes: "In section 3.3.1 I pointed to the importance of Dewey's notion of situation, where situation is not equivalent to the objective environment, but includes the agent or experiencing subject in such a way that there is no way for the agent to gain an objective perspective on the situation. This is reflected in the idea that by perception alone the organism doesn't know or control its own viability conditions. It discovers them and can control them only by taking action" (Gallagher 2017: 129–30).
6. Physicist and dialogue theorist, David Bohm, also uses the term coherence to describe what happens in a well-functioning system. I take the term fragmentation from his work. See Bohm 1980 and 1996.
7. This is one of the three articles of faith in democracy that John Dewey defends (Dewey 1939).
8. My appreciation goes to Jennifer Hall for insightful comments on an earlier draft.

References

Barthold, Lauren Swayne (2010), *Gadamer's Dialectical Hermeneutics*. Lanham, MD: Rowman and Littlefield.

Barthold, Lauren Swayne (2020), *Overcoming Polarization in the Public Square: Civic Dialogue*. New York: Palgrave Macmillan.

Bohm, David (1980), *Wholeness and the Implicate Order*. New York: Routledge.

Bohm, David (1996), *On Dialogue*. Edited by Lee Nichol. New York: Routledge.

Brownstein, Michael and Jennifer Saul (eds.) (2016a), *Implicit Bias and Philosophy, Volume 1: Metaphysics and Epistemology*. New York: Oxford University Press.
Brownstein, Michael and Jennifer Saul (eds.) (2016b), *Implicit Bias and Philosophy, Volume 2: Moral Responsibility, Structural Injustice, and Ethics*. New York: Oxford University Press.
de Geuss, Eelco (2020), "Sensing the dialogue field," presentation at the Academy of Professional Dialogue annual conference, November.
Dewey, John (1939), "Creative Democracy: The Task Before Us." *The Later Works* SIU Press: 14: 227–33.
Gadamer, Hans-Georg (1992), *Truth and Method*. Second Revised Edition. Translation revised by Joel Weinsheimer and Donald G. Marshall. New York: Crossroad.
Gallagher, Shaun (2017), *Enactivist Interventions: Rethinking the Mind*. New York: Oxford.
Isaacs, William (1999), *Dialogue and the Art of Thinking Together*. New York: Currency.
Kögler, Hans Herbert (1999), *The Power of Dialogue*. Translated by Paul Hendrickson. Cambridge, MA: MIT.
Kögler, Hans Herbert (2000), "Empathy, Dialogical Self, and Reflexive Interpretation: The Symbolic Source of Simulation." In *Empathy and Agency: The Problem of Understanding in the Human Sciences*, edited by Hans Hebert Kögler and Karsten Stueber. Boulder CO: Westview Press.
Kögler, Hans Herbert (2012), "Agency and the Other: On the intersubjective roots of self-identity." *New Ideas in Psychology*, 30: 47–64.
Kögler, Hans Herbert (2014), "Ethics and Community." In *The Routledge Companion to Hermeneutics*. Edited by Jeff Malpas and Hans-Helmuth Gander. New York: Routledge.

11

Dialogue in a Polarized World—Is There a Way Out?

Randi Gressgård

In *Populocracy*, Catherine Fieschi (2019) reflects on her research experience from the Netherlands over the past few years. All of multiculturalism's basic tenets, she remarks, were taken as the signs of an intellectual posturing clearly at odds with common sense:

> One of the key insights ... was just how reluctant people were to have to explain themselves; and part of it was that they were reluctant to spell out the "obvious." But part of it was something else, it was growing unease with conversation and dialogue. Dialogue had come to mean ... bending over backwards to make themselves understandable, when in fact they had not changed.
> Fieschi 2019: 78

Multiculturalism, with its euphemisms and dissimulations, was considered inauthentic. Perhaps the most important function performed by this notion of authenticity is to connect to the experience of "the people" (Fieschi 2019: 37), perceived as a homogenous group based on ethnocultural or racial traits. Authenticity allows for a politics rooted in instinct; claims to "being right" must be the product of "instinct," or they are not to be trusted (35, 36). But far from creating trust, Fieschi remarks, the striving for authenticity (through quasi-Rousseauian transparency) tends to create permanent doubt, fostering deep mistrust and suspicion (160).

The aforementioned populist ideas are, in key respects, the inverse of Kögler's (1999) critical hermeneutics and what my 2010 book—informed by his *The Power of Dialogue*—details as the conditions for multicultural dialogue (Gressgård 2010). If shared truth is a criterion for the acceptance of the other, Kögler (1999: 147) contends, then the other of dialogue merely becomes the mirror image of self. If we do not introduce a dimension of symbolic order between the meaning of a statement and its truth value, we remain imprisoned within its own horizon of meaning (143). In a word, whereas right-wing populism strives for truth-oriented immediacy, critical hermeneutics seeks to achieve an immediate unfamiliarity.

By the time my book was published, multiculturalism had become a proxy for a set of racialized anxieties about immigration and minority populations subsumed into the mainstream, and as political idea(l) it had been declared dead by European right-wing populists and mainstream politicians alike. Given this new political landscape in which multiculturalism is deemed a failure and drastic racial disparities continue, the question is, where do we go from here? In an opinion piece in the *Guardian*, Ghassan Hage (2019) valiantly proposes that we go back (to where we came from) and restart the argument. If multiculturalism has failed, he says, it surely has to do with liberals dismissing the *radical* critique of white entitlement twenty years ago. Apparently, multiculturalism lost its political edge when co-opted by liberal governments' managerial diversity politics. In response to prevalent trends of right-wing populism, therefore, Hage does not lament late-liberal politics of recognition as much as calling for more radical symbolic disempowerment. Transposed to Kögler's conceptual apparatus, this could be taken as an argument for the need to resuscitate dialogical critique in terms of defamiliarization; disclosure of symbolic orders; re-examination of modes of though and behavior, etc.

Going back and restart the argument is hardly viable, though, without taking seriously the strong current of criticism against established critical thinking in the humanities and social sciences over the past decades. The by now commonplace "end of critique" trope signals that issues of epistemology must give way to affective affirmation of what *is* in ontological terms, highlighting life's immanent potential for generative newness, in place of the faith in knowledge as foundation for political action. As Ben Anderson (2014: 165; 2017a: 594) notes, the affective turn in academic circles has been inseparable from a renewed concern with the multifaceted concepts of life and living, an affirmative vision of life centering on change in terms of immanent creative forces, the "otherwise" immanent to any arrangement of the actual. However, before discussing affect theory's relevance for present anti-racist struggles, it may be helpful to recollect some of the arguments advanced by critical scholars in the context of multiculturalism, including Kögler's and my own work on dialogue.

Critical Dialogue

In the preface to *Multicultural Dialogue*, I picked a contentious political phenomenon as starting point for my critical reflection on the status of cultural difference, namely, the popular vote in Switzerland in 2009, where fifty-seven percent of the electorate voted in favor of a constitutional ban on constructions of new minarets on mosques (Gressgård 2010: xi). This referendum was indicative of a growing populist right-wing tendency by which Muslims were homogenized and cast as a threat to national and European values, presumably supported by liberal elites in the name of multiculturalism. Right-wing leaders across Europe saw the Swiss vote as both a major blow struck against multiculturalism and a triumph for the people against the elites. A few years earlier, the so-called Danish cartoon affair[1] got extensive media coverage across the world for much the same reason, and became the focus of scholarly debate in *Is Critique Secular?*—a volume involving Talal Asad, Saba Mahmood and Judith Butler, edited by Wendy Brown. In the Introduction, Brown (2009: 13) notes that there is both a theoretical and political incitement of this particular inquiry, a combination that itself herald the work of critique. This crucial statement, which implies that academic critique in the politicized field of multiculturalism is all but "detached" from the world, is emblematic of the critical literature to which Hage points when suggesting that we go back and restart the argument, and it serves as a guiding principle for my discussion of critical dialogue here.

It is important to note that the public responses to *Jyllands-Posten*'s publication of the Muhammad cartoons revealed a striking lack of appreciation of difference in modalities of belief and interpretation—an almost total lack of recognition of the injury they caused for many Muslims. Brown (2009: 17) comments, echoing Kögler, that "the debate remained locked in an unreflexive and one-sided hermeneutic taken to be the only hermeneutic." From a critical hermeneutical perspective, such solipsism "excludes *self-distanciation* and a *new evaluation* of one's own customary and unthematic assumptions, practices and orientations" (Kögler 1999: 140). Kögler explains that the identification of a common subject matter or meaning—such as the Muhammad cartoons and the meaning of blasphemy—may not imply a communality of evaluative standards (155). Even though each interpretation *must* posit a common point of reference within the meaning context to be understood, he points out, corresponding assumptions and "epistemic orientation" may nevertheless be completely different (165). Drawing on Foucault's work, he goes on to argue that it is crucial to frame and pursue historical or cultural understanding in such a way that it can engender an illuminating contrast to one's own symbolic assumptions by reconstructing other meaning structures such that they retain their alterity (174).

In my own discussion of how to obtain a critical evaluative distance, I draw on *The Power of Dialogue* to probe how a dialogically open understanding can make incommensurable differences in world views appear. In line with Kögler's (1999: 241, 242) argument that we cannot universally define the specific ideas and expectations constituting an acceptable existence for people, and that we should take into consideration whether they suffer under the given conditions, I make the case that the catalyst for critical dialogue is a sense of injustice, a sense that something is wrong—a malaise of sorts. Engaging also with Jean-François Lyotard's (1988) work, I am interested in the human capacity to be affected by others, which facilitates a demand—beyond normative justification—to find new idioms when faced with insurmountable difference. The conflict that emerges when no overarching or universal framework can do justice to all involved parties in an encounter—what Lyotard terms the "differend"—amounts to an *aporia* (Derrida 1993). However, the irreconcilable conflict is always immediately smothered and reduced to a solvable litigation through the ways that language works pragmatically. In relation to multicultural dialogue, I suggest that postponement of judgement could make us attentive to this kind of silencing mechanism: the injustice occurring when the "regulation" of a conflict is done in the idiom of one part, while the wrong suffered by the other part is "forgotten" insofar as there is no way it can be expressed in that idiom (Lyotard 1988: §12). A "wrong" is, in brief, a damage accompanied by the loss of the means to prove it (§7). Alluding to Spivak (2004), we may infer that "righting" wrongs is at once an impossible and indispensable task, a critical-dialogic ethos—a sensibility of sorts. The latter bears affinity to what Kögler (1999: 272, 274) calls a dialogical attitude, understood as a consciously adopted ethos of interpretation, only with a different inflection, as I am chiefly concerned with the feelings that move us, indistinguishably tied to the (incommensurable) differences that escape signification in the process of interpretation.

Kögler (1999: 163) is careful to explain that incommensurability is not to be equated with untranslatability. But if we consider dialogue as a task of "cultural translation," in accord with Judith Butler's (2009) approach, dialogue comes to mean—paralleling Kögler's critical hermeneutics—a process of yielding our most fundamental categories. Through comparative interrogation, with no direct standards of comparison, one framework is interrupted by another, whereupon we become (reflexively) aware that our conceptions are located in a given framework (Butler 2009: 104f., 108). Because the conflict that emerges is one between competing schemes of evaluation (i.e., incommensurable evaluative norms), translation is not merely a matter of suspending the question of evaluation or judgment in a temporal sense but a critical inquiry into the ways in which knowledge is organized prior to specific acts of knowledge and judgment (115). In this framing, cultural translation involves an investigation of the conditions that make judgment possible, separate from (the acts of) judgment itself. If we now connect back to Kögler's conception of dialogue as a consciously adopted ethos, it is possible to argue— from this reconfigured critical perspective—that incommensurable frames of evaluation oblige us to search for novel representations and new possibilities for action.

In a political culture of intense polarization, on the other hand, nurturing directed and reflective social action by way of dialogue (Kögler 1999: 275) is demanding, to say the least. Polarization entails not merely increased alienation of certain sectors of the population but are also characterized by narrowed political options and available vocabularies. The choices may be so simplified that actors feel violence is the only option left for them (Glynos and Howarth 2007: 57). Still, as Jason Glynos and David Howarth emphasize, even if people are likely to affectively invest in discourses and ideologies that induce "forgetting" of difference when their modes of being are experienced as disrupted or in a crisis, unsettling experiences might also provoke dialogue and critique, given that they call upon subjects to confront the contingency of social relations (110) and thus destabilize consolidated trajectories of past, present and future. Although there is a major difference between political discourse and what is commonly understood as hermeneutical conversation, this critical perspective resonates with Kögler's (1999: 272) assumption that "the confrontation with another meaning sets into motion a process of becoming reflectively aware of hitherto hidden assumptions and practices." To the extent that dislocation results in heightened alertness to one's social environments, to difference in particular, increased receptiveness to others and reflexivity are as likely as negative responses. Either way, experiences of volatility and unpredictability—collective affects formative of many encounters today—appear to compel critical scholars to seek a fuller understanding of affects as both impediment to and impetus for dialogue.

Affects and Critique

As mentioned at the outset, the relationship between knowledge and political action, or the link between critical thinking and social transformation, has come under scrutiny amongst a growing number of scholars announcing the "end of critique" or pointing to a "post critique" political culture. For instance, Eve Cherniavsky (2017) suggests that ideology critique has lost its political traction and sunk deeper into obsoleteness. The post-critique political culture manifests most distinctively in right-wing populism, since one of the favorite tactics of partisan politicians is to antagonize and divide, often refusing to acknowledge the legitimacy of their political opponents and showing outright contempt for "the views and groups that do not fit with the majoritarian meaning of the 'people'" (Urbinati 2019: 3–4).

In her influential essay "Paranoid reading and reparative reading," Eve K. Sedgwick (2003) sets the tone, preparing the ground for "post critique" academia. She comments: "it's strange that a hermeneutics of suspicion would appear so trusting about the effects of [a paranoid project of] exposure" (138–9), before rhetorically asking: "What does a hermeneutics of … exposure have to say to social formations in which visibility itself constitutes much of the violence?" (139–40). Interpretative projects of unveiling hidden power seem increasingly futile amid a surge in blatant racism and xenophobia, Sedgwick continues. At least we must admit, she asserts, that the efficiency of demystification projects does not reside in their relation to knowledge per se (141).

Despite important differences among proponents of the turn to affect, they all, in one way or another, oppose the privileging of the epistemological in scholarly literature—questions of discourse; knowledge; truth; interpretation, etc.—over questions concerning sensations; intimate textures of everyday life; experiences of world forces that cannot be contained within meaning's frame, etc. Robyn Wiegman (2014: 6, 7) describes it as a split between the (paranoid) critics' authority to know what things really mean on the one hand and privileging of the object's wordly inhabitations and needs on the other. When *knowing* is no longer the means for knowing what *to do*, the argument goes, we need to shift our attention from "critique" to affective affirmation.

Commenting on the early debates on epistemology versus affect, Clair Hemmings (2005) expresses concern over the reductive "grand shift" narratives typical of academic turns (cf. Gressgård and Lozic 2020). In celebrating the "new" that bears no resemblance to the past, pioneer proponents of affect theory portray epistemology as a closed social system of theory and knowledge, a dead-end, while offering affect as a "way out," a way of breaking free of Theory's straightjacket (Hemmings 2005: 555ff). Unlike those positing affect as a radically different order of experience to the epistemological, locating it entirely outside the reach of interpretation, Hemmings (2012) is interested in how affective experiences *can* become a sense of injustice that prompts reflexivity and political action. Conceptualizing politics as that which moves us, as opposed to that which confirms us in what we already know (151), she suggests that reflexive politicization might be based on a desire for transformation out of the experience of discomfort or dissonance (158). Yet, while maintaining that affect can be an impetus for dialogue and solidarity, she is also wary of its perils, pointing to the antagonism that is likely to arise from an inequality of location (153). Hemmings, in line with Glynos and Howarth referred above, cautions that we do not quite get at the possibility of hostility as a genuine affective condition of some intersubjective encounters (whatever our intentions), which severely impinges on the conditions for dialogue.² Hostility, she notes, might signal a lack of any real intersubjective connection (152, 153).

To discern how affects can motivate as well as constrain dialogic encounters, let us dwell on the notion of encounters for a moment. In a paper contesting the presumption of symmetry of exchange prevalent in so-called modern, western societies, Leonie Ansems de Vries and Doerthe Rosenow (2015) draw attention to Gilles Deleuze's (1988) Spinoza-informed notion of the "encounter" which is regarded as the ground for affective relationships, hence operating at the level set before the organization required by human perception (Haynes in Ansems de Vries and Rosenow 2015: 1119). Residing in the register of the sensational—that which is direct and not removable from experience—the encounter is characterized by fundamental indeterminacy; the "outcome" cannot be given in advance (1129). However, as Ansems de Vries and Rosenow see it, invoking the encounter as a *concept* not only allows us to pursue indeterminate line of flight but also enables us to shed light on what happens when "sense" hits taken-for-granted categories and, in so doing, puts into question (the binary logic of) these categories and the violence that brought them about (1120, 1130). While this conceptualization points to an immanent critical potential of actual encounters, bringing to the fore how their "sensation" is related to dominating configurations of thought and practice, the concept of encounter simultaneously suggests that what has been disrupted will always be reordered within new frames of recognition (1120). In this regard, pursuing encounters does not offer a "way out" of the epistemic requirements of representation as much as it entails an occasional dispensation of judgment and nurturing of affective relationships (1130). For Anderson (2017a: 594), the latter amounts to a micropolitics of learning "how to act in the midst of ongoing, unforeclosed situations and experiment with ways of discerning and tending to the 'otherwise.'"

To the extent that such micropolitics involves, as Anderson (2017a: 594) puts it, a temporal reorientation of knowledge practices to the emergent and prospective— through the promise of inaugurating (through a practice of judgment) some kind of disruption or interruption in the existing organization of the actual—we could regard it as a critical practice/ethos. It is not, however, tantamount to opposition or resistance (593–4). Hemmings (2012: 157) similarly notes that affective experiences of dislocation or dissonance cannot guarantee a resistant mode. As marginalized subjects might not be enraged at inequality but may instead affectively invest in sustaining relations of domination (154), thereby eschewing expectations of intersubjective reciprocity and mutual understanding (152), the pressing question is how to decenter congealed, violent beliefs about superiority (recall Hage's plea for symbolic disempowerment), while also enabling subjects to identify differently (Glynos and Howarth 2007: 79). The salient question for Kögler would be how to go beyond contextual self-interpretation and break from the immediate self-understanding of situated subjectivity. How can encounters possibly become a "starting point for directed and reflective social action" (Kögler 1999: 275)?

Sustaining a balance between critical hermeneutics and critical political theory, I would suggest that we call attention to the ways in which subjects are gripped by certain discourses and ideologies (Glynos and Howarth 2007: 79), how ideology is operating experience (Spivak 1988a). The need to reorient the "distorted vision of situated subjects" (Kögler 1999: 265) by way of "ideology critique" is hardly an argument for more reasoned, rational deliberations, though.[3] If knowledge is equated with rationality or an unbroken attitude toward truth, as Kögler puts it, then Sedgwick is right in claiming that the efficiency of demystification projects does not reside in their relation to knowledge per se. To avoid conflating critique (demystification) with realist notions of revealing illusions (cf. Cherniavsky 2017), it seems equally important, therefore, to separate knowledge—and, by extension, (ideology) critique—from enlightenment notions of reason. As Brown (2009: 13) points out, the dominant understanding of critique in a western context has for more than 150 years been contrasted with an idea of "religious illusion" (even when religion is not the expressed target of critique). Critique would seem to carry a tacit presumption of (enlightenment) reason's capacity to unveil error, and therein lies part of the problem (9).

It appears that Sedgwick, at least in part, alludes to a realist notion of critique when deflating interpretative projects of unveiling hidden power (or ideology). But if critical thinkers and proponents of the affective turn concur on this view, each in their own way repudiating the idea of reason's capacity to expose illusion, then it might prove more fruitful to identify points of convergence between them than detecting incompatibilities. That brings me back to Butler's (2009) intervention. For her, critique is indeed affectively invested, involving the sense that something is wrong or unfair, ultimately concerning that which we need to live (a livable life). To the extent that critique is bound up with survival, with living on, it is a truly existential issue, which is markedly different from criticism considered a random, negative and judgmental operation (110). It is also, and most importantly, irreducible to "paranoid reading" in Sedgwick's articulation, or what Anderson (2017a: 594) describes as a style of critique habitually reducing "the present and near future to another expression of a supposedly settled and named source of harm or damage."

Engaging with Foucault's (1997a) essay "What is Enlightenment?," in which he reiterates Kant's formulation of enlightenment as "a way out," Butler (2009) wonders whether he means by this that Kant provides a way out, or that Foucault, through his very citation of Kant, seeks to establish a way out of Kant. What seems clear is that "a way out" does not mean breaking free of Theory's straightjacket (as Hemmings puts it). Butler clarifies: "Although Foucault attributes to Enlightenment the injunction, 'dare to know', he clearly takes distance from the idea that knowledge is an exclusive function of reason" (112), which means that Foucault decisively breaks with Kant's notion that "reason" is the substance of critique. Characterizing the operation of critique as an attitude—a mode of relating to reality—and an ethos, Foucault establishes instead a close link between knowledge and sensibility.

> By "attitude," Foucault means a mode of relating to reality or, alternatively, an ethos—a way of acting and behaving that belongs to a certain culture or community, that signals that belongingness, and that is also an ongoing process and which presents itself as an obligation and a task.
>
> Butler 2009: 113

In the lecture "What is Critique?," Foucault (1997b) states that the task of critique is to call into question established frameworks of evaluation (cited in Butler 2009: 114; see also Butler 2000). Even in Kant, Butler (2009: 115) notes, critique is an inquiry into the conditions of possibility that make judgment possible. If the Kantian approach to critique suggests that our ways of knowing are structured prior to the possibility of our judgment, then Foucault's take on this would be to ask how knowledge is organized by specific historical schemes and how our judgments rely on those prior organizations of knowledge.[4] In the context of the Danish cartoon affair, Butler takes critique to be a process of delimiting and naming the conditions of possibility for "affective and evaluative" response. The task of critique, then, is to question the taken-for-granted ways that dominant Euro-Atlantic schemes circumscribe the domain of understanding and evaluation, how those specific schemes "inform and move us" (107, 115, 116). This is one way of attending to the ways in which subjects are gripped by certain discourses and ideologies.

Paraphrasing Foucault on the relation between life and power, Anderson (2014: 167), meanwhile, underscores that "affects may be instruments or effects of apparatuses, but also they may be impediments or irritants." While taking inspiration from non-representational theories that conceive of life as an impersonal force, he does not consider these life forces as "a guarantee that things might be different and better or necessarily oppositional to modalities of power" (168), but nor does he take ordering processes as a product of some form of determining structure. Neither bodily capacities to affect and being affected (emerging from encounters), nor collective affective conditions (mediating how life is lived and felt), can be explained by reference to some external social factor (168). With this interdependent and indeterminate relationship between affects and symbolic orders in mind, let us now return to the relationship between critique and the world—to specify and redirect our questions.

Critique and the World

It should be clear by now that it is somewhat misleading to depict critique as an exercise confined to the domain of abstract Theory, detached from experience and intersubjectivity, and conversely, it seems mistaken to locate affects in a register entirely outside the reach of critical interpretation. Even so, the question remains as to whether the practice of (ideology) critique is dissociated from the material world by readily reducing matters of fact to matters of concern, as Bruno Latour (2004) argued already two decades ago. From a non-representational point of view, critical thinking's privileging of epistemology detaches it not only from concrete experiences but also from the concrete world of facts. In response, Butler (2019) asserts that the critical project does not take leave of the world of facts as much as it recognizes that it is a world, finding modes of dynamic engagement with it (3). Caught up in the temporal vector of past, present and future, "we think within a mode of thought formed in, by, against—and even for—the impress of the world" (4).

This line of reasoning does not merely suggest that critique is historically conditioned and situated; it is—more substantially—suggestive of a particular temporal modality in the ways that "the world acts on us and exercises a historical demand on thought" (Butler 2019: 4). To the extent that critique emerges from situations experienced as urgent, the "critical" can perhaps best be understood through the temporality of crisis—for which Brown's (2005) chapter "Untimeliness and punctuality: Critical theory in dark times" seems particularly instructive. By reference to Reinhart Koselleck's (1988) seminal work, *Critique and Crisis*, Brown (2005) points to the etymological link between the two terms and their shifting historical relationship (from ancient times onwards). I shall not attempt to recapitulate Brown's detailed argument here; suffice it to say that, in its "original" meaning, there could be no such thing as "mere critique," insofar as the project of critique was inherently bound up with action. This meaning lingers in the medical designation of "critical" conditions, as well as in political crises designated as critical. "A critical condition is a particular kind of call: an urgent call for knowledge, deliberation, judgment, and action to stave off catastrophe" (7). Because a political crisis demands judgment about appropriate interventions, the underlying temporality is one of continuity amid temporary moments of interruption (associated with affects such as anxiety, fear and insecurity). The temporally finite nature of a crisis indicates that critique has a restorative as much as a transformative function. Critique involves an affirmation of this world and this time, Brown (16) notes, although not in terms of a "return to normal" but a reorientation and reconfiguration of time to open the present (14).[5]

The term "crisis" is of course closely related to "emergency" in the manner through which it relates to the past, present and future. In his conceptual discussion of emergency as a term and technique of government, Anderson (2017b) discerns between four interrelated temporalities around which emergency is organized: exceptionality; urgency; interval; and hope. It does not come as a surprise that exceptionality is the most discussed among these, considering the excessive use of force typically accompanying political declarations of states of exception/emergency (cf. Gressgård 2019). But the sense of urgency described by Brown resonates more with the presence of—or construction of a sense of—a compressed time for decision and action, a "now" that requires immediate response (Anderson 2017b: 469–70). Much like Brown's (2005: 13) assertion that the call for (decisive) response issued from a critical condition "stills time" (not to be confused with a "frenetic standstill" as famously articulated by Hartmut Rosa (2013)), Anderson further emphasizes the interval or break during which emergency action can still make a difference: "If action is decisive and happens at the correct time, then the emergency can be brought to an end without loss, harm or damage" (2017b: 470). Inseparable from the category of emergency, therefore, is hope. Though the outcome of an event or situation is uncertain, correct action may avert that which is threatened (considered worthy of protection) (470).

Importantly for our purposes, the language of emergency has for some time now been instrumental to non-governmental groups in documenting and generating a sense of urgency around entrenched structural violence precipitating and legitimating situational violence. For instance, the Black Lives Matter (BLM) movement has increasingly drawn attention to ordinary conditions harming and damaging people of color, concurrent with (fatal) police violence disproportionately affecting black people.

Although the BLM uprising in 2020, prompted by the police killing of George Floyd, focused mostly on police brutality and institutionalized contempt for black people, the ensuing interventions also highlighted temporally extended processes of "slow death" (Berlant 2007) in which the temporality of emergency coexists and folds with the temporality of that which endures (Anderson 2017b: 472; cf. Gressgård 2019). In naming the systemic racism as a series of emergencies, BLM activism does not merely make suffering more palpable; it blurs the very boundary between the endemic and the eventual. When the endemic and eventual (or the non-event and event) become indistinct in this way, it becomes abundantly clear that there is no normal or non-emergency situation to return to (Anderson 2017b: 472). This strategic use of emergency brings to the fore how "the distinction between everyday and emergency has only ever been available to some and is produced at the cost of making life into a perpetual emergency for others" (473).

Another way of putting this would be that the vocabulary and technique of emergency is a critical intervention in the present aimed at disrupting the unlivable conditions that have become ordinary over time. Consider the story of Belly Mujinga, a black woman who became ill with Covid-19 and died in April 2020 in London after being assaulted by a white man allegedly spitting at her and her colleague when at work in Victoria station, yelling "I've got Covid—I'll give it to you." The story attracted massive attention after reaching the media in May, when Covid-19's impact on people of color was becoming increasingly clear. An article in the *Guardian* poignantly states that Belly's story was enraging because it was a familiar one:

> Most of the public anger is directed at Belly's assailant. But the story is bigger than that ... Almost every aspect of the ... story is upsetting. Layers of injustice are buried inside each other, like Russian dolls. There is the alleged assault, which is straightforwardly contemptible. Then there is the question of why a woman with underlying health conditions was working in a public-facing role in the midst of a pandemic ... Why wasn't she listened to, if, as her union representative says, Belly told her supervisor she had been assaulted, and did not want to go back out to work? Why wasn't a report made to the police immediately? The list goes on.
>
> Kale 2020

Anderson (2017b: 473) points out that "[n]aming the everyday as an emergency is, in part, a bearing witness to and making present how otherwise invisible, silent, violences result in Black lives not mattering." He maintains that this is not only an attempt to step out of the continuous time of the linear production of the everyday emergency (475), but also a way of positively affirming that Black lives matter, which makes it an act of hope (albeit without guarantees) (474). However, "bearing witness" also risks eliding the inequality of position noted by Hemmings, hence inadvertently exacerbating it. She explains: "Witnessing has a whiff of innocence about it, one that locates its subject outside rather than caught up in the conditions that make intersubjective recognition impossible in the first place" (Hemmings 2012: 153).

While we can agree with Brown (2005: 13) and Anderson (2017b: 475) that the temporality of crisis or emergency—the urgent *now* and the *interval* pertaining to "stilled time"—opens the present from the continuum of history and embodies a hope for other futures, there is an imminent risk of being too hopeful, as it were.[6] With a strong emphasis on the possibility of bringing crisis to an end without loss, harm or damage, critique works on the assumption that bearing witness to the ordinary as a series of emergencies might help solving the problem, provided that appropriate action is taken. For Lyotard (1988), on the other hand, there cannot be "reparations" of damages in the absence of a common frame of judgment. The urgent if exacting task lies instead in bearing witness to damages that are *not* reparable owing to incommensurable standards of evaluation. Another dialogic way of proceeding, therefore, would be through cultural translation. In any event, radical conflicts, which are routinely ignored or pragmatically "resolved," are invisible or silent in a manner significantly different from the unrecognized non-events characteristic of what Lauren Berlant calls "crisis ordinariness" (cited in Anderson 2017b: 474).[7]

Different World Views, Different Worlds

To take alterity seriously, some would argue, it is not satisficing to affirm this world and time alone; we must (re)locate radical difference at the level of ontology, acknowledging "the existence of multiple, different worlds, rather than merely accepting multiple perspectives of THE ('one') world" (Rosenow 2019: 84). Ontological multiplicity, Rosenow explains, comes about when we encounter the clashing of different worlds, which is—as indicated above—an affectively unsettling and dislocating experience with the potential for creating new, emancipatory projects (84). This turn to ontology (primarily in anthropology and decolonial thought) coincides with the affective turn in its emphasis on discomforting experiences of dislocation, but the understanding of worlds as ontologically plural—also called "pluriverse"—takes us one step further away from representations of cultural difference, toward affirmation of the plurality of what *is*: the clashing of different worlds means encountering different modes of existence, not merely conflicting world views. Referring to Christina Rojas (2016), Rosenow (2019: 87) notes that a genuine "world dialogue" would be a relational activity of openness to the other, based on encounters rather than on attempts to know (abstractly) cultural difference. Knowledge is, on this account, a product of the world working on us (Chandler and Reid 2019: 93), although not in the Butlerian meaning outlined above. The sense of opening to the world through concrete encounters involves geo-situated or bodily situated knowledges that are truly immanent: knowing is being.

As David Chandler and Julian Reid (2019) forcefully argues, however, the ontological turn's focus on "other worlds" runs the risk of essentializing and reifying non-western ways of being in the world or enacting the world. So-called pluriversal approaches conceive of different worlds as separate, and typically profess received wisdom (especially indigenous ways of knowing/being in the world), thereby perpetuating ideas of authenticity, even as they foreground alterity. In Chandler and Reid's (2019: 92) view, the problem with pluriversal approaches is that all objects-subjects are understood as irreducibly within their own world of experience and sensation. That means, in Kögler's (1999: 270) terms, that subjects cannot distance themselves from their lifeworldly, situated selves—much like populist notions of authenticity (although their underlying premises are of course fundamentally different). There is simply no external point of view from which to gain insight into the specific structuration of world pictures (212) due to the limits of knowing. The limits to the knowledge claims made by the situated subject will in fact never be clear, Chandler and Reid (2019: 93) remark, "as the mechanism of 'geo- or body-knowledge production' cannot be reflected upon without paradoxically stepping outside of the limits of knowing." Accordingly, it is the very claim to (abstract) knowledge in western, modernist social sciences and humanities that becomes problematic, not so much the conditions of possibility enabling problematic knowledge claims (89)—recall here Butler's (2009) emphasis on the conditions of possibility for acts of knowledge and judgment in her conceptualization of critique.[8] Put differently, the denouncement of western knowledge as colonializing appears to be centered on the problem of representation per se, leaving largely untouched the long-established social arrangements and power hierarchies underpinning (specific) western, modernist representations (see Chandler and Reid 2019: 89). In so doing, pluriversal approaches also risk invoking the very separation between academia and the world that they purport to dissolve. But for all that, inspired by Anderson's account of the language of emergency being strategically deployed by BLM activists, thus reckoning with the politically saturated conditions for dialogue, I shall round off the discussion by venturing into and reconfigure the plural-worlds vocabulary as a form of strategic essentialism (Spivak 1988b)—aimed at radical symbolic disempowerment.

World Dialogues—a Way out of this World?

By way of conclusion, I shall advance the argument that radical symbolic disempowerment—the interruption of unlivable conditions that have become ordinary over time—hinges on the possibilities of dismantling the master's house, to borrow Audre Lord's (2007) legendary phrase: the world of common humanity and single horizon of sense. The "world" in a strong sense, Clair Colebrook (2020: 181) posits, "is an inherently enlightenment notion, bound up with a concept of human as properly geared toward unified understanding and a common history." The global project of humanity is a world in which all humankind can affirm each other in difference, and in such a world, fragmentation or polarization jeopardizes the tenors of liberal democracy and cosmopolitanism.

I have so far addressed the problem of right-wing populism as though it was the sole source and defining feature of polarization (stoking fear and division), but we cannot view the events and damaging effects of a "polarized world" through the prism of populism alone. We should also take into consideration anti-populist responses that tactically use disaster metaphors to evoke and convey a sense of existential threats to "our" democracy, society or humanity posed by "irrational and irresponsible" voters (Glynos and Mondon 2016: 7ff). Anti-Brexiters in Britain and anti-Law and Justice (PiS) campaigners in Poland (Gressgård and Smoczynski 2020), to mentions but a few, conjure the image of "barbarian" or "backward" voters in what they claim is a struggle for our existence; our way of life is on the line. Being invested in preserving this world as we know it, confirming us in what we already know (recall Hemmings), anti-populists are hardly any more intent on changing the conditions for people living in a world without the possibility of living a livable life than are their populist (right-wing) counterparts. Ultimately, saving *this* world relies upon some lives not mattering, blackness being the most flagrant example—with black life chances being obstructed and warped on a daily basis. There is, importantly, more to this than saying that black lives don't matter, or that "they" are valued less than "us," as it tells us that the very concept of world (or life) is composed by negating and destroying black life (Colebrook 2020: 188).[9] If, as Colebrook asserts, blackness marks an unthinkable non-being that cannot be held within humanism—the assumption of a common humanity (197)—then destruction of this world might be more of a necessity than an imminent threat. The question is, "if the world were to see and feel this violence, would it be able to survive?" (190).

Without adhering to the notion of worlds as ontologically separate (and knowing as being), we could perhaps find a "way out" of this particular if universalized world through dialogues that take radical difference seriously, acknowledging that "many who exist in this world do not experience it as a horizon of meaning and possibility, but as a system that constantly requires their non-being" (Colebrook 2020: 183). Rather than positively affirming that black lives matter premised on the idea(l) of worth (i.e., a polity built on worth) (193; cf. Gressgård 2010),[10] and peaceful coexistence as the primary relation among different "worlds" (Wakefield 2020: 174), genuine "world dialogues" would indeed take seriously clashes between different modes of existence, including what Hemmings describes as a lack of any real intersubjective connection.[11] Our main concern, then, would be not so much a polarized world as a "one world" world predicated on racialized death-politics, spectacular and eventual as well as slow and ordinary.

Acknowledgment

I would like to thank Ľubomír Dunaj and Kurt C.M. Mertel for organizing the *Hermeneutics, Critique and Dialogue* conference at the University of North Florida in February 2020. I also want to thank the other participants, including Kögler, for stimulating discussions while gathered in Jacksonville, and finally, I owe a note of gratitude to Dunaj and Mertel for editing this volume.

Notes

1   The *Wikipedia* article reads: "The *Jyllands-Posten* Muhammad cartoons controversy (or Muhammad cartoons crisis) [...] began after the Danish newspaper Jyllands-Posten published 12 editorial cartoons on 30 September 2005, most of which depicted Muhammad.... The newspaper announced that this was an attempt to contribute to

the debate about criticism of Islam and self-censorship. Muslim groups in Denmark complained, and the issue eventually led to protests around the world, including violent demonstrations and riots in some Muslim countries." Available at https://en.wikipedia.org/wiki/Jyllands-Posten_Muhammad_cartoons_controversy.

2 Worse still is a political climate in which partisan political supporters find community by rejoicing in the suffering of racialized others, as highlighted in Adam Serwer's (2018) essay, "The cruelty is the point."

3 Following Althusser's (1971) lead, ideology is here taken to represent the imaginary relationship of individuals to their real conditions of existence. Its function is to constitute concrete individuals as subjects, involving the twin operation of recognition and misrecognition. On the one hand, ideology "imposes" an obviousness in our relation to the world by way of naturalization or normalization, while on the other, it leads to misrecognition of social reality, as the production of obviousness and normality covers over the ultimate contingency of social existence. Insofar as ideologies are understood to be part of the very structures of society—which is a far cry from seeing ideology as (false) consciousness—the system of representation and practices constituting the ideological instance of a social formation can never be erased in the name of a society completely transparent to itself (Glynos and Howarth 2007: 117–18). "Ideology critique" is hence not aimed at revealing the truth behind ideology by way of exposure.

4 At this juncture, we might ask why Kögler does not engage with Foucault's notion of critique along similar lines, especially when "dialogical attitude" is concerned. While Kögler (1999: 173) states that Foucault can serve as a guiding thread for the theory and methodology of a critical hermeneutics, he draws mainly on Foucault's earlier writings. Kögler notes that Foucault, in his later (genealogical) analyses, emphasizes power at the cost of "meaning" as the fundamental concept, and explains that he—in *The Power of Dialogue*—seeks to rework insights from Foucault's earlier works by proceeding from a hermeneutically conceived problematic (175). For an engagement with Foucault's genealogical work, see Kögler (2017). Here, Kögler draws attention to Foucault's epistemological reflections on an "epistemic coalition" between the position of the discourse analyst in academic genealogy and the situated position of the agent, "so as to build a bridge between his own genealogical approach and what he calls *local knowledges*" (253–4, emphasis in original). Linking this notion of epistemic coalition to hermeneutic reciprocity, Kögler proposes a general theory of reflexive social agency which centers on the social and normative conditions for (critical-hermeneutical) dialogical exchange. For a more comprehensive discussion of Foucault's works, including his notion of critique (as an attitude and an ethos), see Kögler (2004) (German edition).

5 This speaks to the critical-theoretical assumption that discourse can alter its terms by reorganizing or reorienting time (and consequently meaning). Paraphrasing—while also distorting ever so slightly—James Martin (2020: 7), we could argue that critique is not merely a response to a situation of crisis but seeks also to transform it, making it amenable to certain kinds of action by, for instance, (re)framing some issues as urgent while disrupting other temporal frames that enclose certain transformations (8, 9). This underlines that critical practices are not separate from, but rather immersed in, the situations in which they seek to intervene. Nevertheless, it could also be argued that such interventions display what Derrida calls "an untimeliness that comes on time" (cited in ibid.: 9). Like Brown, Martin refers to Derrida's (2002) riffing of the line from Shakespeare's *Hamlet*, "the time is out of joint," to stress the "risk" or temporal

instability of meaning: how interpretation happens by way of negotiation in the space between the regular (convention) and the irregular (the unknown future), the commensurable and the incommensurable (Martin 2020: 11f.). Brown, for her part, is less interested in radial hermeneutics and more in how a polity in crisis is living out its time dissynchronically: "When a polity is in crisis, the times are unhinged, running off course; time itself lacks its capacity to contain us and conjoin us" (2005: 8).

6   On a general analytical level, this line of reasoning seems to resonate with Derrida's (1995) argument that any language act, by committing to something in the future, entails a certain structure of the promise. A promise is, on this account, always without guarantees, as it works on the condition that it can fail or be broken. However, insofar as Derrida's argument concerns the structure of language as such, it is not entirely compatible with the aforementioned "hope without guarantees" argument. See Martin (2020) for a discussion of the "promissory" quality of speech (and writing) with reference to Derrida. For another take on "hope without guarantees," see Hirsch (2015). By associating it with chance (and genuine uncertainty), Alexander Hirsch conceives of hope as an opportunity opening up when all available options for action appear exhausted. While chance offers a way of "going beyond," he explains, it is not a way out. Taking a chance is instead a way of responding when there is no way out (4). The will to chance thus consists in excising promises, forsaking all guarantees (or anticipation of the future), which is to say that hope promises nothing (5). In the context of migration and multiculturalism, Hage's work on hope emphasizes the inequality of its production and distribution, and when reflecting on its reception, he puts the problematic of exploitation at the center of his concerns: "certain available hope for someone is built on the sucking of the very possibility of hope from someone else's" (Hage 2016: 466). These various registers of hope—its indeterminate potentiality-character and the inequality of its specific (colonial) formations—come together in the critical perspective I propose in the present chapter.

7   See also Das (2006) on how violence has descended into the ordinary instead of constituting an interruption of life to which we simply bear witness. Another parallel can be drawn to Ann Stoler's (2013: 7ff) discussion of enduring damages in terms of cumulative debris and imperial formations—processes of decimation, displacement and reclamation. These political forms endure beyond the formal exclusions and are hence often less available to scrutiny and less accessible to chart. However, they are discernible and definable providing we, through critical analysis, make historical and structural connections that are not otherwise readily visible (18; cf. Gressgård 2019).

8   It is worth mentioning that Chandler and Reid (2019: 32, 35–6, 73) also criticize one of Butler's works on account of her concept of dispossession (see Butler and Antanasiou 2013), apparently chiming with pluriversal approaches to knowledge as product of the world working on us—worlds in which knowers dissolve themselves (Chandler and Reid 2019: 93). However, as our discussion suggests, a more careful reading could offer a more nuanced understanding of Butler's critical approach.

9   Ta-Nehisi Coates' (2015) award-winning book, *Between the World and Me*, tells us exactly that.

10 "Does the ideal of equality legitimate inequality?" I ask in my discussion of multicultural paradoxes (Gressgård 2010: 37ff), as part of a wider discussion of how modern egalitarian ideologies (classical liberal and republican) involve hierarchization (Chap. 2, "Non-modern holism and modern totalitarianism"). For a similar discussion from a historical perspective, see Chap. 2, "The rise of modern racism(s)," in Fredrickson (2002).

11 This experience is aptly described by Reni Eddo-Lodge (2017) in *Why I'm No Longer Talking to White People about Race*.

References

Althusser, L. (1971), *Lenin and Philosophy, and Other Essays*, New York: Monthly Review Press.
Anderson, B. (2014), *Encountering Affect: Capacities, Apparatuses, Conditions*, London: Routledge.
Anderson, B. (2017a), "Hope and micropolitics," *Environment and Planning D: Society and Space* 35 (4): 593–5.
Anderson, B. (2017b), "Emergency futures: Exception, urgency, interval, hope," *The Sociological Review* 65 (3): 463–77.
Ansems de Vries, L. and Rosenow, D. (2015), "Opposing the opposition? Binary and complexity in political resistance," *Environment and Planning D: Society and Space* 33 (6): 1118–34.
Berlant, L. (2007), "Slow death (sovereignty, obesity, lateral agency)," *Critical Inquiry* 33: 754–80.
Brown, W. (2005), *Edgework: Critical Essays on Knowledge and Politics*, Princeton: Princeton University Press.
Brown, W. (2009), "Introduction," in Asad et al. (eds.): *Is Critique Secular? Blasphemy, Injury, and Free Speech*, 7–19, Berkeley: University of California Press.
Butler J (2000), "What is critique? An essay on Foucault's virtue," Cambridge University Raymond Williams Lecture. Published in longer form in Ingram D (ed.): *The Political: Readings in Continental Philosophy*. London: Blackwell, 2002. Available online: https://transversal.at/transversal/0806/butler/en (accessed 1 August 2020).
Butler, J. (2009), "The sensibility of critique: Response to Adad and Mahmood," in Asad et al. (eds.): *Is Critique Secular? Blasphemy, Injury, and Free Speech*, 101–36, Berkeley: University of California Press.
Butler, J. (2019), "The inorganic body in the early Marx: A limit-concept of anthropocentrism," *Racial Philosophy* 2 (6): 3–17.
Butler, J. and Antanasiou, A. (2013), *Dispossession: The Performance in the Political*, Cambridge: Polity.
Chandler, D. and Reid, J. (2019), *Becoming Indigenous: Governing Imaginaries in the Anthropocene*, London: Rowman & Littlefield.
Cherniavsky, E. (2017), *Neocitizenship: Political Culture after Democracy*, New York: New York University Press.
Coates, T-N. (2015), *Between the World and Me*, Melbourne: Text Publishing.
Colebrook, C. (2020), "What would you do (and who would you kill) in order to save the world?," in D. Chandler, K. Grove, and S. Wakefield (eds.): *Resilience in the Anthropocene: Governance and Politics at the End of the World*, 179–99, London: Routledge.
Das, Veena (2006), *Life and Words: Violence and the Decent into the Ordinary*, Berkeley: University of California Press.
Deleuze, G. (1988), *Spinoza: Practical Philosophy* (trans. R. Hurley), San Francisco: City Lights Books.
Derrida, J. (1993), *Aporias* (trans. T. Dutroit), Stanford, CA: Stanford University Press.
Derrida, J. (1995), "Passages—from traumatism to promises," in *Points . . . Interviews*,

1974–1994 (ed. E. Webber, trans. P. Kamuf), 372–95, Stanford, CA: Stanford University Press.

Derrida, J. (2002), *Specters of Marx: The State of the Debt, the Work of Mourning and the New International* (trans. P. Kamuf), London: Routledge.

Eddo-Lodge, R. (2017), *Why I'm No Longer Talking to White People about Race*, London: Bloomsbury Circus.

Fieschi, C. (2019), *Populocracy*, Newcastle: Agenda Publishing.

Foucault, M. (1997a), "What is enlightenment?" (trans. C. Porter), in S. Lotringer (ed.), *The Politics of Truth*, 97–119, Los Angeles: Semiotext(e).

Foucault M. (1997b), "What is critique?" (trans. L. Hochroth), in S. Lotringer (ed.), *The Politics of Truth*, 41–82, Los Angeles: Semiotext(e).

Fredrickson, G.M. (2002), *Race: A short History*, Princeton: Princeton University Press.

Glynos, J. and Howarth, D. (2007), *Logics of Critical Explanation in Social and Political Theory*, London: Routledge.

Glynos, J. and Mondon, A. (2016), "The political logic of populist hype," *POPULISMUS Working Papers No. 4*.

Gressgård, R. (2010), *Multicultural Dialogue: Dilemmas, Paradoxes, Conflicts*, New York: Berghahn Books.

Gressgård, R. (2019), "The racialized death-politics of urban resilience governance," *Social Identities*, 25 (1): 11–26.

Gressgård, R. and Lozic, V. (2020), "The shifting status of failure and possibility: Resilience and the 'shift' in partnership-organized prevention in Sweden," *Politics*, 40 (3): 332–47.

Gressgård, R. and Smoczynski, R. (2020), "Noble Polish sexuality and the corrupted European body," *Intersections: East European Journal of Society and Politics*, 6 (3): 13–32.

Hage, G. (2016), "Questions concerning a future-politic," *History and Anthropology*, 27 (4): 465–7.

Hage, G. (2019), "The politics of white restoration has to 'go back where it came from,'" *The Guardian*, July 19. Available online: https://www.theguardian.com/commentisfree/2019/jul/20/the-politics-of-white-restoration-has-to-go-back-where-it-came-from (accessed July 20, 2019).

Hemmings, C. (2005), "Invoking affect," *Cultural Studies*, 19 (5): 548–67.

Hemmings, C. (2012), "Affective solidarity: Feminist reflexivity and political transformation," *Feminist Theory*, 13 (2): 147–61.

Hirsch, A.H. (2015), "Hope without guarantees: Mourning, natality, and the will to chance in Book XXIV of the *Iliad*," *Theory & Event*, 18 (1): 1–8.

Kale, S. (2020), "'I feel she was abandoned': The life and terrible death of Belly Mujinga," *The Guardian*, August 25. Available online: https://www.theguardian.com/society/2020/aug/25/i-feel-she-was-abandoned-the-life-and-terrible-death- of-belly-mujinga (accessed August 25, 2020).

Koselleck, R. (1988), *Critique and Crisis: Enlightenment and the Pathogenesis of Modern Society*. Cambridge, Mass: The MIT Press.

Kögler, H-H. (1999), *The Power of Dialogue: Critical Hermeneutics after Gadamer and Foucault* (trans. Paul Hendrickson), Cambridge, Mass: The MIT Press.

Kögler, H-H. (2004), *Michel Foucault* (Zweite Auflage), Stuttgart: J.B. Metzler/Springer.

Kögler, H.H. (2017), "A discursive view from somewhere: Foucault's epistemic position," in B.B. Janz (ed.): *Place, Space and Hermeneutics*, 239–60, Cham: Springer.

Latour, B. (2004), 'Why has critique run out of steam? From matters of fact to matters of concern," *Critical Inquiry*, 30: 225–48.

Lord, A. (2007/1984), "The Master's tools will never dismantle the master's house," in *Sister Outsider: Essays and Speeches by Audre Lorde*, 110–14, Berkeley, CA: Crossing Press.

Lyotard, J-F. (1988), *The Differend: Phrases in Dispute* (trans. G. van den Abeele), Minneapolis: University of Minnesota Press.

Martin, J. (2020), "Rhetoric, discourse and the hermeneutics of public speech," *Politics* (OnlineFirst), 1–15. Available online: https://journals.sagepub.com/doi/full/10.1177/0263395720933779 (accessed 1 August 2020).

Rojas, C. (2016), "Contesting the colonial logics of the international: Toward a relational politics for the pluriverse," *International Political Sociology* 10 (4): 369–82.

Rosenow, D. (2019), "Decolonising the decolonisers? Of ontological encounters in the GMO controversy and beyond," *Global Society* 33 (1): 82–99.

Rosa, H. (2013), *Social Acceleration: A New Theory of Modernity* (trans. J. Trejo-Mathys), New York: Columbia University Press.

Serwer, A. (2018), "The cruelty is the point," *The Atlantic*, 3 October. Available online: https://www.theatlantic.com/ideas/archive/2018/10/the-cruelty-is-the-point/572104 (accessed August 1, 2020).

Spivak, G.C. (1988a), "Can the subaltern speak?," in C. Nelson and L. Grossberg (eds.), *Marxism and the Interpretation of Culture*, 271–313, Basingstoke: Macmillan Education.

Spivak, G.C. (1988b), "Subaltern Studies: Deconstructing historiography," in R. Guha, and G.C. Spivak (eds.): *Selected Subaltern Studies*, 3–32, Oxford: Oxford University Press.

Spivak, G.C. (2004), "Righting wrongs," *The South Atlantic Quarterly*, 103 (2–3): 523–81.

Stoler, A.L. (2013), "Introduction: 'The rot remains': From ruins to ruination," in A.L. Stoler (ed.), *Imperial Debris: On Ruins and Ruination*, Durham: Duke University Press.

Urbinati, N. (2019), *Me the People: How Populism Transforms Democracy*, Cambridge, MA: Harvard University Press.

Wakefield, S. (2019), "More of the same? Life beyond the liberal one world world," in D. Chandler, K. Grove, and S. Wakefield (eds.), *Resilience in the Anthropocene: Governance and Politics at the End of the World*, 162–78, London: Routledge.

Wiegman, R. (2014), "The times we're in: Queer feminist criticism and the reparative 'turn,'" *Feminist Theory*, 15 (1): 4–25.

Conclusion

Social Ontology, Dialogic Recognition, and Contemporary Challenges: A Reply

Hans-Herbert Kögler

The hermeneutic process consists of the understanding and interpretation of the meaning, expressed as a view about a subject matter, of another agent who articulates herself symbolically or actively in some form. The hermeneutic situation is defined by certain background conditions that exist formally on both the interpreter and the interpretee's side and that allow for the "epistemic access" to the meaning of the Other. Hermeneutic interpretation is thus defined by an equality in difference: the distance or divide between one's own pre-understanding and assessment of the issue needs to be "mediated" or related to the other's perspective; the articulation of a sensible account of what was said or done and why and how it is made possible by some shared understanding of what is provided by different contexts. Philosophical hermeneutics sets out, based on its long trajectory from the beginning of modernity, to reconstruct the conceptual, methodological, and normative grounds on the basis of which such a process can be taken to create valid knowledge, and thus contribute to a culture and society's self-understanding. Culminating in Hans-Georg Gadamer's approach, the essential nature of an interpreter's pre-understanding as a condition for interpretation, the dialogic nature of the interpretive process, and the essential openness and non-closure of our hermeneutic being came into focus. Critical hermeneutics sets out to advance and develop those insights in the spirit of critical social theory. The project consists both of an immanent critique of hermeneutic thought and, more importantly, in the transformation of core tenets such that they serve the goals of a reflexive self-realization in power-defined situations and practices.

The harmonious and tradition-preserving tendencies of hermeneutics are thus transformed into a critical and distanciating attitude that acknowledges one's radical and inescapable situatedness in cultural contexts, while the Enlightenment ideals of a self-determining subject, capable of exercising agency in light of objective conditions and realizing free and equal conditions, are re-emphasized. Yet the ideals of self-determination, equality, and solidarity are now re-envisioned against the background of (a), the hermeneutic insights of one's inescapable social situatedness; and (b), a set of critical philosophies that, roughly, continue the project of a modern ethos while emphasizing its radical altered and transformed conditions. Most importantly rank here Habermas' critical dialogue with Gadamer's philosophical hermeneutics, the poststructuralist dismantling of naively universalist and essentialist conceptions of reason, science, and normativity, and the pragmatist onslaught on core concepts of the philosophical tradition like the correspondence theory of truth or the referential theory of meaning. All three movements point toward the need for a redefinition of the inherent logic and validity of hermeneutic understanding. Heeding this call, critical hermeneutics undertakes a systematic reintegration of social theory with hermeneutic situatedness via the analysis of the hermeneutic background and the role of agency, context, and power in the formation of the interpretive process. In all that, to make it clear, critical hermeneutics aims to *reconstruct*, not *deconstruct*, our commitment to the truth of interpretation, the normative recognition of the Other as an insurmountable orientation of one's actions, and the overall goal of a just and egalitarian society. Yet its stubborn starting point is now, in good hermeneutic spirit, the interpretive situation between me and the Other, from which a detailed reconstructive process unearths universally shared features; it thus aims to enable a renewed philosophical appropriation of the important hermeneutic tradition in philosophy in order to reposition critical theory.

The immensely rich contributions in this volume testify to the depths and productivity of this approach by further advancing it. I owe a considerable debt to the editors Ľubomír Dunaj and Kurt C.M. Mertel not only for assembling and motivating such an outstanding and diverse group of scholars, but for also envisioning this project before I did. In my view, the essays provide important developments and inspirations as they specifically point to three constructions sites: reconstructing a hermeneutic social ontology, articulating the normative implications of dialogic interpretation, and assessing the sources of critique in current society and politics. With regard to the transition from a "linguistic ontology" (Gadamer) to social ontology, the body, social power, and the role of social-cognitive capabilities prove central, as Simon Susen, Rainer Winter and Stephen Turner articulate (1.). As to the normative entailments of dialogic interpretation, the chapters by Karsten Stueber, Werner Delanoy, Paul Healy and John Maraldo move from an analysis of the moral implications of critical hermeneutics to its natural unfolding in a dialogic cosmopolitanism and to the role of religion in public dialogue (2.). Finally, Frédéric Vandenberghe, William Outhwaite, Lauren Barthold and Randi Gressgård engage what we may call "dialogue in difficult times," i.e., the social and political challenges that current contexts present for the dialogic ethos (3.). The sophistication and scrutiny with which all of them engage the impetus and implications of critical hermeneutics fills me with humility and gratitude—and with the modest hope that this approach may provide a unified sense of purpose, or at least some orientation and guidance, within the complex and diversified fields of critical theory and cultural studies.

Part I: From Hermeneutics to Social Ontology: Body, Power, Capabilities

Hermeneutic thought, itself the reflexive appropriation of the reflexivity entailed in interpretation, focuses on the formal presuppositions of how we understand. Since understanding something as something both encompasses the intentional disclosure of phenomena in the world and its potential thematization as a world-constituting process, it is essentially defined by language. "Being that can be understood is language" (Gadamer 1989: 474) because only through symbolic mediation achieves thought its inner articulation, becomes capable of "symbolic pregnance" (Cassirer 1955) and shared world-orientation. This process entails the potential for *self-reflexivity*, as my intentional focus on something can itself become the focus. But it is usually oriented toward *something "in the world"* and as such allows for a fixed and "objective" construction of world in the first place. This world-orientation is embedded and actualized in the *social use* of language, as the shared linguistic meaning is what creates an *invisible bond* among subjects. Language allows for an *intersubjective interpenetration* among speakers as individuals, as Wilhelm von Humboldt so suggestively put it, "a circle whence it is possible to exit only by stepping over at once into the circle of another one" (Humboldt 1999: 60). For Humboldt language consists in the constant re-actualization of a dialectic between subjective agency, in which I as an agent address you (and vice versa) vis-à-vis our perspectives toward a shared world, and an objectively structured medium of common concepts and assumptions. Language is both *energeia*, the agentive force to always name, define, reinvent, and rethematize what's at stake, and the underlying *ergon* on which we draw in order to make ourselves understood, and which underlies the possibility to even exist in this shared medium of meaning.

I have presented these *linguistically grounded* aspects of critical interpretation because they are indispensable to establish the critical-hermeneutic project with regard to its agency-enabling and normative dimensions. But if separated from the overall reconstruction of the hermeneutic background, they can create the misguided impression that understanding is here idealized again, that my approach errs on a preponderance of "language and reason," as Simon Susen alleges. It is true, as Stephen Turner suggests, that the approach builds in important aspects on the "idealistic tradition" broadly constructed, and it is therefore also apt, as Rainer Winter proposes, to reconsider the role of the body especially with regard to critical social thought. The challenge, it seems, that an approach that aims to rebuild critical theory from the grounds of the reflexive hermeneutic process confronts, is whether it can convincingly integrate precisely those dimensions of social (and cognitive) reality that *prima facie* seem to evade the hermeneutic self-understanding of situated agents. Inasmuch as this non-ideal, material, bodily, or cognitive "unthought" would be essential for hermeneutic and social thought, without them critical hermeneutics would at best be incomplete, and at worst be an epiphenomenon of social reality, itself in need to be explained by truly critical, objective social theories. So how do our intuitive, situated, first and second person self-understandings relate to the material dimensions of social reality, i.e., to the embodied effects of social fields, systems, and institutions? How does the body and its material, non-symbolic reality figure in both the agent-based and the socially imposed construction of meaning? How are agents—who interpret themselves in tradition-bound lifeworldly categories—capable of reflexively relating to and thematizing such dimensions, such that they do neither deny their entailed potential for reflexive agency nor over-idealize their existent power-shaped reality as social selves? How are social selves—who are hermeneutically dependent on certain cognitive presuppositions—able to establish a situated sense of interpretive autonomy and an adequate self-understanding?

It is highly instructive to enter these challenges, as Simon Susen does, with my critique of Bourdieu's two epistemological breaks: the first needed to transcend the phenomenological "intra-lifeworld" vision of situated agents who would otherwise remain stuck, so to speak, in their contextual first-person acquired comprehension of themselves, the world, and others. Ethnomethodology would be the full-blown endorsement of such a view and its alleged self-sufficiency. Critical hermeneutics and an objectifying sociology agree that the initial first-order reflexive stance needs to be overcome, that structural features of power, operating in fields and institutions and establishing themselves via habitualized "system-conform" dispositions and assumptions, would otherwise not be recognized as meaning-constitutive and socially determining. Yet the second step that Bourdieu undertakes makes the difference between a critical-hermeneutic and "reflexive" sociology clear:

- Bourdieu remains at the height of sociological objectification to explain the actualization of agents' practices via their functional integration and success, relative to hierarchical positions within fields (accomplished via different types of capital).
- Critical hermeneutics, in contrast, reapplies and reintegrates the objectifying insights with the situated first and second person *self-understanding* of the agents.

The hermeneutic reconstruction of this core-situation of (self-) understanding guarantees that what becomes visible as macro-structural effects and influence, however individually habitualized, is nevertheless only relevant and also ontologically existent relative to the agent. Rainer Winter emphasizes rightly that we need a theoretical analysis of social fields and macro-processes: "Bourdieu emphatically shows that sociology is above all about exploring the social meaning, which does not arise from the intentions of the agents but is instead determined by the relations in the social field" (Winter 81). But while this is true insofar as the meaning-constitutive background is always prior to the individually interpreting self, it is nevertheless *only through these individual acts that socially shared meaning is reproduced*. This inevitable needle thread through which meaning must pass to *exist as meaning* should prevent us ontologically from hypostasizing "social meaning"—as most dramatically done in Luhmann's social systems theory—into an abstract, self-sufficient, ontologically independent layer of reality. The "epistemic access" to objective social meaning contexts is only possible by intentionally relating to the expressed beliefs, assumptions and values, and thus in a hermeneutically participatory fashion. The reconstruction of objectively shared assumptions in a context does not change this hermeneutic ontological fact.[1]

Thus Susen seems overhasty in suggesting that my account "misses" the essential species-constitutive features of action but is right in that my focus on the concrete hermeneutic core-situation made me emphasize its most universal features less clearly than I should have. Indeed, the hermeneutic account entails a *social ontology* which is expressed by the relation between an intentional world-orientation, which is itself intersubjectively constituted and mediated, and a three-layered background of individual-biographic, symbolic-cultural, and practical-institutional spheres. Susen does a formidable, almost exegetical job in reconstructing these layers, including dialogic intersubjectivity, the theorist-agent relation, and the dialectic between a social "me" and a self-asserting "I." These "species-features" are captured in my hermeneutic humanism, as Winter and Turner (and Susen himself at times) understand. Drawing on the rich tradition of Humboldt, Schleiermacher, Dilthey, Heidegger and Gadamer, with the due criticism that I develop, makes sure that the idealistic heritage is both preserved *and* critically reconstructed. It is therefore problematic to accuse me "to overstate the role of *language* and *reason*, including their pivotal role in dialogic processes, and to understate the role of other attributes that are . . . *species-constitutive* in that they make us human . . . If critical hermeneutics focuses almost exclusively on the socio-ontological significance of language and reason, then it fails to do justice to the complexity, multiplicity, and convergence of factors that define the human condition" (Susen 35, 36). Since in my account the hermeneutic background is transformed, in contrast to Gadamer's linguistic ontology, into an *individually irreducible* existence, *mediated* by symbolically articulated and socially assumptions and values, which are themselves grounded in *embodied and institutionalized practices and fields*, no such ontological overstatement exists.

Susen thus mistakes the emphasis on the *reflexive medium* within which social meanings in their complexity are articulated with their *ontological constitution*. The theoretically informed and linguistically articulated critique of such meanings—which is motivated by their intrinsic definition by practices of power and domination—is the most *explicit* way in which social criticism can proceed. But neither are the sources and modes of critique thereby limited to nothing but social *theory*, nor is the reality that is targeted reduced to nothing but *intentional* meaning. The linguistic medium presents us with, if you wish, the closest mode of self-understanding within which we can make objective meaning, social power, structures of domination, embodied habitus, etc. *known to ourselves*. As such, it is also the site where we seem to feel a certain *interpretive autonomy* as it is us *in thought* who now reflexively articulate "what happens to us"— not in the hybris that it has already been our spirit, Geist, the truth—or even God— that guided and undergirded us, but as a mode of *symbolic resistance* by rejecting the phenomenologically given view and advancing toward a higher, a structural self-reflexivity. Denying the epistemic significance of this reflexive process not only misses this source of autonomy. It also robs us of essential normative and motivational resources for resistance. Only if we succeed in relating social critique back to the embedded and culturally inherited self-understanding of agents—ourselves, really!— do we stand a chance to oppose the modes of power and domination that pervade our lifeworld. Yet still, Susen's and Winter's challenges to fully integrate and accommodate the insights of Bourdieu's (and others') objectifying social theory, and thus to account more fully for the role of power and domination in understanding, need more concrete answers. I will specifically address the issue of the role of the body, the conceptualization of power and domination, and the resources of critique via cognitive capabilities—the latter a theme that Stephen Turner has convincingly reintroduced.

The Body

Rainer Winter's chapter makes an invaluable contribution by reconstructing the rich Frankfurt background with its diverse orientations, traditions, and perspectives, all united in the attempt to reconstruct critical theory, to keep Horkheimer's spirit in unifying empirical social research and normative philosophical concepts alive. While Outhwaite presents us with a nice step-by-step reconstruction leading up to my critical hermeneutics (see Outhwaite 2022, 195–8), Winter's interest is in grounding and practicing Cultural Studies, of which he is one of the leading representatives in Germany. Our decade-long interactions have now reached a new level as he here articulates, much in agreement overall and endorsing my approach, the perceived need to refocus the role of the body. Winter develops this need organically out of a sophisticated reconstruction of my approach, which he sees in need of a double transcendence: First, Bourdieu (just as for Susen) serves Winter as a placeholder for a power-impregnated body, and as such for an objectifying sociological approach that focuses on the socio-functional integration of the self via the body: "Social order is expressed in the bodily dispositions. In [Bourdieu's] opinion, the habitus is 'the durable and transposable systems of schemata of perception, appreciation, and action that result from the institution of the social in the body (or in biological individuals)' ... which has been structured by a social field and therefore navigates within it" (Winter 2022, 80). Winter keenly observes that Bourdieu's account does not entail a blunt determinism, that agents, in need to "navigate" their social worlds, are capable of devising strategies, which they can do "to the extent that they consciously master the relations they entertain with their dispositions (Bourdieu/Wacquant 1992: 137)." Winter is certainly also right that embodied dispositions ingrain themselves deeply into an agent's self-identity. Bourdieu's empirical studies on the social habitus impressively demonstrate how one's intuitive preunderstanding may thus be shaped by specific class and social context factors. Those acquired dispositions can certainly *not* be shed and overcome *ad hoc* or by a simple dialogic procedure; rather, they usually ground the intuitions and preferences that fuel such exchanges. With all this I couldn't agree more: yet what is at stake in the hermeneutic-practical starting point is simply that an agent's practical and symbolic skills and capabilities enable not just a tactical and strategic attitude vis-à-vis one's own "second nature," but that they allow for such a thematization in light of practices and experiences that are *irreducible* to the logic of unconscious adjustments, social mobility and success within pre-existing fields. Agents are "integrated" into social fields in multiple ways, including their conscious (however idealistic and thus to some extent ideological) value-orientations. For instance, the dialogic presuppositions of mutual respect and rational reciprocity can serve as regulative ideals to adjust and transform the practices within a field and thus the associated habitus.[2]

A normative transcendence of social power is ultimately also the aim of Winter who proceeds, in an original turn invoking Alfred Lorenzer, to introduce the body as a positive, power-challenging dimension. Bourdieu's somewhat externally and power-induced construction of the habitus from social relations is now matched by a quasi-internal source of agency, the "self-will of the body." "The body does not merge [as in Bourdieu] with the field" (82). As such, it represents a constant source of resistance, which, moreover, always presents itself as a both socially induced and uniquely individual, ontogenetic "base." Lorenzer's approach avoids a macro-ontological essentialism of "the body" as an abstract theoretical category. In this "hermeneutics of the body," the early pre-linguistic forms of interaction are seen as constituting the always uniquely mediated instinctual "nature" of the self. The subsequent linguistic socialization is seen as the more or less successful matching up with these early inscribed desires. Repression is the exclusion of those early individually formed desires and impulses that do not fit. But the challenge against social norms is always there. Winter's suggestion thus goes beyond my Neo-Median reconstruction of the relation between a power-induced "Me" and a transgressive, rebellious, instinctually pushed (yet not instinctually controlled) "I." Mead thinks of this pre-linguistic reservoir of urges and desires as a deep motivational source. I have given this a discourse-analytic turn by suggesting that we can never "reach" or assume a level of uncontaminated immediate impulses (Kögler 1997; 2012). Winter's approach invites us to go further and to attempt to think of the bodily dimension as itself willfully structured, as forming an endorsable source of resistance, of "grounding" the conscious reflexive self in a pre-linguistic identity whose *rediscovery* may challenge societal norms and practices.

In the critical-hermeneutic framework, this would mean to understand one's own life trajectory in a new and revealing manner, and that the agent's voice and self-understanding is both respected and potentially transformed.[3] What counts most here is that the self acquires not only new insights provided by and then accepted by the theorist, but that she develops the *reflexive capacity* to listen to her body, always aware that its voice is itself the co-product of social practices and inculcations. Ultimately, such a listening would have to place itself reflexively in a wider normative framework that situates one's own desires and needs in a social context that is both defined by power and the normative challenge to respect others as free and equal. For Winter, our pre-linguistic nature as uniquely socialized selves "embodies concepts of life and forms of practice that are incompatible with existing relationships of power and domination, which are not recognized by them and which defy and challenge them" (82). Yet short of turning this pre-linguistic field of bodily urges and impulses into a *utopian reservoir* of rebellious resistance, critical hermeneutics would insist that all such constructions are, inescapably, undertaken within our conceptually developed post-linguistic existence. The normative resources thus need to be developed from this evolved position without denying the need to take to bodily dimension reconstructively into account. The body cannot become a new transcendental signifier of a better life *per se*. It forms, as Winter forcefully reminds us, a reservoir of desires which both drive us and may need more fully recognition. Yet the "true status" of our urges, impulses, and desires will always have to be relative to what we can justify as an overall acceptable and good life.

Power and Domination

Simon Susen raises important points concerning power and domination, both with regard to my appropriation of Bourdieu and Foucault and specifically with regard to critiquing the perceived universality of domination. Clearly the gist of this latter idea is in my own interest, as Susen's own account of my approach concerning the inevitable ontological implications of freedom and resistance within power-saturated contexts shows. Yet he takes, first, issue with some of my characterizations of Bourdieu as entailing a "totalizing theory of power" or Foucault merely presenting "a heuristics of power." While I would still defend, despite occasional remarks to the contrary by both, that the former aims to establish a scientific-structural theory of social reality as such, and the latter displays a much more historicized, localized, and "interventionist" self-understanding, quibbling over such terms or self-assessments seem little fruitful. What is rather at stake here is the systematic use of theoretical and empirical insights by Bourdieu and Foucault. What I attempted to do is to free certain notions like "habitus" or "disciplinary power" from their embeddedness in their contexts of origin in order to preserve their productivity and without having to buy into the downsides of their home theories. Differently put, I extract and transform conceptions of habitus and power in order to integrate them into a hermeneutic social ontology. My remarks about a totalizing account of power in Bourdieu do not deny his overall complexity and subtlety—which I myself utilized and emphasized—but do remind us that the full experiential and hermeneutic resources of agency are still foreclosed in his objectifying approach. Vis-à-vis Foucault, the claim of a heuristics is meant to pave the way toward a hermeneutically sensitive theory of power, i.e., one that pays attention to how power is specifically instantiated and practiced in different social and historical contexts. In the end, both theories serve as quarries for a critical hermeneutics in need of tools to objectify one's own situatedness in power and domination.

Susen finds it "ironic" that despite my hermeneutic efforts to re-establish agency and critical reflexivity, "Kögler appears to overstate the power of power when asserting, for instance, that every power struggle and every open strategy are already engaged in a field of pregiven relations of domination. It is, at best, an exaggeration or, at worst, a misrepresentation to affirm that all power struggles and all strategic modes of action are embedded in relations of domination ... it is erroneous to assume that all power relations—including the struggles and strategically motivated actions taking place within them—are relations of domination" (Susen 2022, 37). Now "being embedded in domination" is obviously something different from "power being identical to domination." What is at stake is that in a functionally differentiated and decentralized society, i.e. one defined by a plurality of fields or systems (as prominently explored by Bourdieu or Luhmann, for example), agents are to a large extent situated within social institutions (like corporations, universities, political organizations, etc.) as the socially articulated contexts of fields (like the economy, science and education, the state, etc.). Social fields are in turn internally structured by status-functions derived from positions related to the "mission" or "value-orientation" of such fields (like CEO, employee, professor, teacher, student, president, citizen, etc.; see Searle 2009). This in turn means that the concrete intersubjective encounters between agents—the ones where they can influence each other as agents based on their free and responsive agency—are generally "embedded in" hierarchically defined positions: CEO-employee, professor-student, politician-citizen, etc. The agentive power that a subject can exert is thus pre-circumscribed by such roles, as participants very well know, having internalized both the status-related scopes of authority and power as well as the gratification and recognition that comes with a higher status within a context. Such an institutional framework delimits what can be said, done, and often felt and perceived—yet it does not take the creativity and agency away from the subjects. Foucault thematized this with a remark referring to the nineteenth century status of women in this regard: women could not vote or get divorced, but *within existing* institutions like the marriage, they could withdraw and deny sex, cheat, etc. Frameworks of domination pervade all institutions *without* fully *determining the agency within it*. They may express themselves in symbolic forms of power, like the veil in traditionally Muslim societies, but such a "sign" of one's identity may then be reinterpreted in other contexts and by specific subjects as a rebellious, anti-Western, anti-colonial way of asserting one's unique identity.

We thus have to distinguish between the institutionally established status-functions, which are usually *legitimized* by some kind of competence or intrinsic authority vis-à-vis the field's value-orientation, and the intersubjective agency-relations. Susen is clearly right to define the latter as (a) not all susceptible to domination per se, as I myself have just argued, and (b) to suggest that not all intersubjective relations are defined by power, since the status functions entail epistemic and cognitive competences and are therefore also defined by their intrinsic value-orientation. Yet power (not domination, which pre-regulates what agents can do within fields) is here defined as the attempt to impose my will on the will of another as such, i. e. to subject (subordinate) another's acts, feelings, desires, self-images, etc. to a project that derives from my own interest, attitudes, value-orientations, etc. Thus I do agree that, in the language of Habermas, not all intersubjective relations are defined by *strategic rationality*, i.e., the attempt to overpower the other—or as Susen says, to exert "power-over." Yet I am hesitant to quickly assent, as Susen suggests, to a new foundationalism that distinguishes a primordial "power-to" from a lesser foundational "power-over." Susen proclaims that "power-to is an ontological precondition for the emergence of social order: subjects need to be able to exert a minimal amount of 'power to,' in order to construct, and to reconstruct, both the symbolic and material elements of their existence" (37). Such an ontological pragmatism, tied as it were to a subject-object scheme of productive agency, does not do justice to the co-primordiality of practical *and* intersubjective relations within human existence. Susen defines "power-to" as "an entity's capacity to do something and/or act upon the *world* in a particular way ... as a *productive* form of power." "Power-over" is, in contrast, "an entity's capacity to exercise influence, or even control, over something or somebody in a particular way and to a specific extent ... it may be interpreted as a *coercive* power" (37).

In my account, both "practical" and 'intersubjective" attitudes toward the world and others have to be seen as intertwined and co-constitutive of social reality. The concept of power is reserved for the intersubjective relations that are aimed at imposing one's will upon another. Agency itself is defined as the capacity to exert one's will in a causally efficacious way upon the world, doing so consciously, and being able to distinguish one's own impact from external causal sources (Kögler 2012). Inasmuch as agency is linguistically mediated (upon reaching a certain developmental stage, as we'll see in Turner), it is able to dialogically relate to co-subjects and thus to distinguish different modes of self-other relations, among them a dialogically open and truth-oriented one and a deceiving, self-interested and strategic one. The crucial attitudinal difference that comes into play here vis-à-vis power—i.e., the relation between subjects aiming toward having an impact on one another—is located at the *intersubjective* level. This intersubjective power relation (which can tilt toward domination by attempting to fix the Other's subordinate status) is embedded in institutional contexts and thus tied to status functions. These status functions, as we said above, are usually *legitimized* in terms of cognitive or epistemic competency: this is the way that "power-to" comes into play in critical hermeneutics. The term "power-to," however, somewhat covers up that what is really at stake are *capacities* to accomplish certain tasks, to display skills and cognitive capabilities. In the Habermas/Gadamer debate, this issue arose with regard to the term "authority," which both entails the *social status-function* (and thus has the smell of power qua domination), and the *cognitive competence* to be capable to do the job, to actually fulfill the expectation of the status role (and thus refers to epistemic capabilities) (Kögler 2021). Both aspects have to be thought together to bring out the specifically hermeneutic approach to power, which thereby addresses the legitimacy and justifiedness of agents as holders of status-functions via their capability to fulfill the attributed value-oriented tasks. Because of this, I am hesitant to call those capabilities "power-to" and assimilate them rhetorically to a type of power; in my view, they rather constitute *cognitive and practical capabilities* which may indeed by colonized and adapted by social power relations and structures of domination, for instance when certain skills in self-presentation via make-up and clothes become functional in the maintaining of, say, gender-defined types of domination.[4] The reflexive thematization of precisely these entanglements of power, domination, and embodied skills and capabilities is a challenge that critical hermeneutics aims to present vis-à-vis existing modes of power and domination.

Acquiring Hermeneutic Capabilities

How to best theorize the acquisition and exercise of cognitive capacities is the topic of Stephen Turner's contribution. In a first to my knowledge, he confronts a highly informed and elegantly synthesized account of cognitive science with hermeneutic philosophy as represented by my approach. Perhaps slightly overstating the contrast, he defines my intentions as derived from the "rich traditions of German idealism" with which the "naturalist" cognitive science approach is to enter into dialogue, nicely put as the quest for translation opportunities. Neither the critical hermeneutic background context of realizing cognitive acts as an interpretive resistance against power and domination, nor the normative orientation toward a recognition of the Other, are explicitly taken up. But Turner addresses the project of an "authentic intercultural understanding" rightly as requiring, in my view, a reconstructive approach vis-à-vis the full complexity of a symbolically mediated self-understanding. Only thus,

I claim, can the cultural specificity (the "cultural niche" allowing special "affordances," in Turner's lingo), together with the other agent's capacity to reflexively situate herself in a context of power/meaning relations, be addressed. And there is no doubt that a *naturalist* account of *developmentally* pre-linguistic capacities challenges the reconstructive hermeneutic account that quasi-transcendentally analyzes the unavoidable presuppositions an interpreter has to make in order to adequately understand and interpret another agent. So how can a naturalistic approach that reconstructs cognition from a third-person perspective as derived from pre-linguistic states and capacities be possibly reconciled with hermeneutic insights? How could the latter be translated back into hermeneutic categories? What can critical hermeneutics learn from developmental cognitive science in order to advance its approach?

Productive impulses can indeed be derived with regard to the deep intersubjective constitution of selfhood, the precarious, both enabling and limiting role of linguistic mediation, and the enduring openness and transformability of our ingrained cognitive habits. Just like in Neo-Median accounts like Axel Honneth's or my own reconstruction of Mead's dialogical subjectivity, cognitive research suggests a deeply interwoven, pre-linguistic dependency of understanding oneself and another (Mead 1934; Honneth 1995; Kögler 2012). Yet importantly, as Turner shows, such a mutual dependency does not necessarily entail a "theory" of "the mind:" children learn about love, emotional recognition, and mutual reliance long before they develop the capacity to attribute mental states as states to the other: "When children learn about themselves, they learn about others, and learn the two in parallel. But what they do tacitly and what they do explicitly turn out to be two different things.... "the capacities for understanding others are not innate, though they are based on innate capacities, [they are] a matter of social learning" (Turner 2022, 90, 91).[5] For a hermeneutic conception which takes *cultural mediation* to be essential, the question arises as to the impact of such a pre-linguistic sociality. Here Turner turns to the role of *play* as a crucial medium in which the symbolic stance can be learned. Rather than suggesting that a theory of mind, or a "hermeneutics in the crib," simply pops up or has to be transcendentally (and for Turner thus obscurely) imputed, he suggests that *play* exemplifies the social setting where the *pretend stance*—i.e., the cognitive capacity to interpret something standing in or "being" something else—is first exercised and developed. Suggesting "I am the mother" imaginatively substitutes oneself for something/someone else, and thus articulates a symbolic "representation;" yet it does so in the context of role-taking, emerging from an *emulation of others* in social roles received from the environment. Taking a banana for a phone or a stick for a horse are thus "symbolic" acts exercised and made possible in social settings. Adopting a symbolic stance thus emerges from embodied, practical, and socially interactive contexts (Bruner 1990; Harris 2012).

To be sure, for the reflexive self-other differentiation, much more has to happen, and here linguistic mediation still proves central. Turner presents a host of important reflections and insights concerning the necessary entailments of articulating the respective cognitive skills, but importantly, he connects these back to the hermeneutic emphasis on language vis-à-vis intercultural understanding. What is most instructive here is Turner's *dialectical* view, which both recognizes the immense advancement that the step toward linguistic self-understanding entails, as much as the loss and limitation that comes with it: "To enter into the linguistically rich world of the language of motherhood is to gain the power to evoke responses in strangers, in symbolic forms, in print, and to avail oneself of the affordances supplied by people's habits of mind, mental associations, sentiments, emotions, and so forth, and to do so much more reliably because these things are linguistically ordered. This is the important truth in Kögler's argument" (98). Yet such an elevation also comes at a price: with regard to cultural differences, "we lose emotional responses, connections, modes of empathy, as we gain mastery of the affordances of our cultural niche" (99). Turner here succeeds in rephrasing the critical-hermeneutic core situation of being located in *particular cultural contexts* as a necessary take-off context in order to make sense. But most importantly, he hints toward an enduring mediation of pre-linguistic skills and linguistic mediation that both elevates and constrains their exercise. "There is something more than language. Language builds on and transforms things that are already there" (99). And the enduring presence or force of such capacities may indeed be re-activated within the context of intercultural understanding: "it is not in merging of fixed horizons, of different culturally constructed "realities," that understanding becomes possible, but rather in the open and improvisational interactions that more closely resemble play. It is in the recapturing of this mode, rather than in the appeal to universal standards of validity, that authentic dialogue becomes possible" (100). This raises the issue how the reactivation of imaginary perspective-taking and symbolic representation as embodied cognitive skills is possible within a full-fledged hermeneutic *recognition* of the Other, and furthermore: can we reconstruct on these grounds a moral stance of recognition and respect?

Part II: Dialogic Recognition as a Cosmopolitan Moral Stance

Hermeneutic thought holds substantial promise to refine our ethical and moral sensibility. The normative implications of understanding and interpretation evoke the original term of "moral sciences" for human sciences and cultural studies. The core of its moral substance is, naturally, entailed in the dialogic situation. To spell out its normative implications relates social-scientific interpretation back to a normative framework of critical theory, but also establishes a moral conception of agency. Indeed, in critical hermeneutics the hints that we can find in Gadamer are walked back toward their agentive source. For Gadamer, overcoming the misguided objectification of a historical consciousness that reflects itself out of its own traditional situatedness means acknowledging that the ontological nature of history and culture expresses a moral core. Tradition can only be "accessed" via a dialogic approach: i.e., I have to first-personally invest my own pre-understanding on a subject matter in order to understand the meaning of the text, as "meaning" *is* a view on an issue. The text appears as another subject's expression, so interpretation becomes the *recognition* of the other's perspective by relating my view to the second person. "Hermeneutic experience is concerned with *tradition* . . . But tradition is not simply a process that experience teaches us to know and govern; it is language—i.e., it expresses itself like a Thou" (Gadamer 1989: 358). Since interpretation is thus defined by the first and second person relation, it entails a *normative* dimension: "It is clear that the *experience of the Thou* must be special because the Thou is not an object but is in relationship with us.... Since here the object of experience is a person, this kind of experience is a moral phenomenon" (ibid.). The other's expression needs to be *recognized and respected* as such.[6] Respect via recognition is entailed in the dialogic situation since I have to relate the symbolic expressions of the Other to my own taken-to-be-true assumptions and values in order to even begin to make sense. Dialogic interpretation thus entails the projection of the Other as a rational and reflexive self. Hermeneutic recognition means that I never reduce the Other to her background, circumstances, social power, or other heteronomous factors, but always also address her own claims as potentially valid and meaningful. Such an ontological framing of the interpretive process addresses the Other as an end-in-herself, as a rational co-subject, as a being with intrinsic self-worth that has "something to say to me."[7]

The critical-hermeneutic project reconstructs this insight as an "Ethos toward the Other" based on the full ontological constitution of the self, without denying the Other her rational capacity for self-determination (Kögler 2010). Such a self-determination, to be sure, is always situated, thrown into complex heteronomous conditions, affected by power and domination. Yet such contexts are also always symbolically mediated, they form the background of intentional and self-reflexive agents. Since interpretation cannot begin to make sense of the Other without taking into account the Other's self-understanding, it exerts the first basic step toward dialogic recognition. But the precarious vulnerability of agents thus situated, their complex and diverse cultural, social, and historical backgrounds, as well as the macro-structural institutional and practical influences that factor into their concrete social existence, demand a more radical transformation of the hermeneutic moral stance that takes those factors explicitly into account. Here, the core idea consists in a reconstruction of the symbolically mediated situatedness of human agents as entailing the potential for moral recognition and self-determination despite their embeddedness in contexts of power, and to do so by taking seriously the *actual cognitive capacities* to understand oneself and the Other.

Empathy or Dialogic Recognition?

Reconstructing basic capacities which enable a critical and reflexive process of interpretive understanding ties the normative projection of the Other to real cognitive psychological sources and thus grounds moral understanding in empirically detectable roots. It thus claims too, like Karsten Stueber's approach, to be a naturalism. Yet my hermeneutic naturalism is reconstructive, as it analyzes the presupposition of the situated hermeneutic interpreter. It thus avoids the third-person perspective of an objective psychological process by tapping into the rich and symbolically mediated background of the interpreting self. But Stueber is right to emphasize the many convergences between our views, as imaginative perspective-taking, the role of empathy for moral understanding, and certainly the sticking to a moral universalism are shared concerns (the latter sets me apart, as he supportively notes, from other "social constructivists"). Yet Stueber also challenges some basic claims of mine, including that a social-ontological reconstruction of the "debt we owe to the other" can carry the weight of grounding the universal perspective of moral recognition.

Stueber couches his approach in the "sentimentalist" tradition of the seventeenth and eighteenth centuries, specifically Adam Smith, as he sees them turning the epistemic role of empathy into moral purchase: "It is Smith's great contribution—building on the insights by David Hume—to understand empathy as the primary psychological mechanism that allows us to become embedded in a social context within which human beings constantly judge each other" (Stueber 2022, 111,112). Morality is exemplified by moral judgments which in turn are grounded in our psychologically shared empathetic "human nature:" "Empathy is something human beings crave of each other since it is in this manner that their existence as a human being is recognized and acknowledged" (112). This statement conflicts with my designation of *dialogic recognition* since it grounds the moral recognition as such in *shared sentiments*, whereas critical hermeneutics conceives it as the capacity to imaginatively adopt another's stance as recognizing the Other's *interpretive and reflexive agency*. The dialogic stance is intrinsically symbolically mediated, i.e., not to be merely conceived as carried by an "underlying psychological mechanism," but as taking the interpretive perspective of another *toward a subject matter or issue*, such that their claims and beliefs come into focus as possible truth claims. The capacity to adopt such a stance is prefigured in our psychological being by enabling us to feel, see, appreciate, etc. phenomena like others do. But once we *advance* toward the linguistically mediated level of agency, as Turner agrees, we intentionally disclose reality from *within* such intentional perspectives—and thus need to enter and address them to fully recognize and "understand" how another understands herself. Assuming a strict division between an operative level of psychological capacities and linguistically articulated reasons does not do justice to how agents intentionally experience life. Stueber grants that "interpretation is always mediated by cultural context and differences between those contexts" and acknowledges "that after becoming initiated into such structure our thoughts and emotional sensitivities are very much couched and conceptually structured in a certain manner" (116). But his insistence that the *reasons* agents have for their own emotional responses need to be taken into account, foremost in the cases when we cannot accept that other's response, does not go far enough.[8] Understanding culturally situated agents means adopting the other's perspective *as an intentional and thus reflexive agent situated in a social environment*, which essentially involves symbolically articulated assumptions and embodied dispositions. The anger the "natives" experienced upon the return of Captain Cook requires taking into account the symbolic order and the previous complex beliefs and habits that led to his subsequent death. Truly understanding another, even in her emotional responses, requires situating oneself within her full symbolico-practical context, even if imaginatively.[9]

Stueber also challenges how my intersubjectivist social ontology conceives of the moral self. "Kögler's considerations take an ontological turn via Mead's considerations about the intersubjective, social, and dialogical constitution of the self and self-consciousness in order to reveal the normative source of this presupposition of any concrete interpretive encounter" (117). What I call the "ontological debt toward the Other" cannot, in Stueber's view, carry the full normative weight of recognizing the Other morally. But the reflexive reconstruction of the intersubjective roots of self-identity provides those grounds precisely by creating a rich enough source of moral agency, and by reflexively appropriating one's relational existence as an *essential openness toward the Other*. The core idea is the need for intersubjective recognition in order to develop a self at all (Mead 1934; Honneth 1995; Kögler 2012). One's own agency is defined via a socially constructed "Me" and a transgressive, creative, non-objectifiable "I." Reconstructing the intersubjective recognition that leads to the "Me" (via internalized adopted expectations of significant others) shows that the Other who recognizes "me" can only be the Other's "I"—objects and tools do not have that power. But this means that the "Other's irreducible agency is constitutive of the self's capacity to establish an identity" (Kögler 2012: 47). Empathy (as any normative attitude toward the Other) does not proceed from a Cartesian self-enclosed self which extends its "empathy" toward other minds, equally separated and enclosed. Rather, the "open self" is always already intrinsically oriented and indebted toward others. This suggests that an equal recognition of the Other as irreducible self is built into my own. This intrinsic openness can then be reflexively appropriated and motivate actual recognition and dialogic openness. But the process of self-other relations is in any event constitutive for the unfolding of the actually socially recognized self (and of course the Other). It "entails that other people can help me figure out who exactly I am: I never have 'an absolutely privileged position vis-à-vis the meanings that make up [my own] self.'... It also entails that there is no definite end to this process of interpreting either myself or the other; every such interpretation is open to further challenge and revision" (Fleischacker 2019: 44). The insight in the developmental *Other-dependency of the self* thus transforms into a dialogically open and other-oriented ethos.

Yet Stueber takes further issue with the culturalist implications of this position. Samuel Fleischacker, who sees strong parallels between my "dialogically divided self" and his account of Adam Smith, suggests that "finally, according to Kögler, ... our conceptions of our selves and others are culturally mediated from the get-go. As we are socialized into communicative practices, we are *ipso facto* socialized into specific modes of communication" (ibid.). Here Fleischacker raises the interesting point that I may see these cognitive processes—which are actualized within concrete cultural practices—problematically as themselves culturally dependent. Fleischacker rightly emphasizes that in my developmental account, the conversational competence to take turns, i.e., imaginative perspective-taking, is what develops *alongside linguistic competence* and seems thus to be tied to specific languages, whereas for him, *languages* and *conversational competence* should be distinguished. The former are culturally specific and express cultural particulars (see also Turner's account of justifications), while the latter entail the universal capacity to enter into "symbolic world-disclosures" via *conversational perspective-taking*. I can accept this clarification, since it dovetails with my own Humboldtian account: while the *ergon* of language expresses the symbolic orders of cultures, the dialogical *energeia* cuts across and activates a universal intersubjective potential. The co-dependency of the "psychological" and the "linguistic" cognitive development establishes that the moral self here is the fully competent, linguistically mediated agent. Yet Stueber holds against this the prevalence of pre-linguistic capacities for self-identification, such as distinguishing one's own "Leib" from other human bodies and also other objects, and the capacity of infants to recognize their faces "immediately" in the mirror. But these core-capacities of self-identification are under-complex to account for the self-identity of human agents. Self-understanding is a narrative affair of attributing one's acts, beliefs, and emotions to one's own self *as identical in practice*. As Korsgaard rightly says, and Frankfurt developed with his concept of second-order desire, whether I "see" *myself* in certain dispositions, feelings, or actions is due to a reflexive and thus hermeneutic process: I can always reject certain immediate (or acquired) desires or endorse them (Korsgaard 1997). What enables the moral self is thus a linguistically mediated, "dialogically divided" self which defines its identity in ongoing and intersubjectively negotiated *acts*. This hermeneutic competence toward selfhood draws on universal capacities such as perspective-taking fused into a specifically situated self-identity.

Stueber's perhaps strongest challenge consists in questioning whether my situated dialogic account can deliver what the "moral stance" as such requires: a truly *universal standpoint*, a "cosmopolitan normative structure" transcending cultural particulars in order to establish an impartial perspective. To be sure, how to transcend local affinities and loyalties is a problem for *any* postmetaphysical moral stance, i.e., one that cannot claim access to a transcendental "kingdom of ends" (or any other divine, eternal, or metaphysical foundation). For neo-Medians, the ascendance to such a stance usually moves, in a moral-developmental account, from the stage of play—where I align myself with particular roles and positions—to the stage of game—where I understand the rules of the game as such and take the position of any possible role or player, the *Generalized Other*. My dialogic account gives this a specifically hermeneutic twist: any access or reference to the Generalized Other will always be mediated by one's concrete location. But this does not foreclose the reference to the *regulative ideal of universal recognition and inclusion*. Stueber challenges the ontological debt toward others since he assumes that it ties my account to such particulars, which do not even necessarily accord with recognition: "After all, teenagers do not seem too much obliged toward their parents in recognizing that their parents are their creators" and thus deserve some credit (117). *Pace* Confucianism, which turns such familial bonds into a major ground of ethical respect, the issue of how to generalize from such concrete dependencies can only, I agree with Stueber, proceed through a *reflexive universalizing step*.[10] Understanding that we are all someone's daughter or son, brother or sister, or parent, may jump-start a process to put myself universally into concrete positions of another. The universal capacity to assume those roles grounds a shared recognition that we all are equal in our capacities and thus deserve equal recognition. The fact that it is in each case "I" who assumes these roles, preserves the *universal human dignity* of all of us as self-interpreters assuming our concrete roles in cultural settings. *But since we are also all mediated by such contexts, our own interpretations and assumptions how to best conceive of the universal values and grounds can never claim absolute validity*: the situated background qualifies any such claim and similarly motivates that I respect the claims and contributions of any other such situated agent. By being thus, through my own limits, drawn toward the recognition of the Other, I also realize that a truly rational and egalitarian recognition of the Other requires recognition as an equal subject *in concrete dialogue*: "The dignity of persons ... is the second-personal authority of an equal: the standing to make *claims and demands* of one another as equal free and rational agents, including as a member of a community of *mutually accountable* equals" (Darwall 2006: 121, emphasis added).

Stueber himself arrives at the "universal moral stance" via a reconstruction of conflicting claims (based on ethical and cultural difference) and suggests as an answer (with Smith) the position of the "impartial spectator." But evoking this neutral view, popping up like a rabbit from the hat, does not explain how it is possible, given that the conflict arose in the first place: Stueber must assume that, suddenly and mysteriously, the moral self (one's own self or the other's?) is granted some immediate access to the shared universal dispositions. But if they are so shared, why the conflict? How is it that their understanding did not evolve equally in all cultures? If cultural sentiments (and interest and goods)—or their interpretation and justification—differ, which culture to prefer? Whom should we grant the right to decide? In the dialogic account, these questions are not obscurely left undecided, or left to the authority of the self-as-interpreter (who may only duplicate her own cultural biases). Rather, the mutual situatedness in cultural contexts is received *as a call to come to a real mutual understanding*, involving both agreement and dissensus about the values and assumption through dialogic interpretation and real exchange. Rather than catapulting oneself out of the *interpretive* process, plunging into it *together* seems the best way to accommodate and figure out what we share, what we all deem universal, and what *we all* may reject as possibly grounded in some arbitrary cultural norms and power practices.

We owe it to Karsten Stueber that the moral stance of critical hermeneutics can be so clearly envisioned, as its dialogic grounding does entail the challenge to advance, from this source, a *universal* moral perspective that realizes itself as a *dialogic cosmopolitanism*. The next three chapters do not compete with this framework, but rather productively apply and advance it. Werner Delanoy succeeds in articulating subtle and essential aspects by integrating its core insights into the educational scientific analysis of foreign language learning. Paul Healy articulates a dialogic approach toward religious voices in the public sphere in critical affront to Habermas whose spearheading role in this domain is recognized. John Maraldo further advances inter-religious hermeneutics by complementing an overly textual-based and -oriented hermeneutics with the collective experience of religious rituals and practices, which provide a unique mode of social experience and solidarity.

Linguistic World-Disclosure, Dialogic Cosmopolitanism, and Cognitive Capabilities

Werner Delanoy's cosmopolitan grounding of foreign language education makes a strong case to advance an already complex notion of linguistic understanding. Learning to speak another language is here, from the get-go, conceived as entering into other symbolic worlds, as acquiring new capabilities of cognitive and moral sensibility, and most importantly, perhaps, as acquiring a reflexive sense of how language enables both our "being-in-the-world" *and* a uniquely distanced and reflexive, freedom-enabling self-understanding: "Language learning is not treated as an end in itself, but as a medium for furthering democratic, ecological, transnational, and (self)-critical life-perspectives" (Delanoy 2022, 123). The medial character of world-disclosure can be preserved without buying into the detrimental misunderstanding of a transsubjective *Seins-* or *Überlieferungsgeschehen* by appropriating dialogue and agency from critical hermeneutics. Language grounds us in particular contexts and "worlds," yet it reproduces itself through the intersubjective acts of *dialogue,* and thus points beyond its immediate horizon toward shared yet differently disclosed world-relations of situated agency. Learning a "foreign" language, therefore, means more than referring to the exact same items in a different vocabulary, or expressing the exact same emotions in an alternative lingo: rather, subjects become aware of the perspective-character of language, of its internal framing and scaffolding (Turner), of how different linguistic settings disclose the same subject differently. A language is thus not acquired as a "system of rules," as a grammar entailing syntax and lexicon, but rather as a new world-relation and disclosure: "those who know nothing of foreign languages know nothing of their own" (Goethe) could be Delanoy's slogan, as lacking this decentered perspective implies being unawares of language's mediating nature. Yet becoming aware may now entail the enhanced challenge that *more than just one such world has become conceivable*!

Indeed, Delanoy's real aim is to push the boundaries of foreign language education toward a full-blown *cosmopolitan self-understanding.* His reflections on dialogue, amplified by our emphasis on symbolic world-disclosure as its hidden ground, establish the linguistically mediated imaginary perspective-taking as a cognitive capacity. (Foreign) language learning turns a universal capacity into a real capability. It does so by taking up new symbolic perspectives. It is grounded in a cognitive capacity to do so. "Linguist competence" is in truth a hermeneutic competence to take the perspective of the Other. Now when Delanoy turns to cosmopolitanism, he encounters what he calls two somewhat opposed genealogies: one grounded in a Western notion of moral universality, traced back to the Greek Stoa, culminating in Kant, and emphasizing universal human rights and moral values; the other dating from the sixteenth century with "the emergence of the Atlantic commercial circuit, the genocide of the Indians, the massive appropriation and expropriation of land by European monarchies and the massive slave trade and exploitation of labour" (128). While Delanoy himself remarks that attempts to synthesis and cross-over exist, a more explicit connection to the "grounded category of cosmopolitanism" that he rightly attributes to my approach would have allowed for an even more organic synthesis. *Dialogic cosmopolitanism* actualizes its potential not only by symbolic perspective-taking, but, as I suggested above, also by committing to universal norms and values *and* by critically reflecting on pervasive power and domination, especially in conjunction with one's allegedly universal values. Moreover, all such "values" and "norms" bear the stamp of concrete historical roots and contexts.

The *genealogical* task for any possible cultural horizon is thus, in my view, twofold: on the one hand, to reconstruct one's own relation and source for universal respect and recognition; and on the other hand, to critically reflect on the practices of oppression, exclusion, domination, etc. that have prevailed in one's culture and tradition. The critical-hermeneutic view synthesizes the "Western" and the "post-colonial" approaches by basing both, together with the empathetic openness to other cultures and traditions, on socio-cognitive capabilities that any true cosmopolitan self-understanding—and thus also foreign language learning—would have to consider and integrate (Kögler 2005). Such an approach finds its own genealogy in the Axial Age discourse, according to which—at multiple locations in human history about 2500 years ago— crucial cognitive insights and normative distinctions became possible: the distinction between political legitimacy versus mere power; the distinction between a universal and eternal truth versus temporal experiences; and the distinction between the universal value of the human individual versus her social status (Jaspers 1953; Bellah/Joas 2005; Assmann 2018; Habermas 2019). Interestingly, for Habermas the axial age values are, *mutatis mutandis* their postmetaphysical and fallibilistic reconstruction, still influential for our contemporary democratic public sphere (Habermas 2019; Kögler 2020b). For critical hermeneutics, the development of cognitive capabilities, the recognition of the diverse cultural traditions, and the deconstruction of power and domination are crucial. Yet the normative orientation toward a shared public sphere in which these desiderata can unfold is a necessary precondition as well.

Recognizing Religion's Symbolic Claim in the Public Sphere

How we may conceive concretely the dialogic recognition of diverse cultural traditions within a shared public sphere is, with a special focus on the recognition of religion, the topic of Paul Healy's chapter. The target is Habermas's account which for Healy falls short to ensure equal recognition of religious voices and discourses within the democratic public sphere. Healy articulates, based on an impressive set of literature critical of Habermas, a strong plea for a truly dialogic approach of religion. Such a stance would *not*—as he sees Habermas doing—prescribe *secular* norms and conditions *up fronte* to religious participants. It would rather allow for a "genuinely complementary learning," a conjoining process of a mutually enriching listening, thus taking both sides into account and so doing justice to the "distinctive voice of religion," to religious experience and insight (see also Joas 2013). Since Healy professes being influenced by the critical-hermeneutic approach to dialogue I proposed, it might first seem ironic that I feel the need to defend Habermas, at least to some extent. Yet a more dialogical reading of Habermas' own "distinctive voice" may help better bring out what's at stake here—namely how we can best reconstruct the shared egalitarian and respect-based grounds of a public sphere which truly *recognizes* the manifold social, cultural, and religious backgrounds of the participating citizens. With regard to religion, Habermas grants Rawls with having brought the subject matter of religion back on the agenda. Rawls and Habermas are deeply motivated by the need to *legitimize* a political culture in which the participants debate and decide on legal and policy issue *with reasons that all can reasonably endorse*. Both Habermas and Rawls take religious doctrines to *not* provide such reasons, at least *prima facie* as far as their metaphysical justifications are concerned. They consider religious beliefs as grounded in "comprehensive doctrines" or metaphysical worldviews that do not *per se* fit into the pluralistic and egalitarian framework of a postmetaphysical democratic public sphere. Habermas deepens and expands the Rawlsian account by theorizing religion more fully *and* by integrating it more deeply into the public sphere. To do so, Habermas suggests certain cognitive presuppositions so as to enable religion to "fit into democracy"

(1), a *translation proviso* that would ultimately dissolve or "translate" *religious* truths into generally shared insights (2), and the distinction between the informal and the formal public sphere which would allow religious discourse to thrive in the former but be excluded from the latter.

(1) For Habermas, accepting the truth claims of empirical science, endorsing a universal morality, respecting individual life-choices (not a pre-ordained "good life" politics), and reflexively tolerating the pluralism of metaphysical and religious "worldviews" are *non-negotiable premises for a democratic public sphere and society*. On an epistemic and normative level of discourse, it seems hard to reasonably argue with those assumptions. Healy himself clarifies that he does not oppose the first three principles but insists that his "concern is rather with their precondition for religious citizens as such" (Healy 2022, 154, fn6). For Healy, complementing the normative endorsement of these principles with the requirement of a "cognitive mind set" that religious subjects have to adopt amounts to a militant secularism and undermines the proclaimed openness to religion; he rejects the symbolically violent imposition that religious citizens have to accept "the priority of *secular* reasons in the 'political arena'" (142, see also 141, 148). But do we really have to interpret these rules as "violent impositions" on the *self-identity* of citizens? Are they not better understood as accepting certain norms and values without which the *democratic game we play* would make no sense? Rather than constituting "cognitive usurpations" onto the totality of religious minds, don't they rather amount to "gateway checks" about the understanding of basic democratic rules? Healy suggests that Gadamer's endorsement of "openness" would do better here. But the mere "openness" as a precondition may shiver between asking both too little and too much: too little, as openness may imply the acceptance of anti-scientific or non-universalistic positions, which Healy himself rules out; and too much, as a fundamentalist Christian or Muslim may find "openness" toward heretics, infidels, immoral subjects such as LGTBQ or abortionists just as unacceptable as the Habermasian strictures. Healy also underplays in my view the strong burden that Habermas and critical hermeneutics complementarily place on science and secularism. To undercut these viewpoints overplaying their hand as quasi-worldviews, i.e., as *scientism*, they are held accountable to a reflexive rethinking of their attitudes (Habermas 2019; Kögler 2020a). Accepting religious voices as potentially rational and fruitful dialogue partners is by no means an easy feat for everyone.

(2) Healy and Habermas both share the concern that religious voices be more fully "listened to," that they be capable of fully participating in the democratic public sphere. Such a full participation, however, Healy sees curtailed by Habermas' *translation proviso*. Habermas' aim is indeed to have a full-blown dialogue in the "informal" public sphere, and have the formal public sphere be "reserved" for secular reasons and justifications. This is based on the Rawlsian/democratic ground that the *reasons have to be comprehensible, endorsable, and acceptable by all*. Healy seems to suggest that no such proviso is needed. He assumes that the process itself would take care of that without the need for a "firewall" between artificially constructed spheres. As for the "formalized spheres" of parliament, government, and courts (including the supreme court), there exists, so Healy, a "common awareness that different styles of discourse and modes of argumentation befit different institutional contexts, such as the academic,

scientific, parliamentary, and judicial," and that such a socially shared pre-understanding is sufficient to ensure that the language used is "appropriate to the context in question without the need of additional, potentially discriminatory distinctions affecting designated worldviews such as the religious" (151). I take Habermas' aim to merely articulate basic conditions of possibility for mutually respectful discourse *in all these spheres*. They require indeed an orientation toward values like openness, as Gadamer, Simone Chambers, and Healy rightly assert, but reasonably allow for a little more articulation as to what such "openness" may or may not entail. What Healy considers to be both superfluous and potentially repressive *socio-cognitive* presuppositions are perhaps less trivial and "taken-for-granted" if one looks at the Christian right in the US, and also at the analysis that I have undertaken regarding the inherently authoritarian potential of religious discourse (Kögler 2017a, Kögler 2020a), and they may appear less "violent" if we emphasize that they remain oriented toward enabling an ethos of democratic deliberation so that religious citizens can determine *for themselves* how to approach controversial issues in search for a common answer.

(3) To be sure, Healy contrasts the alleged assimilating force of Habermas' "crypto secularism" with the repeated emphatic plea for the "distinctive voice of religion." Habermas is criticized for streamlining the multiplicity of religious attitudes, creating a problematic and homogenous ideal type that ultimately leads to a uniform need for *assimilation* toward the secular regime and its secular justifications. This is Healy's strongest point of critique. But the "distinctive voice" of *religion* remains strangely vague and undefined in his account. What exactly is the distinctive contribution that religion can make to a mutually open and truly transformational and genuine dialogue? Habermas at least suggests two distinct features of religious discourse and experience. On the one hand, religion entails for him an "inviable core of revealed truth that is resistant to discursive thematization or justification." If not integrated as a respected core conviction *within* a deliberative public sphere, such a non-discursive metaphysical root may be abused and function as a source of authoritarian fundamentalisms. Religion thus calls for a postmetaphysical or hermeneutic reformulation of its self-understanding (Habermas 2019; Kögler 2020a). On the other hand, Habermas focuses on religious experience as maintained in the exclusive communities of world religions, which collectively replenish their faiths through continued ritualistic practices. For Habermas, rituals and sacred ceremonies express a deep connection to an archaic solidarity which still awaits a full secular understanding or "translation." Accordingly, as a practical reservoir of collective self-affirmation, religious practices may fuel a hope for our postmetaphysical condition and its secular life-form as a potentially reinvigorating source for a renewed ethical and moral spirit. While Healy's interest is lies in advancing a more radical openness toward the *symbolic* claims of religious traditions—a highly worthwhile project as every agent's background deserves the fullest possible, and most possibly unrestrained, recognition in a pluralistic democracy—Habermas' ultimate interest lies in the pre-linguistic collective practices as *resources for moral renewal*, awaiting their transmission into an idiom all can share. This practical dimension of religious experience is addressed by John Maraldo's chapter.

Recognizing Religion's Practical Claim in Intercultural Understanding

Accordingly, we may ask whether the challenge faced by divergent *symbolic orders* is the only real challenge posed by religious understanding. Is the ethical recognition of a plurality of religious traditions even best accounted for in terms of *linguistically expressed* truth claims? Is the hermeneutic recognition of religion identical to, or rather more complex than *dialogic interpretation*? In fact, that the understanding of religion *cannot* be reduced to language is the core thesis of John Maraldo. He rejects—via a succinct and sovereign engagement of Heidegger, Gadamer, and Ricoeur—the textualistic obsession of classical philosophical hermeneutics in order to advance an "alternative notion of understanding." Maraldo makes a compelling case that religious experience is more than "language," that its (full) understanding must be based on embodied, engaged, and situation-bound practices. He aligns himself with my own multilayered background analysis of hermeneutic understanding that reconstructs the embodied and practical dimension as one layer of pre-understanding: purely focusing on expressed articulated truth claims thus hovers above the whole complexity of dialogic understanding and fails to capture the whole *Lebensvollzug* of interpretation. In line with Delanoy's account of language as well as with ideas found in Turner and Barthold, he reconstructs *linguistic meaning and experience itself* as an embodied, practical, less "text-or sentence-based" type of understanding: "one learns how language is used in concrete situations, and that usage involves situationally dependent elements that are not coded in grammar or vocabulary—elements like tone of voice, gesture, and facial expression ..." (Maraldo 2022, 171). Maraldo mobilizes the experiential importance of a practical approach vis-à-vis religion to adequately capture "activities like prayer, meditation, chanting, or participating in other religious rituals ..." (169) His contribution expands dialogic understanding toward an account of "practical understanding" that complements and advances the scope and power of hermeneutics.

Maraldo thus productively aims to unearth a hermeneutic approach "distinct from understandings that are merely intellectual, textual, or empathetic" (171). Yet in carving out the role of practical "meanings," he seems to conceive "linguistic dialogue" in terms of a detached, non-participatory, and objectifying third-person representation, whereas the practical and embodied "understanding" is identified with an engaged and first-person attitude. For him, the world of the *text* is abstract and universalizing (171) as the "sentence structure" allows for a distanced approach, whereas practical understandings "engage the body more consciously and disengage discursive thought. We *cannot employ* such embodied practices as we do concepts or judgments that form beliefs about the world. In the case of judgments, we may merely mention them while standing back and remaining detached, or we may assent to them and direct our beliefs accordingly while still remaining bodily disengaged. In contrast, practices *in the alternative sense* require coordinated bodily and mental attention" (170, emphasis added). Yet I would argue that the first-and-second person approach contrasts with a third-person approach in *both* linguistic and bodily practices. With regard to linguistically articulated beliefs and assumptions, hermeneutics taught us that only through a *relation to our own symbolically mediated pre-understanding* can beliefs and judgments be accessed. We may decide to suspend judgment and reconstruct the other's internal coherence, but to begin to make sense at all, a dialogic relationing to our own views about the subject matter is a *sine qua non* for understanding. And complementarily vis-à-vis the body, we may find the specific mind-body fusion that Maraldo asserts for religious practical experiences compelling, but even with regard to the body, the engaged or dialogic attitude needs to be *reflexively* taken. Here, too, we have to enter into the practical experiences *in the right way*, i.e., such that we do not objectify our body, which may happen either in practice—as, say, sex workers do in an extreme manner, but also all "service personnel" by adopting "fake" professional embodied attitudes—or in theory, as in Bourdieu's conception of habitus, here as a theoretical reconstruction of objective social relations. Maraldo's embodied practical understanding aims to relive and experience the bodily dimension from the *first-and-second-person-perspective* as meaningful and experientially rich, and is precisely in this sense a uniquely "hermeneutic" approach.

While both language and body may thus be *either* objectified *or* dialogically engaged, the subsequent question arises whether there is a "distinct" and somewhat separate mode of understanding apart from an already symbolically disclosed practice. Does Maraldo suggest that there is a deep layer of "purely" bodily practices which inculcate or define a unique stratum of meaning? Or does he, like critical hermeneutics, see both dimensions as inextricably intertwined while not reducible to one another? I submit that the practices he mentions, like prayers, meditation, religious ceremonies (rituals), and even chanting or dancing, "make sense" fully only within the whole mode of religious world-disclosure. Maraldo introduces the highly original move to point to these embodied practices as *intrinsically meaningful*, as semantically self-referential and thus self-fulfilling: "Such activities may indeed have an objective, but the objective is not external to the activity that achieves it.... The intention of Benedictine chanting may ultimately be to glorify God, and that of Zen chanting be to concentrate the mind and embody the Dharma, but the intention is repeatedly fulfilled in the very act of chanting" (170). Religious ceremonies or rituals are taken to "transcend" the everyday utilitarian mode of goal-oriented thought and practice; they create a space apart, devoted to and enabling the sacred, which ultimately celebrates and endorses the community in its mutually shared social existence. For Habermas, rituals have in this way preceded the symbolic articulation of myth (Habermas 2019). Rituals are early forms of an embodied appropriation or "thematization" of our collective social interdependence, which is evolutionarily basic for the human species (Tomasello 2008). Myth constitutes the symbolic world disclosure which emerged *later* as associated with rituals, which thus preserve, just as Maraldo argues, a *pre-linguistic core* of shared ceremonial collectivity. For Maraldo, plausibly, the participation in religious practices is a core element of religious experience, which if rendered in symbolic "truth claims" alone would lack an essential experiential dimension. While the whole of religious experience corelates rituals with symbolic frameworks, the embodied and shared togetherness expressed in the rituals as such reveals a potentially deep-seated layer of social reality.

It is almost as if the ritualistic underbelly of cultural and religious practices is the *phylogenetic* equivalent to the transgressive and impulsive bodily dimension that

Rainer Winter, Stephen Turner, and Randi Gressgård invoke at the *ontogenetic* level. Yet here as there, the full appropriation requires a reflexive sensibility with regard to how those pre-discursive dimensions of sociality are channeled into the dialogically defined and morally articulated modes of recognition. Maraldo couches his emphasis on the embodied and practical sense as being ultimately required to adequately understand religion, i.e., to do it justice. To the concern of critical hermeneutics vis-à-vis the potentially authoritarian dimension of religious faith, "especially as they seek to root their authority in vertical and transcendental sources" (174, fn4), Maraldo positions his own approach as complementary: "The religious interactions I explore are by nature horizontally rooted in certain practices that are intersubjectively grounded and neither private nor directed toward reception by a public sphere" (20). In the meantime (Kögler 2020a), I have argued that the hermeneutic access to sacred texts allows for a reconstruction of universal and egalitarian intuitions as built into the cultural appropriation of tradition. Accordingly, both Maraldo's practical and the critical-hermeneutic approach seek to locate resources of an intersubjectively constituted, mutually recognizing and social practice, albeit vis-à-vis different strata of our hermeneutic self-understanding. Maraldo's approach allows for a broadening of the critical-hermeneutic perspective to include embodied religious practices. His approach may also question whether "translating" the embodied strata, as Habermas demands (and about which Healy cautions us), is the only or even the right path here. Finally, we may ask whether such modes of social solidarity must be, or are plausibly restricted to, "religious" practices in the narrower sense. Certainly, collective experiences of solidarity in aesthetic, cultural, and political contexts may equally serve as a source against today's individualizing, fragmenting, and alienating systems of social domination (Matustik 2019; Mendieta 2018).

Part III: Contemporary Challenges for the "Ethos of Dialogue"

The normative recognition of the Other follows from the intrinsic dialogic relation that entails a projection of the Other as subject. It reveals itself reflexively by reconstructing what is involved in the hermeneutic process. But what kind of force can such a reflexive reconstruction really have? Critical hermeneutics operates in the post-Hegelian context, has forsaken the metaphysical hopes of a "philosophy of history," understood as the necessary developmental unfolding of progressive learning stages toward the ideals of the Enlightenment, equality, autonomy, solidarity. Furthermore, the focus on dialogue has been liberated in critical hermeneutics from the idealistic context of an appropriating and truth-conserving tradition and plunged into the power-defined and domination-structured context of social practices and institutions. Yet the challenge as to how "the principle of dialogue" can be more than just another "principle of hope" stands. How can a dialogic approach to self, culture, and society prove to unleash a situated yet critical force of resistance? How can the "ethos of dialogue" be more than the trite ideological reference to a process of an all-too-pleasant, all-too-accepting "recognition" as appreciation of otherness? How can critical hermeneutics present a "realistic" case that its cognitive and normative resources have a chance to make an impact—in the real social and historical contexts of today?

Methodological Premises of a Hermeneutic Ontology of the Present

Frédéric Vandenberghe responds to the "realistic challenge" by constructing a three-step argument how the social sciences may regain their importance via morphing into an "ontology of the present." Sociology is to realize itself as a radical *Zeitdiagnose* enlisting cultural studies. Vandenberghe suggest three major revisions in the disciplinary self-understanding of "sociology" to live up to this challenge. In a first step, Vandenberghe criticizes sociology's loss of a unifying and orientating function, which he traces to the lack of a theoretical grounding. What is needed is a "dynamic synthesis," for which Karl Mannheim's work serves as a paradigmatic orientation: "In [Mannheim's] vision of a dynamic and synthetic sociology, the painter is an unattached intellectual who floats freely between the disciplines to try to understand what is happening in the world, with nature, with culture, and with societies when there is no longer (or not yet) a philosophy of history" (Vandenberghe 2022, 182, 183). My concern would here be that Mannheim's vision of a "free-floating intellectual" does not sufficiently ground the theorist in the full ontological and normative background situation of her own existence; contrary to the "painter's view" floating above the landscapes of worldviews, her own pre-understanding will, in spite of academic reflexivity, still exert a substantial influence, and thus needs to be consciously included in the hermeneutic process (Kögler 1997). Vandenberghe asserts that sociology "must maintain its autonomy as a science to defend the values that are its own—communism, universalism, disinterestedness and organized skepticism" (183). But the concrete interpretations of social scientists necessarily mediate particular assumptions and value-interpretations with their "scientific approach," which thus requires a reflexive—and not just detached—attitude on the side of the theorist. The reflexive turn, by revealing subjective, normative, and symbolico-practical background layers of meaning in the theorist's as well as the agent's background, in fact nicely dovetails with Vandenberghe's ultimate concern that sociology "succeeds in resuming the dialogue with critical theory and the Studies, as well as philosophy" (184). Importantly, this rearticulates Horkheimer's early formulation of the unique status of a critical theory of society as a mediation between *empirical* social research and *normative* philosophical ideas (Kögler 2017b).

Vandenberghe's second step consists in the advancement toward a *Zeitdiagnose*. In order to address the concrete challenges of current social life—the privatization of markets, the return of authoritarian states, the twin challenge of neoliberalism and populism, and dramatically what he calls "the structures of the system collapsing in real time" (191)—Vandenberghe proposes, "following Foucault … an ontology of the present as a critical reflection on our 'historical mode of being'—understanding 'the events that have led us to become who we have become' so as to open up 'the possibility of no longer being, doing, or thinking what we are, do, or think'" (185). He imaginatively invokes the Portuguese and Spanish distinction between "ser" (essential enduring being) and "estar" (temporal states of being) to clarify that an "ontology of ourselves" is to occupy itself with *contemporary* understandings, practices, and institutions. It does not aim at the question of Being itself. Here I would contend that the distinction between a social ontology, understood as a philosophical reflection on the universal premises of our self-understanding, and the "ontology of the present," understood as the reflexive appropriation of current patters of actions, thought, and feeling, does not pose itself as an Either/Or. Both modes of reflexivity must maintain a conversational flow between what seems philosophically necessary and insurmountable and what seems currently dominating and pervasive, in order to correct false generalizations on the one side, but also mistaken reductionisms on the other side. A hermeneutic social ontology, for instance, reminds us that

> it is indeed the social actors who make history, even if they do not make it in the circumstances they have chosen and even if it inevitably escapes them. Together, the order of things (truth), the analytics of power (norms) and the practices of the self (subject) configure a "historical ontology of ourselves in modernity" (Kögler 1994: 9) that is susceptible to change.
>
> (185)[11]

Vandenberghe's third step involves the proposal to loosen the "disciplinary matrix" of sociology and engage with cultural studies. Clearly, those "Studies" superseded traditional social science vis-à-vis the engagement of current tendencies. He proposes to apply the dialogical model to this interdisciplinary exchange: "Listen, learn, read and teach, all this in the dialogical spirit that characterizes the hermeneutic encounter with the other that is at the very heart of all of Hans-Herbert Kögler's writings...If we transpose the 'ethos of hermeneutic dialogue'... from intercultural understanding to interdisciplinary communication, there's no reason to assume that understanding across and between disciplines will necessarily fail" (187). Yet, again I want to emphasize that such a dialogue stands under certain normative constraints. Besides the "agency-constraint" that we just mentioned stands importantly the "mediation-constraint" which serves as a bulwark against naively pursued affective and ontological turns in cultural studies (also addressed by Gressgård). The crucial implication of the self-reflexivity invoked in critical hermeneutics involves that the individuo-subjective level of agency is preserved at the object side of theory, thus never eliminated from the socio-ontological core of basic concepts. Ontological theories of social experience—say of affects, emotions, life, death—that bypass the reconstruction of their symbolic and practical mediation in specific contexts are problematic: "The question for a hermeneutically inspired theory of practices is whether affects can really be disconnected from all processes of representation and signification ... The relation between the body and the mind, the intention and the execution, the pre-predicative and the linguistic is not disjunctive" (189).[12]

For Vandenberghe, the current social processes point to a "second post-modernity," defined by the most dramatic constellation of our times, the axis of *neoliberalism* and *populism*, the true challenge of our *Antropocene*—i.e., the status of human society and its moral, cultural, and social prospects of progress versus survival. Deeply engaged and personally authentic, Vandenberghe writes under the impact of Bolsanaro's regime and its devastating "death politics" in Brazil. Importantly, he himself presented a compelling *Zeitdiagnose* of the decline and destruction of democracy under Bolsonaro in which he traces the diverse economic, political, institutional, security-based, and ecological roots of the crisis in this "Democratorship" (Vandenberghe 2019). No doubt a pessimistic undertone is justified, as "everything solid melts in the air" in a time of disarray, dissolution, "the very structures of the global system are unravelling ...," or with Gramsci: "The old is dying, the new cannot be born: during this interregnum we observe the most varied morbid phenomena" (191). To be sure, it is exceedingly difficult to assess the true significance of a time in its present: Gadamer's theorem of the *Zeitenabstand* understands this much. Similar suggestion like "reflexive modernization" (Giddens, Lash, Beck), "late modernity" (Habermas), or "new axial age" (Jaspers) should thus be read less as propositional claims *tout court*, but rather as probing suggestions what this age may tend to, as dominant tendencies to be endorsed or opposed. The emphasis on possible change, on a new horizon, on a transformed basis for subjectivity, sociality, and meaning, marked already the Foucauldian attempt. Vandenberghe, almost heroically, invokes Gramsci's dictum to combine "the pessimism of the intellect" with "the optimism of the will," similar to Horkheimer's characterization of critical theory as theoretically pessimistic and practically optimistic. Does "the principle of dialogue" have something—a glimmer of hope—to offer here?

The Limits of Dialogue in Real Time Politics

The force of the dialogic model is put to a thorough test by William Outhwaite's exceedingly *quellenreiche* and subtly reflective chapter on the impact of current populist and identity-based modes of politics, specifically related to "understanding" Brexit, i.e., those who supported and opposed it. The somewhat pessimistic undertone of this chapter suggests that we may have to wait for a generational turn-over, a "demographic renewal to take its toll on authoritarian populism," based on that vast support for "remain" from younger voters and for Brexit from the older ones. While "there may be no alternative to sticking with a critical hermeneutic framework, and rational deliberation as a practice, ... we should perhaps be aware of over-estimating their effectiveness" (Outhwaite 2022, 207). I fully agree with an initial sentiment to not over-idealize our trust in "the dialogic attitude;" yet in order to adequately answer Outhwaite's skeptical thoughts, we would do best to first take a step back in order to distinguish three different levels of conceptualizing the *dialogic sources of democratic deliberation*. Outhwaite aims to confront a dialogic cosmopolitanism with the persistence of "anti-cosmopolitan nativist conceptions of identity and nationalism," and specifically reconstruct the empirical "realistic" basis for such attitudes. I take up his challenge by reemphasizing the relevance of the capabilities approach to dialogue (1), revisit the normative grounding of a democratic public sphere and deliberation (2), to finally address the question as to how to "be dialogic" (or not!) in the public realm (3).

(1) It is certainly fair to reconstruct my dialogic approach, as Outhwaite does, from a Habermasian angle, especially in political contexts, albeit my conception derived in its immanent critique from Gadamer's concept of hermeneutic experience. Yet for

both accounts, the emphasis that I place on *cognitive capabilities as essential presuppositions* overcomes a naïve trust in traditions or a somewhat idealized orientation at validity claims. What is crucial is not, as in a structural-intersubjectivist model, that validity claims may be raised—that the speaker always has the abstract option to say Yes or No—but instead how the *actual agents* develop and can *actualize* the entailed resources, i.e. the communicative potential entailed in symbolically mediated interaction. To be sure, Habermas grounds validity claims in real life-contexts when he reconstructs the explicit raising of such claims, in good pragmatic fashion, as emerging from problem situations; and his recent interest in a "mind-set analysis" when it comes to religious and secular participants in public discourse points in my view in the right direction. But my conception of a "grounded cosmopolitanism," while oriented at the desirable universal values of mutual recognition (as culturally particular, as universally dignified, and vulnerably situated), makes specific *cognitive capacities* central, and thus puts the focus on the resources, rules, and contexts within which these can become actual individuo-based *capabilities* (Kögler 2005). How does this relate back to Brexit? The scandalous lack of critical capabilities to see through the deceptions used by political players dramatically enforces the need to focus on *developing* those capabilities. We can't just wait on a quasi-natural replacement of one generation by another. Realizing how capabilities are needed to actualize adequate public deliberation puts *educational efforts and policies* on top of the political agenda: The mere dissemination of "information," itself embedded in an overkill of such information and facing subjects caught in communication bubbles unable to critically differentiate, is not sufficient. Surely such a development of critical capabilities is not subject to critiques of social engineering, as it develops precisely those critical skills that would allow for a self-determined and informed participation in public forums.[13]

(2) The next level of discourse concerns the normative conception of public dialogue, i.e., its internal goals, procedures, practices, vis-à-vis the democratic and egalitarian value-orientations. While the struggle for capabilities is fought on the level of social policy and reform, this fight is fought on the level of political theory. Outhwaite invokes Chantal Mouffe's model of an "antagonist" public versus an "agonistic" one, with which she importantly aims at a more radical pluralism than Habermas' consensus-oriented model (or Rawls' conception of public reason, for that matter), based on the real "populist" fractions, antagonisms, different interests, life-situations, etc. (Mouffe 2000). While inspired by Carl Schmitt, Mouffe stops short at defining politics as a mere struggle over power, to determine who is friend and who foe (Schmitt 1996); yet Mouffe's taming of Schmitt via a political realm that knows "adversaries" but no "enemies" leaves open on what basis the recognition of the Other here proceeds. Her "agonism" aims for pluralism but fails to show on what shared basis the mutual recognition of respect as co-citizens can proceed. This opens the door to Bourdieu's glib remark that "public opinion does not exist" (due to the social stratification of citizens). In the critical-hermeneutic approach, the public sphere is neither idealized as a detached and "pure realm" of reasons, i.e., not conceived as an "abstracted" "logico-public space of political reasons" (as in Habermas or Rawls), nor is it reduced to the social-Darwinistic clash of different existential life-projects and interest groups (as in Schmitt and potentially in Mouffe). The hermeneutic capabilities approach, instead,

transforms the mutual dialogic orientation from a mono-linear assessment of the "non-coercive force of the better argument" into a shared realm within which the particular existential cultural backgrounds provide crucial resources of understanding. *Difference is constitutively included*—but from a mutually appreciative, perspective-exchanging view (not as an insurmountable antagonism). It entails a mode of dialogic interpretation that avoids the "symbolic violence of immediate judgment" by reconstructing *first* the underlying basic beliefs and assumptions of the Other *before* arriving at a final evaluative judgment. It foregoes the assumption that we always already share basic (pre-) ontological premises and puts special effort on their reconstruction so as to fully represent and recognize the particular experiential and symbolic perspective of the Other. This approach further ameliorates our conception of a shared yet plurally engaged public sphere by reconstructing major cultural traditions and movements, such as the "worldreligions" emerging from the axial age, and the diverse secular traditions such as unions, socialism, communism, peace movements, etc. as background contexts from which the particular and diverse viewpoints emerge. Such reconstructions of existing traditions and movements not only enhance mutual understanding but replenish motivational sources to participate productively in the public sphere.

(3) Yet Outhwaite's skeptical doubts concerning dialogue also concern a third dimension: the here and now of dialogic engagements, whether deliberation can be effective, make sense at all, in light of the hardened attitudes of Brexiters, Trumpists, etc.. This directly practical or "applied" problem, however, can come best into focus by drawing on the former two dimensions. Clearly, for the hermeneutic attitude, the recognition of the Other's self-understanding and their "claims" is a *default* position, an *original intuition*; but as we saw, in order to fully realize the true potential of dialogic interaction, (a) socio-cognitive capabilities in the individual and (b) a respective social sphere of mutual engagement, respect, and perspective-taking, have to be established. This means in turn that when the conditions are *not* met, dialogue may be futile, maybe "postponed until further . . .," and replaced by an "objectifying" and explanatory approach that reconstructs how and why the lack of true dialogic opportunity and condition exists. It is also clear that such an assessment is always highly volatile and contextual; yet so is all understanding. The question whether to actually enter into a dialogue has to answered *in practice*; critical theory can only pinpoint possible guidelines and presuppositions as to whether dialogic conditions are in place. Whether members of a political party enter public discussions with the aim to accept their deliberative or majoritarian results (or just make a strategic use of public domains to establish visibility and "reputation"); whether subjects truly engage in a hermeneutic reconstruction of their background and vulnerability so as to enable mutual respect and recognition (or whether they use such references for their "innocence" merely to ignore the special experiences and vulnerability of the excluded, abnormal, marginalized); whether claimants of enlightened truth, "woke" subjects, rightly approach those who appear to cement an unreflective *status quo* of whiteness as racist (or whether those who are targeted could be differently understood), for example, always requires concrete interpretations, and thus real dialogues. Those dialogues should be governed by one's own fore-conception of implicit biases, but address the Other—at least initially—with

the same assumption of capability that one grants oneself to critically reflect on them. The customary use of linguistic formula may carry deep-seated collective projections of inferiority of some groups and members, but the very fact of a holistic unthematic background as constitutive of *all* of our pre-understanding may invite a collective and reflexive effort toward reconstruction, rather than moralizing and individualizing attributions of guilt and failure by some toward some others.[14]

Challenging Dialogic Experience as Enabling Reflexive Distanciation

Lauren Barthold poses a challenge to critical hermeneutics from another angle: whether its reliance of an empathetic conception of imaginary perspective-taking remains overly entangled in Cartesian background assumptions and thus ultimately fails to deliver the emancipatory understanding that, in a contrast she draws, an enactivist conception of empathy can provide. "We are all familiar with [Descartes'] efforts to secure a truth that ultimately would be accessible only by an individual's purely rational cognition thus curtailing any forms of doubt and uncertainty stemming from the unruly power of institutions. While this rendition obviously is lacking in subtlety, I think we can recognize how it functions as the ancestor of many forms of critique today" (Barthold 2022, 216). Any such general tracing of "current forms of critique" to Cartesian roots—we may remind ourselves of Foucault's appropriation of an Enlightenment ethos that aims at transformation rather than grounding, the pragmatist critique, Habermas's communicative turn in critical theory, last not least the hermeneutic attempts—may already seem problematic. Barthold specifies her concerns by lasering in on the role of "distanciation" and generally "critical reflexivity" as core features of the hermeneutic process. While she emphasizes that my approach "has much to offer, in particular [in] the way it addresses the objection that once we insist in dialogically engaging the common ground of our humanity neither agency nor emancipatory understanding is possible" (216), she also maintains that "we hermeneuts should stop worrying about how to access a 'critical reflexive' agency to gain freedom and truth…" (216). Barthold opposes a *distanciating critique* in favor of "true dialogic connectedness… Emancipatory understanding occurs when all dialogic participants experience freedom as a result of their fully engaged playful connection with the whole dialogic event" (216). Instead of a mere cognitive realization, as it were encapsulated in the individual interpreter's mind, enactivist empathy enables a "visceral experience stemming from a genuine dialogic encounter with the other *qua* human" (216). The "reflective standpoint," unhappily inheriting Cartesian vices, is rejected for an enactivist account of empathy in which connection trumps distanciation, coherence overcomes fragmentation, detached and abstract thought is replaced by a brain-body-mind engulfing "dialogic event" in which our shared humanity is literally both realized and felt. However, as attractive as this vision may sound, I will briefly highlight why neither the charge of Cartesianism holds true (1) nor that reflexivity can be dispensed with as an essential moment of the hermeneutic process (2).

(1) Critical hermeneutics is neither ontologically nor methodologically "Cartesian," albeit it admittedly strengthens the epistemic and reflexive role of the situated agent. But just as little as Gadamer's "historically effected consciousness," *pace* Heidegger,

represents such a regression, critical reflexivity cannot be construed as defined by a separate "mental realm," a cognitive homunculus sphere of pure thoughts and ideas. Indeed, as our previous discussions made abundantly clear (see esp. Winter, Turner, and Stueber), the "sense of self" is an emergent category, co-developing with and dependent on the Other; it marks a self-reflexive pole within a constitutive intersubjective and dialogic situation. Yet it does not, as I made already clear against Gadamer in the *Power of Dialogue*, entail the complete abandonment of reflexive self-understanding. As an outcome of dialogic experiences, and then, as its own mode of *Bildung*, it rather emerges from hermeneutic events. Gadamer himself calls this the negativity of all hermeneutic experience in relation to which the self learns to profile itself—its "self." These processes are not "launched" from an inner encapsulated sphere, but, as in Dewey and Mead, triggered by encountered problem situations.

I specifically emphasize in the *Power of Dialogue* the productive experience of culturally and historically situated Others, as this enables the unique mode of realizing how whole frames of experience, mediated symbolically and practically embodied, may challenge my own world disclosure. And while I recognize the high level of problem-consciousness in Gadamer regarding the tension between the necessary disclosure of the Other's meaning and background based on *one's own pre-understanding*, and the need to prevent and protect the Other from mere *assimilation*, I insist on the need for a more reflexive orientation toward the Other's background assumptions. To that purpose I employ Foucault's discourse analysis and genealogy of power to carve out two layers of such background dimensions; later I realized that my approach is even better served, without giving up the Foucauldian tools, if we reinterpret the "theoretical" reconstruction of such layers as a form of perspective-taking (Kögler 2000; 2012; 2017c). Indeed, I can now claim with early hermeneutics, especially with Humboldt and Schleiermacher, that the capacity to take the perspective of the Other becomes a linguistically mediated capability to assume the Other's situational and interpretive perspective toward the world, others, and oneself. True, such an imaginary perspective-taking is always a "fusion of horizon" (Gadamer), and yet it does not focus on the consensual reaching of a shared truth; it foremost opens itself toward the Other through a thorough reconstruction of the internal coherence of the Other's background, thus pushing further the process of self and other differentiation. It does this without denying the intentional validity-orientation at work in the Other's world, nor does it preclude a possible consensus—it is just not assuming it *immediately* based on one's own perspective. A heightened sense of one's own assumptions and those of the Other sets in, event-like and "playfully," just as Gadamer and Barthold rightly emphasize. While it begins with the explicit methodological aim to do justice to the Other *in her self-understanding*, the process will eventually take over: whether my first assumptions are ultimately productive, what's "on target" and what's "misguided," *emerges* via an open and "uncontrollable" process—and is thus indeed more a "play" and less a "method." Accordingly, it is the process—and not the methodical control of an individual interpreter—which brings productive insights and interpretations to light; what comes to light are not pure beliefs shut-off and represented in individual minds, but individually embodied perspectives in socially and symbolically mediated practices and life-contexts.

(2) Assuming that we grant *reflexivity* to be thus situated and emergent, must we, however, assume that it is needed for "emancipatory understanding?" Is a reflexive understanding of difference, even of power-induced backgrounds and interests, not creating more fragmentation and polarization rather than the experience of our common humanity, as Barthold seems to contend? Recall that understanding the perspective of the Other explores not only the conscious beliefs, but also the respective whole life-context, including power relations, of the Other; it is therefore that I claim that the reflexive reconstruction of background power is an important dimension of ethico-political recognition (Taylor 1995; Searle 2009) As the discourse concerning "whiteness" shows, the oblivious arrogance of occupying an "innocent" or "normal" view on life can be understood as the mirror-image of socially inculcated ignorance concerning other life conditions. It can only be truly challenged by exposure to the marginalized and excluded voices and positions. One's own privilege is the luxury of the non-understanding of differently situated agents. *Reflexivity is recognition.* Understanding others in their vulnerable circumstances is the first step toward a decentering of one's own dominant view. Recognizing the life-circumstances of subordinated or marginalized subjects means to give a "hearing" to them, it engages in concrete listening, openness, and turn-taking.

The critical-hermeneutic attitude therefore suggests and motivates such a *reconstructive perspective-taking*. The approach is based on a (shared) situatedness in (different) holistic backgrounds. As such, it does take the *whole* dialogic situation into account and is not merely, as Barthold alleges, "dyadic." Yet the adequate reconstruction of the involved backgrounds, due to their complex multilayered structuration, requires an *explicit* reconstruction of the diverse viewpoints and embodied perspectives, because the diverse backgrounds entail power and domination, which operates via the inculcation, as poststructuralist studies have shown, into social selves and their habitus. Concrete interpersonal engagements, like in "The Color of Fear" (a reflective group-dynamic experience), show that making these implicit presuppositions explicit is not an abstract, cold, and detached process (for discussion see Kögler 1999b); still, the concrete encounter of differently situated subjects can and must be the source of a *detachment*—a reflexive distanciation—from once previously and naively occupied *social* location and *status* (see also Gressgård 2010). If the source of reflexive distanciation is thus a concretely recognizing multicultural dialogue, the further reflexive appropriation can prevent the fragmentation and lack of unifying coherence Barthold is rightly concerned about. On the one hand, the loosing of the grip of everyday-ideologies opens the space of inserting and expanding one's own historical, cultural, and social knowledge, bringing critical theory to bear on one's life situation, and thus to radically expand one's horizon. The alternate "public sphere" of the humanities and social sciences provide in their vast teaching potential the currently best context here. On the other hand, such a process activates universal human capacities which it applies to the concrete contexts and capabilities of subjects in different life-circumstances. It thus mediates particularity and universality, abstract human being and concrete human existences—and thus does not fragment at all, but rather unifies-in-difference, creating a *shared bond* with the actually existing communities and groups, rather than with an abstract subject "*qua human*."

Yet Barthold's most serious challenge to this reflexive dialogic practice may in fact be her claim that when "the focus is on dyadic empathetic exchanges, the deeper level wherein the latent prejudices and fears operate remains untouched, leaving ideologies of individual hearts (!) and systematic structures unchallenged" (221). Invoking in-group ethical solidarity (like Stueber did), she finds deep-seated biases resistant to change, closing off out-group ethical recognition: "We are simply less responsive to out-group members ... in-group members fail to understand out-group member actions ... the more dehumanized the out-group is, the less intuitive the grasp of out-group member intentions and actions" (224). While this assessment makes plausible why Barthold assumes that "volitional efforts by an individual (whether on an epistemic or ethical level) to shift a horizon prevent true change" (222), the stated fact that we "simply" "display significantly less motor cortex activity when observing out-group members" smacks of a problematic reductionism. It is granted, with Barthold and Gallagher, that human dispositions are shaped in holistic brain-body-mind-environments in which a neat separation of mind and world is not possible: their constitution (and reproduction, I would add) is relational; but this does not mean that we have to take the initial dispositions for granted. The transcendence of the usual dispositions—these social habitus, we may say with Bourdieu—is especially in order when they delimit and structure the possible range of thoughts, perceptions, and acts of embedded selves in *non-egalitarian* and *unjust* ways. We should thus take Barthold's problem how to best approach fully situated subjects seriously. The hermeneutic capabilities approach conceives of social and pedagogical practices which entail role-taking exercises, foreign language- and world-learning, as well as discursive and genealogical reconstructions, so as to widen and unleash the actual capabilities which are exercised in limited ranges (Delanoy 2022; Burkitt 2002).

Barthold suggests instead a conception of enactivist empathy that suffers from over-ambition and under-definition. There is a lot that seems highly attractive, like the need for a more listening-oriented than argument-winning conception of dialogue; the correction of an overly cognitivist conception of holism (as merely a *belief* of belonging) in favor of a visceral connection with all; and the collectivist understanding of dialogic outcomes as the process-results of all and not based on genial achievements of individuals. But regardless, the very dispositional engraving of group-based attitudes that she herself invokes makes the immediate and spontaneous *willingness* to subject oneself to such dialogic self-understanding a total mystery, and thus is in no better position here than the hermeneutic capabilities approach. Furthermore, the mere will to plunge oneself into the visceral collective enactment—into this enticing bodily in-between of true dialogue—leaves unclear how the deep-seated prejudices that Barthold mobilized against the reflexive perspective-taking suddenly disperse themselves into thin air and make space for a truly shared "common humanity" via agreement. Finally, and perhaps most importantly, such a melting pot of all cultural differences in the enactivist haven of liquefied dispositions does not do justice to the rich and diversified self-identities that *demand recognition*, and that require mediation and perhaps reconciliation through an engaged and mutually respectful dialogue *recognizing difference*! Barthold certainly unearthed an important sub-cognitive dimension of possible dialogic fusion and sharing; yet her radical opposition and resistance to integrate her insights into a position that takes political and moral selves as reflexive agents into account, severely hampers her claim, at least for now, to enable a truly "emancipatory understanding."

The "Ethos of Dialogue" Revisited: On Grounding "Critique"

Yet how may we then assess the force of critical dialogue in times in which the fragmentation and polarization of the public sphere is ubiquitous? How could the attempt to engage in reflexive critiques, especially if premised on perspective-taking, gain traction given that cultural and political contexts seem defined by a pervasive dominance of populist, authoritarian, and other types of enclosed identities and ideologies? Randi Gressgård poses a subtle response to these challenges, taking off from our shared previous endorsement of the need and potential for reflexive dialogues (Gressgård 2010). By addressing the affective and ontological turns in cultural studies, she reimagines a "critique" that is by no means oblivious to emotional or embodied experiences. By focusing on disrupted and displaced situations of *crisis*, the potential of an affective challenge to the *status quo* becomes tangible: "Even if people are likely to affectively invest in discourses and ideologies that induce "forgetting" of difference when their modes of being are experienced as disrupted or in a crisis, unsettling experiences might also provoke dialogue and critique given that they call upon subjects to confront contingency of social relations and thus destabilize trajectories of the past, present, and future ... this critical perspective resonates with Kögler's ... assumption that 'the confrontation with another meaning sets in motion a process of becoming reflectively aware of hitherto hidden assumption and practices'" (Gressgård 2022, 234). Gressgård acknowledges a deep ambivalence as "affects can motivate as well as constrain dialogic encounters" (236), [they] may be instruments or effects of apparatuses, but also they may be impediments and irritants" (238). And yet, the grounding of critique in real life contexts is necessary since the current crisis cannot be overcome or "solved" by "liberal" or "validity-oriented" modes of recognition. Her forceful plea for a radicalized mode of critique integrates deep crisis so as to challenge the unspeakable power and oppression operative in the ordinary, the normal, the *status quo*. True "world dialogues" would thus be less concerned with the apparent polarization and fragmentation but rather focus on overcoming the exclusion of marginalized voices based on the "lack of any real intersubjective connection ... predicated on a racialized death-politics, spectacular and eventual as well as slow and ordinary" (243). I will take up Gressgård's reflections as an opportunity to reconstruct central aspects of the critical-hermeneutic notion of critique.

(1) The concept of critique informed by hermeneutic insights is always radically situated, responsive to concrete challenges, problem contexts, triggered by real events. Heidegger's reconstruction of explicit symbolic representation from a break-down of smooth functioning in practical settings (Heidegger 1969), and Gadamer's emphasis on the negative-dialectical feature of true hermeneutic experience brought this out (Gadamer 1989).[15] Characterizing "ideology critique" in this perspective as a theoretical, academic exercise detached from real life-contexts, like Sedgwick and supporters of the *affective turn* do, amounts to a misguided caricature; after the

detranscendental turn, but also after the fall of the Hegelian master-narrative, the theorist is herself a situated, context-bound, partial agent. Yet this does not mean, as Gressgård keenly notes, that the triggered affective challenges can escape (re-) conceptual integration, or are even best theorized as such: emphasizing concrete affectual embodied encounters should "refrain from locating affect entirely outside of the reach of interpretation" (235), as "the concept of encounter also suggests that what has been disrupted will always be rendered in new frames of recognition." (236) The task of critical hermeneutics is precisely to sensibilize the epistemic perspective for that which may escape it, for its affectual and situational origins, to assist agents to pick "it" up, as it were, in the spirit of an emancipatory project. In this vein, Axel Honneth drew on Dewey's theory of emotion to explain how feelings of injustice and misrecognition may serve as a potential source of resistance and social transformation (Honneth 1995). Similarly, for Judith Butler "critique is indeed affectively invested, invoking a sense that something is wrong or unfair, ultimately concerning that which we need to live (a livable life). To the extent that critique is bound up with survival, with living on, it is a truly existential issue, which is markedly different from criticism considered as a random, negative and judgmental operation" (237).

(2) While affect theory allows us to reconsider the emotional and experiential sources of triggered feelings of distrust, disruption, crisis, it is important that the realization of its explicit modes—i.e., the reintegration in and connection to conceptual and symbolic levels of self-understanding—is not undertaken in an *immediate* mode of empathetic projection. Butler's reflections on critique as different from transcendental or universalist groundings (and as immersed, fragile, transformative, with explicit reference, as Vandenberghe, to late Foucault) were articulated in a discussion concerning the "secular roots of critique" (Brown 2010). While Butler emphasizes how critique challenges (and not just confirms!) our Western roots and self-understandings, Saba Mahmoud challenges how the parameters for empathetic understanding often still derive from a Western, i.e., partial perspective, as when social meanings are conceptualized as contingent and constructed, and thus easily separable from the entrenched symbolic representations, for instance of Mohamed (Mahmoud 2009). For a Muslim believer, however, such post-conventional detachment is *prima facie* not in the cards, since not being part of her symbolic order. To be sure, this does neither question the normative standard of true reciprocity and perspective-taking, nor does it ignore the multiple reflexive self-understandings within the Muslim communities (Mahmoud 2005). But it does challenge a biased and uneven application of perspective-taking as well as attribution of reflexivity. True perspective-taking would emphatically take the *ontological* self-understanding of symbolic representations into account and aim to ameliorate and assess the conditions of a respectful yet free and open dialogue *on that basis*. Accordingly, the critical-hermeneutic perspective does not merely assert the role of affect, emotion, and sensational experiences as triggers for renewed self-evaluation. It rather extends those empathetic states and attitudes into the experiences and worlds of the Other, always aware and reflexively reconstructing how the agents in the respective symbolic and practical background contexts would themselves disclose these phenomena.

(3) The *crisis situation* that breeds disruption vis-a-vis the *status quo* is conceived with practical intent. Gressgård projects a politically oriented crisis motivation with

Brown as an invitation to act: "A critical condition is a particular kind of call; an urgent call for knowledge, deliberation, judgment, and action to starve off catastrophe" (239). For Gressgård, the true disaster is the invisibility and normality of oppression, unbearable suffering covered under the camouflage of the unavoidable, self-inflicted, or simply "normal" condition. The discourse of emergency can thus have an awakening effect: it invokes "exceptionality; urgency; interval; and hope" (239). What is crucial for me is that such a proposal avoids the defeatist discourse on emergency as a sole tool in the hand of bio-power and unassailable macro-structures of domination. Gressgård's mobilization of a discourse of emergency integrates agency and critical reflexivity into the domain of a transgressive politics, without failing to mediate any such politics with the need of a concretely recognizing, empathetic, and intersubjectively oriented understanding.[16]

(4) In order to not fall victim to the existing illusion of an "unrestrained dialogue" or the mere idealizing presupposition of such, the actual being-in-the-world of differently positioned agents needs to be explicitly addressed. But Gressgård rightly objects to the "ontological turn" that it identifies a justified critique of limited inclusion and "representation" with a complete rejection of representationalism. If "the denouncement of western knowledge as colonializing is centered on the problem of representation per se, [it leaves] largely untouched the long-established social arrangements and power hierarchies underpinning (specific) western, modernist representations" (242). Instead of bridging "real life" and "academic discourse," here both get "ontologically separated" from one another, instead of critically related to one another. Indeed, in order to critically "analyze" western modes of power, some "account," thus i.e., some mode of representation or description of power-induced social practices and structures of domination, seems urgent; furthermore, the ontological turn seems to close itself off to any possible analysis and critique of power in the domains that are seen as outside of the "Western" sphere, thus artificially reducing the full scope of a mutually reciprocal and inclusive critique. Yet invoking "ontological worlds" has for Gressgård still the potential—if employed in a strategic way—to challenge a complaisant "one world" conception of liberal cosmopolitanism.[17] In the end, the critical-hermeneutic reappropriation of one's power-defined existence and Gressgård's strategic challenge vis-à-vis a liberal cosmopolitanism intend the same thing: they make visible the excluded world of a radical, racialized, ostracized Other and to challenge one's own taken-for-granted horizon of background assumptions and practices when approaching a cultural and socially Other. Gressgård's plea to envision radical Otherness reaffirms the essential aspects of a dialogic conception of critique:

- Critique emerges against the backdrop of taken-for-granted beliefs, assumptions, and practices in which some phenomenon or event appears as a challenge, invokes a negation of accepted "habits of thought," creates a crisis of sorts, and thus allows for the open space of a challenge vis-à-vis the *status quo*.
- Such critical encounters or engagements are not detached academic exercises of theoretic thought, but embodied, engaged, even visceral forms of detachment and disorientation, which can as such become the source of a reorganization and renewal of one's own interpretive schemes and presuppositions.

- Critique itself enacts the dialogic experience of the Other via empathetic and linguistico-experiential modes of perspective-taking, in which the theorist reconstructs and relives the situated agents' perspective and self-understanding. While such a process is always mediated by a particular situated theorist's perspective and background, it allows for a mutual detachment and distanciation precisely by staying engaged vis-à-vis one another's experiential outlooks.
- Critique thus grounds itself in the lifeworld, moves from situated moral, political, social, and otherwise experiential challenges; yet by thus opening up a horizon of transcendence, it allows for the influx of methodological and theoretical instruments that further expand the localized perspectives and transcend the "immediate" cultural and social horizon. It is ultimately in this horizon-expanding power that critical hermeneutics grounds its qualified hope for a radical and emancipatory understanding.

Is it really a surprise, then, that democracy could not exist without critique? That critique is the ultimate ground of possibility of any democratic politics?

Notes

1   See my detailed criticism of Bourdieu in Kögler (1997a). To remain on the individual perspective-level would miss the socially constitutive background, while the objectifying and mis-recognizing detachment of the result of discourse and sociological analyses from our reflexive situation would miss the Humbolditian interdependency of language as energeia-and-ergon, of agency-and-structure within meaning constitutive, i.e., human practices.
2   Critical hermeneutics would equally claim Dewey's approach of adjusting "bad habits" with "better habits," and not just by mere abstract ideals or "imperatives;" instead, such adjustments may be undertaken precisely by the reflexive appropriation of what is entailed in dialogic practices. See Dewey 2015: 37ff; for a Deweyan conception of habitus, see Burkitt 2002.
3   Lorenzer's approach also famously entails the need to have the theoretical reconstructions provided by the analyst endorsed and accepted by the agent herself. Habermas famously adopted Lorenzer's interpretation of this kind of theoretically induced self-reflexivity for his own early model of a therapeutic social critique. (Habermas 1972)
4   See Sandra Bartky's Foucauldian analysis of gendering body-technics (Bartky 1997).
5   Compare Wittgenstein's reflection of the "natural understanding" of emotional expressions which do not require a theoretical assessment, which indeed come prior to such an assessment and for that reason constitute the possibility to understand others and their emotional and "mental" states (Wittgenstein 1953).
6   Gadamer is interested in reconstructing the "claim of the tradition," i.e. that we let ourselves be addressed by it, in order to reestablish the life-orienting and grounding force (or "validity") of tradition. Objectifying social-scientific as well as individualizing hermeneutic approaches destroy this peculiar bond we may entertain vis-à-vis our cultural legacy; through their objectification they miss the specifically moral type of recognition that preserves the Other as a non-objectifiable, intentionally

oriented co-self in relation to us. See Kögler (2010) for a sympathetic yet also qualifying discussion.

7   Since I have to correlate my own taken-to-be true beliefs, assumptions and values to those of the text in order to make sense at all, I necessarily project a rational pre-assumption toward the Other and her expressions. What Gadamer calls a "fore-conception of completeness" articulates this aspect of the moral phenomenon of interpretation.

8   Stueber's suggestion of "additional information needed" indicates that for him there exists a basic, somewhat direct and immediate process of enacting another's belief and emotional state and that only subsequently, culturally specific constructs have to be taken into account when conflicts arise. Regarding such a case, he states that a "disapproval merely based on us finding somebody unintelligible also does not have to be taken very seriously from the perspective of the target of empathy, if it is not fully understanding the relevant differences between the empathizer and her target" (114).

9   See Sahlins 2003. The Other is only fully recognized if we take this interpretive capability to situate and understand herself *in this manner* into account, and not merely by emotionally grasping her state of mind, only to be added by "reasons" once something disturbing or "unintelligible" occurs.

10 For how to possibly reconstruct critical and normative values *from Confucianism itself*, see Dunaj 2016.

11 Vandenberghe even suggests "a little optimism to think that underneath the rubble there are living forces just waiting to get history back on track"—or as we in the *Undogmatische Linke* in Frankfurt used to say: "Unter dem Plaster liegt der Strand."

12 See the analyses of Rainer Winter and Randi Gressgård with regard to this issue in this volume.

13 For a compelling account of Adorno's reflections on how best to challenge bad cognitive habits in a power-defined public, especially emphasizing the enhanced need for educational interventions and pedagogical practices, see Dahms 2020; John Dewey's approach to orient education toward the formation of "reflective judgment" and the associated necessary capabilities exemplifies a promising model of how to conceive the relevant pedagicial practices and resources (for background see Dewey 2015; also Burkitt 2002).

14 In other words, in the critical-hermeneutic approach, it is okay to criticize or challenge the Other with regard to hidden or unreflective assumptions of biases, say of a racist, classist, or gender-biased nature. But it is important to conceive of these challenges as *shared opportunities for reflexive insights*, rather than as essentialist accusations vis-à-vis the Other, say as a horrifically racist or ignorant *subject*. The deconstruction of micro-aggressions may not lead to a neo-constructivism of micro-essentialisms.

15 For an excellent analysis of current challenges as well as potentials of a "left-Heideggerian" social ontology, especially with regard to early attempts like Herbert Marcuse's—and opposed to current tendencies to create a superficial contrast between a transgressive "political ontology of the event" and a "static" and apolitical "social ontology"— see Mertel 2017.

16 At the same time, such a politics still needs to include a macro-theoretical and (self-) objectifying lens of Agamben or the "bio-political" Foucault which is needed to transcend the interactional focus on power and bring into view structures of domination that predate and prevail it amidst the concrete intersubjective settings (Agamben 1998; Foucault 1976).

17 It is only here where I feel the need to part with Gressgård's otherwise highly instructive analysis: to employ the assumption of plural worlds in a strategic-essentialist attitude à la Spivak seems both an unhappy and unnecessary "way out:" it is unhappy, as the strategic use of neo-essentialisms re-establishes the superior attitude of a theorist (who blinks to her peers "knowing" there are of course no completely separate cultural worlds); it is also unnecessary since grounded cosmopolitanism already entails the assumption of diverse socio-cultural lifeworlds, shaped by globalization but differing in worldreligions, civilizations, historical experiences, etc. I earlier invoked the axial age conceptions of diverse religious traditions, on which the approach to multiple modernities builds. If coupled with a genealogical approach toward reconstructing power relations in one's own respective tradition, i.e., plurally and mutually, radical differences and unacknowledged invisibility could continuously be challenged.

References

Agamben, Giorgio (1998), *Homo Sacer. Sovereign Power and Bare Life*. L.A.: U. of California Press.
Assmann, Jan (2018), *Achsenzeit. Eine Archäologue der Moderne*, München: C.H. Beck.
Barthold, Lauren (2022), "Playing more seriously: an enactivist critique of Kögler's critically reflexive dialogue" (in this volume).
Bartky, Sandra Lee (1997), "Foucault, Femininity and the Modernization of Patriarchal Power," in Katie Conboy, Nadia Medina, and Sarah Stanbury (eds.), *Writing on the body: Female embodiment and feminist theory*, New York: Columbia University Press, 129–54.
Bellah, Robert (2011), *Religion and Human Evolution. From the Paleolithic to the Axial Age*, Cambridge: Harvard University Press.
Bellah, Robert/Joas, Hans (eds.) (2013), *The Axial Age Discourse and its Consequences*, Cambridge: Harvard University Press.
Bourdieu, Pieree/Wacquant, Loic (1992), *An Invitation to Reflexive Sociology*, Chicago: U. of Chicago Press.
Butler, Judith (2009), "The sensibility of critique: Response to Adad and Mahmood," in Asad et al. (eds.): *Is Critique Secular? Blasphemy, Injury, and Free Speech*, Berkeley: University of California Press, 101–36.
Burkitt, Ian (2002), "Technologies of the Self: Habitus and Capacities," *Journal for the Theory of Social Behaviour*. 32.
Bruner, Jerome (1990), *Acts of Meaning*, Cambridge, Harvard University Press.
Cassirer, Ernst (1955), *Philosophy of Symbolic Forms, Vol. 1: Language*, Chicago: Chicago University Press.
Dahms, Harry (2020), "Adorno's Critique of the New Right-Wing Extremism: How (Not) to Face the Past, Present, and Future," in *disclosure*, Vol. 29, 129–179.
Darwall, Stephen (2006), *The Second-Person Standpoint. Morality, Respect, and Accountability*, Cambridge, MA: Harvard University Press.
Delanoy, Werner (2022), "Dialogue, Cosmopolitanism and Language Education" (in this volume).
Dewey, John (2015), *Human Nature and Conduct*. Independent Publishers.
Dunaj, Ľubomír (2016), "Towards critical aspects of Confucianism," *Ethics & Bioethics*, 6 (3–4), 135–45.

Fleischacker, Samuel (2019), *Being Me, Being You. Adam Smith and Empathy*, Chicago: Chicago University Press.
Foucault, Michel (1976) *Discipline and Punish*. New York.
Foucault Michel (1997a), "What is enlightenment?" (trans. C. Porter), in S. Lotringer (ed.): *The Politics of Truth*, 97–119, Los Angeles: Semiotenxt(e).
Foucault, Michel (1997b), "What is critique?" (trans. L. Hochroth), in S. Lotringer (ed.): *The Politics of Truth*, 41–82, Los Angeles: Semiotenxt(e).
Gadamer, Hans-Georg (1989) *Truth and Method*, New York (New York: Crossroads Publishing Company.
Gressgård, Randi (2010), *Multicultural Dialogue: Dilemmas, Paradoxes, Conflicts*, New York: Berghahn Books.
Gressgård, Randi (2022), "Dialogue in a polarized world—is there a way out?" (in this volume).
Habermas, Jürgen (1972) *Knowledge and Human Interest*, Boston: Beacon Press.
Habermas, Jürgen (2008), "Religion in the Public Sphere: Cognitive Presuppositions for the 'Public Use of Reason' in Religious and Secular Citizens," in *Between Naturalism and Religion*, Cambridge, UK: Polity Press, 114–47.
Habermas, Jürgen (2008) *On the Logic of the Social Sciences* (Cambridge: MIT Press, 2008).
Habermas, Jürgen (2019) *Auch eine Geschichte der Philosophie, vol. 1: Die okzidentale Konstellation von Glauben und Wissen*; vol. 2: *Vernünftige Freiheit. Spuren des Diskurses über Glauben und Wissen,* Berlin: Suhrkamp Verlag.
Harris, Paul (2012), *Trusting What You're Told. How Children Learn from Others.* Cambridge, MA: Harvard University Press.
Healy, Paul (2022), "Secularity, Religion, and Dialogue: Rethinking the Conditions of the Possibility for Genuine Complementary Learning" (in this volume).
Hellweg, Joseph (2020), "Religion in—and as—the Public Sphere: A West Africa/based Critique of Critical Theory of Democracy," *Berlin Journal of Critical Theory*, Vol. 4, n.2, 81–106.
Honneth, Axel (1995) *The Struggle for Recognition*, London: Polity Press.
Humboldt, v. Wilhelm (1978), *On Language*, Cambridge: Cambridge University Press.
Jaspers, Karl (1953) *The Origin and Goal of History* (Newhaven/London: Yale University Press.
Joas, Hans (2013), "The Axial Age Discourse as Religious Discourse," in Bellah/Joas (eds.) *The Axial Age and Its Consequences*, Cambridge: Harvard University Press, 9–29.
Korsgaard, Christine (1996), *The Sources of Normativity*, Cambridge, MA: Harvard University Press.
Kögler, Hans-Herbert (1997), "Alienation as Epistemological Source. Reflexivity and Social Background in Mannheim and Bourdieu," *Social Epistemology*. Vol. 11, n., 141–69.
Kögler, Hans-Herbert (1999a), *The Power of Dialogue. Critical Hermeneutics after Gadamer and Foucault*, Cambridge: MIT Press.
Kögler, Hans-Herbert (1999b), "New Arguments for Diversifying the Curriculum: Advancing Students' Cognitive Development," in *Diversity Digest*, ed. Association of American Colleges and Universities (AAC&U), Washington D.C.
Kögler, Hans-Herbert (2000), "Empathy, Dialogical Self, and Reflexive Interpretation: The Symbolic Source of Simulation," in *Empathy and Agency*, Kögler, Hans-Herbert/Stueber, Karsten (eds.), Boulder, Co: Westview Press, 194–221.
Kögler, Hans-Herbert (2004) *Michel Foucault*, Stuttgart/Weimar: Metzler Verlag.

Kögler, Hans-Herbert (2005), "Constructing a Cosmopolitan Public Sphere. Hermeneutic Capabilities and Universal Values," *European Journal for Social Theory*, 3 (8): 297–320.

Kögler, Hans-Herbert (2010), "Being as Dialogue, or: The Ethical Consequences of Interpretation," *Consequences of Hermeneutics*, Malpas, Jeff/Zabala, Santiago (eds.) Evanston: Northwestern University Press, 343–67.

Kögler, Hans-Herbert (2012), "Agency and its Other: on the intersubjective roots of self-identity," *New Ideas in Psychology*, 30, n. 1, Elsevier, 47–64.

Kögler, Hans-Herbert (2017a) "The Religious Face of Evil," *Berlin Journal of Critical Theory (BJCT)*, Vol. 1, n. 2, 21–46.

Kögler, Hans-Herbert (2017b) "A Critical Hermeneutics of Agency: Cultural Studies as Critical Social Theory," *Hermeneutic Philosophies of Social Science*, Babich, Babette (ed.), Berlin/Boston: De Gruyter, 63–88.

Kögler, Hans-Herbert (2017c), "A Discursive View from Somewhere: Foucault's Epistemic Position," *Place, Space, and Hermeneutics*, Janz, Bruce (ed.), Cham: Springer International Publishing, 239–60.

Kögler Hans-Herbert (2020a), "Tradition, Transcendence, and the Public Sphere: A Hermeneutic Critique of Religion." *Berlin Journal of Critical Theory (BJCT)*, Vol. 4, n. 2, (2020b), 107–46.

Kögler, Hans-Herbert (2020b) "A Genealogy of Faith and Freedom." *Theory, Culture, and Society (TCS)*, 37 (7-8): 37–46.

Kögler, Hans-Herbert (2021), "Dialogue on Dialogue. Gadamer and Habermas," *The Gadamerian Mind*, Locke, Theodore, Heiden, Gert-Jan v.d. (eds.), London: Routledge, 288–303.

Mead, George Herbert (1934) *Mind, Self and Society*, Chicago: Chicago University Press.

Mahmoud, Saba (2005), *The Politics of Piety*, Princeton: Princeton University Press.

Mahmoud, Saba (2009), "Religious Reason and Secular Affect: An Incommensurable Divide?", in Asad et al. (eds.): Is *Critique Secular? Blasphemy, Injury, and Free Speech*, Berkeley: University of California Press, 58–94.

Maraldo, John (2022), "The Limits of Interreligious Hermeneutics and the Need for Alternative Understanding" (in this volume).

Martustik, Martin (2020), "Which Axial Age, whose rituals? Habermas and Jaspers on the 'spiritual' situation of the present age," *Philosophy and Social Criticism*, 1–14.

Mendieta, Eduardo (2018), "The Axial Age, social evolution, and postsecular consciousness," *Critical Research on Religion*, 6 (3): 289–308.

Mertel, Kurt C.M. (2017), "Two ways of being a left-Heideggerian: The crossroads between political and social ontology," *Philosophy & Social Criticism*, 43 (6): 1–19.

Mouffe, Chantal (2000), *The Democratic Paradox* (London: Verso, 2000).

Outhwaite, William (2022), "Cherche pas à Comprendre: Cosmopolitan Hermeneutics in Difficult Times" (in this volume).

Rawls, John (1993), *Political Liberalism*, New York: Columbia University Press.

Sahlins, Marshall (2003), "The Apotheosis of Captain Cook," in *Between Belief and Transgression*. Ed. M. Izard, P. Smith, Chicago: University of Chicago Press.

Schmitt, Carl (1996), *The Concept of the Political*, Chicago: University of Chicago Press.

Searle, John (2012) *Making the Social World. The Structure of Human Civilization*, Oxford: Oxford University Press.

Stueber, Karsten (2022), "The Moral Stance, Our Moralizing Nature, and the Hermeneutic and Empathic Dimension of Human Relations" (in this volume).

Susen, Simon (2022), "The Case for a Critical Hermeneutics: From the Understanding of Power to the Power of Understanding" (in this volume).

Taylor, Charles (1995), "Multiculturalism and the Politics of Recognition," Princeton: Princeton University Press.
Tomasello, Michael (2008) *Origins of Human Communication*, Cambridge, MA: The MIT Press.
Turner, Stephen (2022), "Naturalizing Kögler" (in this volume).
Vandenberghe, Frederic (2020), "Demokratur in Brasilien. Versuch einer Lehre vom Systemzusammenbruch," in *Leviathan*, 48.Jg. 4, 637–54.
Vandenberghe, Frédéric (2022), "Sociology, the Studies, and the Ontology of the Present" (in this volume).
Winter, Rainer (2022), "Power, the Body, and Reflexivity. Hans-Herbert Kögler's Hermeneutics in the Context of Critical Sociology" (in this volume).
Wittgenstein, Ludwig (1953), *Philosophical Investigations*, New York: Macmillan.

List of Contributors

Lauren Swayne Barthold teaches philosophy at Emerson College. Her current research explores the scope and power of dialogue. She is the author of *Overcoming Polarization in the Public Square: Civic Dialogue* (2020), *A Hermeneutic Approach to Gender and Other Social Identities* (2016), and *Gadamer's Dialectical Hermeneutics* (Rowman Littlefield 2010). She is the co-founder and program developer for the Heathmere Center for Cultural Engagement, a non-profit that engages marginalized communities through dialogue and the arts.

Werner Delanoy is Associate Professor of English Language Education in the Department of English and American Studies at the University of Klagenfurt. His main areas of research are inter- and trans-cultural learning perspectives, literature and language education in a digital age, and contemporary British culture and literature. His main publications include *Fremdsprachlicher Literaturunterricht: Theorie und Praxis als Dialog* (2002), *Cultural Studies in the EFL Classroom* (2006; with Laurenz Volkmann), *Future Perspectives for English Language Teaching* (2008; with Laurenz Volkmann) and *Learning with Literature in the EFL Classroom* (2015; with Maria Eisenmann and Frauke Matz).

Ľubomír Dunaj is Assistant Professor of Philosophy at the University of Vienna and Research Fellow at the Centre of Global Studies of the Institute of Philosophy, Czech Academy of Sciences. He obtained his Ph.D. from the Comenius University and spent time as a DAAD doctoral and post-doctoral research fellow at the Goethe University, Frankfurt am Main, and as a Fulbright Scholar at the University of North Florida. He is editor-in-chief of *Pragmatism Today* and member of the international editorial board of *Contradictions: A Journal for Critical Thought*. His areas of specialization are social and political philosophy and social theory.

Randi Gressgård is professor at the Centre for Women's and Gender Research (SKOK), affiliated with the research unit International Migration and Ethnic Relations (IMER), at the University of Bergen. Her research interests span the fields of migration and minority studies, gender and sexuality studies, and urban studies. Among her publications is *Multicultural Dialogue: Dilemmas, Paradoxes, Conflicts* (2010/2012), which was debated in *Dialogues in Human Geography*'s book forum in 2012.

Paul Healy is currently Adjunct Research Fellow (Philosophy) in the School of Arts, Social Sciences, and Humanities at Swinburne University of Technology. Before that, for many years he was Head of the Swinburne Philosophy program and Convenor of the Swinburne Bachelor of Arts program. His research has focused primarily on utilizing key insights from continental philosophy, especially hermeneutics and critical theory, for exploring contemporary problems in political philosophy, epistemology, philosophical psychology, and intercultural relations. He has numerous publications in these areas, many of which build on the framework developed in his *Rationality, Hermeneutics and Dialogue* (2017/2005).

Hans-Herbert Kögler is Professor of Philosophy at the University of North Florida, Jacksonville, and regular guest professor at Alpen-Adria University, Klagenfurt, Austria. Major publications include *The Power of Dialogue: Critical Hermeneutics after Gadamer and Foucault* (1999); *Michel Foucault* (2nd ed., 2004, 2016); *Kultura, kritica, dialog* (2006; 2014); the co-edited *Empathy and Agency. The Problem of Understanding in the Human Sciences* (2000; 2018); *Enigma Agency* (2019); the edited *Reconceiving Religion in the Postsecular Public Sphere"* (2020). Numerous essays in critical hermeneutics, critical social theory (Frankfurt School), philosophical hermeneutics, philosophy of language, poststructuralism, cultural studies, and social and political philosophy.

John C. Maraldo is Distinguished Professor Emeritus of Philosophy at the University of North Florida. He has held guest professorships at the University of Kyoto, the Catholic University of Leuven, and Nanzan University, respectively. In addition to numerous articles in comparative hermeneutics, phenomenology, and Japanese philosophy, his publications include: *Japanese Philosophy: A Sourcebook* (co-edited with J.W. Heisig and T.P. Kasulis, 2011); *Japanese Philosophy in the Making 1: Crossing Paths with Nishida* (2017) and *2: Borderline Interrogations* (2019), and *The Saga of Zen History and The Power of Legend* (2021).

Kurt C.M. Mertel is Assistant Professor of Philosophy in the Department of International Studies at the American University of Sharjah. He obtained his doctorate from Northwestern University and was previously a DAAD doctoral fellow at the Institute for Social Research (Frankfurt am Main) and post-doctoral fellow at the Czech Academy of Sciences, respectively. His research lies at the intersection of philosophical anthropology, ethics, and social and political philosophy and his work has been published in English, German, and Spanish. He is currently working on two book projects that provide the foundations for a Heideggerian approach to critical social theory.

William Outhwaite is Fellow of the Academy of Social Sciences (London). He taught at the universities of Sussex and Newcastle, where he is emeritus professor of sociology. He is the author of *Understanding Social Life: The Method Called Verstehen* (1975, 2nd edn. 1986), *Concept Formation in Social Science* (1983), *New Philosophies of Social Science: Realism, Hermeneutics and Critical Theory* (1987), *Habermas* (1994), *The Future of Society* (2006), *European Society* (2008), *Critical Theory and Contemporary Europe* (2012), *Social Theory* (2015), *Europe since 1989: Transitions and Transformations* (2016), *Contemporary Europe* (2017), *Transregional Europe* (2020) and (with Larry Ray) *Social Theory and Postcommunism* (2005).

List of Contributors

Karsten R. Stueber is Professor of Philosophy at the College of the Holy Cross. He works at the intersection of philosophy of mind, the philosophy of the social sciences, and metaethics. Among others, he is author of *Rediscovering Empathy: Agency, Folk-Psychology, and the Human Sciences* (2006). Together with Hans-Herbert Kögler he has edited *Empathy and Agency: The Problem of Understanding in the Human Sciences* (2000) and has more recently co-edited *Ethical Sentimentalism: New Perspectives* (2017). At the moment, he is finishing up a new book project on the moralizing animal, that is, us humans, and the relationship between empathy and morality.

Simon Susen is Professor of Sociology at City, University of London. Before joining City in 2011, he held lectureships at Birkbeck, University of London (2010–2011), Newcastle University (2008–2010), and Goldsmiths, University of London (2007–2008). He received his PhD from the University of Cambridge in 2007. Prior to that, he studied sociology, politics, and philosophy at a range of international universities and research centres—including the University of Cambridge, the University of Edinburgh, the Colegio de México, the Facultad Latinoamericana de Ciencias Sociales in Mexico City, and the École des Hautes Études en Sciences Sociales in Paris. He is Affiliate Professor of Sociology at the Universidad Andrés Bello in Santiago, Chile. In addition, he is Associate Member of the Bauman Institute and, together with Bryan S Turner, Editor of the *Journal of Classical Sociology*.

Stephen Turner is Distinguished University Professor at the Department of Philosophy, University of South Florida, where he is also director of the Center for Social and Political Thought. He has held visiting professorships at Boston University, the University of Notre Dame, Virginia Tech, and the University of Manchester, and fellowships from the US National Endowment for the Humanities and the Swedish Collegium for Advanced Studies. His current research interests are in cognitive science and aspects of democratic theory, especially relating to issues of knowledge and expertise.

Frédéric Vandenberghe is Professor of Sociology at the Federal University of Rio de Janeiro (IFCS-UFRJ), where he also directs the Social Theory Lab (Sociofilo). He has published widely on the history of ideas and various aspects of social theory in English, French and Portuguese. His most recent book is (with Alain Caillé): *For a New Classic Sociology. A Proposition*, followed by a Debate (2021).

Rainer Winter is Professor of Media and Cultural Theory at the Institute for Media and Communications, Alpen-Adria University of Klagenfurt. His background is in sociology, psychology and philosophy. He is the co-author and co-editor of more than 30 books.

Index

Adorno, Theodor 71–3, 83, 182, 186, 196, 286 n.13
affect 188–9, 223, 226–7, 232, 234–9, 241, 274, 282–3
    affective turn 188–9, 232, 237, 241, 274, 282–3
    theory 232, 235, 283
agency 3, 7, 71, 78, 81, 83, 89, 91–2, 107, 117, 134, 226
agreement
Albert, Hans 72
alterity (otherness) 233, 241
Althusser, Louis 186
Anderson, Ben 232, 236–42
Anthropocene 4, 188, 191–2
anthropology 80–1, 110, 130, 185, 187–9, 241
    evolutionary 110
    philosophical 4
Appiah, Kwame 126, 128–9
Arendt, Hannah 128
Aristotle 114
autonomy 10, 21, 32, 78, 82, 87, 252–3, 272
axial age 267, 277, 287 n.17
    new 275

background
    assumptions 93
    knowledge 74
    understanding 2
Beck, Ulrich 128–9, 130, 191, 275
being 2, 32, 33, 38, 75–6, 163–7, 169, 174–5 n.11, 185, 219, 234, 241, 243, 249, 251, 265, 273–4, 282, 284
    estar/ser 185, 273–4
    non-being 243
belief 90, 96, 112, 124–7, 130, 142, 145, 149, 159–61, 170, 172–3, 204–5, 215, 217, 221–2, 224–8, 233, 252, 262, 264, 270, 277, 279–81, 284; 286 nn.7–8

false belief problem 90–1
    religious 267
Black Lives Matter 239–40, 243
body 3, 71, 79–82, 117
Bolsonaro, Jair Messias 192 n.1, 274–5
Bourdieu, Pierre 8, 10, 71, 76, 79–82
    epistemological break 7–10, 39, 41, 252
    habitus 10–12, 36, 71, 79–82, 253–6, 271, 280–1
Braidotti, Rosi 124
Brexit 198–206, 275–7
Brown, Wendy 232–3. 237, 239–41, 283–4
Butler, Judith 188, 232, 234, 237–9, 241–2, 283

capability
    capabilities approach 130–1
    cognitive 2, 107–8, 133
    dialogic 131
    discursive 125
    symbolic 126, 132
capitalism 127, 131, 188, 192, 197
Cherniavsky, Eve 235, 237
climate change 128, 131, 183–4, 191–2, 202, 204
cognitive
    preconditions 140–5
    science 87–9, 95–6
colonialism 187–8
Comte, August 186
complimentary learning
    between religious and secular 139, 141–4, 146, 148, 150–2
concept/conception (conceptual) 88
conditional dependence 92–5, 98–9
consensus 27, 75, 144, 145–6, 201, 279
Corbyn, Jeremy 206
coronavirus pandemic 181, 183–4, 191, 202, 240

cosmopolitanism 3, 123–5, 127–35, 190, 198, 242, 249, 265–7, 275–6, 284
critical theory 1
    as critical hermeneutics 7
critique 3, 75, 219, 232–4, 237–42
cultural studies 2, 83, 83 n.3, 183, 186–9

Deleuze, Gilles 186–7, 236
democracy 126, 129, 198–9, 151–2, 184, 186, 192, 202, 205, 242, 267–9, 275, 285
Derrida, Jacques 186–7, 195, 233, 245 n.6
Descartes René 80, 216, 278
    Cartesian 171, 216, 221, 278–9
        self 217, 263
    Cartesianism 225, 278
Dewey, John 220, 223–4, 279, 283, 285 n.2
dialogue 1, 3, 71, 73, 77–9, 82–3, 87, 117, 123–5, 130–3, 140, 146, 166–7, 215, 224–8, 232–3
    intercultural dialogue 2, 100, 116
    interreligious 159–62, 169
    as play 4
dignity 106, 204, 264–5
Dilthey, Wilhelm 164, 168, 183, 195–6, 253
Diogenes the Cynic 127
discourse 10, 14, 78, 141–2, 150–1, 168–9, 185–6, 197–8, 216, 226–8, 234–8, 244–5 n.5, 255, 268–9, 276, 279, 282, 284
    religious 140–2, 149, 267–9
doxa 12, 20, 30, 39–40, 91
Durkheim, Emile 182, 186

Eagleton, Terry 124
emancipation 18–19, 39, 41, 216
emergency 239–42, 281
empathy 3, 88–9, 99, 106–7, 109–16, 219–23, 226–7
    enactivist empathy 216, 219–23, 226–8, 278, 281–2
    hermeneutical Empathy 219–23, 226–7
empiricism 87
emulation 97–9
enactivism 4, 215–16, 221–6
Enlightenment 128–9, 131–2, 185, 215–16, 225, 237, 242, 249, 272, 278

equality 73, 143–4, 249–51, 272
    comparable validity and dialogical equality 143–4, 146–7, 149–53
    inequality 11, 236
exploitation 127–9, 132, 187, 245 n.6, 266

fake news 198, 200, 208 n.17
Fieschi, Catherine 231
Fleischacker, Samuel 107, 112, 117, 263
Floyd, George 240
foreconception (of completeness) 286 n.7
foreign language education 3, 123–6, 132–5, 164, 171–3
fore-structure of understanding needed
Foucault, Michel 73, 75–8, 81, 83
    archaeology 75
    Foucauldian 2, 3
    genealogy 75, 78
Frankfurt, Harry 264
Frankfurt School 1, 2, 73, 83, 183, 188, 197, 254
freedom 11, 16–18, 31, 78–9, 108
    academic 204, 216, 224–5, 228, 256, 265–6, 278
    Buddhist and Islamic traditions of 129, 196–7
Frege, Gottlob 169
Freud, Sigmund 82, 183
    Freudian 92, 197
Fromm, Erich 197

Gadamer, Hans-Georg 3, 74–5, 77, 83, 107, 115–16, 123–5, 144, 146, 163–7, 171–2, 186–7, 195–7, 201–2, 215–16, 219–22, 225, 227, 249–51, 253, 258, 260–1, 268–70, 275–6, 278–9, 282, 285–6 n.6
    fusion of horizons 30–1, 75, 116, 146, 164, 219–21, 279
Gallagher, Shaun 222–4, 226, 281
genealogy
    Foucauldian 2, 127–8
    genealogical intertwinement of religious and secular 141, 145–6, 148–9
German idealism 87, 92, 258

globalization 128, 135, 190–2
Gopnik, Alison 88, 90, 93–4, 96
Gramsci, Antonio 191, 201, 275

Habermas, Jürgen 1, 72–5, 139–53, 181, 190, 195–8, 201–3
habitus 10–12, 36, 71, 79–82, 253–6, 271, 280–1
Haidt, Jonathan 111, 118 n.4
Hay, Colin 198–9
Hegel, George Wilhelm Friedrich 32, 184, 196–7
   Hegelian 1, 2, 282–3
      post-Hegelian 272
      subject, 217
Heidegger 3, 32, 162–6, 168, 172, 174–5 n.11, 182–3, 185–6, 189, 253, 270, 278–9, 282
Hemmings, Claire 235–7, 240, 243
hermeneutic(s) 2
   attitude 32, 277, 282
   circle 93, 132, 162, 216
   confrontation 10, 124, 234, 282
   critical 1, 2, 4, 71, 76–9, 81–3, 118, 195–7, 201, 207, 215–16, 219, 226, 231–4, 236–7
   experience 14, 20, 196, 260, 275, 279, 282
   in-depth 71–4, 81–2
   interreligious 3, 159–62, 169–73
   intercultural 88, 97, 123
   non-textual 159, 162, 169–70, 171–3, 270–2
   objective 72
   philosophical 2
   as social theory 3
   of suspicion 185–6, 235
Hierocles 127–8
historicity 21
holism 99, 281
Holocaust 128
   denial 200, 204
Honneth, Axel 2, 73, 78, 118 n.2, 197, 259, 283
Horkheimer, Max 72–3, 83, 186, 254, 273, 275
Hoy, David 74–5
human and social sciences 89
Humboldt, Wilhelm Von 92, 251, 253, 279
   Humboldtian 263

Hume, David 106–7, 111–12, 198, 262
Husserl, Edmund 169

ideology 40, 127, 220–1, 225, 227, 236–8, 280–1, 244 n.3
   critique 123, 196, 235, 237, 282–3
individual(ity) 19, 21, 38–9, 76–7, 81, 124, 225, 227
intentionality 77, 90–1, 111, 172, 221–2

justice 105, 111, 128, 185, 228
   injustice 130, 233, 235, 240, 283
   testimonial 209 n.27

Kant, Immanuel 107–8, 128–9, 131, 196–7, 237–8, 266
   Kantian 1–2, 35, 106, 109, 116, 128, 131, 148–9, 184
   Neo-Kantianism 89, 92
   sensus communis 3, 107, 115
knowledge
   prelinguistic 91
   tacit 94
Kögler, Hans-Herbert 1, 2, 4, 139, 146
   agency 83, 107, 115–16, 130, 216, 219–22
   critical hermeneutics 181, 186
   critical theory 197
   dialogue 87, 126, 134, 159, 187–8, 195, 198, 201–2, 217–22, 228
   on empathy 4, 88–9, 113, 116–17, 215–16, 219–24, 226–7, 260–3
   intersubjectivity 91–93, 96
   other 153
   and power 4, 8, 10, 71, 75, 77–80, 123, 185
   resistance 73
Korsgaard, Christine 106, 109, 264
Koselleck, Reinhart 239

language 71, 73–5, 82, 91–9, 162–9, 189, 196
   first signal system 92, 94
   second signal system 92–5, 98–9
   see also discourse
Latour, Bruno 189, 191, 238
lebensphilosophie 91–2

Leibniz, Gottfried Wilhelm 80
Lévi-Strauss, Claude 9–10
lifeworld 8–9, 16–17, 20, 24–7, 29–32, 77–8, 190, 242, 252–3, 285
linguistic idealism 196
Lorenzer, Alfred 71–4, 81–2, 255, 285 n.3
Lukács, György 183
Lyotard, Jean-François 195, 233, 241

Mahmoud, Saba 282–3
Mannheim, Karl 181–3, 186, 273
Marx, Karl 32, 72, 182, 186, 207
    Marxism 187, 292
    Marxist(s) 148–9
        economics 197
        sociology 183
mass migration 128, 188
materialism 92, 94
Mauss Marcel 9–10
May, Theresa 206
Mbembe, Achille 188
Mead, George Herbert 34, 78, 81, 107, 117, 220, 223, 229 n.1, 255, 259, 262–3
    me and I 7
meaning 8, 9, 75, 77, 79, 163–9, 174–5 n.11, 221, 223, 231, 234
Meltzhoff, Andrew 89–90
Merleau-Ponty, Maurice 79, 189, 220, 223
mirror neurons 88, 119 n.10
modernity 126–30, 133–5, 181, 184–6, 189–90, 249, 274–5
morality 105
    in group loyalty 105, 111, 118
    Kantian 106
    moral community 106, 116
    moral judgments 105–8, 113, 262
    the moral stance 105–10, 113, 115–18, 118 n.2, 119 n.7, 119 n.10, 260–5
    moralizing attitudes 105–6, 111, 118 n.4, 263
Mouffe, Chantal 198, 276
multiculturalism 231–3, 245

nationalism 133, 198, 206, 275
naturalism 3, 88, 106–8, 115–17, 140

neoliberal
    hegemony 190
    neoliberalism 191–2, 273–4
    technology 188
Nietzsche, Friedrich 32–3, 106
    Nietzschean 2, 24
nine eleven (9/11) 190
Nussbaum, Martha 128, 130–1

object permanence 97–8
objectification 77, 89, 252, 261, 271, 285–6 n.6
    self 31
    see also tradition
objectivism (scientific) 9–11
Oevermann, Ulrich 72–3
ontology 14, 36, 241
    of the present 181, 184–5, 187, 191, 192 n.1, 273–4
    social, 250, 253, 256, 262, 274, 286 n.15
openness 12, 78, 99–100, 125, 130, 146, 154–3, 156 n.19, 215, 218, 222, 227–8, 241, 250, 259, 262–3, 266–9, 280
Oppenheimer, Robert 99
oppression 23, 28, 224, 227–8, 266, 282, 284
    oppressed 15, 24
other see also alterity 75, 78, 95, 219
    otherness 125

Parsons, Talcott 181, 186
perspective taking
    dialogic 147, 201–2
    empathetic 130, 133
    imaginary 110–16, 215, 221, 223, 225, 227
    impartial spectator perspective 106–7, 110, 113–16, 119 n.6, 264–5
philosophy (of history) viii
Piaget, Jean 205
play 4, 92–5, 98–100, 215–16, 219, 220–2, 225–6, 259–60, 264, 278–9
Plato 166
politics
    anti-democratic 4
    political philosophy 4

political polarization 4, 182, 184–5,
    198–201, 204–5, 224–6, 228,
    234, 242–3, 280–2
Popper, Karl 72
populism 4, 183, 188–9, 191–2, 199–200,
    205–7, 208 n.12, 231–2, 235,
    242, 273–5
postcolonial(ism) 125, 127, 129–32
postmetaphysical thought 141–2, 148–9,
    264, 267, 269
postmodern
    postmodernism 186, 188
    postmodernity 181, 189–91, 197
    second postmodernity 181, 189–92,
        274–5
postsecularism 139–40, 143, 148
poststructuralism 1–2, 33, 124, 186–9, 197,
    219, 250, 280
power 2, 3, 8, 11, 117, 185, 187, 197,
    217–18, 238
    dispositifs 75
    and domination 7, 73–4, 76–8, 81–3,
        129, 183, 187
practical sphere 7
practices
    cultural 78–9
    embodied 159, 165, 169–73, 270–2
    religious 159–60, 169–70, 172–3,
        270–2
    social 9, 77, 82, 89, 111, 126, 185–6,
        217
praxis 3, 9–11
predictive processing 96–7
preunderstanding 2, 12–15, 22–3, 25, 33,
    74–8, 124, 172, 175 n.14,
    249, 254, 260, 269–71, 273,
    278–9
Pritchard, H.A. 108
psychoanalysis 72–3, 81–2, 183
psychology (developmental)
public sphere 3, 141–5, 148–53, 183, 202,
    253, 265, 267–9, 272, 275–7,
    280, 282

race 106, 187–9
    racism 4, 35, 128, 200, 231, 235–6
        anti-racism 188, 218, 232
        systemic racism 239–40
Rawls, John 148, 196, 267–8, 276

reality 10–11, 14–18, 25, 40, 98, 126, 160,
    182, 186, 188, 196, 237,
    252–3, 262
    social 10, 12, 36–7, 72, 182, 251, 256–7,
        271
reason
    critique of, 101
    secular 141–3, 148, 150
    universal
    recognition 3, 73, 90
reciprocity 10, 38, 98, 139, 146–7, 187–8,
    236, 254, 283
reductionism
reflexivity 87, 219, 234
    critical 2, 33, 219, 256, 278, 279, 284
    cultural 82
    hermeneutic 7, 71, 77, 79, 81
    self- 134
relativism 22
religion 3, 139–40, 144–5, 147–8, 159, 237,
    250, 267–72
    religious belief 141, 145, 160–1,
        204, 267
    religious discourse 140–4, 149, 267–9
    religious doctrine 163
    religious teachings 160–1, 163
    religious traditions 140–1, 143, 270
    world religions 159, 161–2, 169–70,
        269, 277
repression 82, 255
resistance 3, 7, 18–21, 41, 73, 76–8, 81–3,
    187, 197, 199, 236, 253–6,
    258, 272, 283
respect 106, 116–17, 125, 129–30, 151, 204,
    254–5, 260–1, 264, 266–7,
    276–7
Ricoeur, Paul 2–3, 163, 165–9, 270
Rorty, Richard 187–8

Said, Edward 132
Sartre, Jean-Paul 79
scaffolding 97
Schleiermacher, Friedrich 164, 168, 253,
    279
Schütz, Alfred 196
Sedgwick, Eve 235, 237, 282–3
self 89, 92, 117, 185, 219
    hermeneutic nature of viii
    understanding 150, 217–18

self-distanciation 22–4, 29, 76, 217, 233, 215–17, 224, 233, 228
Sen, Amartya 129
situatedness 2, 77, 81, 124, 128, 130, 217–19
  see also tradition
Smith, Adam 106–7, 109–18, 262–3, 265
  empathy 3
sociology 4, 8, 71–2, 80–1, 83
solidarity 15, 140–3, 149, 151–2, 235, 249–50, 265, 269, 272, 281
Spencer, Herbert 95, 180
Sperber, Dan 88, 95
Spivak, Gayatri Chakravorty 233, 236–7, 242
Straub, Jürgen 74–5, 82
subjectivity 10, 71, 77–8, 125, 217–18, 225
  dialogic 7
  subjective sphere 7
  see also individuality/individual(s)
symbolic
  horizon 8
  order 76, 98, 217–18, 231–2, 238
  sphere 7
  see also worldview

terrorism 130, 183
theory 1, 7, 88, 93–4, 235, 237
  critical 72–3, 81, 90, 159, 183, 188, 196–7
  social 10, 87
  theorist-agent dualism 217
theory of mind 88, 90, 94
  representational 215, 221–2, 226
tradition 74–5, 124, 126–7
translation (proviso) 139, 141–3, 146–52, 155 n.11
Trendelenburg, Friedrich 93

Trump, Donald 190–1, 198, 200–1
Trumpism 200
Trumpists 277
truth 8–9, 10, 13, 20–1, 22–4, 74–5, 94, 98, 124, 141, 145, 160, 169–70, 182, 185, 216–17, 225, 227, 229 n.2, 231, 235, 237, 250, 253, 258, 262, 267–71, 277–9

understanding 88–9
  critical 73–4, 76
  intercultural, 87, 99, 115, 187
  intersubjective 89–94, 98, 107, 110, 218
  mutual 139, 144, 147, 151, 159, 201, 215, 218, 221–2, 224–6, 236
  practical 164–5, 169–73, 270–2
  self-understanding 8, 9, 10, 11, 77, 130, 160, 168–9, 187–8

Vygotsky, Lev 92

Wallace, Jay 106
Weber, Max 182–3, 186
Weigman, Robyn 235
Western tradition
  Eurocentrism 129–30
  West 129, 132
  see also tradition; axial age
Wittgenstein, Ludwig 92, 174 n.6, 196, 285 n.5
world-disclosure 2, 8, 18, 20, 92, 165–6, 168–9, 263, 265–6
  religious 154–5 n.10, 271
worldview 20, 23, 143, 145–52, 183, 186, 200, 268, 273
  religious 147, 161, 268–9

zeitdiagnose 182–3, 192 n.2, 273–5, *zeitdiagnostiche* 4
Zima, Peter 81, 123–6, 132

www.ingramcontent.com/pod-product-compliance
Lightning Source LLC
Chambersburg PA
CBHW070751020526
44115CB00032B/1619